E/2009/50/Rev.1
ST/ESA/319

Department of Economic and Social Affairs

World Economic and Social Survey 2009

Promoting Development, Saving the Planet

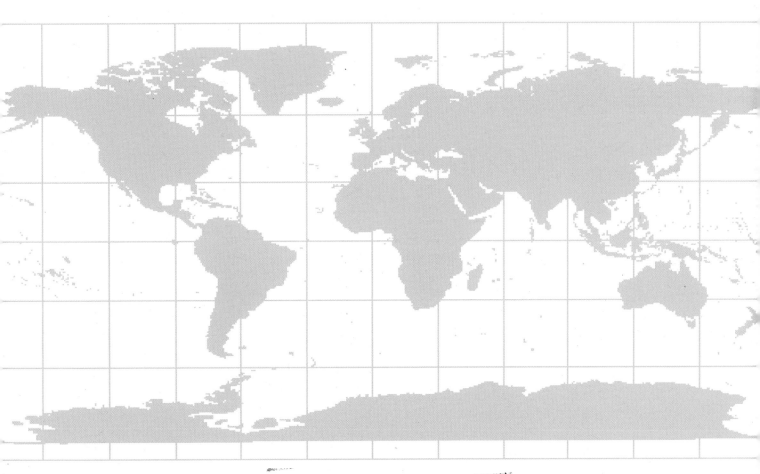

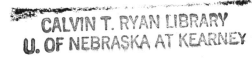

United Nations
New York, 2009

DESA

The Department of Economic and Social Affairs of the United Nations Secretariat is a vital interface between global policies in the economic, social and environmental spheres and national action. The Department works in three main interlinked areas: (i) it compiles, generates and analyses a wide range of economic, social and environmental data and information on which States Members of the United Nations draw to review common problems and to take stock of policy options; (ii) it facilitates the negotiations of Member States in many intergovernmental bodies on joint courses of action to address ongoing or emerging global challenges; and (iii) it advises interested Governments on the ways and means of translating policy frameworks developed in United Nations conferences and summits into programmes at the country level and, through technical assistance, helps build national capacities.

Note

Symbols of United Nations documents are composed of capital letters combined with figures.

E/2009/50/Rev.1
ST/ESA/319
ISBN 978-92-1-109159-5

United Nations publication
Sales No. E.09.II.C.1
Copyright © United Nations, 2009
All rights reserved
Printed by the United Nations
Publishing Section
New York

Preface

Unprecedented steps have been taken to halt the global financial meltdown and to enable the world to recover from the economic crisis that emerged in 2008. But the world also faces a climate crisis which has been building over a much longer period of time. If we do not bring to this challenge the same determination and sense of common cause with which we have addressed the economic crisis, not only will the climate catastrophe feared by the scientific community occur, but recovering from it will be an impossibility. Fortunately, the appropriate responses to the climate crisis can also contribute to long-term economic prosperity.

Scientists warn that global emissions must peak within a decade or we will face grave consequences, particularly in the developing world, where the vast majority of humanity live and where the vulnerability to climate impacts is greatest. If rising incomes in the developing world are to be achieved through high-emissions growth, such as that pursued by today's developed countries, then our environmental fabric will be stretched to the breaking point.

Indeed, the tremendous scale of the climate challenge reflects two centuries of unchecked emissions growth. Continuing along this route is not what was promised under the Kyoto Protocol to the United Nations Framework Convention on Climate Change. The sad fact is that we have missed multiple opportunities to change course. Developing countries are the first—and worst—sufferers from a problem for which, from a historical perspective, they bear the least responsibility. Issues of equity and burden-sharing must be addressed.

The United Nations Climate Change Conference, to be held in Copenhagen in December 2009, will provide an unprecedented opportunity to map out a more sustainable economic future. As the advanced economies have the resources and the responsibility to lead the way, they will be required to make bold commitments to reducing their emissions and helping developing nations undertake mitigation and adaptation.

Climate change represents a global challenge whose impact can be addressed only through open, inclusive and frank dialogue. The United Nations is at the heart of that dialogue. The *World Economic and Social Survey 2009* makes the case for meeting both the climate challenge and the development challenge by recognizing the links between the two and proceeding along low-emissions, high-growth pathways.

There is no single blueprint for achieving these goals. The *Survey* examines the key building blocks in order to assess the best possible options available to countries at different levels of development. At the same time, it rejects the polarization of mitigation and adaptation and the notion that one must choose between them. Both are essential, as are the financial and technological resources needed to support them.

There are huge synergies to be generated through big investments in energy efficiency, renewable energy, reduction of vulnerability and broader development projects. This will necessitate truly integrated policy responses, as well as enormous adjustments in the global economy. Yet, we must demand no less of ourselves if we are to put the world on a more sustainable path of development. The onus is on the international community to deliver the resources and leadership required to ensure that whatever is feasible becomes both practical and fair. The present *Survey* makes a timely contribution to that effort, and I commend it to a wide global audience.

BAN KI-MOON
Secretary-General

Acknowledgements

The *World Economic and Social Survey* is the annual flagship publication on major development issues prepared by Department of Economic and Social Affairs of the United Nations Secretariat (UN/DESA). This year's *Survey* was prepared under the general supervision and leadership of Rob Vos, Director of the Development Policy and Analysis Division (DPAD) of UN-DESA. Richard Kozul-Wright led the team that prepared the report. The core team at DPAD included Imran Ahmad, Piergiuseppe Fortunato, Nazrul Islam, Alex Julca, Oliver Paddison and Mariangela Parra. Alex Izurieta, also of DPAD, provided the model simulations presented in chapters I and IV. Important guidance for the overall analysis was provided by Tariq Banuri of the Division for Sustainable Development (DSD) of UN-DESA, who, together with David O'Connor, Chantal Line Carpentier and Fred Soltau, provided the principal inputs to chapters II and V of the report. Manuel Montes and Frank Schroeder of the Financing for Development Office of UN-DESA provided principal inputs to chapter VI. Jan McAlpine and Barbara Tavora-Jainchill of the secretariat of the United Nations Forum on Forests provided inputs to chapters III and VI.

Inputs and comments were also gratefully received from funds and organizations across the wider United Nations system, including the Global Environment Facility, the International Finance Corporation, the International Labour Office (Employment Strategy Department), the United Nations Development Programme (Bureau for Development Policy, New York), the United Nations Environment Programme (Division of Technology, Industry and Economics, Paris), the United Nations Environment Programme Risø Centre (Copenhagen) and the United Nations Framework Convention on Climate Change secretariat (Bonn). Specific inputs were also received from researchers at the Australian National University, Tufts University and the University of Oregon and from the South Centre, Geneva.

The analysis benefited from a number of background papers prepared especially for the *Survey* by a number of prominent experts on climate change and development. Those background papers are available at http://www.un.org/esa/policy/wess.

Helpful overall guidance was provided by Jomo Kwame Sundaram, Assistant Secretary-General for Economic Development at UN-DESA.

Overview

Addressing climate change is the concern of all

The central message of the *World Economic and Social Survey 2009* is that addressing the climate challenge cannot be met through ad hoc and incremental actions. In the first place, it requires much stronger efforts by advanced countries to cut their emissions. The fact that in this regard more than a decade has been lost since the adoption of the Kyoto Protocol to the United Nations Framework Convention on Climate Change[1] only adds urgency to those efforts. However, even if advanced countries begin to match their words with deeds, their efforts are, by themselves, unlikely to be sufficient to meet the climate challenge. The active participation of developing countries is now required and such participation can occur only if it allows economic growth and development to proceed in a rapid and sustainable manner.

This *Survey* argues that switching to low-emissions, high-growth pathways in order to meet the development and climate challenge is both necessary and feasible. It is necessary because combating global warming cannot be achieved without eventual emissions reductions from developing countries. It is feasible because technological solutions that can enable a shift towards such pathways do in fact exist. It is, however, neither inevitable nor inconsequential. Such a switch would entail unprecedented and potentially very costly socio-economic adjustments in developing countries—adjustments, moreover, that will have to be made in a world more rife with inequalities than at any time in human history. If it is to happen, the switch will require a level of international support and solidarity rarely mustered outside a wartime setting.

The *Survey* also argues that achieving such a transformation hinges on the creation of a global new deal capable of raising investment levels and channeling resources towards lowering the carbon content of economic activity and building resilience with respect to unavoidable climate changes. Most developing countries do not currently have the financial resources, technological know-how and institutional capacity to deploy such strategies at a speed commensurate with the urgency of the climate challenge. Failure to honour long-standing commitments of international support in those three areas remains the single biggest obstacle to meeting the challenge. Bolder action is required on all fronts.

The *Survey* contends that, in line with common but differentiated responsibilities, the switch will demand an approach to climate policy in developing countries different from that in developed ones. It will, in particular, require a new public policy agenda —one that focuses on a broad mix of market and non-market measures while placing a much greater emphasis than has been seen in recent years on public investment and effective industrial policies, to be managed by a developmental State. The mix in developed countries is likely to entail a larger role for carbon markets, taxes and regulations.

Finally, issues of trust and justice will need to be taken much more seriously so as to ensure fair and inclusive responses to the climate challenge. The *Survey* argues that one determinant of success will be the capacity of developed and developing countries to create a more integrated framework and joint programmes with shared goals on, inter alia, climate adaptation, forestry, energy (including energy access), and poverty eradication.

---

1   United Nations, *Treaty Series*, vol. 2303, No. 30822.

Projections and principles

The climate challenge for developing countries

Even if the annual flow of emissions were to stabilize at today's level, the stock of greenhouse gas emissions in the atmosphere would be twice the pre-industrial level by 2050, entailing a high probability of dangerous temperature rises, with potentially destabilizing economic and political consequences. The latest findings of the Intergovernmental Panel on Climate Change (IPCC) suggest the following:

> For many key parameters, the climate is already moving beyond the patterns of natural variability within which our society and economy have developed and thrived. These parameters include global mean surface temperature, sea-level rise, ocean and ice-sheet dynamics, ocean acidification, and extreme climatic events. There is a significant risk that many of the trends will accelerate, leading to an increasing risk of abrupt or irreversible climatic shifts.[2]

In light of these findings, the Survey recognizes a maximum temperature increase of 2° C above pre-industrial levels as the target for stabilizing carbon concentrations at a level that prevents dangerous anthropogenic interference in the climate system. This corresponds to a target greenhouse gas concentration (in terms of carbon dioxide equivalents (CO_2e)) of between 350 and 450 parts per million (ppm) and to global emission reductions of the order of 50-80 per cent over 1990 levels, by 2050. In terms of actual emissions, this would be equivalent to a reduction from roughly 40 gigatons of carbon dioxide ($GtCO_2$) at present to between 8 and 20 $GtCO_2$ by 2050.[3]

This challenge is the consequence of over two centuries of unprecedented growth and rising living standards, fuelled by an ever increasing quantity and quality of energy services. Traditional (biomass) energy sources were initially replaced by coal and (beginning in the early 1900s) by oil. Today, fossil energy sources provide for some 80 per cent of total energy needs.

However, the activities that utilize these services have been very unevenly distributed, resulting in a sharp divergence of incomes between the developed and the developing world and huge economic and social disparities globally (figure O.1). Moreover, as a result of this uneven development, the advanced countries have, since 1950, contributed as much as three quarters of the increase in emissions despite the fact that they account for less than 15 per cent of the world's population.

It follows that the response to climate change in developing countries will necessarily unfold in the face of vastly more daunting challenges than those confronting developed countries and in a far more constrained environment. The major challenge remains that of economic growth. Economic growth is important not only for achieving poverty eradication but also for bringing about a gradual narrowing of the huge income differentials between the two groups of countries. The idea of freezing the current level of global inequality over the next half century or more (as the world goes about trying to solve the climate problem) is economically, politically and ethically unacceptable.

---

2   Key message 1: (Climatic trends) from the International Scientific Congress Climate Change: Global Risks, Challenges and Decisions, Copenhagen, 10-12 March 2009.

3   A gigaton is equal to 1 billion metric tons.

Figure O.1
The income gap between G7 and selected regions, 1980-2007

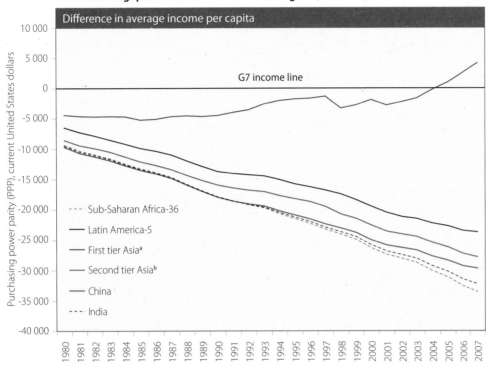

Source: DESA/DPAD/DSP calculations, based on WB-WDI online database.
a Hong Kong Special Administration Region of China; Republic of Korea, Singapore; Taiwan Province of China.
b Indonesia, Malaysia, Philippines, Thailand.

Synergies between the climate and development challenges

Is it possible to combine high economic growth in developing countries with a radical lowering of their emissions trajectory? The literature on climate and development encompasses two different approaches to this issue. Proponents of the "top-down" approach focus on the global challenge and what kind of emissions trajectories and targets for developing countries would be consistent with meeting this challenge. This approach has also been used to calculate representative costs of climate action. Proponents of the alternative, "bottom-up" approach focus on the concrete actions that are being undertaken by developing countries, in the context, for example, of energy efficiency, pilot programmes in renewable energy, and afforestation projects. This approach has also been used to develop cost estimates of specific mitigation. However, there are very few studies that translate both these approaches into the kind of strategic programmes that would put the economy on a sustainable development trajectory.

Combining the two approaches leads to the conclusion that it is indeed possible to integrate the climate and development agendas, although this would require a very different stance on climate policy in developing countries than the one that has emerged in developed ones. While there will be similarities between the two groups of countries in terms of a subset of national policy instruments (smarter incentives, stronger regulations), developing-country Governments would need to steer resources mobilized for large-scale investments into new production sectors and new technologies. While the emphasis in developed countries is on the development of the carbon market, the preferred option for developing countries should be an emphasis on active industrial policies. This combination of large-scale investments and active policy interventions requires strong and sustained political commitment embodied by a developmental State and, as critically, sizeable and effective multilateral support with respect to both finance and technology.

Synergies between developed and developing country actions

The search for synergies between developed and developing countries in respect of climate action has led to three rather different approaches. Application of the first approach means that developing countries follow the example of developed countries, either voluntarily or through some form of coercion, by adopting emissions reduction targets. Under the second option, either setting targets or undertaking actions is conditional on the availability of finance and technology from developed countries. Under the third option, developed and developing countries jointly adopt both climate and development targets.

The *Survey*'s conclusion is that the first approach is bound to fail. The second approach is a necessary one, but it runs the risk of producing only incremental action on a project-by-project basis. Quite understandably, this approach has focused attention on the question of financial transfers through official development assistance (ODA). If ambitions with respect to meeting the climate challenge were more modest, this approach would suffice; given, however, the scientific consensus on the dangers of climate change, it is most likely inadequate. It is the third approach that is in fact best suited for reconfiguring the development trajectory. As it turns out, the recent multiplicity of food, energy and financial crises may have created just the context in which such cooperative action could take root. While the origins of those crises may be distinct, like the climate crisis they pose a common threat to actions still to be completed under the agenda for achieving economic development and poverty eradication.

In response to the global economic and financial crisis, steps have been taken to bring about recovery, to prevent a return to the financial excesses of "casino capitalism" and, through the inclusion of green investments in stimulus packages, to address environmental concerns, including those pertaining to climate change. While these initiatives do not yet add up to a long-term sustainable solution, they do point in the right direction. Still, much more needs to be done. There has been, in particular, a reluctance to acknowledge both the scale of the adjustments that developing countries will be required to make to pull their economies out of the global recession and shift onto low-emissions pathways, and the resulting economic and political costs. If developing countries are to undertake such adjustments, a much greater level of international cooperation will be needed.

Burden-sharing

The climate crisis is the result of the very uneven pattern of economic development that evolved over the past two centuries, which allowed today's rich countries to attain their current levels of income, in part through not having to account for the environmental damage now threatening the lives and livelihoods of others. Indeed, it has been estimated that for every 1° C rise in average global temperatures, annual average growth in poor countries could drop by 2-3 percentage points, with no change in the growth performance of rich countries. It is even possible that the advanced countries will actually benefit from temperature rises in the medium term thanks to, for instance, improved agricultural yields (due to carbon fertilization) and lower transportation costs (across ice-free arctic shipping routes). That uneven pattern of development is reflected in per capita emissions, which are still on average 6-7 times greater in advanced than in developing countries.

Working these considerations into a consistent climate framework has proved a difficult task. Since the United Nations Conference on Environment and Development, held in Rio de Janeiro in 1992, it has been agreed that countries have "common but differentiated responsibilities" for dealing with the climate challenge. (The principle was restated at the thirteenth session of the Conference of the Parties to the United Nations Framework Convention on Climate Change,[4] held in Bali, Indonesia, in December 2007). It has been difficult to reach a consensus on what this means in practice, however, because rich countries do not want to give too much significance to past actions that would place the bulk of the responsibilities on their shoulders, while developing countries fear, for the same reason, giving too much importance to current and future emissions.

Correcting a market failure …

A breakthrough of sorts occurred with the Stern Report released in late 2006 by the Government of the United Kingdom of Great Britain and Northern Ireland, which identified greenhouse gases as "the greatest market failure the world has ever seen" and provided the first serious attempt to model the cost of doing nothing in comparison with the cost of adopting an alternative strategy which would hold emissions below a manageable threshold. From this perspective, a form of climate ethics emerges around the need to realign social and private cost by making the polluters pay for the damage they inflict on others. The Stern Report concluded that it was possible to ensure that future generations would be much better off at relatively little cost to present generations.

Stern's analysis has triggered a heated debate among economists about the right methodology for costing climate damage and the most efficient mechanisms for correcting the underlying market failure. That debate has encouraged policymakers to think more clearly about the management of climate risk under conditions of imperfect information and uncertainty, and to develop a sense of both historical considerations (regarding how far back the polluter-pays principle should reach) and geographical ones (regarding whether the polluter is the producer or the consumer of the goods that add to the stock of greenhouse gases).

The resulting "top-down" metrics have generated complicated country schedules for bringing carbon emissions down to sustainable levels. So far, however, this approach has provided surprisingly little policy guidance on how countries might manage transformative change, with discussion in this regard being limited to the subjects of the distribution of emission rights and the determination of the right price for carbon.

Creating carbon markets and establishing a predictable carbon price will be part of the policy mix, but they do not address the development dimension of the challenge. For instance, the cap-and-trade system has been designed to conform to the policy experience, institutional capacity and economic conditions of rich countries. By default, this provides significant advantages to them, as the essential baseline is the current emissions of the high-emitting countries.

---

4   United Nations, *Treaty Series*, vol. 1771, No. 30822.

… or promoting development rights

Others have argued that the economists' focus on market failure is overly reliant on cost-benefit calculations and thereby underestimates the threat of catastrophic climate shocks and understates the plight of the most vulnerable communities. The rural poor in the developing world will likely face the largest adjustments to climate change and helping them meet their adaptation challenge should be an essential feature of a fair climate framework.

However, divergent growth and rising global inequality over the past 60 years make the development policy challenge into something much bigger than that of eliminating extreme poverty (United Nations, 2006). Moreover, over that period, advanced countries, in their climb to the top of the development ladder, have used up a good part of the atmospheric space for greenhouse gas emissions. Given the close link between energy use and economic growth, there is a real concern that the sustainable development ladder has already been kicked away and with it any real chance of combining climate and development goals.

A possible framework based on the idea of "greenhouse development rights" combines a measure of responsibility and ability to pay as a possible basis for sharing the burden of climate change that is consistent with the scale and urgency of the climate challenge as well as development objectives. This would be realized by establishing the right to be exempt from sharing the burden of climate protection up to a given world average income of $9,000 (purchasing power parity (ppp)). This figure is above the current global average and represents a threshold consistent with the situation of more diversified economies and beyond which further income increases have little effect on human development indicators. Individual citizens above that income threshold in a country whose average income fell below it would be expected, however, to share in meeting that burden. In essence, this makes the capacity to pay similar to that determined by an income tax with a personal exemption of $9,000.

While this threshold is only illustrative, on any realistic calculation, developed countries will assume a much more significant share of the global costs of climate protection, while developing countries will assume only more responsibilities in line with their level of development. It is possible that some arrangement along these lines will eventually emerge from discussions on common but differentiated responsibilities. On the other hand, this approach still tends to avoid discussing the specifics of policy design in moving towards low-emissions, high-growth development pathways and the kinds of international mechanisms needed to effect such a transition.

Greening catch-up growth

Policies designed to deal with the threat of dangerous climate change are lagging far behind the scientific evidence. At the same time, existing international commitments have fallen well short of promises and progress on new commitments is moving slowly. This represents a dangerous impasse as developing countries strive to accelerate growth through industrial development and rapid urbanization. The only way to make tangible progress is to approach the climate challenge as a development challenge.

An investment-led approach

All economic success stories have enjoyed a sustained burst of growth, on the order of 6-8 per cent per annum, allowing them to raise living standards and close the income gap with the developed countries. Growth, moreover, is strongly correlated with a broad set of social indicators, including poverty reduction, which together describe a more sustainable and inclusive development path. But this path does not emerge spontaneously. Even after a period of rapid growth, countries can get stuck or even fall back. Others struggle just to take off.

A rapid pace of capital accumulation, accompanied by shifts in the structure of economic activity towards industry, is usually a critical factor behind a sustained acceleration of growth. A good deal of early development policy analysis was focused on raising the share of investment to a level that would trigger a virtuous circle of rising productivity, increasing wages, technological upgrading and social improvements. The successful versions of this "big push" concentrated on selective leading sectors whose development would attract a further round of investment through the expansion of strong backward and forward linkages. As described, the development policy challenge was less about detailed planning and more about strategic support and coordination, including a significant role for public investment in triggering growth and crowding in private investment along a new development path.

In the 1980s and 1990s, investment-led development models had been abandoned in favour of market-oriented economic reforms. However, for most developing countries, freer markets and greater exposure to global competition did not produce the outcomes expected by the proponents of those reforms, particularly with respect to investment performance.

A return to an investment-led approach in developing countries makes sense once the climate challenge is properly integrated with the development challenge. Such an approach has already begun to take shape in richer countries with the inclusion of green investments in stimulus packages designed to create jobs in the face of a severe economic downturn. For developing countries where the shift to new sources of energy must take place in the context of their need to urbanize, strengthen food production and diversify into competitive industrialization, the challenge is of an even larger magnitude.

The mitigation challenge

Reducing greenhouse gas emissions will require large and interconnected investments across several sectors, with the aim, inter alia, of halting deforestation and land degradation, retrofitting buildings to make them more energy-efficient and redesigning transportation systems. But it is an energy transition that will be at the core of an alternative integrated strategy for meeting climate change and development goals. Energy use is responsible for 60 per cent of total greenhouse gas emissions, all stabilization scenarios indicate that a huge share of emissions reductions, perhaps as much as 80 per cent, will have to come from the reshaping of energy systems. Figure O.2 depicts the historical evolution of the energy system and one possible future development path towards decarbonization, one that would limit the increase in global average temperatures to about 2° C by the end of the century. The figure illustrates the much-needed transformational change of the global energy system. The ultimate goal of such a transition must be to improve energy efficiency and reduce reliance on fossil fuels, especially oil and coal, and to increase reliance on renewable sources of energy, especially wind, solar and advanced (non-food) biofuels.

Developed countries have mature economies, in which there is adequate (and even excessive) availability of modern energy services. They do not need to undertake a massive expansion of their energy infrastructure. However, lifestyle changes and sizeable investments will still be needed to turn their energy system away from the current dependence on fossil energy towards a complete decarbonization by the end of the century, or earlier. Developing countries, on the other hand, are severely handicapped in terms of modern energy infrastructure, and will require sustained large-scale investments in this sector to meet existing demand and promote economic development.

It follows from this that developed economies may need, and will be able to afford, a substantial increase in the price of energy, especially fossil-based energy, in order to provide the right market signal to potential consumers and investors. In contrast, all developing countries face the urgent challenge of expanding the energy infrastructure and making energy services widely available at affordable prices. The estimated number of people lacking such access ranges between 1.6 billion and 2 billion, mainly in rural areas. At least for the foreseeable future, developing countries will need to subsidize energy for their middle- and lower-income groups in order to make these services affordable.

Connecting those people to energy services will cost an estimated $25 billion per year over the next 20 years. This is a large sum for the poorest of the developing countries and is several times larger than the amount of aid spent on energy services.

A range of technological options will be relevant to the mitigation challenge, from the diffusion of existing low-emissions technologies, through the scaling up of new commercial technologies, to the development and diffusion of breakthrough technologies. Some of these will be cost-saving immediately or over a short time span. However, the production of larger amounts of clean energy in line with industrial and urban development will require very large investment with a long gestation period.

Figure O.2
Historical evolution of, and a possible future for, the global energy system, in the context of the relative shares of the most important energy sources, 1850-2100

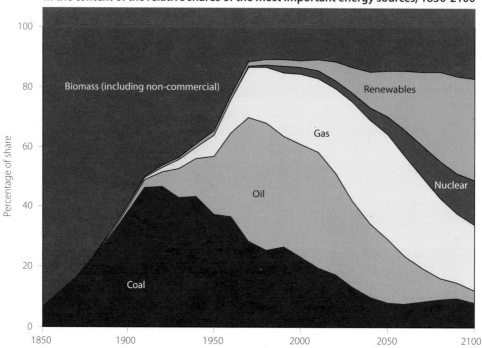

Sources: Grübler, Nakicenovic and Riahi (2007), and Nakicenovic and Riahi(2007), and International Institute for Applied Systems Analysis (2007).

To realize scale economies and the potential benefits of technological learning, "upfront" investments would need to be made in new and advanced carbon-saving technologies, which would, after scale-up and adoption, lower the mitigation costs and increase the mitigation potentials. Complementary investments in research and development and related skills development would also be needed to improve the performance of carbon-saving technologies and reduce their costs.

The potential size of the energy market in developing countries along with the possibility of making improvements to already installed capacity serves as an indication of how important investment opportunities could be. However, as the initial costs and risks are likely to deter private investors, the public sector would be left with a leading role, at least in the early stages of expansion. The current investments in the global energy system are estimated at some $500 billion per year. The sustainable scenario depicted in figure O.2 would require at least twice this effort during the coming decades—about $1 trillion per year or $20 trillion by 2030.

Resilience through diversity: the adaptation challenge

For many developing countries, environmental constraints and shocks are already part of a vicious development cycle which traps them at a low level of income, undermines their resource base and constrains their capacity to build resilience with respect to future shocks. Even if policymakers can quickly effect the transition to a low-emissions growth path, unavoidable rising global temperatures will bring serious environmental shocks and stresses, through spreading drought conditions, a rising sea level, ice-sheet and snow-cover melting, and the occurrence of extreme weather events. In the coming decades, these phenomena will threaten and destroy livelihoods around the globe, in particular the livelihoods of already vulnerable populations, including in developed countries.

Humanitarian groups have expressed concern for some time regarding the potential linkages between low or negative economic growth rates, higher levels of unemployment in the workforce, and stressed land and marine ecologies. A changing climate would engender, in already fragile contexts, additional stress factors such as more intense hurricanes in the Caribbean, above-average warming impacting glacier-dependent river flows in Central Asia, and drought-induced water scarcity impacting the fragile economies of Northern Africa.

Adapting to climate change will have to be a central component of any comprehensive and inclusive climate agenda. Poor health of populations, lack of infrastructure, weakly diversified economies, missing institutions and soft governance structures expose poorer countries and communities not just to potentially catastrophic large-scale disasters but also to a more permanent state of economic stress from higher average temperatures, reduced water sources, more frequent flooding and intensified windstorms.

Those threats are particularly common in rural communities where more than one third of households globally must confront the precariousness of their livelihoods. In sub-Saharan Africa, that proportion is over 60 per cent, and in some areas, heat-related plant stresses will contribute to reduced yields in key crops, by as much as 50 per cent. Strategies to avoid crop failures will include diversity farming, which is potentially one of the most important strategies for achieving food security in a changing climate, and the utilization of new crop strains that are more weather-resistant and have higher yields. More generally, economic policies to promote agricultural development should focus on extending support services, particularly for smallholders, and improving infrastructure (such as roads and storage facilities along with irrigation networks).

Forests are a source of livelihoods for close to 25 per cent of the world's peoples, many of whom are under threat from climate change. Important elements of forest protection encompass not only improved climate forecasting and disease surveillance systems but also strategies for preventing and combating forest fires, including the construction of fire lines, controlled burning and the utilization of drought- and fire-resistant tree species, such as teak, in tropical forest plantations. Measures aimed at assisting forests in adapting to climate change encompass, for instance, facilitating the adaptive capacity of tree species mainly by maximizing silvicultural genetic variation, and also management approaches such as reduced-impact logging. More generally, investments in economic diversification and employment creation, as well as improvement of land, soil and water management, will be part of a more integrated strategy.

The impacts of a changing climate on health and sanitation will be just as significant. While warming has already contributed to an additional 150,000 deaths annually in low-income countries, higher temperatures will further increase the survival and replication rates of bacterial contaminants of food and water sources, exacerbating the impact on health. Further, increased water scarcity will worsen already inadequate sanitation and hygiene standards; in Africa alone, 200 million people are already facing water stress. In many cases, water management is made all the more difficult by the variability in water availability, a consequence of both population increases and a changing climate, a situation that requires increased resilience in water management systems. Although efforts are already under way to strengthen those systems in a number of developing countries, significant public investment will be needed to achieve sustainable results.

More than half of the world's population now live in urban areas. City dwellers are expected to make up three quarters of the world's population by 2050, with almost all the growth in the developing world. Urban environments face their own adaptation problems, linked, in particular, to the quality of social infrastructure and building. In rapidly expanding coastal cities, for example, protection against sea-level rises and increased wind strength is an urgent priority. A combination of poverty, population density and poor social services makes for particularly vulnerable communities for which sudden climatic shocks can prove devastating. As things currently stand, most of the risk to urban areas is associated with the incapacity of local governments to, inter alia, ensure the development and protection of infrastructure and the adequacy of disaster risk reduction and disaster preparedness.

Combined large-scale investments, information management and collective action have already been undertaken by countries and communities with advanced economies that are vulnerable to the threat of climatic shocks. For many developing countries, however, the core of adaptation is still closely tied to the need to diversify their economies away from reliance on a small number of activities, particularly those in the primary sector that are sensitive to climatic shocks and changes. The Government of Mozambique, for example, has drawn up ambitious plans for the sustainable development of the coastal region, including infrastructure (transportation, drainage and water supply), land-use changes, and soft options to manage beach erosion. Such plans, which present unique opportunities for an infusion of massive development projects, need to deal with climate risks in an integrated manner, across seasonal, inter-annual and multi-decadal time scales. A combination of public investment, cheap credit and access to appropriate technology will be essential to meeting the adaptation challenge.

Towards an integrated agenda

Though the number of calls for a mainstreaming of climate policy is growing, the response cannot be one of simply grafting adaptation and mitigation goals onto the objectives of development policy that are currently being discussed. Rather, the two big challenges of development and climate change have to be connected through the long-term management of economic and natural resources in a more inclusive and sustainable manner. This should be viewed not as a quick—and certainly not as a costless—fix but rather as a multidimensional task in which large and long-term investments will play a pivotal role in enabling economies, at all levels of development, to switch to low-emissions, high-growth pathways. Policymakers will need to confront historical legacies, contemplate alternative economic strategies and embrace a more collaborative political discourse. Moreover, they will have to do so as the world tries to recover from the biggest economic shock since the Great Depression.

The current shocks and the resulting crisis have provided an opportunity for fresh thinking about the public policy agenda, and have served as a reminder that Governments are the only agents capable of mobilizing the massive financial and political resources required to confront large systemic threats. Large-scale resource mobilization will certainly be needed at both the national and the global levels in order to achieve combined climate and development goals. The big policy challenge lies in ensuring that these investments trigger more virtuous growth circles, through which to crowd in private investment and initiate cumulative technological changes in dynamic growth sectors, thereby supporting economic diversification and creating employment opportunities.

Public policy challenges

The big push towards cleaner, more diversified and more resilient economies will be supported or hindered through Government policies. Because many of the required investments will be large and complementary, price signals and regulatory measures (including building codes, fuel efficiency standards and mandates for renewable energy use), will need to be predictable. In the face of the initial cost disadvantages, the adoption of new cleaner technologies through Government subsidies, feed-in tariffs and other support measures, can be facilitative.

Some developing countries have begun to develop alternative policy frameworks through, for example, national adaptation plans. These have focused on climate-proofing infrastructure projects, such as transport and irrigation systems, improved disaster monitoring and management and better land-use planning; but difficulties in scaling up projects, because of funding and institutional shortcomings, as well as the failure to adopt a more broadly developmental approach, still need to be overcome. More lasting success will depend on adopting smarter development policies which link adaptation more tightly to ongoing efforts to remove existing vulnerabilities and constraints on growth and development. Such approaches will need to use large-scale adaptation projects in both the rural and urban sectors to create jobs, achieve economic diversification and trigger faster growth.

A missing element in the current discussion—one central to achieving a more integrated approach—is industrial policy, consideration of which has been out of fashion in recent years on the grounds that "picking winners" has a long history of failure, particularly in developing countries. However, at a time when developing countries must industrialize to meet their development goals even as they strive to achieve climate goals, it is difficult to imagine an integrated approach which does not take industrial policy seriously. Stronger intellectual property rights and efforts to attract foreign direct investment (FDI) are no substitute for sound industrial policies in developing countries.

The development of new low-emissions technologies will respond to supply-push (such as targeted cheap credit) and demand-pull (such as a policy-induced price of carbon) factors. The sooner these are adopted, the faster cost savings will be linked to learning and wider diffusion. The longer the wait, the higher the required emissions reduction will be and the slower the cost buy-downs. Leapfrogging, through the import of such technologies, holds out the possibility of more vigorous improvements in energy efficiency, from supply to end use, expanded shares of renewables, more natural gas and less coal, and early deployment of carbon capture and storage.

Such transformational changes in the energy system need support from research, development and deployment (RD&D), removal of trade barriers, and effective capacity-building. Centres for low-emissions technology innovation could have an important role to play. At least in the initial stages, the centres are likely to be publicly funded, though the precise details of the mix of donor, public and private funding would vary across countries and over time. What combination of basic research, field trials, business incubator services, venture capital funding, technical advice and support, and policy and market analysis is adopted will also be very much contingent on local conditions and challenges. In some cases, regional centres might represent the best way to benefit from economies of scale and scope.

A New Deal?

Those organizing a more integrated policy approach to the development and climate challenges could certainly learn from the experience connected with introducing the New Deal policies in the United States of America in response to the Depression of the 1930s. In particular, the interconnected investments in energy, transportation, agriculture and health laid the foundations not only for a return to full employment but also for a strong industrial take-off in some of the most underdeveloped parts of the United States, crowding substantial private investment into new sources of job creation.

Since 1945, successful developing countries have also used a mixture of market incentives and strong State interventions to generate rapid growth and structural changes. Such support was often guided by an encompassing development vision that judged policy interventions in terms of their contribution to diversifying economic activity, creating jobs and reducing poverty.

By contrast, many developing countries have suffered from a rollback of the role of the State during the lost decade of the 1980s. As a result, the ability of the public sector to provide effective and innovative leadership in such a complex area as climate change is severely strained. Those countries will need support in rebuilding the State infrastructure in order to be able to discharge the additional responsibilities attendant upon achieving the objectives of the climate agenda.

Adjusting through investment

An integrated approach entails not only finding solutions in situations involving traditional market failures but also dealing with systemic threats and managing large-scale adjustments in economic activity. The only sensible response is to mix market solutions with other mechanisms, including public investment.

It is important to see investments in both adaptation and mitigation as part of a larger shift to a new investment path involving a broad number of sectors and regions, and aimed at weakening the climate constraint on global growth. If history is any guide, industrial-scale production and distribution of cleaner energy should exhibit scale economies and trigger a range of complementary investment opportunities in different sectors of the economy and in new technologies. Figure O.3 presents some of the major technologies involved and how soon they might be ready for large-scale deployment. Related investments, in many developing countries, will be needed to raise agricultural productivity, improve forest management, and ensure, along with a more reliable water supply and a more efficient transport system, the steady expansion of green jobs.

In the short and medium run, however, mitigating and adapting to climate change increase the cost of development. Perhaps as much as $40 billion might be needed to make existing investments climate-proof, and the figure for ensuring resilience in the face of future developments will be much larger. The United Nations Development Programme (UNDP) has estimated that this would require $86 billion annually (by 2016) and failure to act quickly on mitigation will only add to that figure. Investment in mitigation will be of a much higher order. Estimates by McKinsey & Company, a global management consulting firm, suggest that additional investments of up to $800 billion annually by 2030 would be needed to meet stabilization targets. The *Survey* argues, however, that many of these investments will have to be front-loaded. The figure is likely to be in excess of one trillion dollars.

Financing these investments will be among the big constraints on the shift to low-emissions economies in most developing countries, particularly where domestic markets for low-emissions technologies are small. Macroeconomic policies will need to be consistently pro-investment; and institutional reforms, including the revival, recapitalization and refocusing of development banks, will need to be adopted. However, such constraints serve as an important reminder that this time around, any "green new deal" will need to have a global dimension.

Figure O.3
Technology development and CO$_2$ mitigation for power generation

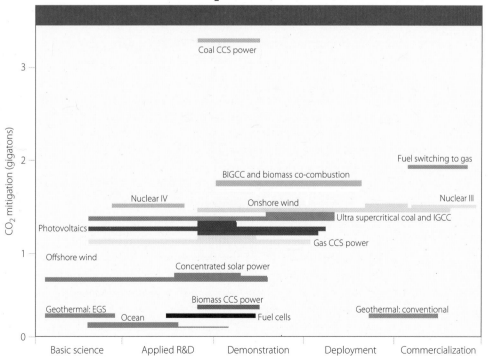

Source: International Energy Agency (2008a).

Abbreviations: CCS, carbon capture and sequestration; IGCC, integrated gasification combined cycle; BIGCC, biomass integrated gasification combined cycle; EGS, enhanced geothermal systems.

A Global Sustainable New Deal

The search for sustainable alternatives that counter the threat of dangerous climate change must at the same time deal with a legacy of highly uneven economic development and a growing level of insecurity linked to interrelated crises in the supply of food, energy, water and finance.

A Global Sustainable New Deal should seek to establish a new public policy agenda aimed at placing countries on a different developmental pathway—one that protects the natural resource base in an equitable manner without compromising job creation and catch-up growth. Such a goal can be achieved only if Governments of rich and poor countries alike come together in collaborative initiatives.

Such initiatives should follow basic principles in order to maximize their contributions to development goals. They could be pursued, in part, by using the resources mobilized by the stimulus packages of developed countries, but reform of the multilateral financial and trading systems will be needed, over the medium term, to support a more stable global economy and promote investment-led growth in a low-emissions economy. Over the longer term, that growth will be sustainable only if developing countries are able to mobilize sufficient domestic resources.

Managing the Global Sustainable New Deal

In order for the combined challenges of development and climate change to be met, nothing less than a fundamental transformation as regards financial and technological support to developing countries is needed. Such a transformation would involve moving beyond the long-standing promises of such support from developed countries, to a full-blown strategy of how they will support the investments developing countries would have to undertake to shift quickly to a low-emissions, high-growth path.

What also needs to change is the intergovernmental process on climate change, whose evolution has been governed largely by principles of environmental protection. This has meant that the consideration of development has been left to other forums and institutions. A new focus on development needs to be engendered and the regime and governance mechanisms need to build appropriate linkages and processes around sustainable development at the international level, which would encompass:

- *An investment-based approach.* A low-emissions growth trajectory will not be created through prudent macroeconomic policies and rapid market liberalization. Instead, massive investments (from the public and private sectors) in new infrastructure, new capacities and new institutions will be needed to meet mitigation and adaptation challenges
- *A collaborative agenda.* Inherent trust among developed and developing countries is a central need in tackling a global challenge: Weak performance on mitigation obligations by high-emitters in the North, combined with minimal operational support for technology and finance, has resulted in a large trust deficit. This must change, as solving the climate problem without participation of the South is no longer possible. This collaboration requires a consistent focus on a fairer world order and a system of global governance that is open transparent, participatory and responsible

- *A commitment to phasing out high-emissions growth.* "Dirty" subsidies have been estimated at $250 billion or (0.5 per cent of world gross product) in 2005. Redirecting these to clean energy sources—but not at the expense of access to energy services in developing countries—would boost the transition to low-emissions high growth. Moreover, the rights of countries that depend on the extraction of fossil fuels, which have been recognized in the United Nations Framework Convention on Climate Change, should be an important determinant of the policies chosen.

New financing mechanisms

The difficulty of access to appropriate and predictable levels of finance, at an acceptable cost, has been a consistently binding constraint on investment and growth in poor countries. While the estimates for meeting the mitigation and adaptation challenge cover a wide range, the figures suggested earlier will pose a major obstacle to climate progress in many developing countries. Currently, the financing needed to meet the climate challenge that is available to developing countries from bilateral and multilateral sources is estimated at about $21 billion. That amount will have to rise manifold, and sooner rather than later. This is a daunting challenge.

If private investment is to fulfil its role, predictable long-term signals will need to be established based on the price of carbon, using a combination of taxation, emissions trading and regulation. However, the limited evolution of carbon markets and the current financial crisis will discourage private investment in the short and medium term at a most critical time, since new infrastructure projects will be producing emissions for decades. Resource mobilization for public investment, from both national and international sources, needs to be pursued more vigorously, and on a much larger scale.

Funding of the large public investments required to meet the challenge, particularly with respect to mitigation, where the front-loading of investments is essential, is unlikely to come through ODA even if donor countries live up to their commitments. Utilization of new funding sources, such as "government green bonds" and special drawing rights (SDRs) from the International Monetary Fund, needs to be considered. Global levies or taxes on bunker fuel for air and ship transport, air travel or financial transactions will also have a role. However, administrative obstacles and concerns about their possibly regressive nature have still to be addressed.

It is widely understood that there is need for an enhanced financial mechanism to deal with the massiveness of the scale of the transfers required for mitigation and adaptation in developing countries. There remains considerable disagreement however, regarding whether new institutional arrangements, including funds, are needed, or existing arrangements and funds, suitably reformed and scaled up, would suffice. Concerning the governance of such a mechanism, the crucial question is *who will decide what* with respect to the management and allocation of financial resources.

Funding the incremental costs of adaptation will, in most cases, be linked to development-related funding, for example, for infrastructure investment and diversification efforts in developing countries. The closeness of the link may partly explain why institutions like the World Bank have set up their own climate funds. The scale of such funding remains woefully inadequate and scaling up is an urgent challenge.

The scale of the financing needed to make the big push to a low-emissions development pathway is several orders of magnitude greater than that available through current financing arrangements. Financing the mitigation challenge might therefore warrant making more radical changes in the existing international architecture. Some possible measures include:

- *A global clean energy fund.* In light of the urgency of this challenge, a new global fund to address climate change mitigation in developing countries, established outside the existing multilateral financing institutions and with a governance structure acceptable to all parties to the United Nations Framework Convention on Climate Change, needs to be considered. In time, existing mitigation funds could become part of this larger mechanism

- *A global feed-in tariff regime.* A global feed-in tariff programme could provide guaranteed purchase prices to producers of renewable energy in developing countries over the next two decades. This mechanism would lead to an automatic drawdown of subsidies over time as production and incomes increase. Delivery mechanisms would have to be carefully designed so as to ensure a level playing field for all competing technologies and on-grid and off-grid operators and benefit targeted low-income consumers. The programme should be accompanied by provision of support to local renewable components industries to ensure that national production capacities are spurred and countries are able to satisfy a growing share of the increased demand for renewable energy locally, thereby benefiting from additional job creation

- *A reformed Clean Development Mechanism.* The United Nations Framework Convention on Climate Change Secretariat estimates that, by 2020, offsetting could yield up to $40.8 billion per year, although this is still only a fraction of estimated incremental costs in developing countries. The present deficiencies of the Clean Development Mechanism for facilitating large-scale resource transfers are widely acknowledged. Much attention has focused on reforming the Mechanism in such a way as to replace its project focus with a programmatic and/or policy focus, in the expectation of larger impacts, shorter funding cycles and lower transaction costs

- *Forest-related financing mechanisms.* Forestry accounts for about 17 per cent of global greenhouse gas emissions. Several new financing initiatives have been launched to help reduce emissions from deforestation and forest degradation, including the World Bank Forest Carbon Partnership Facility and the United Nations Collaborative Programme on Reducing Emissions from Deforestation and Forest Degradation in Developing Countries (UN-REDD Programme). Sustainable forest management is the right approach to dealing with mitigation in the forest sector as well as other forest sector challenges; financing should enable not only climate change mitigation but also adaptation.

Technology transfer

Existing best-practice technologies for a low-emissions economy are already in place in advanced economies and further breakthroughs are likely. Technology transfer is therefore a critical international public policy issue. At the same time, developing countries will need support in building their own technological capacity so as to ensure that they both undergo a smooth transition to a low-emissions economy and maintain competitiveness in an open global economy. The supporting architecture for dealing with these dimensions of the challenge is still poorly developed and in need of urgent attention focused on:

- *A climate technology programme.* An operational programme, supported by a Secretariat and various panels of experts, needs to be established, possibly under the auspices of the Conference of the Parties to the United Nations Framework Convention on Climate Change to examine the various dimensions of the technology challenge in developing countries and, where appropriate, to provide technical assistance with respect to, inter alia, energy efficiency in buildings; greening industrial supply chains; deployment and maintenance of renewable energy infrastructure; integrated waste management; water and sanitation; and extension services to promote sustainable agriculture

- *A global research, development and deployment fund.* Current trends have not been favourable for technology development and demonstration. Public expenditures in countries members of the Organization for Economic Cooperation and Development (OECD) on energy-related research, development and deployment have declined to some $8 billion from about $12 billion two decades ago, while private expenditures have declined to $4.5 billion compared with almost $8 billion a decade ago. This means that in the world today we are investing barely $2 per person per year in energy-related research, development and deployment activities. This needs to increase by a factor of 2 to 3 in order to enable the transition towards new and advanced technologies in energy systems. Given the interrelated threats of climate change and food security, special attention may need to be given to the challenges facing agriculture in the developing world in the context of the green revolution

- *A balanced intellectual property regime for technology transfer.* The parties to the United Nations Framework Convention on Climate Change need to agree on the role of intellectual property in the transfer of technology. There are several flexibilities available within the framework of the Agreement on Trade-related Aspects of Intellectual Property Rights[5] such as compulsory licences, exceptions to patents rights, regulating voluntary licences, and strict application of patentability criteria. These measures may enable access to technologies to a certain degree but their use is limited to specific circumstances and they are usually more difficult to operationalize in developing countries. Options such as allowing developing countries to exclude critical sectors from patenting, as well as a global technology pool for climate change, merit serious consideration, as these options would provide certainty and predictability in accessing technologies and further enable much-needed research and development for local adaptation and diffusion, which would further reduce the cost of the technologies. In addition, modalities for access to publicly funded technologies by developing-country firms need to be explored.

---

5   See *Legal Instruments Embodying the Results of the Uruguay Round of Multilateral Trade Negotiations, done at Marrakesh on 15 April 1994* (GATT Secretariat publication, Sales No. GATT/1994-7).

Trade

Serious discussion of the links between trade and climate change has been stymied by the impasse in the Doha Round of negotiations. As Governments are becoming serious about addressing climate change, the old trade and environment debates on how to distinguish between legitimate environmental and health protection measures as allowed under the rules of the World Trade Organization and disguised trade protectionism measures need to be revived.

Trade is important because environmental technologies and know-how are generated primarily in developed countries and transferred to developing countries mainly through embodied technologies in imported goods and services, FDI or licensing. If Governments of Annex I countries should choose to pursue border measures (for example, border tax adjustments) to protect their energy-intensive industries based on the carbon directly and indirectly emitted in the production of a product, it would become necessary to address the unresolved issue of how to treat processes and production methods. Because subsidies are and will continue to be used to support the development of alternative energies, the issue of determining how to handle those subsidies and which ones are non-actionable under the rules of the World Trade Organization will also have to be dealt with.

Last but not least, these issues need to be resolved taking into account the principle of common and differentiated responsibilities as embodied in the United Nations Framework Convention on Climate Change and its equivalent within the framework of the World Trade Organization, namely, special and differentiated treatment for developing countries. If these issues are not resolved adequately, they may result in protracted trade disputes.

Sha Zukang
Under-Secretary-General
for Economic and Social Affairs
June 2009

Contents

Boxes

Figures

Tables

Explanatory notes

The following symbols have been used in the tables throughout the report:

..   **Two dots** indicate that data are not available or are not separately reported.

–   **A dash** indicates that the amount is nil or negligible.

-    **A hyphen (-)** indicates that the item is not applicable.

-    **A minus sign (-)** indicates deficit or decrease, except as indicated.

.   **A full stop (.)** is used to indicate decimals.

/   **A slash (/)** between years indicates a crop year or financial year, for example, 1990/91.

-    **Use of a hyphen (-)** between years, for example, 1990-1991, signifies the full period involved, including the beginning and end years.

     Reference to "dollars" ($) indicates United States dollars, unless otherwise stated.

     Reference to "billions" indicates one thousand million.

     Reference to "tons" indicates metric tons, unless otherwise stated.

     Annual rates of growth or change, unless otherwise stated, refer to annual compound rates.

     Details and percentages in tables do not necessarily add to totals, because of rounding.

The following abbreviations have been used:

AAUs	assigned amount units	EU	European Union
ACP	African, Caribbean and Pacific Group of States	EU ETS	Emission Trading Scheme of the European Union
APEC	Asia-Pacific Economic Cooperation	FAO	Food and Agriculture Organization of the United Nations
BAU	business-as-usual		
BIGCC	biomass integrated gasification combined cycle	FDI	foreign direct investment
boe	barrel of oil equivalent	FFV	flex-fuel vehicle
CAIT	Climate Analysis Indicators Tool	FIT	feed-in tariff
CCS	carbon capture and sequestration	GATT	General Agreement on Tariffs and Trade
CDIAC	Carbon Dioxide Information Analysis Center	GCCA	Global Climate Change Alliance (European Commission)
CDM	Clean Development Mechanism		
CERs	certified emission reductions	GDP	gross domestic product
CFCs	chlorofluorocarbons	GDRs	Greenhouse Development Rights
CFI	Climate and Forest Initiative (Norway)	GEF	Global Environment Facility
CFLs	compact fluorescent lamps	GFDRR	Global Facility for Disaster Reduction and Recovery
CIF	Climate Investment Fund		
CIS	Commonwealth of Independent States	GHG	greenhouse gas
CO2	carbon dioxide	GIS	geographic information system
CO2e	carbon dioxide equivalent	GNP	gross national product
CSP	Concentrating solar power (Global Environment Facility)	GPM	United Nations Global Policy Model
		GPS	Global Positioning System
EPA	United States Environmental Protection Agency	Gt	gigatons
EPPs	environmentally preferable products	GtCO2	gigatons of carbon dioxide
ESTs	environmentally sound technologies	GtCO2e	gigatons of carbon dioxide equivalent
ETF-IW	Environmental Transformation Fund-International Window (United Kingdom)	GW	gigawatt
		GWh	Gigawatt-hours

HS	Harmonized Commodity Description and Coding System (World Customs Organization)	PV	photovoltaic
HVAC	heating, ventilating and air conditioning	R&D	research and development
IAEA	International Atomic Energy Agency	RD&D	research, development and deployment
ICI	International Climate Initiative (Germany)	REDD	reduction of emissions from deforestation and forest degradation
IEA	International Energy Agency	RFPs	renewable portfolio standards
IFC	International Finance Corporation	RGGI	Regional Greenhouse Gas Initiative (United States)
IFCI	International Forest Carbon Initiative (Australia)	SCCF	Special Climate Change Fund (Global Environment Facility)
IGCC	integrated gasification combined cycle	SDRs	special drawing rights
IISD	International Institute for Sustainable Development	SECCI	Sustainable Energy and Climate Change Initiative (Inter-American Development Bank)
ILO	International Labour Organization	SGP	Small Grants Programme (Global Environment Facility)
IMF	International Monetary Fund	SPA	Strategic Priority on Adaptation (Global Environment Facility)
IOE	International Organisation of Employers		
IPCC	Intergovernmental Panel on Climate Change	SRES	Special Report on Emissions Scenarios (Intergovernmental Panel on Climate Change)
ITUC	International Trade Union Confederation	tCO_2e	ton of carbon dioxide equivalent
kg	kilogram	3CEE	Three-Country Energy Efficiency Project (Brazil, China, India)
km2	square kilometres		
kW	kilowatt	TRIPS	Agreement on Trade-related Aspects of Intellectual Property Rights
kWh	kilowatt-hours	TVA	Tennessee Valley Authority
LDCs	least developed countries	TWe	terawatts electric
LDCF	Least Developed Countries' Fund (Global Environment Facility)	UNCTAD	United Nations Conference on Trade and Development
LPG	liquefied petroleum gas	UN/DESA	Department of Economic and Social Affairs of the United Nations Secretariat
LTMS	long-term mitigation scenarios		
MDGs	Millennium Development Goals	UNDP	United Nations Development Programme
MIT	Massachusetts Institute of Technology	UNEP	United Nations Environment Programme
mm	millimetres	UNFCCC	United Nations Framework Convention on Climate Change
MOC	meridional overturning circulation		
MW	megawatt	UN/HABITAT	United Nations Human Settlements Programme
NAFTA	North American Free Trade Agreement		
NAMAs	nationally appropriate mitigation actions	UNHCR	Office of the United Nations High Commissioner for Refugees
NAPA	National Adaptation Programme of Action		
ODA	official development assistance	UN-REDD	United Nations Collaborative Programme on Reducing Emissions from Deforestation and Forest Degradation in Developing Countries
OECD	Organization for Economic Cooperation and Development		
OPEC	Organization of the Petroleum Exporting Countries	USSR	Union of Soviet Socialist Republics
OTA	Office of Technology Assessment (United States Congress)	WGP	world gross product
		WHO	World Health Organization
ppm	parts per million	WIPO	World Intellectual Property Organization
PPMs	processes or production methods	WMO	World Meteorological Organization
ppmv	parts per million by volume	WTO	World Trade Organization
ppp	purchasing power parity		
PRSPs	Poverty Reduction Strategy Papers		

The designations employed and the presentation of the material in this publication do not imply the expression of any opinion whatsoever on the part of the United Nations Secretariat concerning the legal status of any country, territory, city or area or of its authorities, or concerning the delimitation of its frontiers or boundaries.

The term "country" as used in the text of this report also refers, as appropriate, to territories or areas.

For analytical purposes, unless otherwise specified, the following country groupings and subgroupings have been used:

Developed economies (developed market economies):

Australia, Canada, European Union, Iceland, Japan, New Zealand, Norway, Switzerland, United States of America.

Subgroupings of developed economies:

Major developed economies (Group of Seven):

Canada, France, Germany, Italy, Japan, United Kingdom of Great Britain and Northern Ireland, United States of America.

European Union (EU):

Austria, Belgium, Bulgaria, Cyprus, Czech Republic, Denmark, Estonia, Finland, France, Germany, Greece, Hungary, Ireland, Italy, Latvia, Lithuania, Luxembourg, Malta, Netherlands, Poland, Portugal, Romania, Slovakia, Slovenia, Spain, Sweden, United Kingdom of Great Britain and Northern Ireland.

EU-15:

Austria, Belgium, Denmark, Finland, France, Greece, Germany, Ireland, Italy, Luxembourg, Netherlands, Portugal, Spain, Sweden, United Kingdom of Great Britain and Northern Ireland.

New EU member States:

Bulgaria, Cyprus, Czech Republic, Estonia, Hungary, Latvia, Lithuania, Malta, Poland, Romania, Slovakia, Slovenia.

Economies in transition:

South-eastern Europe:

Albania, Bosnia and Herzegovina, Croatia, Montenegro, Serbia, the former Yugoslav Republic of Macedonia.

Commonwealth of Independent States (CIS):

Armenia, Azerbaijan, Belarus, Georgia, Kazakhstan, Kyrgyzstan, Republic of Moldova, Russian Federation, Tajikistan, Turkmenistan, Ukraine, Uzbekistan.

Developing economies:

Africa, Asia and the Pacific (excluding Australia, Japan, New Zealand and the member States of CIS in Asia), Latin America and the Caribbean.

Subgroupings of Africa:

Northern Africa:

Algeria, Egypt, Libyan Arab Jamahiriya, Morocco, Tunisia.

Sub-Saharan Africa, excluding Nigeria and South Africa (commonly contracted to "sub-Saharan Africa"):

All other African countries except Nigeria and South Africa.

Southern Africa:

Angola, Botswana, Lesotho, Malawi, Mauritius, Mozambique, Namibia, South Africa, Swaziland, Zambia, Zimbabwe.

East Africa:

Burundi, Comoros, Democratic Republic of the Congo, Djibouti, Eritrea, Ethiopia, Kenya, Madagascar, Rwanda, Seychelles, Somalia, Sudan, Uganda, United Republic of Tanzania.

West Africa:

Burkina Faso, Benin, Cape Verde, Côte d'Ivoire, Gambia, Ghana, Guinea, Guinea-Bissau, Liberia, Mali, Mauritania, Niger, Nigeria, Senegal, Sierra Leone, Togo.

Central Africa:

Cameroon, Central African Republic, Chad, Congo, Equatorial Guinea, Gabon, Sao Tome and Principe.

Subgroupings of Asia and the Pacific:

Western Asia:

Bahrain, Iraq, Israel, Jordan, Kuwait, Lebanon, Occupied Palestinian Territory, Oman, Qatar, Saudi Arabia, Syrian Arab Republic, Turkey, United Arab Emirates, Yemen.

East and South Asia:

All other developing economies in Asia and the Pacific (including China, unless stated otherwise). This group is further subdivided into:

South Asia:

Bangladesh, Bhutan, India, Iran (Islamic Republic of), Maldives, Nepal, Pakistan, Sri Lanka.

East Asia:

All other developing economies in Asia and the Pacific.

Subgroupings of Latin America and the Caribbean:

South America:

Argentina, Bolivia (Plurinational State of), Brazil, Chile, Colombia, Ecuador, Paraguay, Peru, Uruguay, Venezuela (Bolivarian Republic of).

Mexico and Central America:

Costa Rica, El Salvador, Guatemala, Honduras, Mexico, Nicaragua, Panama.

Caribbean:

Barbados, Cuba, Dominican Republic, Guyana, Haiti, Jamaica, Trinidad and Tobago.

Least developed countries:

Afghanistan, Angola, Bangladesh, Benin, Bhutan, Burkina Faso, Burundi, Cambodia, Central African Republic, Chad, Comoros, Democratic Republic of the Congo, Djibouti, Equatorial Guinea, Eritrea, Ethiopia, Gambia, Guinea, Guinea-Bissau, Haiti, Kiribati, Lao People's Democratic Republic, Lesotho, Liberia, Madagascar, Malawi, Maldives, Mali, Mauritania, Mozambique, Myanmar, Nepal, Niger, Rwanda, Samoa, Sao Tome and Principe, Senegal, Sierra Leone, Solomon Islands, Somalia, Sudan, Timor-Leste, Togo, Tuvalu, Uganda, United Republic of Tanzania, Vanuatu, Yemen, Zambia.

Small island developing States:

American Samoa, Anguilla, Antigua and Barbuda, Aruba, Bahamas, Barbados, Belize, British Virgin Islands, Cape Verde, Commonwealth of the Northern Mariana Islands, Comoros, Cook Islands, Cuba, Dominica, Dominican Republic, Fiji, French Polynesia, Grenada, Guam, Guinea-Bissau, Guyana, Haiti, Jamaica, Kiribati, Maldives, Marshall Islands, Mauritius, Micronesia (Federated States of), Montserrat, Nauru, Netherlands Antilles, New Caledonia, Niue, Palau, Papua New Guinea, Puerto Rico, Saint Kitts and Nevis, Saint Lucia, Saint Vincent and the Grenadines, Samoa, Sao Tome and Principe, Seychelles, Singapore, Solomon Islands, Suriname, Timor-Leste, Tonga, Trinidad and Tobago, Tuvalu, United States Virgin Islands, Vanuatu.

Parties to the United Nations Framework Convention on Climate Change:

Annex I Parties:

Australia, Austria, Belarus, Belgium, Bulgaria, Canada, Croatia, Czech Republic, Denmark, Estonia, European Community, Finland, France, Germany, Greece, Hungary, Iceland, Ireland, Italy, Japan, Latvia, Liechtenstein, Lithuania, Luxembourg, Monaco, Netherlands, New Zealand, Norway, Poland, Portugal, Romania, Russian Federation, Slovakia, Slovenia, Spain, Sweden, Switzerland, Turkey, Ukraine, United Kingdom of Great Britain and Northern Ireland, United States of America.

Annex II Parties:

Annex II parties are the parties included in Annex I that are members of the Organization for Economic Cooperation and Development but not the parties included in Annex I that are economies in transition.

Chapter I
Climate change and the development challenge

Introduction

We are living in the best of times and in the worst of times. Over the long sweep of its history, our world has never been more prosperous, inventive or interconnected than it is today. Yet, economic insecurity has become ubiquitous (and was becoming so even before the financial meltdown), social divisions are greater than ever, and the health of the planet has never been so fragile. These are interrelated challenges that can be effectively addressed only through cooperation and collective actions, at both the national and international levels.

In recent years, collective actions have been hampered by technocratic complacency, which privileged private means over public ends. A combination of deregulation, at both the national and international levels, and corporate leadership skills was deemed all that was needed to find the quickest and most efficient solutions to a wide range of contemporary policy challenges, from health-care provision and urban renewal to poverty alleviation and climate change. This mindset has been dominated by the rhetoric of targets, partnerships, synergies, etc., which, draining policy discussion of much of its substance, inevitably tends to ignore or gloss over the conflicts and difficult trade-offs that accompany all big policy challenges.

Climate change will be among the biggest of those challenges over the coming decades. It is, at a very profound level, an existential threat. Recent estimates suggest that 300,000 people are dying each year as a result of global warming and the lives of 300 million more are being seriously threatened. We know a good deal more than ever before about why this is happening. The Intergovernmental Panel on Climate Change (IPCC), established in 1988 by the United Nations Environmental Programme (UNEP) and the World Meteorological Organization (WMO), has proved an invaluable source of information and analyses concerning why and how our climate is changing and with what consequences. The members of the wider scientific community have backed up their efforts with a mountain of supportive evidence and modelling exercises. Theirs is a sobering picture of how the stretching of our environmental fabric due to the emission of man-made greenhouse gases (GHGs) has already led to serious tears and is getting closer to a snapping point. The race to keep global temperatures within safe bounds is now a race against time. By 2050, there needs to be a cut in global emissions, in the order of 50-80 per cent, which is equivalent to a reduction in carbon dioxide (CO_2) levels from roughly 40 gigatons (Gt) per year (at present) to 8-20 Gt.

So far, however, increased scientific understanding and greater public awareness have not translated into a focused policy response. This is particularly true in today's advanced industrialized countries: although it is two centuries of their carbon-fuelled growth that lies behind the warming trend, they have failed to commit the resources and the ambitious political will needed to establish an alternative development pathway. At the same time, the international community—most recently at the thirteenth session of the Conference of the Parties of the United Nations Framework Convention on Climate Change,[1] held in Bali, Indonesia, in December 2007—has reaffirmed that growth and

An estimated 300,000 people are dying each year as a result of global warming and the lives of 300 million more are being seriously challenged

The failure of advanced countries to match words with deeds in respect of the climate challenge has made it difficult to convince developing countries to turn to alternative (and expensive) energy sources

development remain the overriding objectives of the vast majority of people on this planet. The failure of advanced countries to match words with deeds in respect of the climate challenge has made it difficult to convince developing countries to now turn to alternative (and expensive) energy sources to meet their own (significant) development objectives.

In 2009, a new round of climate negotiations is expected to move the agenda a big step forward. Some key questions will likely shape those negotiations, namely, How much emissions reduction should take place, and where and by when? How much will it cost to meet the targets and how will they be covered? How should a proper and enhanced global adaptation response be framed in light of the significant impacts of climate change?

The present *Survey* does not try to provide any hard-and-fast answers to these questions. The answers can be found only through open, inclusive and frank negotiations among all the contracting parties. But even assuming that an agreement is reached, the work of translating it into an effective programme of transformative change will be an ongoing process which evolves through adjustments, continuous consultation and response to persistent policy challenges. Accordingly, the *Survey* has chosen to assemble agreed building blocks of a long-term solution—mitigation, adaptation, technology and finance—in order to consider what is being asked of developing countries in terms of adjustments, trade-offs and challenges, and what the international community must do to ensure that those countries are able to contribute to meeting the climate challenge without jeopardizing their development goals.

The *Survey* proceeds essentially by working back from 2050, by which time there will be another 3 billion people on this planet, the vast majority of whom will be urban-dwellers and living in the developing world. If current trends continue, not only will most of them still be poor and insecure but they will also be much more vulnerable to climate-related threats posed by warmer temperatures.

Developing countries pursuing catch-up growth and industrialization must find alternatives to the profligate energy model of the past

A necessary part of the solution lies in lowering the level of emissions released into the atmosphere, which is feasible to the extent that the technological know-how that can help build low-emissions pathways exists or will exist shortly. This shift, however, is neither inevitable nor inconsequential. In advanced countries, significant emissions reduction has to be accompanied by a return to full employment and a search for energy security. In developing countries, pursuing a low-emissions path must be compatible with catch-up growth, industrialization and urban expansion.

Since the focus of this publication is to a great extent on the interrelated climate and development challenges facing policymakers in the developing world, it consequently pays particular attention to the mitigation challenge linked to energy use (chap. II). But inasmuch as building resilience with respect to climate threats is, for many poor countries, just as, or even more, important (chap. III), the *Survey* seeks to avoid fostering the erroneous notion that countries must choose between mitigation and adaptation. To this end, it spells out the shared opportunities and synergies to be derived from investment-led responses to both these challenges, from forging truly integrated strategies and from reviving the role of an effective developmental State (chap. IV).

A level of international support and solidarity rarely mustered outside a wartime setting is required

The adjustments that are being asked of developing countries are unprecedented and will carry heavy investment costs, particularly in the initial stages of the transition. Those costs present the major obstacle to the development of low-emissions, high-growth pathways. But if properly managed, the investments involved can provide developing countries with a productive basis for mobilizing their own resources to meet the climate challenge. Still, if such a transition is to happen, it will require—so as to ensure both sufficient technological transfers (chap. V) and sufficient access to financial resources (chap. VI)—a level of international support and solidarity rarely mustered outside a wartime setting.

Development in a warming world

The development challenge

The industrial revolution beginning in the late eighteenth century inaugurated two processes of far-reaching consequences. Through the first, a select group of countries were enabled to embark on a modern economic growth path and thereby break the constraints on development imposed by the immutable rhythms of the natural environment and the localization of economic activity. New levers of wealth creation emerged around market specialization, innovation and scale economies, and in the context of industrializing, urbanizing and the greater interconnection of communities. In the wake of this transformation, the income gap between the group of early starters and the rest of the world widened rapidly, all the more so to the extent that the exploitation of resources and markets by colonizers suppressed economic opportunities in many countries and communities across the world for a century or more.

Through the second process, the relation between human society and the natural environment was transformed: instead of merely adapting, humans now dominated the environment. The result has been ever increasing demands on the environment in the service of expanding output. In particular, the traditional energy sources (biomass, water and wind) utilized to complement manual labour and animal transport were replaced, initially by coal and then (beginning in the early 1900s) by oil, for the purpose of powering increasingly sophisticated machines and means of transport. Access to these cheaper fossil fuels has been a critical stepping stone on all modern development pathways. However, the full cost of exploiting carbon-based fuels, and other natural assets, has often gone unrecorded.

Over the past 50 years, developing countries have been caught up in a process of trying to close the economic gaps opened over the previous two centuries. The process has not been smooth, nor has success been automatic. External constraints and shocks have persistently upset efforts in many countries, holding back growth prospects. While some developing countries, particularly those in East Asia, have been successful (as evidenced by their having gotten close to or, in some cases, their having surpassed the G7 countries in terms of per capita income), they have been atypical (see figure I.1). In fact, as documented in *World Economic and Social Survey 2006* (United Nations, 2006), beginning with the debt crisis of the late 1970s, constraints had tightened and shocks intensified, which led to a fragmented and divergent pattern of global growth. The most notable success story through all this has been China, whose uninterrupted growth over the past 30 years explains many of the positive aggregate trends in social and economic performance in the developing world over that period. Between 2002 and mid-2008, unprecedented strong growth was registered almost everywhere, including in the least developed countries, reflecting, in part, the growing economic interactions among developing countries themselves. However, that phenomenon came to an abrupt end with the onset of the most severe economic crisis since the 1930s. The heavy reliance on debt which fuelled much of that growth has proved an unreliable substitute for sound development strategy (see United Nations, 2009).

Government leaders in many developing countries are concerned that climate change is being used by those at the top of the development ladder—and who gorged excessively on the global carbon budget to get there—to again constrain the efforts of their countries to climb higher. How developing countries can achieve catch-up growth and economic convergence in a carbon-constrained world and what the advanced countries must do to relieve their concerns have become leading questions for policymakers at the national and international levels.

Figure I.1
The income gap between G7 countries and selected regions, 1980-2007

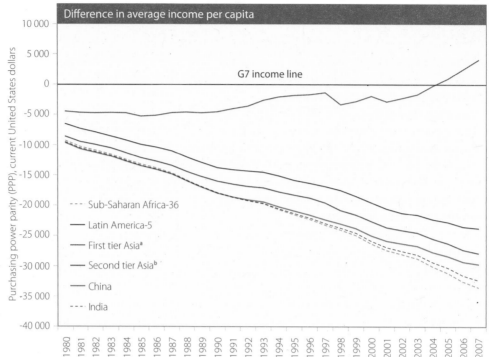

Source: DESA/DPAD/DSP calculations, based on WB-WDI online database.
a Hong Kong Special Administration Region of China; Republic of Korea, Singapore; Taiwan Province of China.
b Indonesia, Malaysia, Philippines, Thailand.

The climate challenge

The science behind the assertion that our climate is changing for the worse, thanks to human activity, is unequivocal. The climate challenge arises from interference in the natural warming effect of the planet: by causing an increase in the flow of greenhouse gases in the atmosphere, human activity has led to an increase in the concentration of those gases from a pre-industrial level of 250 parts per million (ppm) of carbon dioxide equivalent (CO_2e) to 430 ppm and is causing a major disruption in the natural climatic process of the planet. These gases have a long gestation cycle in the atmosphere; in other words, once emitted, they remain there for decades.

Carbon is the main component of the greenhouse gases that are the leading contributors to global warming. Emissions have reached levels that concern the scientific community principally as a result of energy use by rich countries. Today fossil energy sources provide some 80 per cent of total energy needs. However, they are not the sole source of the problem (table I.1). Globally, forest ecosystems contained 638 billion tons of carbon in 2005, with half of that amount (321 Gt) in forest biomass and deadwood. The estimated average global rate of forest carbon depletion per year is 1.6 Gt, or about 0.25 per cent of total forest carbon. Deforestation and forest degradation are the primary sources of carbon emissions from some developing countries. In 2004, the forest sector accounted for the release of approximately 8.5 gigatons of carbon dioxide equivalent (GtCO_2e),[2] mostly from deforestation, which contributes 17.4 per cent of all human-generated CO_2 emissions.

Emissions have reached levels that concern the scientific community principally as a result of energy use by rich countries

---

2   A gigaton is equal to 1 billion metric tons.

Table I.1
Greenhouse gas emissions (carbon dioxide, methane, perfluorocarbons, hydrochlorofluorocarbons and sulphur hexafluoride) by sector, 2000a

Sector	Megatons of CO_2	Share (percentage)
Energy	24 731.2	59.4
Electricity and heat	10 296.0	24.7
Manufacturing and construction	4 426.5	10.6
Transportation	4 848.1	11.6
Other fuel combustion	3 563.3	8.6
Fugitive emissions	1 597.4	3.8
Industrial processes	1 369.4	3.3
Agriculture	5 729.3	13.8
Land-use change and forestry	7 618.6	18.3
Waste	1 360.5	3.3
International bunkers	829.4	2.0
Total	**41 638.4**	**100.0**

Source: Climate Analysis Indicators Tool (CAIT), version 6.0 (Washington, D.C., World Resources Institute, 2009).

Note: Data on nitrogen dioxide were not available.

a   Including land-use change and international bunkers.

The consequences of rising emission levels are now becoming clear. Global average surface temperature increased by almost 1° C between 1850 and 2000, with a noticeable acceleration in recent decades (see figure I.2). The global average sea level has

Climate change is significantly affecting forests largely owing to changes in temperature and rainfall

Figure I.2
Increase of global mean temperature since 1850

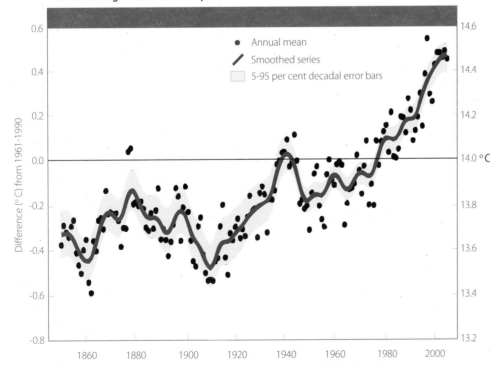

Source: Intergovernmental Panel on Climate Change (2007a).

increased at an average rate of 1.8 millimetres (mm) per year over the period 1961-2003. In the more recent period 1993-2003, this rate of increase has risen to 3.1 mm per year. There have been large changes in the pattern of precipitation, with significant increases in eastern parts of North and South America, Northern Europe, and northern and Central Asia, and decreases in the Sahel, the Mediterranean, Southern Africa and parts of South Asia. The area affected by drought has increased. Extreme weather events have increased in number, scope and intensity. Climate change is significantly affecting forests: there have been changes in their physiology, structure, species composition and health, largely owing to changes in temperature and rainfall. Many tropical forests in Latin America have experienced losses in biodiversity. Increased temperatures and drought result in more frequent outbreaks of pest infestations, more forest fires and increasing alterations in populations of plant and animal species, severely affecting forest health and productivity.

The latest findings of the Intergovernmental Panel on Climate Change suggest that:

> For many key parameters, the climate is already moving beyond the patterns of natural variability within which our society and economy have developed and thrived. These parameters include global mean surface temperature, sea-level rise, ocean and ice-sheet dynamics, ocean acidification, and extreme climatic events. There is a significant risk that many of the trends will accelerate, leading to an increasing risk of abrupt or irreversible climatic shifts.[3]

That the situation will worsen is no longer in doubt, the only question is by how much. Table I.2 below presents the emission scenarios identified by the Intergovernmental Panel on Climate Change and their likely impact on temperatures and sea level by the end of this century.[4] Generally speaking, the A1FI scenario involves the greatest amount of emissions and hence the greatest change in climate, while the B1 scenario entails the least amount of emissions and hence the smallest change in climate.

Moreover, as the Intergovernmental Panel has noted, the scenarios described in its *Special Report on Emission Scenarios* (Nakicenovic and others, 2000) (SRES scenarios), as well as most post-SRES scenarios, fail to take into account the uncertainties with respect to various aspects of "climate processes and feedbacks". These include (a) transmission of heat to lower depths of ocean, causing thermal expansion, (b) contraction of the Greenland ice sheet, (c) contraction of the western Antarctic ice sheet, (d) reduction in the terrestrial and ocean uptake of atmospheric CO_2 as the CO_2 level rises, a phenomenon referred to as "positive carbon cycle feedback", (e) cloud feedback, (f) slowing down or even reversal of the meridional overturning circulation (MOC), etc. These feedbacks add another layer of complexity (and uncertainty) to future projections; however, the Intergovernmental Panel suggests that the impact of climate change will likely be more severe, or even catastrophic.

---

3   Intergovernmental Panel on Climate Change, Key message, "Climatic trends", from the International Scientific Congress on Climate Change: Global Risks, Challenges and Decisions in Copenhagen, 10-12 March 2009.

4   Intergovernmental Panel on Climate Change broadly identified four possible economic pathways (or "storylines"), referred to as A1 (a convergent world with fast economic growth); A2 (a non-convergent world with slow economic growth); B1 (a convergent and more environment-friendly world); and B2 (a non-convergent but environment-friendly world with an intermediate rate of economic growth). In addition to the above four broad storylines, the following three sub-variants of A1 have been distinguished, depending on the energy composition of economic growth: A1FI (relatively greater dependence on fossil fuels); A1B (a more balanced dependence on different energy sources); A1T (a greater reliance on non-fossil energy sources).

Table I.2
Emission scenarios and their impact

Case	Greenhouse gas concentration in 2100 (ppm of CO_2e)	Temperature change (in ° C) in 2090-2099 relative to 1980-1999		Sea-level rise (metres) in 2090-2099 relative to 1980-1999
		Best estimate	Likely range	Model-based range (excluding future rapid dynamical changes in ice flow)
Constant year 2000 concentration		0.6	0.3-0.9	..
B1 scenario	600	1.8	1.1-2.9	0.18-0.38
A1T scenario	700	2.4	1.4-3.8	0.20-0.45
B2 scenario	800	2.4	1.4-3.8	0.20-0.43
A1B scenario	850	2.8	1.7-4.4	0.21-0.48
A2 scenario	1250	3.4	2.0-5.4	0.23-0.51
A1FI scenario	1550	4.0	2.4-6.4	0.26-0.59

Source: Intergovernmental Panel on Climate Change (2007a), table 3.1.

What seems certain is that even if the annual flow of emissions were to stabilize at today's rate, the stock of greenhouse gas emissions in the atmosphere would reach double the pre-industrial level by 2050, resulting in a high probability of dangerous temperature rises, with potentially destabilizing economic and political consequences. The most recent modelling exercise, using the Massachusetts Institute of Technology (MIT) Integrated Global Systems Model, a detailed computer simulation of global economic activity and climate processes, suggests that without massive policy action, there will be a median probability of surface warming of 5.2° C by 2100, with a 90 per cent probability range of 3.5-7.4° C. This can be compared with a median projected increase of just 2.4° C in an earlier (2003) exercise.[5]

Even if the annual flow of emissions were to stabilize at today's rate, the stock of greenhouse gas emissions would reach double the pre-industrial level by 2050

The interdependency challenge

The climate and development challenges are inextricably linked. When the overriding policy priority is economic growth, expanding the reach of energy and transportation infrastructure and making them available to an increasingly urban population and industrial workforce are unavoidable. So are major land-use changes. If developing countries simply replicate the path followed by today's rich countries, the impact on the earth's climate will be devastating.

If developing countries simply replicate the path followed by today's rich countries, the impact on the earth's climate will be devastating

At the same time, prospects for a more sustainable development are likely to be undermined by the direct and indirect impacts of climate change on economic growth; and the resulting diminution of the resources available to undertake actions to achieve effective diversification and resilience will heighten vulnerability to future climate trends and shocks. This vicious circle is already apparent in many arid and semi-arid countries in Africa. Adverse impacts on food and water supplies as well as on health conditions are likely to tighten growth constraints in other parts of the world.

---

5   See *Journal of Climate*, American Meteorological Society, vol. 22, No. 10 (May 2009).

An understanding of the complex ways in which economic development and climate variables interact is still evolving. However, the cumulative and unstable nature of that interaction poses obvious challenges for policymakers. This *Survey* seeks to build its assessment of that challenge around the pivotal role of investment and to examine some of the linkages and feedbacks that, from this starting point, can help define development strategies in a warming world.

From free-riding to burden-sharing

The Stern Review on the Economics of Climate Change (Stern, 2007) launched by the Government of the United Kingdom of Great Britain and Northern Ireland in October 2006 identified climate change as "the greatest market failure the world has seen" and provided the first serious attempt to model the cost of doing nothing in comparison with the cost of adopting an alternative strategy which would hold emissions below a manageable threshold. From this perspective, a form of "climate ethics" emerged centred around the challenge of providing a "global public good" and the need to realign social and private cost by making the polluters pay for the damage they had already caused and would cause in the future if there was no change of course. The Stern report concluded that future generations could be made much better off at relatively little cost to present generations.

Difficult distributional issues, rooted in a very uneven historical pattern of economic development, are obscured by the global public good terminology

Depicting a stable climate as a global public good allows one to make an important rhetorical point about the systemic nature of the challenge and the need for collective action to overcome it. On the other hand, the public good parallel is far from perfect; for one thing, the qualities of non-rivalled and non-excludability do not apply easily to the interrelated challenges of climate change and development. Problems of externalities, of vested interests and market power, and of uncertainty certainly mar this interrelationship, making the market by itself an imperfect instrument for managing these challenges. Moreover, difficult distributional issues, rooted in a very uneven historical pattern of economic development, are obscured by the global public good terminology.

Historically speaking, it is mainly the emissions produced by the currently developed industrialized countries that have caused the dangerous rise in greenhouse gas concentrations. Table I.3 presents the shares of various countries in the cumulative stock of greenhouse gas emissions since 1840; it is estimated that the share of the cumulative total generated by Annex I countries has been three fourths (Raupach and others, 2007). The picture is even starker if per capita emissions are used (see figure I.3).

China's current level of per capita emissions is equivalent only to the level reached by the United States at the time of the First World War

As the concept of burden-sharing is often discussed on the basis of current total emissions, the fact of historical culpability, as reflected in the wide differences in per capita emissions, is sometimes overlooked. Much attention has been given to several big developing countries that have had large emissions in absolute terms in recent years, and much has been made, for example, of the fact that China has replaced the United States as the largest greenhouse gas emitting country. However, their per capita emissions levels remain far below those of the developed countries (and in fact, below those of many other developing countries); indeed, China's current level of per capita emissions today is equivalent only to the level reached by the United States at the time of the First World War.

Moreover, given the dominant economic and political influence of wealthier countries, there exists the potential for a further round of adverse spillover effects from the actions and policies that these countries adopt in response to the climate crisis. The adoption of policies in developed countries could have negative implications for international

Table I.3
Per capita emissions in 2005 and share in cumulative emissions during 1840-2005, selected developed and developing countries and economies in transition

	Share of global cumulative metric tons of carbon emissions 1840-2005 (percentage)	*Per capita emissions in 2005 (metric tons of carbon)*
Developed countries		
United States	27.8	5.3
France	2.7	1.7
Germany	6.7	2.6
United Kingdom	5.9	2.5
Japan	3.6	2.6
Canada	2.0	4.5
Economies in transition		
Poland	1.9	2.2
Russian Federation	8.0	2.9
Developing countries		
China	8.1	1.2
India	2.4	0.3

Source: UN/DESA/DPAD calculations, based on Marland, Boden and Andres (2008), Carbon Dioxide Information Analysis Center (CDIAC) database; and UN/DESA/statistics population database.

Note: The share of the Russian Federation has been computed from data for the former Union of Soviet Socialist Republics (USSR) and is based on the current share of the Russian Federation of emission of the Commonwealth of Independent States (CIS).

Figure I.3
Annual per capita emissions, selected regions, 1950-2005

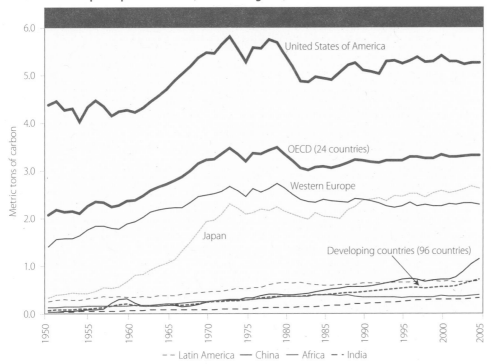

Source: See table I.3.

trade, financial flows and commodity processes, and ultimately for growth in developing countries. Sectoral policies, with respect, for example, to biofuels, can also have serious consequences for the incentives facing developing countries. Policies with respect to the transfer of technology, such as those involving intellectual property rights, will likely have a significant impact on developing countries (see chap. V).

To possibly label developing countries "free riders" for resisting commitments imposed against this backdrop does not make much sense and in fact a much more nuanced framework will be needed within which to address the issue of managing the burden of protecting the climate on an equitable basis. Several proposals for advancing the discussions are currently on the table (see box I.1).

Box I.1

Burden-sharing proposals

Numerous burden-sharing mechanisms have been introduced both in the literature on climate and development and in the global climate negotiation process. A few of the most common proposals include:

- *Equal per capita emissions rights*. Every person has an equal right to the global sink for greenhouse gases. A limit is set on world annual emissions. This limit is divided by world population to arrive at an equal per capita right to emit. Each country is allocated a level of emissions calculated by multiplying the per capita emissions right by the country's population. The limit on global emissions would be reduced over time to achieve a desired stabilization trajectory (Agarwal and Narain, 1991; Narain and Riddle, 2007)

- *Individual targets*. This approach assigns equal emissions rights (or a "universal cap") to individuals in order to meet a desired stabilization trajectory. Each nation's emissions allocation is the sum of its actual individual emissions, for all residents with emissions less than the cap, and its target individual emissions, for all residents with emissions equal to or greater than the cap. In this way, high emitters in a low-emissions country do not free-ride by de facto absorption of low emitters' unused rights (Chakravarty and others, 2008)

- *Contraction and convergence*. This plan combines equal rights to emit with grandfathering (or assigning of rights based on past emissions: the higher the past emissions, the larger the grandfathered emissions rights). Each country is allocated emission rights based on its past emissions. Countries that exceed desired per capita global emissions have their allocation reduced in each succeeding year, while countries that emit less than this target receive a higher allocation each year. Over time, global emissions contract while high- and low- emitting countries converge on the same target per capita emissions (Global Commons Institute, 2008)

- *One standard, two convergences*. Each country is allocated a right to a total contribution to greenhouse gas concentrations based on equal per capita cumulative allowances targeted to meet a desired stabilization trajectory. Differentiated annual emissions ceilings for industrialized and developing countries are adjusted each year to achieve convergence. A relatively high ceiling (in comparison with current emissions) for developing-country emission allows these countries to increase their annual emissions so as to achieve economic growth before having to decrease emissions to stay within their cumulative cap. Trading of emissions rights makes it possible for all developing countries to use their entire allowance (Gao, 2007). A few burden-sharing plans reject the assumption that each country must pay for its own abatement and include a more explicit discussion of who pays for abatement and where

- *Greenhouse development rights*. The burden of emissions reductions is shared among countries according to their capacity to pay for reductions and their responsibility for

Box I.1 (cont'd)

past and current emissions. Each of these criteria is defined with respect to a development threshold so as to explicitly safeguard the right of low-income countries to economic growth; only individuals with incomes above this threshold have a responsibility to pay for emissions abatement. Each country is assigned an emissions allocation based on per capita rights. In addition, each country is assigned an obligation to pay for abatement—whether at home or abroad—based on its share of cumulative emissions starting from a base year (such as 1990) and the cumulative income of its population with incomes above the development threshold (Baer, Athanasion and Kartha, 2007)

- **Revised greenhouse development rights**. Formulated by a team of researchers at Tsinghua University in a report prepared by the Chinese Economists 50 Forum, the revised greenhouse development rights builds on the work of Baer, Athanasion and Kartha (2007) by including cumulative emissions going back to 1850, and accounting for emissions based on consumption (rather than on production) within each country. The result is a greater responsibility on the part of industrialized countries for paying for emissions reductions around the world (Fan and others, 2008).

Source: Ackerman and Stanton (2009).

Still, in a very real sense the future of the planet rests with the efforts of the developing world. Already, the share of rich countries in total global population is less than one sixth and almost all of the additional 3 billion people to be added to that population over the next four decades will reside in the developing world. Developing countries will be central to any international action to protect "their future" (Stern, 2009, p. 13). At the same time, developed countries will have to bear a disproportionately larger share of the initial costs of ensuring that future, in keeping with both the cumulative history of emissions and the differences in economic resources. By the same token, the developing countries themselves will have to take measurable and verifiable steps towards securing that future.

While it is impossible to escape history, in terms of the responsibility for contributions to climate change, it is also prudent to remain focused on potential synergies over the coming decades between the efforts by advanced countries to cut the stock of existing emissions and those aimed at attenuating and eventually reversing the higher emissions that will accompany higher growth, industrial development and urban expansion in developing countries.

Developing countries' scepticism regarding participation in international mitigation efforts has been driven as much by developed countries' recent performance regarding multilateral responses to climate change as by their past developmental record. For example, the Clean Development Mechanism, established under the Kyoto Protocol to the United Nations Framework Convention on Climate Change,[6] which was supposed to be an important link between developed countries' emission reduction efforts and efforts of developing countries, has failed to live up to expectations, in terms of both quantity and quality. Similarly, the level of support provided to various funds set up to help developing countries in respect of adaptation has up to now remained very low and has not matched the scale of the problem (see chaps. III and VI). Lack of bold and generous leadership has given rise to a lack of trust, which now represents a serious obstacle to mustering the international cooperation needed to deal effectively with the climate challenge.

Charles Kindleberger (1986, p. 10) observed that in a world of interdependent nation States with widely differing access to economic resources and political power, effective multilateral cooperation depends on "positive leadership, backed by resources and readiness to make some sacrifice in the international interest". He also recognized that

The level of support provided to various adaptation funds has up to now remained very low and has not matched the scale of the problem

The urgency of the climate crisis certainly calls for a renewed leadership role from those countries most responsible

the leadership role often goes unapplauded, particularly at home, and has a tendency to retreat or atrophy, but that, particularly in a time of crisis, the hallmark of leadership is the willingness to assume responsibility. The urgency of the climate crisis certainly calls for a renewed leadership role from those countries most responsible.

International cooperation does not, however, hinge on leadership alone. Strong State capacities are needed, at all levels of development, to help shape a common and inclusive vision, to ensure that the conceding of national sovereignty in some areas is balanced by the opportunities opened up in others, and to guarantee effective participation in the negotiation and implementation of international rules, regulations and support mechanisms. In this respect, the erosion of State capacity in recent years, particularly in developing countries, represents an obstacle to international cooperation and has contributed to the lack of transparency and democratic accountability in many multilateral institutions, particularly those dealing with the development challenge. Correcting this is an urgent priority if real progress on the climate issue is to occur at the required pace (for further discussion, see chap. IV).

The policy response

Scientists, dreamers and defunct economists

The policy response to climate change is complicated by the fact that, so far, it has been a slow-moving process—one whose impact has certainly been less perceptible than that of other shocks and crises confronting policymakers in the "normal" political cycle. Moreover, its consequences have been easier to ignore to the extent that their brunt has been borne by the poorest countries and communities.

Climate scientists have begun to close these gaps with a vast array of evidence and analyses demonstrating the unprecedented historical scale and speed of greenhouse gas increases, the signs of acceleration, the damage that has already been done to the climate, and the risks of getting locked into irreversible pathways if trends continue. This has led some countries to adopt ambitious targets for emissions reduction, but opinion surveys suggest that the scientific community has still some way to go towards convincing politicians and the public of the urgency of the challenge (Schmidt, 2009). Along these lines, the Secretary of Energy of the United States, Steven Chu, recently acknowledged that the climate challenge involves a difficult compromise between scientific and political realities —an admission that has elicited some degree of consternation.[7]

The environmental movement has a longer track record than other groups in respect not only of having warned of the dangers of unchecked pollution and the reckless exploitation of natural assets but also of having organized successful campaigns on local environmental issues. The political parties, regulatory reforms and environmental ministries that have often emerged from those campaigns have been responsible for the wider national focus on the environmental challenge, particularly, but not exclusively, in developed countries. Moreover, this community has been on the front lines in the ideological battle against the climate sceptics. On the other hand, it has struggled to forge its own integrated perspective on the economic, political and scientific dimensions of the climate challenge, particularly in moving into the international arena. Even where such a perspective has begun to emerge in richer countries, the implications for the developing world, where rapid growth, industrialization and urbanization remain paramount goals, have not been clearly, or convincingly, spelled out.

7   See "America's new green guru sparks anger over climate change U-turns", *The Observer*, Sunday, 24 May, 2009.

Economists are latecomers to the climate debate and, more generally, have entered the fray with a less-than-honourable record on environmental issues (Dasgupta, 2008).[8] However, they have been quick to fashion policy options. Theirs is a language of risk assessment, measured trade-offs between costs and benefits, marginal price changes, discounting of future outcomes, etc. Their so-called integrated assessment models confer an aura of quantitative rigour and precision on their discussions, in which they typically endorse an overly cautious approach to policy, whether by demonstrating the advantages of going slow on climate action or by offering quick solutions to "externalities" which allow the market to reassume its central role (see box I.2). In the context of climate change, practical policy advice has focused on the mechanics of carbon taxes or trading schemes, and on the dangers of ambitious climate initiatives constraining future growth. Self-regulation has become the mantra, and when policy action is proposed the framework is predisposed to gradualism and delay (Ackerman, 2009).

Economists are latecomers to the climate debate and have entered the fray with a less-than-honourable record on environmental issues

---

Box I.2

The limits of conventional economic models

Good climate policy requires the best possible understanding of how climatic change will impact on human lives and livelihoods, in industrialized countries and in developing countries. Unfortunately, many climate-economics models suffer from a lack of transparency, in terms of both their policy relevance and their credibility. Building a model of the climate and the economy inevitably involves numerous judgement calls; debatable judgements and untestable hypotheses turn out to be of great importance in evaluating the policy recommendations of climate-economics models, and should be visible for purposes of debate.

A good climate-economics model would be transparent enough for policy relevance, yet sophisticated enough to get the most important characteristics of the climate and the economy right. Unfortunately, many existing models fall short on the first count or the second, or both: some are very complex—often to the point of being entirely opaque to the non-specialist—while others represent the climate and the economy incorrectly, as discussed below.

The different types of model structures provide results that inform climate and development policy in very different ways. All have strengths and weaknesses. Many of the best-known *integrated assessment models* attempt to find the "optimal" climate policy, the one that maximizes long-term human welfare. This calculation depends on several unknowable or controversial quantities, including the numerical measurement of human welfare, the physical magnitude and monetary value of all current and anticipated climate damages, and the relative worth of future versus present benefits.

General equilibrium models can be extremely complex, combining very detailed climate models with intricate models of the economy; yet, despite the detail of general equilibrium models, the commonly used assumption of decreasing returns seriously limits their usefulness in modelling endogenous technological change. *Partial equilibrium models* circumvent the problem of increasing returns, at the price of a loss of generality. In some cases, there appears to be a problem of spurious precision in overly elaborate models of the economy, containing, for example, projections of long-term growth paths for dozens of economic subsectors.

Simulation models are well suited to representing uncertain parameters and to developing integrated assessment model results based on well-known scenarios of future emissions, but their policy usefulness is limited by a lack of feedback between their climate and economic dynamics. Finally, *cost minimization models* address policy issues without requiring calculations of human welfare in money terms, but existing cost minimization models may be marred by a spurious precision, a characteristic they tend to share with some general and partial equilibrium models.

Source: Ackerman and Stanton (2009).

---

8 Ackerman (2009, p. 12) notes that researchers in the field of "ecological economics" have examined the economy as embedded in and constrained by the earth's ecosystem but without offering a complete theory of economics and the environment; nor have they had much influence on their colleagues in the wider domain of economics.

The fact that, while being concerned with overall costs and benefits, integrated assessment models generally have little to say about structural inequality or historical development. This has been a long-standing target of criticism of conventional economic models.[9] Perhaps more surprising, however, has been the cavalier attitude of many economists towards climate risk. Helm (2008) has argued that current climate policy and targets are being designed on the basis of current economic structures and of how marginal emissions reductions can be achieved from such a starting point, but with very little attention paid to long-term structural trends. This approach is likely to seriously underestimate the size and cost of the challenge. Stern (2009) acknowledges this bias; but as Weitzman (2009, p. 22) has suggested, economists still seem preprogrammed to react to an impending climate disaster by adjusting their flow instruments to control the stock accumulation that is producing the disaster, a position he likens to "using an outboard motor to manoeuvre an ocean liner away from an impending collision with an iceberg".

The risks of catastrophic global warming merit a significant planetary insurance policy

The probabilities that scientists attach to the occurrence of higher temperatures are given in table I.4; they are of an order that is a good deal higher than what would lead individuals to take out insurance against worst-case scenarios. On this basis, Ackerman (2009) has suggested that the risks of catastrophic global warming merit a significant planetary insurance policy.

Moving the agenda demands an integrated approach, that is to say, a climate-inclusive developmental approach

In light of these various shortcomings, there is a suspicion among many policymakers in developing countries that none of the constituencies shaping climate policy are paying sufficient attention to the kind of adjustments that are being asked of them with regard to meeting the climate challenge. Industrialization and urbanization are hotwired into the development process, hence restricting these processes, and the attendant expansion of the energy sources that they require, is not an option. A low-emissions push in developing countries requires not only a massive injection of renewable sources of energy in the energy mix along with technologies that help improve energy efficiency and prevent deforestation (in affected countries) but also changes in land-use planning, the organization of transport and water management. These requirements are sure to entail major costs for developing countries—costs that explain their objection to the imposition

Table I.4

Probability of exceeding the temperature increase (relative to the pre-industrial level) at different greenhouse gas concentration stabilization levels

Percentage						
Stabilization level (ppm CO$_2$e)	Increase in temperature (relative to the pre-industrial level (degrees celsius))					
	2	3	4	5	6	7
450	78	18	3	1	0	0
500	96	44	11	3	1	0
550	99	69	24	7	2	1
650	100	94	58	24	9	4
750	100	99	82	47	22	9

Source: Stern (2009, p. 26).

Note: The probabilities are based on the Hadley Centre Ensembles and are available from Murphy and others (2004).

---

9   Ironically, conventional economic models have their intellectual roots in the natural sciences of the nineteenth century. However, while natural scientists have moved on to exploring more complex, chaotic and unstable systems, including the threat of dangerous climate change, economists have clung doggedly to the idea of a harmonious system in or close to equilibrium.

of any forced emission commitments. Moving the climate agenda forward demands an integrated approach, that is to say, a climate-inclusive developmental approach: treating climate and development separately, as has largely been the case in the past decade and even earlier, no longer can be deemed the basis of a tenable framework.

Interrelated threats

Climate change and development are closely interconnected and the feedbacks and reactions, particularly through the production and use of energy, are cumulative. Economists, as suggested earlier, have a poor record when it comes to analysing these kinds of feedbacks and cumulative linkages. Policymakers appear predisposed to underestimate both the scale of the threats that are being posed and the cost of removing those threats.

More recently, however, policymakers have shown signs of recognizing the urgency of the situation, which seems to reflect a growing awareness that the international community faces a series of interrelated threats which can no longer be effectively tackled in isolation. A climate crunch, an energy crunch, a food crunch and, perhaps most significantly, a credit crunch have all exposed the danger of subordinating risk management to the self-regulating forces of the marketplace.

Since the summer of 2008, policymakers in more advanced countries have been struggling to deal with the cumulative and interconnected shocks of a housing crisis, excessive energy consumption and financial collapse which have rippled and intensified throughout an increasingly fragile global economy (Klare, 2008). In some communities, these shocks have been further compounded by weather-related disasters. However, the challenges posed by the fact that climate change, economic insecurity and political conflict are interlinked are even greater for developing countries and the consequences are likely to reach well beyond their own borders, as has been made clear by the testimony of the newly appointed United States Director of National Intelligence, Dennis Blair (2009).

Adaptation without mitigation could prove an ineffective response for many developing nations, and the failure to deal with these interrelated threats will almost certainly have much more widespread and damaging consequences. There is real concern that neither the time nor the resources exist for dealing with a multiple syndrome encompassing intensified and interrelated shocks and crises.

> There is real concern that neither the time nor the resources exist for dealing with a multiple syndrome encompassing intensified and interrelated shocks and crises

A New Deal?

Parallels have often been drawn between the climate challenge and the interwar experience of overcoming an economic crisis, defeating fascism and rebuilding ravaged economies. A Marshall Plan to tackle global warming is a logical consideration (Gore, 2007; and chap. VI). The call, however, particularly since the sharp downturn in the global economy starting in the summer of 2008, has been for a global new deal capable of responding to the economic and climate threats simultaneously (New Economics Foundation, 2008; United Nations Environment Programme, 2009; United Nations Department of Economics and Social Affairs, 2009).

Historical analogies always need to be treated with a degree of caution. However, the original New Deal, as noted in chapter IV, certainly did deal with a series of interrelated threats, including threats to the environment, through an expanded and transformative policy agenda of a sort that needs to be revived in light of today's threats and challenges. The scale of the response is also worth recalling. The New Deal had committed 3 per cent of gross do-

> The call has been for a global new deal capable of responding to the economic and climate threats simultaneously

mestic product (GDP) each year between 1933 and 1939, and a good deal more was added to counter the threat of fascism. Moreover, once the fighting stopped, the United States, through the Marshall Plan, committed almost 1 per cent of its GDP each year for five years to rebuild Europe. This constituted a massive resource commitment over a 20-year period.

Economists have suggested that a smaller effort will be needed to counter the threats arising from climate change. This seems an optimistic stance. As Stern (2009, pp. 12-13) indicates, the kind of 30-year strategy that is needed to keep climate risk manageable will involve long-term planning and a massive investment programme and will require the kind of leadership and cooperation that helped defeat fascism and rebuild shattered economies. Moreover, if the shift to low-emissions development pathways is to take place in a timely and orderly fashion, the commitments should be made sooner rather than later.

No country left behind

Making an exact estimate of the economic costs of climate change is a difficult exercise which relies heavily on the kinds of assumptions and scenarios that are used in modelling exercises. Damage functions are difficult to specify and externalities are difficult to price. Moreover, the costs vary with the ambitiousness of the targets. The Intergovernmental Panel on Climate Change has presented some damage estimates using a standard economic model. According to its *Fourth Assessment Report*, the damage inflicted by climate change will entail on average a loss of 1-5 per cent of global GDP. However, the Intergovernmental Panel also notes that globally aggregated figures are likely to underestimate the damage costs because they cannot include many "non-quantifiable impacts" (Intergovernmental Panel on Climate Change, 2007a, p. 69).[10]

It would be misleading to suggest that developed countries will not face adaptation challenges. However, the fact that they have already invested billions of dollars in climate-related adaptation measures and have diversified economies which are consequently more robust in the face of climatic shocks, combined with the fact that many may even extract short-term gains from rising temperatures, could make for increased divisiveness, on top of that already created by their carbon-fuelled past success.

The damage to developing countries from climate change is already perceptible. Indeed, it has been estimated that for every 1°C rise in average global temperatures, annual average growth in poor countries drops by between 2 and 3 percentage points, but with no change in the growth performance of rich countries (Dell, Jones and Olken, 2008). Stern (2009) describes the adverse impact from climate change on developing countries as a "double inequity", given that they carry little responsibility for causing the problem. Table I.5 presents estimates of the damage under a "business-as-usual" (BAU) scenario and, depending on assumptions regarding adaptation efforts, the probability of catastrophic risk and sensitivity to climate change. The likely damage to developing regions (measured as a percentage of respective GDP in 2100) is more than double that for OECD countries excluding the United States, and more than 5 times greater than the damage to the United States. At a further disaggregated level, the damage to Latin America and the Caribbean, Africa and the Middle East, and India and Southeast Asia will be 7, 7.6, and 9.6 times greater, respectively, than to the United States (Evans, 2009).

---

10   The Intergovernmental Panel on Climate Change also indicates that:

Peer-reviewed estimates of the social cost of carbon (net economic costs of damages from climate change aggregated across the globe and discounted to the present) for 2005 have an average value of $12 per ton of CO_2, but the range of 100 estimates is large (from -$3/t$CO_2$ to $95/t$CO_2$). The range of published evidence indicates that the net damage costs of climate change are projected to be significant and to increase over time.

Table I.5
Business-as-usual damages in 2100

A. Mean business-as-usual damages in 2100: "no adaptation" scenario				
	Annual damages as percentage of GDP in 2100			
Region	Economic	Non-economic	Catastrophic	Total
United States	0.3	0.4	0.1	0.8
Other OECD	0.7	1.0	0.2	1.9
Rest of the world	1.6	2.3	0.4	4.3
World total	**1.2**	**1.8**	**0.3**	**3.4**

B. Mean business-as-usual damages in 2100: no adaptation, increased catastrophe risk and increased damage exponent				
	Annual damages as percentage of GDP in 2100			
Region	Economic	Non-economic	Catastrophic	Total
United States	0.4	0.5	0.6	1.5
Other OECD	0.9	1.3	1.6	3.8
Rest of the world	2.0	2.9	3.2	8.2
World total	**1.6**	**2.3**	**2.6**	**6.4**

C. Business-as-usual damages in 2100: 83rd percentile estimates (no adaptation, increased catastrophe risk and increased damage exponent)				
	Annual damages as percentage of GDP in 2100			
Region	Economic	Non-economic	Catastrophic	Total
United States	0.6	0.9	1.2	2.6
Other OECD	1.4	2.0	3.1	6.2
Rest of the world	3.2	4.5	6.3	13.5
World total	**2.5**	**3.6**	**4.8**	**10.8**

Source: Ackerman and others (2008), tables 2, 3, and 4.

Note: The results are based on 5000 runs of the PAGE2002 model. As the impacts are closely but not perfectly correlated, the 83rd percentile of the total damages is slightly less than the sum of the 83rd percentiles of the damages in the individual impact categories.

Climate change is already multiplying vulnerabilities in developing countries by heightening livelihood risks and further weakening adaptive capacities. Rising sea levels are considered a threat for people who live within 60 miles of a shoreline. They make up one third of the world's population and a large number of them live at low altitudes. The threat to people living in small islands and low-lying territories is unequivocal, while extended periods of drought in other areas have been generating a flow of environmental refugees and conflict with neighbouring countries and populations. Similarly, the outbreak of tropical diseases is expected to be larger in areas with increased incidence of heatwaves, thus extending drought-prone areas, while the prevalence of water-related diseases is likely to rise in areas with an increased incidence of floods (see chap. III).

The growing threats from climate change will mainly affect populations that are already challenged by multiple vulnerabilities associated with low levels of economic and human development. Poorer countries and communities with poor health care, lack of infrastructure, weakly diversified economies, missing institutions and soft governance structures may be exposed not just to potentially catastrophic large-scale disasters but also to a more permanent state of economic stress as a result of higher average temperatures, reduced availability of water sources, more frequent flooding and intensified windstorms.

Climate change will deepen inequalities, with least developed countries and small island States being the most affected

By increasing vulnerability in developing countries, climate change will deepen inequalities, with least developed countries and small island States being the most affected. As Dodman, Ayers and Huq (2009, p. 152) puts it: "The uneven distribution of climate change risk mirrors the existing uneven distribution of natural disaster risk—in 2007, Asia was the region hardest hit and most affected by natural disasters, accounting for 37 per cent of reported disasters and 90 per cent of all the reported victims." In other words, people with limited assets and resources and with less reliable access to decent jobs will continue to be the most affected by the adverse impacts of climate change.

The adaptation challenge is essentially a development challenge

The adaptation challenge is essentially a development challenge. It will require significant investments, not only to climate-proof existing projects and ensure effective responses to natural disasters, but also to diversify economic activity and address a range of interrelated vulnerabilities that are already exposing communities to threats from quite small changes in climate variables.

There is some confusion about whether we need mitigation or adaptation—in fact, we need both. For a number of countries, the challenge of adaptation looms very large. However, in many cases, adaptation and mitigation cannot be so clearly distinguished—for example, energy conservation measures could be classified under both mitigation and adaptation. Chapter III develops these arguments.

Common but differentiated mitigation challenges

Procrastination in respect of the need for aggressive climate action has to stop immediately

In light of the accumulating scientific evidence, this *Survey* regards the 2° target for stabilizing carbon concentrations, that is to say, a maximum ultimate temperature increase of 2° C above pre-industrial levels, as appropriate for preventing dangerous anthropogenic interference in the climate system. Global emission reductions of the order of 50-80 per cent by 2050 are deemed essential. Even such estimated emission concentrations pose a risk to the climate, as reported by the Intergovernmental Panel on Climate Change and as clearly demonstrated by other findings in the scholarly literature; hence, procrastination in respect of the need for aggressive climate action has to stop immediately.

As Stern (2009) argues, achieving the transition to a low-emissions economy depends on when we start and the time at our disposal for exploiting the life cycles of investment in and development of new technologies. The current starting point is 430 ppm CO_2e and the longer action is delayed, the greater the costs will be, as the threshold for attaining dangerous levels approaches. Advanced countries will need to do more and quickly (see chap. II) both at home to reduce the stock of emissions and to support the efforts of developing countries to decelerate the flow of emissions and to establish a viable development pathway along which they can eventually begin to decarbonize their own economies (see box 1.3).

Researchers have used both case-study evidence and modelling exercises to better understand the mitigation costs involved. Using the former approach, McKinsey and Company has developed a ranking of mitigation steps in accordance with their costs (for further discussion, see chap. II). Others have identified "wedges" of alternate technologies,[11] each of which could displace a certain amount of emissions each year, thereby stabilizing emissions

---

11   Potential wedges come in many forms, ranging from improvements in efficiency of automobiles, appliances and power plants, and allocation of greater shares in energy supply for nuclear energy, renewable energy and carbon capture and storage, to enlargement of bio-carbon stocks through management of forests and soils.

Box I.3

Carbon indebtedness

Scientific consensus has established a non-catastrophic global warming threshold at 2° C above pre-industrial levels. On one recent assessment (Meinshausen and others, 2009), this translates into a 1,440 gigaton (Gt) (equivalent to 393 gigatons of carbon) limit on the amount of CO_2 that can be emitted in the atmosphere between 2000 and 2050, that is, if we want to have a 50:50 chance of staying within that threshold. To shift those odds to a 75 per cent chance of staying on track, we should emit no more than 1 trillion tons of CO_2 (273 Gt of carbon) in total. Up to 2000, 271 Gt of carbon had already been emitted into the atmosphere,[a] of which 209 GtC (77 per cent of the total) had come from Annex I countries.

One scenario, associated with a 50:50 chance of staying within the 2° C threshold, implies a global reduction of 50 per cent over 1990 levels. The big question is how that happens. Under this scenario, the emissions limit for the period 1850-2050 is 650 GtC. The sharing rule proposed by many European countries to convince reluctant big developing countries to actively cooperate in the post-Kyoto regime (the so-called "shared vision") would make Annex I countries responsible for 85 per cent of the overall emissions reduction burden. That would imply an additional emission of 85 Gt of carbon for that group of countries in the period 2000-2050, and a total emissions of 314 GtC. In other words, these countries would be allowed to consume 48 per cent of the available carbon budget.

This is a figure considerably higher than their share of global population. On those grounds Annex I countries should only consume 21 per cent of the global carbon budget for the period 1850-2050, leaving 79 per cent for non-Annex I countries. That would mean an allocation of 137 GtC for Annex I countries. As they have already used 209 GtC and expect to consume another 85 GtC until 2050, this would mean that they would have consumed 177 GtC over and above their "fair" share. By contrast, non-Annex I countries would have to restrict their emissions to 336 GtC over the whole period. Pricing that debt, moreover, can give an indication of the compensation owed to developing countries under this scenario to help finance their shift to a low-emissions, high-growth pathway.

a Climate Analysis Indicators Tool (CAIT), version 6.0. (Washington, D.C.: World Resources Institute, 2009).

in 2050 and leading to global reductions thereafter (Pacala and Socolow, 2004; and figure I.4) The alternative has been to use integrated assessment-type models to determine mitigation costs. These two approaches are not mutually exclusive, however. Various estimates are considered in subsequent chapters.

While the absolute values of required investment can appear quite high, the costs of inaction are even higher. It is also clear that the lower the stabilization level chosen, the safer the future, but the higher the initial investment costs. As noted above, very broadly, even an annual cost as high as 2 per cent of GDP is small in comparison with the potential damage from following business-as-usual pathways. Thus the benefit-to-cost ratio is hugely in favour of urgent actions taken to mitigate climate change.

While the absolute values of required investment can appear quite high, the costs of inaction are even higher

Defining low-emissions, high-growth pathways

The policy challenges along such a pathway are certain to vary across countries at different levels of development. For advanced countries, the required shift in economic activity to ensure substantive reductions in existing emission stocks will have to be accompanied by a return to full employment and improved energy security. This requirement is at the core of the "green jobs" agenda which has received a boost from recent stimulus packages devised to address the current economic downturn (see box I.4). For many developing countries, diversifying economic activity away from the primary sector and low value added manufacturing combined with efforts to eradicate poverty and ensure a more balanced integration into the global economy, remains essential policy goals.

Figure I.4
Emissions stabilization wedges, 2000-2060

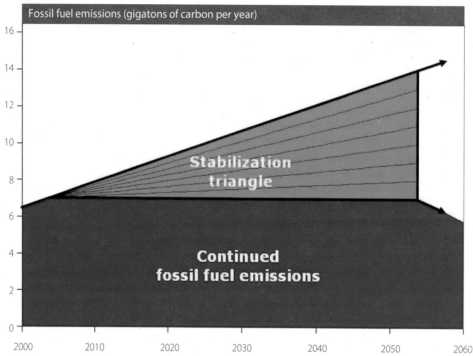

Source: Grubb (2004).

Notes: As compared to a "business as usual" future in which CO$_2$ emissions double from 7GtC/yr to 14GtC/yr by about mid-century, emissions stabilization requires a "stabilization triangle" that grows to save 7GtC/yr by mid-century. Each wedge grows linearly from zero today to 1 GtC/y in 2054.

Box I.4

Green jobs

The Green Jobs Initiative was launched in June 2007 as a partnership between the United Nations Environment Programmes (UNEP), the International Trade Union Confederation (ITUC), the International Organisation of Employers (IOE) and the International Labour Organization (ILO). Its aim is to promote the linkages between environmental sustainability and employment and labour markets.

Green jobs are defined as those that reduce the environmental impact of enterprises and economic sectors, ultimately to levels that are sustainable. Such jobs are found in many sectors of the economy ranging from energy supply to recycling and from agriculture and construction to transportation. They help to cut the consumption of energy, raw materials and water through high-efficiency strategies, to de-carbonize the economy and reduce greenhouse gas emissions, to minimize or eliminate altogether all forms of waste and pollution, and to protect and restore ecosystems and biodiversity. Green jobs can thus play a crucial role in reducing the environmental footprint of economic activity. There is evidence both of the rapid growth of green or greener jobs and of substantial spillover or indirect employment effects: jobs in Germany's renewables sector, for example, rose between three- and fourfold between 1998 and 2006.

A number of observations are of particular importance in the discussion of green jobs. First, there are many that already exist worldwide (table 1); indeed, half of all jobs in renewable energy are in the developing world. Second, some green jobs are associated with new green industries (such as renewable energy), and clearly some of these jobs are also new themselves, for example, that of photovoltaic cell engineer (table 2). On the other hand, in years to come, the far more widespread phenomenon will be the "greening" of existing jobs in what are otherwise traditional occupations.

New occupations and the greening of existing ones will in fact pose a broad challenge to education and vocational training systems, even if the vast majority of green jobs are in the same areas of employment that people already work in today, as demonstrated in the table below. Take, for example, the occupation of automotive mechanic in connection with the introduction of hybrid automobiles. This is a traditional occupation for which new skills will need to be learned. In fact, the absence of adequate or rapid action on the supply side of the labour market through skill "retooling" and upgrading constitutes a constraint on addressing environmental sustainability.

Source: ILO, Employment Strategy department.

Box I.4 (cont'd)

Table 1
Employment estimates in renewable energy, selected countries and the world, 2006

Renewable energy source	World[a]	Selected countries	
Wind	300 000	Germany	82 100
		United States	36 800
		Spain	35 000
		China	22 200
		Denmark	21 000
		India	10 000
Solar PV	170 000	China	55 000
		Germany	35 000
		Spain	26 449
		United States	15 700
Solar thermal	624 000	China	600 000
		Germany	13 300
		Spain	9 142
		United States	1 900
Biomass	1 174 000	Brazil	500 000
		United States	312 200
		China	266 000
		Germany	95 400
		Spain	10 349
Hydropower	39 000	Europe	20 000
		United States	19 000
Geothermal	25 000	United States	21 000
		Germany	4 200
Renewables: total	**2 332 200**		

Source: United Nations Environment Programme, International Labour Organization and others (2008).

a Comprising countries for which information was available.

Table 2
A greener economy with familiar occupations

Strategies for green economy investments	Representative jobs
Building, retrofitting	Electricians, heating/air conditioning installers, carpenters, construction equipment operators, roofers, insulation workers, industrial truck drivers, construction managers, building inspectors
Mass transit	Civil engineers, rail track layers, electricians, welders, metal fabricators, engine assemblers, production helpers, bus drivers, first-line transportation supervisors, dispatchers
Energy-efficient automobiles	Computer software engineers, electrical engineers, engineering technicians, welders, transportation equipment painters, metal fabricators, computer-controlled machine operators, engine assemblers, production helpers, operations managers, auto mechanics
Wind power	Environmental engineers, iron workers and steelworkers, millwrights, sheet metal workers, machinists, electrical equipment assemblers, construction equipment operators, industrial truck drivers, industrial production managers, first-line production supervisors
Solar power	Electrical engineers, electricians, industrial machinery mechanics, welders, metal fabricators, electrical equipment assemblers, construction equipment operators, installation helpers, labourers, construction managers
Cellulosic biofuels	Chemical engineers, chemists, chemical equipment operators, chemical technicians, mixing and blending machine operators, agricultural workers, industrial truck drivers, farm product purchasers, agricultural and forestry supervisors, agricultural inspectors

Source: Pollin and Wicks-Lim (2008).

Incremental change or a big push?

Historical precedents appear to be few for the kind of transition envisioned through the establishment of a low-emissions development pathway. On some counts, the right approach is to create incentives for private businesses to shift gradually from high-emitting activities and make investments in new high-risk, high-return climate-friendly technologies. A good governance agenda that establishes a price for carbon, guarantees strong intellectual property rights and removes distortionary subsidies for high-emitting activities will, it is believed, provide the right investment climate (International Monetary Fund, 2008a).

The nature of the challenge involved in this transition could entail, alternatively, a series of large and long-lasting investments with respect to the generation and consumption of energy, the use of land in the urban and rural context, the organization of transport, etc., which would have to be undertaken simultaneously if they were to have a significant impact on climate change. This is the approach adopted in the present *Survey*. Price incentives by themselves are unlikely to trigger or sustain the required investments. Rather, a "big push" is needed to launch a successful low-emissions development pathway. This revives long-standing questions, familiar from the development literature, about the challenges facing poor countries in mobilizing investment resources and the relative roles of the public and private sectors in leading such an effort. It also draws attention to the scale of the financing challenge that developing countries will face in pursuing a low-emissions, high-growth path. These issues will be discussed in greater depth in chapters II, IV and VI.

A "big push" would be needed to launch a successful low level carbon development pathway and establish a different pattern of integration with respect to the global economy

Does technology hold the key?

The dual challenge of meeting development goals, including through industrialization, while at the same time controlling emissions and reducing carbon dependence will require new, rapidly scalable and powerful technologies in the next 10–20 years—technologies that transform not only the way that energy is produced, distributed and used but also the approaches to helping vulnerable countries adapt to an unavoidable increase in global temperatures. On some counts, a technological fix is all that can be hoped for.

Yet, while there is broad agreement on the central role that technology will play in meeting this dual challenge, there is less of a consensus on how to build technological know-how and capacity, particularly in the face of significant gaps between rich and poor countries. For some, stronger protection of intellectual property rights, both to encourage local innovators and to attract foreign direct investment (FDI), is key to leapfrogging over old technologies onto a cleaner technological highway. Others not only doubt the efficacy of such mechanisms in generating the required level of innovative effort but also view them as a source of potentially significant obstacles for developing countries (see chap. V).

Historical experience indicates that, in important areas of technology development, government support has extended beyond the research and development (R&D) phase to include support to commercialization, for example, through government procurement and such measures as loan guarantees for construction of buildings and investment in equipment. These fall under the broad rubric of industrial policies. Moreover, technological progress is not independent of investment in both physical and human capital. That a strong investment push is likely to embed new technologies serves as a reminder of overlapping policy challenges.

In important areas of technology development, government support has extended beyond the research and development phase to include support to commercialization

Some question the wisdom of this approach, pointing to the costly practice of second-guessing the market and "picking winners", that is to say, using policies like subsidized credit and infant-industry protection to back one industry or technology rather than another. For others, experimentation, whether with new technologies or with older but previously untried ones, involves learning and uncertain outcomes. Such initiatives, whether undertaken by the private or the public sector constitute grounds for socializing the risks involved. These issues are discussed in greater detail in chapters IV and V.

An expanded public policy agenda

If climate does indeed possess the characteristics of a global public good, stopping free-riding, strengthening property rights and ensuring good collective governance would seem to be the main policy challenges stemming from that fact. However, as discussed earlier, such an approach would appear to frame the challenge too narrowly, in part because in the case of climate, rival use is clearly involved, as are distributional issues. Achieving fast growth in developing countries and full employment in advanced countries along low-emissions pathways will also almost certainly entail complex decisions regarding patterns of consumption, settlement, transportation and urbanization, involving difficult choices and trade-offs arising from the competing use of resources. Moreover, the climate challenge is difficult to separate from other challenges—those having to do with food and energy security and global health issues.

> The climate challenge is difficult to separate from other challenges—those having to do with food and energy security and global health issues

A good many of the differences on policy matters stem from diverging views on how best to meet these challenges: should there be a gradual shift away from business-as-usual scenarios or a transformative change? A central question concerns the relative roles of the private and the public sectors in undertaking the investments needed for the low-emissions, high-growth path. One way in which Governments can act is by instituting a carbon price through either a carbon tax or a cap-and-trade policy or some combination of the two, along with strong regulations. Much of the discussion of the climate challenge in developed countries is focused on the relative efficacy of alternative ways of establishing a carbon price. The mix in developing countries is likely to be different, with a much larger role set aside for public investment and targeted industrial policies. In any case, at all levels of development, all policy instruments, ranging from price incentives, taxes and subsidies to regulation, and encompassing fiscal, monetary and financial measures as well, should be fully used as part of the toolkit created to meet these challenges. Moreover, once the scale, complexity and urgency of the challenge are accepted, ensuring the requisite policy space for using the full range of instruments and measures would seem to be a necessary determinant of success.

> A central question concerns the relative roles of the private and the public sectors in undertaking the investments needed for the low-emissions, high-growth path

Is low-emissions, high-growth feasible?

A low-emissions, high-growth scenario

To assess various scenarios for the implications of an investment push given to address the combined challenges of catch-up growth and climate change, an experimental simulation was run with the Global Policy Model (GPM) developed in the Department of Economic and Social Affairs of the United Nations Secretariat. The Global Policy Model was developed to investigate the spillover effects of macroeconomic policy scenarios in an interdependent world economy. The model is centred around standard macroeconomic relations, including complete specifications and econometric estimations of the stock-flow adjustment of real and financial assets and liabilities. An important long-run characteristic is the assumption of endogenous productivity growth generated by economies of scale. Under this assumption, Government policies affecting aggregate demand and market size will have long-term growth effects. When the model hits on supply constraints, it adjusts prices and exchange rates, along with endogenous macroeconomic policy responses (based on past policy behaviour) and adjustments in financial markets. Supply constraints arising from pressure exerted on natural resources and energy will trigger higher world market prices for commodities and fuels, affecting production and consumption throughout the system. The basic version of the model distinguishes 16 countries and country groups.[12]

While mainly macroeconomic in nature, the model does spell out simultaneously energy production and demand for country groups and an international market (a pool) which sets the equilibrium price. Energy demand is estimated based on historical observations, tracing changes in relation to output (income), population and the state of technology measured in the form of relative income per capita, as well as the international price. Energy production is assumed to be determined by domestic energy resource endowments, technology and demand dynamics linked to change in the production structure, consumption patterns and relative prices of energy. The model does not specify carbon emissions linked to economic activity; therefore, inferences regarding climate change scenarios are drawn from trends in energy efficiency and energy use.

The business-as-usual (BAU) scenario used as the basis for the present analysis assumes that the world economy will recover from the financial crisis in 2010. The return to the past pattern of growth, moreover, will lead to a continuation of the current trends in (high-emissions) energy intensity and the economic inequality of past decades. The implication is that, in the business-as-usual scenario, the world would resume growth on a path deemed unsustainable from both a development and an environment perspective.

The alternative, low-emissions, high-growth (LEHG) scenario, having been constructed as a policy-driven departure from the business-as-usual scenario, requires international policy coordination. Three types of policy adjustment are considered as follows:

- Countries worldwide are assumed to increase public spending levels by between 1 and 5 per cent of GDP, with developed countries in the lower end of the range and developing countries in the upper end. The investment push is expected to trigger faster economic growth and will embrace efforts towards energy efficiency, as well as help increase the supply of primary commodities and food at a rate that is consistent with the growth of world income;

- The investment push and international agreements should contribute to reducing high-emissions energy demand (reflecting, for instance, a cap-and-trade mechanism) to yield lower emissions and greater energy efficiency. Such improvements in energy efficiency are consistent with the investment patterns discussed below;

- Economic resilience of developing countries is strengthened by providing those countries, especially the poorest among them, with full and duty-free market access to developed-country markets, leading to greater economic diversification.

---

12   These include the United States of America, Western and Eastern Europe, Japan, other developed countries, East Asian newly industrialized economies, the Commonwealth of Independent States (CIS) (here incorporating all countries of the former USSR for reasons of historical data consistency), China, Western Asia (excluding Israel which is grouped under "other developed" countries), India, other South Asia (Afghanistan, Bangladesh, Sri Lanka, Nepal and Pakistan), East Asian middle-income countries (excluding the newly industrialized countries), other East Asian low-income countries, Central America (including Mexico and the Caribbean), South America, African middle-income countries and African low-income countries.

Energy efficiency and energy diversification

To assess the implications of changing course, levels of public investments in infrastructure, diversification of economic activity and energy provision are raised by Governments in all country groups. As discussed further in chapter IV, after possible financial 'crowding-out' mechanisms are accounted for, such public spending is found on balance to "crowd in" private investment. The assumption that public sector injections have the potential to boost energy efficiency was based on empirical evidence for a number of countries that have made important shifts in the recent past (see table I.6). Energy efficiency is measured here as the rate of increment in kilograms of oil equivalent per dollar unit of output in real terms. The numbers reflect 20-year averages for 1970-1990, a period in which these countries pushed for greater energy efficiency in response to various oil price shocks. Investment in energy-saving led to reductions in the use of energy per unit of output of 50–200 per cent.

The first main element of the low-emissions, high-growth strategy simulated with the global policy model is therefore injections of public investment which, for developing countries, would be at least as decisive as for the cases presented in table I.7. Such positive shocks yield different results according to the inherited economic structure and institutional patterns captured in the econometric specifications. The table summarizes the outcomes as 20-year averages at the end of the simulation period in 2030.

Such results, even if challenging at first sight, are nevertheless reasonable in the context of acknowledged success stories. Developed countries would be achieving very high efficiency improvements, almost as high as in the best of the cases presented above, albeit with slightly higher investment support. Meanwhile, the improvements expected for developing countries would be considerably higher compared with their past performance, but the impulse from investment is also significantly higher and is sustained over the long term. Hence, the elasticities (ratio of change in investment to energy efficiency) would be in these cases half of those in the developed world. This is a reasonable pattern. The catch-up process in technology improvements cannot be expected to yield immediate results. In addition, not all investments are supposed to be allocated to the energy sector and some growth-enhancing might even require greater energy use.

To what extent these improvements in energy efficiency result in effective reductions of fossil fuel production and therefore CO_2 emissions cannot be established with exact precision by the Model in its current state of development. Given the Model's assumptions, the coordinated policy scenario would reduce the global use of energy, measured in millions of tons of oil equivalent, at an annual rate of about 1 per cent between

With the world economy growing at about 5 per cent during 2010-2030, the effective reduction in global energy use per unit of world output will be about 6 per cent

Table I.6
Energy use and total investment, selected country cases: 20-year averages taken in 1990

	Efficiency: change in energy use per unit of output (percentage)	Stimulus: rate of growth of total investment in real terms (percentage)	Elasticity: ratio of impact of investment to efficiency
Switzerland	-1.18	2.10	0.6
Finland	-2.03	4.31	0.5
France	-3.21	3.30	1.0
Sweden	-5.79	2.59	2.2
Japan	-1.98	4.15	0.5
United States	-2.94	3.02	1.0

Sources: United Nations, *Energy Statistics Yearbook*, various years; and *National Accounts Statistics*, various years.

2010 and 2030.[13] As noted in figure I.5 below, with the world economy growing at about 5 per cent during this period, the effective reduction per unit of world output will be about 6 per cent, broadly consistent with the numbers obtained for energy demand given above (see table 1.7).

The scenario presented here would lead to a cumulative reduction in the use of oil and coal of about 50 billion of tons of oil equivalent between 2010 and 2030. This reduction is about three times the level of world consumption of fossil fuels in 2008. Clearly, this is not sufficient to achieve the required 50-80 per cent reduction by 2050 or a

Improving energy efficiency is not enough: it will need to be complemented by massive investments in renewable low-emissions energy sources, leading over time to a drastic change in the composition of energy sources

Table I.7
Energy use and total investment (model output: 20-year averages taken in 2030)

	Efficiency: change in energy use per unit of output (percentage)	Stimulus: rate of growth of total investment in real terms (percentage)	Elasticity: ratio of impact of investment to efficiency
Developed countries	-5.20	2.90	1.80
Japan	-5.00	3.75	1.30
Europe	-4.80	2.92	1.60
United States	-5.40	2.54	2.10
Developing countries	-5.80	6.80	0.90
China	-6.40	6.45	1.00
Least developed countries	-6.65	9.90	0.70

Source: United Nations, Department of Economic and Social Affairs, Global Policy Model.

Figure I.5
Growth of world income and of energy use

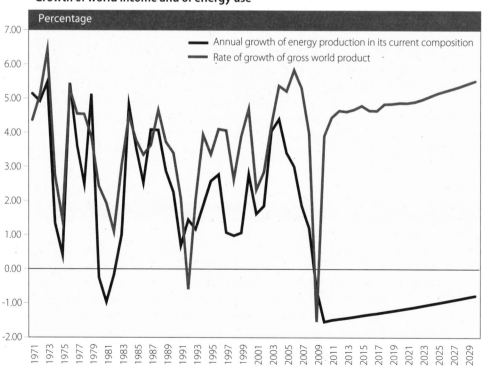

Source: United Nations, Department of Economic and Social Affairs, Global Policy Model.

13 The aggregation into tons of oil equivalent assumes the evolution over time of the current composition of energy production.

commensurate reduction of 25-40 per cent by 2030, as required. In other words, improving energy efficiency is not enough: it will need to be complemented by massive investments in renewable low-emissions energy sources, as assumed in the model simulations, leading over time to a drastic change in the composition of energy sources.

Admittedly, this is an optimistic scenario and the impact of the investment push on energy efficiency may not be as successful as the model outcome signals. Suppose, for example, that the improvements in energy use per unit of output are in the order of 4 per cent per annum instead of 6 per cent. Still, it would be possible to reach the same target for reduction of fossil fuel production (and thus of environmental contamination) if, alternatively, the investment strategies were geared towards the production of non-fossil fuels. This case will require annual increments of low emitting energy of the order of 2 per cent sustained over the long term—a requirement that is not impossible to fulfil. In a study of various country experiences, the Department of Economic and Social Affairs of the United Nations Secretariat and the International Atomic Energy Agency (2007) note that, between 1980 and 2000, Brazil increased the production of biofuels and hydro-electricity (covering about 40 per cent of the total demand for energy) at the rate of 2.25 per cent per annum. Significantly better records have been obtained in France through its shift to nuclear energy.[14] The biofuel or nuclear alternatives are not, of course, free of causes for concern. However, other sources, like wind, solar and hydroelectric, are valid options and are likely to become far more efficient as technologies advance.

Financing or access to markets?

There is no doubt that the low-emissions, high-growth strategy will carry high initial costs for both developed and developing economies. The former, however, are in a better position to advance on this path because they have the financial and technological resources; but even if they do achieve the kind of targets proposed above, this will certainly not be sufficient in terms of meeting global climate goals.

It will therefore be necessary to devise financing schemes through which the resources needed by the developing world to start out on this path are supplied by the developed world. It seems unlikely that developed countries would continue to finance such an investment push for too long. To highlight this difficulty, the global policy model produced an alternative low-emissions, high-growth simulation, fully dependent on external borrowing or aid, which is discussed in greater detail in chapter VI. Worthy of note, however, is the fact that such an outcome might very well leave developing countries still dependent on commodity exports and exposed to sharp price volatility, in addition to being saddled with the accumulation of external debt problems. The scenario also highlights how critical it is for the success of a truly sustainable development strategy that developing countries take significant steps towards attaining diversification into industry and services.

The scenario presented here assumes concerted action by policymakers, particularly in industrialized economies, that strongly encourages improved access of developing countries to the markets of those economies for manufactures and services. If this is accompanied by an international accord that encourages steady-state growth of production of food and primary materials and thus stable terms of trade (as is the case for agricultural

The success of a truly sustainable development strategy requires that developing countries take significant steps towards attaining diversification into industry and services

---

14   United Nations, Department of Economic and Social Affairs, and International Atomic Energy Agency, Energy indicators for sustainable development: country studies on Brazil, Cuba, Lithuania, Mexico, Russian Federation, Slovakia and Thailand (New York, Department of Economic and Social Affairs of the United Nations Secretariat, 2007).

prices in the European Union (EU) and elsewhere), their rapid expansion will benefit not just developing countries themselves but developed countries as well.

However, as indicated in chapter VI, the initial investment push will inevitably require financial support extended from developed to developing countries and, most particularly, to the least developed among them. As soon as there is a plan in place to increase the market share of developing countries in manufactures and services, the need for external resources will diminish sharply. Furthermore, in the absence of an external debt burden, a combination of stable prices of commodities and a sustained growth of income in both the developing and the developed world will contribute to a significantly less dramatic set of fluctuations in domestic prices, interest rates, exchange rates, etc., thus helping to avert sequences of stop-go adjustment-stabilization processes which have been so damaging for long-term development over the last decades.

As soon as there is a plan in place to increase the market share of developing countries in manufactures and services, the need for external resources will diminish sharply

Assessing the simulation results

This empirical exercise aimed at assessing whether the low-emissions, high-growth path postulated is a feasible one from an economic point of view. It clearly is. It succeeds in achieving perceptible improvements in reducing absolute energy consumption despite sustained rates of global economic growth, as discussed above. It also yields significantly higher rates of growth in the developing world and it also allows the developed countries to grow at a faster pace than under the business-as-usual scenario. The critical factor driving these patterns is public investment-led expansion. This is on a significant scale, though not extraordinary compared with some instances and the experience of some countries in the past. In terms of income per capita, this scenario yields an improvement for all blocs and, in particular, it significantly raises poorer countries to a level from which they can proceed in the direction of a smooth and unimpeded convergence. Finally, it contributes to export diversification, stable terms of trade and a smooth reduction of the external imbalances that have proved to be unsustainable. The plots in the annex to this chapter summarize these findings for the above-mentioned variables.

It is critical, however, to stress that the potential shortcomings of this scenario are not to be attributed to the underlying economic principles of the model simulation but rather to the political processes that are required in order for such a big push to take place. Without serious international policy coordination, this scenario cannot work. It is to be hoped that the gravity of the crisis in which the global economy is actually immersed owing to the lack of proactive policy intervention, and the seriousness of the environmental challenge, would be sufficiently powerful to impel policymakers to commit to achieving such a common goal as is exemplified by the low-emissions, high-growth strategy.

The potential shortcomings of the scenario presented here are not to be attributed to the underlying economic principles but rather to the political processes that are required in order for a big push to take place

Conclusion: managing crises

John Maynard Keynes famously remarked that "in the long run we are all dead". Keynes's existential angst was provoked by the stance of policymakers in the early 1920s who were postponing urgently needed action to counter immediate economic hardships in the belief that market forces would (eventually) bring the desired recovery. Similar thinking has informed much economic policymaking during the past three decades. His quip takes on a much more ominous meaning, however, in light of the combined threats to our economic and environmental security.

Price shocks during 2008 in food, fuel and housing markets laid bare the world economy's shaky foundations—excessive debt, unregulated capital flows and rampant speculation. The cost in terms of declining asset values and government bailouts of collapsed financial institutions has been staggering, while more widespread damage is now being felt in the real economies of advanced, emerging and least developed countries alike.

As policymakers seek to turn their economies around, much attention has been given to using economic stimulus packages not just to help meet the short-term goals of creating jobs and securing homes but also to achieve longer-term security goals, including a stable climate. This is a welcome development. However, turning the page on "casino capitalism" and establishing truly sustainable low-emissions alternatives will require policymakers to draw some hard lessons from recent experience.

As pointed out in *World Economic and Social Survey 2008* (United Nations, 2008), a wealth of historical experience and thoughtful reflection has demonstrated that markets—and not only financial markets—do not regulate themselves but depend on an array of institutions, rules, regulations and norms to correct coordination failures, moderate their more destructive impulses and manage the tensions these impulses can generate. There is now agreement that a return to robust economic health will mean breaking with the policy agenda of the past three decades; and while a new consensus has yet to emerge, there is no doubt that active government is back (Rudd, 2009).

The shift to a low-emissions, high-growth development path is a transformative challenge that requires just such a break with recent policy approaches as well as a long-term commitment to a new development path capable of generating full employment in advanced countries and catch-up growth in poorer countries. It will involve smarter incentives, stronger regulations and, above all, significant investments, including in the public sector.

The current crisis serves as a reminder that financial institutions need to get back into the business of securing people's savings and of building stable networks and levels of trust between industry and banking that can support more socially productive investment opportunities. These policy challenges are of long standing in many developing countries, where financial markets have repeatedly failed to build long-term commitments. Adding in the climate challenge only reinforces the urgency of reforming the financial system given the scale of resources that will have to mobilized over the coming decades and the trade-offs that will have to be made if economies are to secure a low-emissions future.

Market forces have an important role to play, but the real leadership will have to build upon a strong public policy agenda and a revitalized social contract—at both the national and international levels. Markets are prone to generate wrong information (risk of mis-pricing), giving rise to perverse behaviour (ranging from moral hazard and free-riding to outright fraud) and undesirable outcomes (excessive leverage, the proliferation of toxic products, hidden accounting practices). In a world of concentrated economic power, distorted information and uncertain outcomes, systemic instability is an ever present threat (Soros, 2008). The strengths and weaknesses of price incentives need to be kept firmly in mind as market-based solutions are extended to meet the climate challenge. Government action to establish a market for carbon, for example, whether through taxation or cap and trade, needs to be guided by an understanding of the limits of price signals with respect to meeting any large and complex challenge—whether it is achieving full employment, engendering catch-up growth, guaranteeing financial stability or tackling the climate crisis—and managing the threat of catastrophic risk.

Turning the page on "casino capitalism" and establishing truly sustainable low-emissions alternatives will require policymakers to draw some hard lessons from recent experience

Market forces have an important role to play, but the real leadership will have to build upon a strong public policy agenda and a revitalized social contract

The current financial crisis has provided a reminder that Governments are the only agents capable of mobilizing the massive financial and political resources needed to confront large systemic threats

The current financial crisis has provided a reminder that Governments are the only agents capable of mobilizing the massive financial and political resources needed to confront large systemic threats. It has also served to demonstrate that policymakers can act with real urgency when faced with such threats. This is encouraging from both the development and the climate angles, given that both challenges involve large resource commitments over the long term, and at both the national and the global levels. Meeting these challenges will entail not only surmounting traditional market failures which occur as a result of externalities and free-riding but also dealing with systemic threats and managing large-scale adjustments in economic activity. The only sensible response is to mix market solutions with other mechanisms, including regulations and public investment.

Annex

Figure A.I.1
Low-emissions, high-growth global scenario: trends in income per capita, by country groups, 1970–2030
(2005 United States dollars purchasing power parity)

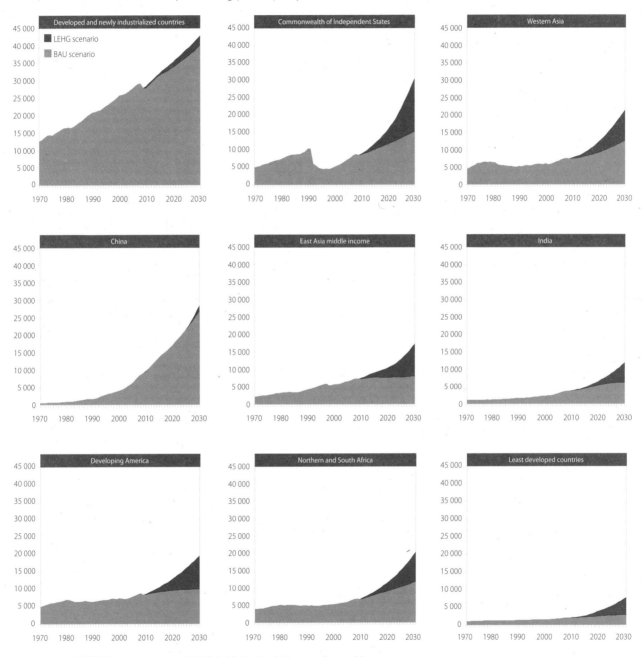

Source: UN/DESA, simulations with UN Global Policy Model (see text for model assumptions).

Figure A.I.2
Low-emissions, high-growth global scenario: GDP growth by country groups, 1970-2030
(long-term income growth, 20 years moving average (percentage))

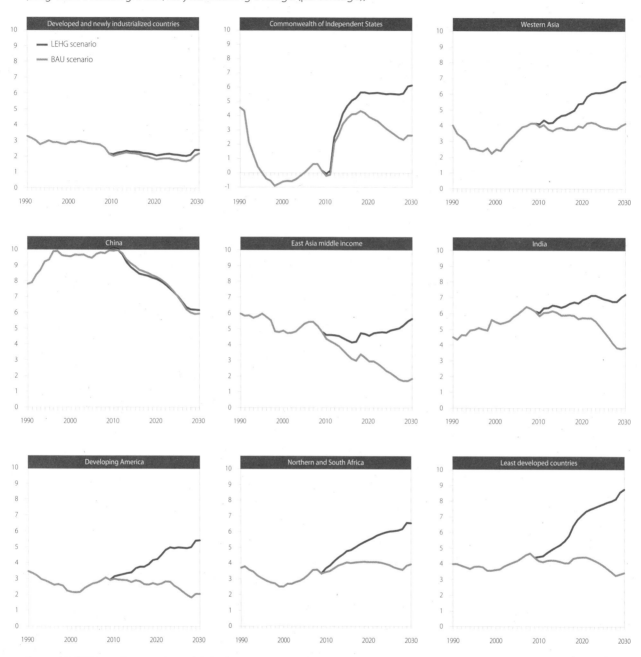

Source: UN/DESA, simulations with UN Global Policy Model (see text for model assumptions).

Figure A.I.3
Low-emissions, high-growth global scenario: growth of real public spending, 1970-2030
(long-term income growth, 20 years moving average (percentage))

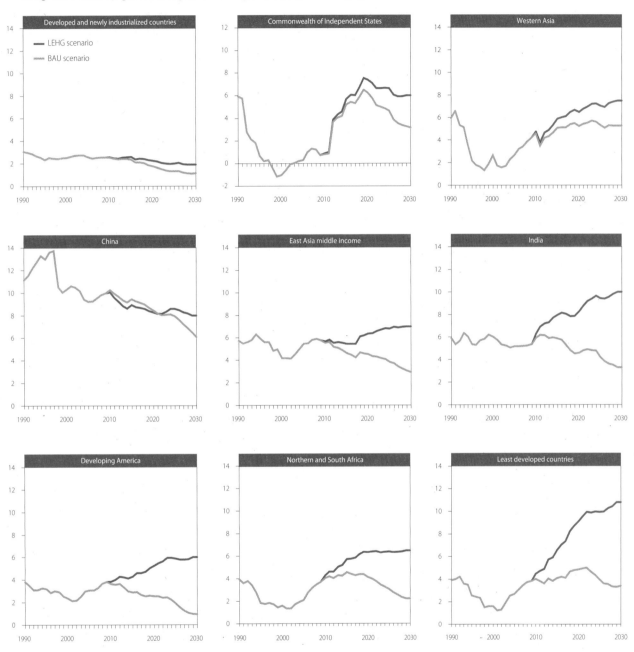

Source: UN/DESA, simulations with UN Global Policy Model (see text for model assumptions).

Figure A.I.4
**Low-emissions, high-growth global scenario: world market prices of
oil, primary commodities and manufactures, 1970-2030**
(relative price indices, 200 = 100)

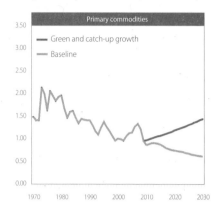

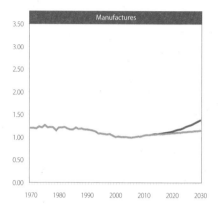

Source: UN/DESA, simulations with UN Global Policy Model (see text for model assumptions).
Note: Commodity price indices were deflated by implicit price deflator of world gross product.

Chapter II
Climate mitigation and the energy challenge: a paradigm shift

Introduction

A maximum temperature increase of 2°C above pre-industrial levels is the consensus target established by the scientific community for stabilizing carbon concentrations at a level that prevents dangerous anthropogenic interference in the climate system. At the same time, developing countries need to achieve a sustained catch-up growth rate of 6-8 per cent per annum to close the income gap with countries at the top of the development ladder. These two broad objectives frame the mitigation challenge facing policymakers at the national and international levels. The present chapter attempts to detail mitigation options that are consistent with convergent economic growth in developing countries.

> Developing countries must achieve a sustained catch-up growth rate of 6-8 per cent per annum

The preceding mitigation target translates globally (in terms of actual emissions reduced) into a reduction from roughly 40 gigatons of carbon dioxide ($GtCO_2$) annually at present to 8-20 $GtCO_2$ by 2050. This is no small undertaking and will involve significant economic adjustments in developed and developing countries. There are certainly win-win options linked, particularly, to energy efficiency; but, as discussed in chapter I, this is necessary but not sufficient to meet stabilization targets. Large-scale and upfront investment in the means of production of electricity along with new sources of renewable energy will be needed, as well as related investments in transportation and construction.

What is required is a gale of "creative destruction" driven by massive investments and innovative technologies. This is not inevitable but will require dedicated and strategic policy action at all levels. The threat is that, by delaying such action, existing investment projects will lock in older technologies for decades, leading to a ratcheting up of the stock of emissions to dangerous levels, and requiring much more costly economic and social adjustments in the future (Stern, 2009).

> What is required is a gale of "creative destruction" driven by massive investment and innovative technologies

In spite of all the accumulating scientific knowledge and growing public awareness of the climate challenge, effective mitigation action has been lacking in developed countries. One of the fundamental reasons for this is a persistent disconnect between environmental objectives and economic goals. This has begun to change with the recognition that the interrelated threats from the financial, energy and climate crises will need to be tackled together (New Economics Foundation, 2008).

> Serious and effective mitigation action is lacking in developed countries

Addressing the challenge of climate change mitigation in developing countries requires not only a change in global and national focus on climate and development policy, but also strategic thinking in terms of the most relevant mitigation options using development as the essential trigger: poverty reduction, rural development, energy access, industrial expansion and infrastructure provision all need to be integrated with mitigation strategies.

The energy sector, broadly defined, accounts for 60 per cent of global emissions (table I.1) and unless significant emissions reductions are achieved from the way energy is produced and consumed, it will not be possible to meet stabilization targets. Energy is, moreover, the pivotal issue at the interface of the climate and development challenges. For this reason, it is the focus of this chapter.

> Energy is the pivotal issue at the interface of the climate and development challenges

Deforestation and forest
degradation in developing
countries are the primary
sources of carbon emissions
from these countries

Deforestation is the other major source of greenhouse gas (GHG) emissions. In 2004, the forest sector accounted for the release of approximately 8.5 gigatons (Gt) of carbon dioxide (CO_2), mostly from deforestation, which contributes 17.4 per cent of all human-generated CO_2 emissions. Deforestation and forest degradation in developing countries are the primary sources of carbon emissions from these countries. Deforestation accounts for 35 per cent of carbon emissions in developing countries and 65 per cent in least developed countries. According to estimates of the Food and Agriculture Organization of the United Nations (FAO), on average, 13 million hectares of forest were lost each year between 2000 and 2005. Over the same period, 5.7 million hectares were added to forest area annually, resulting in a rate of net forest loss of 7.3 million hectares per year, a slowdown from the rate of deforestation experienced between 1990 and 2000.

While we are focusing on the energy sector, at the same time we do not wish to suggest that addressing mitigation options in other sectors like land-use change and forestry, agriculture, transportation, waste and industrial processes is unimportant or irrelevant: these options remain equally important and for some developing countries, they are a key focus. But unless the energy challenge is addressed, as we argue in this chapter, we will experience neither the required mitigation in developing countries nor the catch-up growth needed to allow the transformative change in the economies of developing countries so crucial to their climate and development success.

The next section considers some stablization scenarios and the technological options that will be needed to pursue them. Those options include energy efficiency and new approaches to existing sources, as well as the utilization of new energy sources. This is followed by a discussion of the links among energy, growth and development and what is implied by ensuring income and energy convergence while meeting the climate challenge. The following section considers the big investment push onto a low-emissions growth path. Finally, some elements of an integrated strategy combining energy security, energy access, expanded capacity and research and development are proposed.

Stabilization scenarios and mitigation options

The more than 20-fold
growth in global CO_2
emissions has resulted in
a dramatic increase of its
atmospheric concentrations

The more than 20-fold growth in global CO_2e emissions between 1750 and to present has resulted in a dramatic increase of its atmospheric concentrations from a volume of about 310 parts per million (ppm) to one of almost 430 ppm. Emissions of other radiatively active gases in the atmosphere have accompanied the increase in CO_2. Methane concentrations have doubled over the same period. Chlorofluorocarbons (CFCs) are a fundamentally new anthropogenic addition to the atmosphere. Another indication of the complexities involved is the fact that emissions of sulphur aerosols and particulate matter increase along with energy consumption and emissions of greenhouse gases.[1]

Land-use mitigation
options could provide
15-40 per cent of total
cumulative abatement
over the century

Multi-gas emission reduction scenarios are able to meet climate targets at substantially lower costs compared with CO_2-only strategies (Fisher and others, 2007) and provide for a more diversified approach which offers greater flexibility in the timing of reduction programmes. Including land-use mitigation options as abatement strategies also ensures greater flexibility and cost-effectiveness for achieving stabilization. Even if land activities are not addressed directly in mitigation policies, consideration of land use and land cover are crucial in climate stabilization, given their significant atmospheric inputs

---

1   Aerosol emissions are now regulated in most industrialized countries and are in decline. These
      have actually resulted in regional cooling which has offset some of the climate warming caused
      by increasing concentrations of greenhouse gases.

and withdrawals (through sequestration and albedo effects). Recent stabilization studies indicate that land-use mitigation options could provide from 15-40 per cent of total cumulative abatement over the century (ibid.).

The timing of emission reductions depends on the stringency of the stabilization target. The lower the stabilization target, the sooner the peak of CO_2 and CO_2 equivalent (CO_2e) emissions.[2] In the majority of the scenarios with stringent stabilization targets, (as is the case for category I, with a stabilization level below 490 ppm CO_2e) (figure II.1), emissions are required to decline from around 2015 (at the latest by 2020), dropping to less than 50 per cent of today's emissions by 2050. For somewhat more stringent stabilization levels (for example, below 450 or even 350 ppm CO_2e), global emissions in the scenarios generally peak around the same time, followed by a decline to 80 per cent or more below 1990 levels by 2050. These kind of radical emissions reductions depart fundamentally from the current trends and will require a paradigm-changing transition of the global energy system towards full decarbonization.

Figure II.1 displays global CO_2 emissions from 1940 to 2000 and presents six categories of stabilization scenarios from 2000 to 2100 (left-hand graph); and the corresponding relationship between the stabilization targets and the likely equilibrium global average temperature increase above pre-industrial (right-hand graph). Coloured shadings show stabilization scenarios grouped according to different targets (stabilization categories I to VI). The right-hand graph shows the ranges of global average temperature change above pre-industrial, using (a) "best estimate" climate sensitivity of 3° C (black line in middle of shaded area), (b) upper bound of likely range of climate sensitivity of 4.5° C (red line at top of shaded area) and (c) lower bound of likely range of climate sensitivity of 2° C (blue line at bottom of shaded area). The black broken lines in the left-hand graph portray the emissions range of recent baseline scenarios published since the Special Report on Emissions Scenarios (Nakicenovic and others, 2000). Emissions ranges of the stabilization scenarios encompass CO_2-only and multi-gas (all greenhouse gases and other radiatively active substances) scenarios and correspond to the 10th-90th percentile of the full probability distribution for each.

Figure II.1
Alternative scenarios for CO_2 emissions and equilibrium temperature increases for a range of stabilization levels, 1940-2100

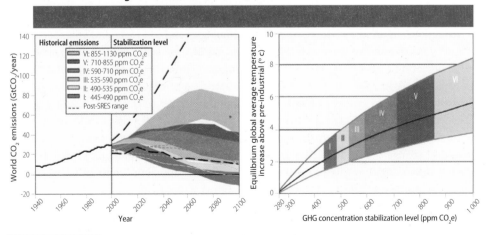

Source: Intergovernmental Panel on Climate Change, (2007c).

Abbreviations: SRES, Special Report on Emissions Scenarios (IPCC).

2   CO_2 equivalent concentration takes into account the radiative forcing of other greenhouse gases besides CO_2 and, often, also other radiatively active substances such as sulphur aerosols and carbon black.

Figure II.1 indicates the urgent need for fundamental changes in the global energy system, land-use patterns and also in human behaviour. Managing those changes will require an integrated policy framework to effect a fundamental paradigm shift from current emissions-intensive patterns of wealth creation to a future low-emissions and decarbonized global economy. Of the utmost importance for achieving stabilization targets and keeping down their cost will be widespread technology improvements adopted on a timely basis, including the diffusion of new technologies, and induced changes to existing technologies.

What seems clear is that drastic CO_2 reduction targets of 50-80 per cent by 2050 (compared with 1990 emission levels) will require reduction in the rate of energy intensity and improvement in carbon intensity by a factor of 2-3 with respect to their historical levels. All stabilization scenarios indicate that a huge share of emissions reductions, in the range of 60-80 per cent, would come from changes in energy systems. It has been found that this will require different sets of mitigation options across regions, with varying shares of renewable energy, nuclear energy, carbon capture and sequestration (CCS), biomass and hydrogen and other advanced energy carriers.

Energy efficiency can play a catalytic role in achieving radical emissions reductions. In a way, it is a prerequisite for increasing shares of zero-carbon energy systems. However, it would be wrong to overestimate its contribution, even in advanced economies (Barker, Dagoumas and Rubin, 2009).

Even efficiency gains will require some investments, though not on the scale required to develop and diffuse new technologies and change existing technologies. Achieving low stabilization levels will require early (upfront) large-scale investments and substantially more rapid diffusion and commercialization of advanced low-emissions technologies. Such investments will need to be made worldwide on the required scale, implying that effective technology and resource transfers will need to be made to those countries lacking those means (see chaps. V and VI for further discussion).

Currently, there are several options for curbing emissions without jeopardizing economic growth, especially in developing countries. These include a switch to renewable energy technologies (of which the most significant is solar energy), the adoption of CCS technologies both to curb emissions from fossil fuel plants and generally to facilitate negative emissions, the enhancement of terrestrial sinks through afforestation in conjunction with sustainable biomass use, and investment in energy efficiency solutions.

The greenhouse gas abatement cost curve developed by McKinsey & Company provides a useful quantitative estimate of both the costs and the actions needed to achieve such reductions (figure II.2). The curve ranks technologies and industrial processes according to the net costs of avoiding a ton of CO_2 emissions, taking into account both the capital costs and the operating costs of low-emissions technologies. Figure II.2 suggests opportunities for negative cost (or win-win) emissions reductions where the upfront capital costs are more than offset by future energy savings. Most of these savings are achieved through improved energy efficiency. Technical abatement opportunities up to a cost of €60 per ton of CO_2e include: energy efficiency, low-emissions energy supply, terrestrial carbon (forestry and agriculture) and behavioural change (figure II.3). The first three options generate a total abatement of 38 Gt CO_2e per year in 2030 relative to annual business-as-usual emissions of 70 Gt CO_2e. Abatement opportunities in these three categories are spread across many sectors of the economy: with approximate figures of 29 per cent for the energy supply sectors (electricity, petroleum and gas); 16 per cent in the industrial sector; 22 per cent in transport, buildings and waste; and 33 per cent in land-use sectors (forestry and agriculture). In all, developing countries have 70 per cent of the reductions opportunities, while developed countries have 30 per cent.

Achieving low stabilization levels will require early (upfront) investments and substantially more rapid diffusion and commercialization of advanced, low-emissions technologies

Figure II.2
Global GHG abatement cost curve beyond business-as-usual, 2030

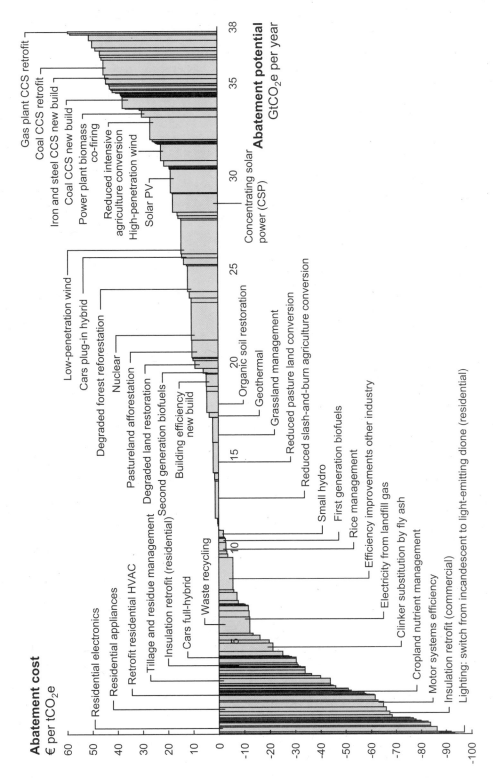

Source: Global GHG Abatement Cost Curve, v2.0.

Note: The curve presents an estimate of the maximum potential of all technical GHG abatement measures below €60 per tCO$_2$e if each lever was to be pursued aggressively. It is not a forecast of what role different abatement measures and technologies will play.

Figure II.3
Major categories of abatement opportunities

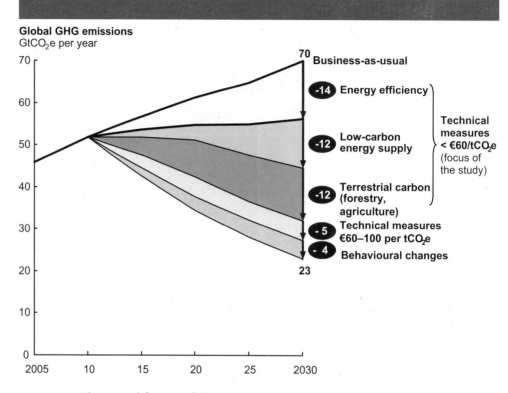

Global GHG emissions
GtCO₂e per year

Sources: Global GHG Abatement Cost Curve, v2.0; Houghton; IEA; and US EPA.

Note: The estimate of behavioural change abatement potential was made after implementation of all technical levers; the potential would be higher if modelled before implementation of the technical levers.

The central feature of these options is that they assume a start date of 2010—a delay of 10 years would almost certainly mean missing the 2°C degree target. Many developing countries are already taking steps on mitigation. However, more action will be required. The policy challenge is to ensure that such action supports, rather than obstructs, the achievement of development goals.

Energy and economic development

The evolution of the energy system

Improved water quality, diet, sanitary conditions and medicine have all contributed to population growth, and all are correlated with increased availability of energy resources

In 1750, the world's population was approximately 750 million, representing a little more than a threefold increase over the population in AD 1 (Maddison, 2006). With the emergence of the industrial revolution, things changed radically. Table II.1 shows that in 1800, global population was still less than 1 billion compared with over 6.5 billion today. This more than sixfold increase corresponds to an annual growth rate of close to 1 per cent per year, and the doubling of the global population every 80 years. This explosive population growth was a result of drastic decreases in mortality and increases in longevity. Improved water quality, diet, sanitary conditions and medicine have all contributed, and all are correlated with increased availability of energy resources.

World gross product (WGP) increased more than 70-fold during the last two centuries, corresponding to an annual increase of 2 per cent per year and a doubling every 35 years. To a large extent, this was made possible by the replacement of human and

Table II.1
**Increases in population, economic activity, energy use,
mobility and greenhouse gas emissions, 1800-2000**

Absolute size and cumulative increases			
	1800	*2000*	*Factor*
Population (billions)	1.0	6.0	x 6
WGP (trillions of US dollars 1990)	0.5	36	x 72
Primary energy use (exajoules)	13	440	x 34
CO$_2$ Emissions (gigatons of carbon)	0.3	6.4	x 21
Mobility (kilometres/person/day)	0.04	40	x 1 000

Source: Nakicenovic (2009).

animal workers with machines fuelled by fossil energy and the resulting release of labour into high-productivity manufacturing activities.

This historical transition is reflected in the enormous increase in global energy needs, by a factor of 34, during the last two centuries. Primary energy increased at half the rate of GDP, meaning that energy intensity of the global economy has declined at the rate of about 1 per cent per year. The CO$_2$ emissions increased even less, indicating a pervasive historical trend towards decarbonization of the global economy at about 1.3 per cent per year.

The energy intensity of economic activities has in fact declined 2-fold but the 72-fold increase in economic activities has required ever more energy. The share of fossil energy sources, taken together, increased (from 20 to 80 per cent) between 1850 and now, as did the emissions of CO$_2$ (as an unavoidable by-product of combustion). Consequently, energy-related emissions of CO$_2$ increased 21-fold to about 6 billion tons of carbon (6 GtC) in 2000. Nevertheless, their increase has remained at a substantially slower pace than that of energy requirements, indicating a strong historical trend towards decarbonization of societies.

Figure II.4 shows how drastically the composition of energy services has been transformed through replacement of traditional (non-commercial) energy sources by fossil fuels—first coal and later oil and natural gas.

In 1800, the world still depended on traditional biomass (mostly fuelwood and agricultural waste) as the main energy source for cooking, heating and manufacturing. Human physical labour and animals were the main sources of mechanical energy, with some, but much more humble, contributions from wind and hydraulic power. By 1850, coal had already provided some 20 per cent of global primary energy needs; the figure peaked to almost 70 per cent by the 1920s. This shift may be characterized as the first energy transition. The coal age brought railways, steam power, steel, manufacturing and the telegraph, to mention just some of the technologies that constituted the coal techno-economic paradigm or the "coal cluster".

Around 1900, motor vehicles were introduced along with petrochemicals, electricity and many other technologies that constituted the "oil cluster". It took another 70 years for oil to replace coal as the dominant source of energy in the world. Today, the global energy system is much more complex, with many competing sources of energy and many high-quality and convenient energy carriers ranging form grid-oriented forms such as natural gas and electricity, and liquids which are mostly used in transportation, to solids (coal and biomass) which are still used in the developing parts of the world (whose one third of global population still do not have any, or any reliable, access to modern energy services). Taken together, fossil energy sources provide some 80 per cent of global energy needs, while fuelwood, hydropower and nuclear energy provide the rest.

By the 1920s, coal provided almost 70 per cent of global primary energy needs ...

... while today, fossil energy sources provide some 80 per cent of global energy needs

Figure II.4
Global primary energy requirements since 1850

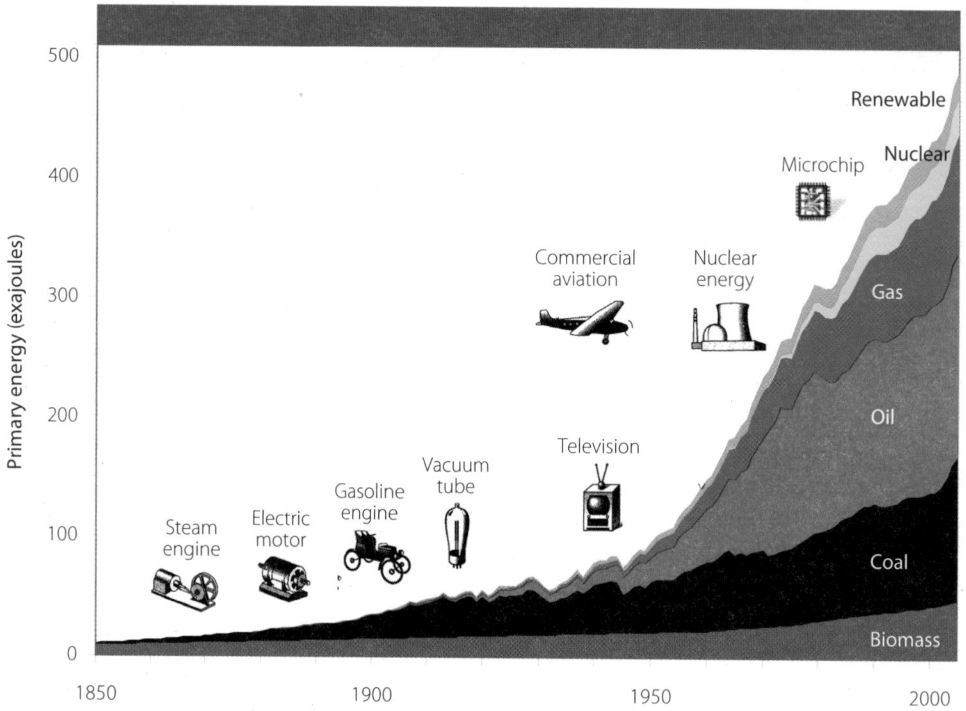

Source: Nakicenovic (2009).

Energy and growth

Energy is the critical link between development and climate mitigation. Access to energy services is distributed almost as unequally as income, with a fairly strong correlation between the two. Up to a point, energy consumption is strongly correlated with human development (see figure II.5). There is, not surprisingly, a strong correlation between economic convergence and energy convergence.

From a policy perspective, significant investments in "social overhead capital" such as the provision of energy services has long been singled out by development economists, in part because of the direct welfare effects of the services provided, but also because of their potential to crowd in other productive investments (Hirschman, 1958; Canning, 1998; Calderón and Servén, 2003).

Returns to these investments are likely to be highest in the early development stages when basic networks are still incomplete. In low-income countries, basic services such as water, irrigation and transport account for most infrastructure spending, while in middle-income countries, telecommunications, and especially electric power, become more important. Once the social overhead capital is in place, more targeted policy incentives can support further diversification and technological upgrading, thereby helping to break remaining constraints on a virtuous growth cycle (Bateman, Ros and Taylor, 2008; United Nations, 2006; Rodríguez, 2007). Indeed, a virtuous circle of strong investment, rising productivity, falling costs, and expanding incomes and markets, leading to further investments and increases in productivity, exhibits the mix of cumulative supply- and demand-side impulses essential to sustained development. Large public investments in social capital, such as energy services, can play a catalytic role in this (Ingram and Fay, 2008; Bindra and Hokoma, 2009).

Energy is the critical link between development and climate mitigation

From a policy perspective, significant investments in "social overhead capital" such as the provision of energy services has long been advocated by development economists

Figure II.5
Per capita energy consumption and human development, selected countries

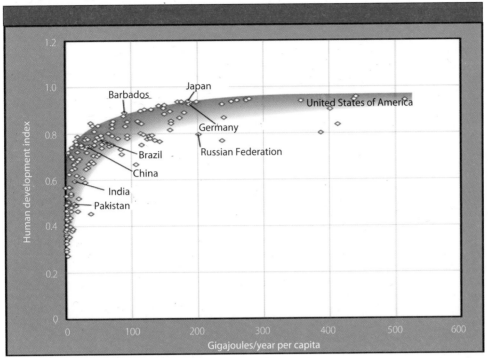

Source: Banuri (2007).

Part of the aim of any big public investment push is to increase the marginal return to private investments in new and more modern technologies by creating rents and market opportunities for the private sector (see chap. IV). Albert Hirschman (1958) recognized that the key to such a push was not just the speed with which cost advantages in the targeted sectors were realized but also the links those sectors established backwards to suppliers of inputs and forward to new activities and markets that used the goods produced by the targeted sector, and whose expansion could trigger new investment opportunities. Hirschman associated these backward and forward linkages mainly with large-scale industrial investment, but he also recognized that the power sector had very strong linkage potential which could trigger cumulative development prospects (see also Toman and Jemelkova, 2003).

The importance of electrification to rural development has long been recognized. Major investments in rural electrification projects, mainly grid extension (United States Congress, Office of Technology Assessment (OTA), 1992) have been an integral part of successful growth experiences. In rapidly developing agricultural regions, electricity helps to raise the productivity of local agro-industrial and commercial activities by supplying motive power, refrigeration, lighting and process heating. Increased earnings from agricultural and local industry and commerce lead, in turn, to greater household demand for electricity. Energy availability for cheaper and better lighting can increase the productivity of education inputs generally and lead to an augmentation effect in human capital provision, as well as raise output by extending the length of the workday.

Increased earnings from agricultural and local industry and commerce lead to greater household demand for electricity

Achieving convergent economic growth and energy consumption

Globally, approximately 31 million tons of oil equivalent are consumed in the form of primary energy every day, equivalent to 55 kilowatt hours (kWh) per person per day. This consumption is distributed very unequally (see table II.2). In countries members of the Organization for Economic Cooperation and Development (OECD), average per capita consumption varies between 100 and 300 kWh per day, divided roughly equally between household and commercial consumption. In the vast majority of developing countries, average per capita consumption is under 35 kWh per day. The exceptions are the countries of

Table II.2
Per capita energy consumption, selected countries, 2005

Country or area	Population (millions)	Primary energy (kWh per capita /day)	Electricity (kWh per capita/day)
Australia	21.0	183.20	28.70
Canada	32.9	265.03	44.13
France	61.7	142.63	19.86
Germany	82.3	133.68	18.28
Japan	127.7	131.84	21.08
Sweden	9.1	182.76	40.21
United Kingdom	61.0	122.50	15.65
United States	302.2	246.92	34.60
Russian Federation	141.7	145.41	15.85
Brazil	189.3	35.27	5.53
Chile	16.6	56.75	7.51
Mexico	106.5	52.85	5.04
Venezuela (Bolivarian Republic of)	27.5	70.60	8.35
Kenya	36.9	14.89	0.38
Nigeria	144.4	22.90	0.30
South Africa	47.9	84.90	11.55
Egypt	73.4	26.61	3.59
Bangladesh	149.0	5.17	0.39
India	1 131.9	15.13	1.25
China	1 318.0	41.51	5.26
Hong Kong SAR[a]	6.9	83.48	15.10
Indonesia	231.6	24.70	1.31
Malaysia	27.2	71.78	9.67
Korea, Republic of	48.5	139.64	20.63
Philippines	88.7	16.05	1.45
Singapore	4.6	208.49	20.92
Taiwan Province of China	22.9	147.19	24.97
Thailand	65.7	49.03	5.17
Viet Nam	85.1	19.21	1.55

Sources: UN/DESA, based on primary energy data from Organization for Economic Cooperation and Development, the electricity data from International Energy Agency (in million kWh per year); and population data from Population Reference Bureau.

a   Special Administrative Region of China.

the Organization of the Petroleum Exporting Countries (OPEC), the newly industrialized countries and regions (Singapore, Republic of Korea, Hong Kong Special Administrative Region of China and Taiwan Province of China, which approach OECD levels), and some emerging economies (such as South Africa at 85 kWh, Malaysia at 72 kWh, and Chile at 57 kWh). Most countries from sub-Saharan Africa, and all South Asian countries consume well under 20 kWh per capita per day. The differences are even wider in the case of consumption of electricity, the pre-eminent form of modern energy service, and the very symbol of modernity and affluence.

The threshold of 100 kWh per capita per day can be used as a convenient dividing line between energy poverty and energy sufficiency. In figure II.5, this consumption level is equivalent to 130 megajoules per capita per year, which corresponds to a human development index of 0.9, somewhat to the left of Japan's. Achieving this human development target would imply a significant expansion of energy infrastructure. Here is where the climate and energy agenda of developing countries begins to diverge from that of developed countries.

In developed countries, there is greater scope for energy conservation and enhancement of energy efficiency, especially since most developed countries consume well over 100 kWh of energy per capita per day, and a scaling down of energy consumption could very well be consistent with the same or higher levels of income and well-being. In developing countries, in contrast, while the energy efficiency agenda is still important, it does not obviate the need for expansion of the energy infrastructure. Enhanced energy efficiency could mean the difference between the desired target indicated here, namely, 100 kWh per capita per day, and, say, 200 kWh per day or higher. Regardless, most countries will need to expand energy services to the threshold level of 100 kWh per day in order to meet the bulk of their human development targets.

> In developing countries, energy efficiency does not obviate the need for expansion of the energy infrastructure

The second reason for divergence hinges on the question of affordability. Currently, the expansion in energy services in developing countries is impeded partly because of the fact that the vast majority of the population is too poor to afford these services without some form of subsidy. Even populations with incomes of $10 per day would not be able to spend more than, say, $1-$2 per day on energy-related expenditures (electricity, cooking, heating, transport). If energy is priced higher than, say, $0.05 per kWh, they would not be able to access adequate amounts of energy services.

> The vast majority of the population in developing countries are too poor to be able to afford energy services without some form of subsidy

This would seem to call for the creation of three complementary agendas. At the aggregate level, it would make sense to set a minimum global target of 100 kWh per capita per day in order to overcome energy poverty. Second, it would also make sense to institute energy efficiency measures in order that this optimal target might correspond to the achievement of economic and human development targets. At the most urgent level, there would also be a need to address "energy destitution", namely the lack of access to modern energy services.

The faster-growing developing countries have been able to follow this trajectory with reasonable success. However, even where the project has been successful—the outstanding example is China, which has doubled energy consumption in five years—it has been based on exploitation of the least-cost energy source, namely, coal, which is also the most polluting energy source in the context of climate change. However, while technological alternatives to coal and other fossil fuels do exist, they are far more costly. If developing countries resort to these resources at other than pilot scales, they would end up putting modern energy services beyond the reach of the bulk of their populations for a generation or more.

That this is a daunting agenda cannot be questioned. Assuming catch-up growth and continuing rates of urbanization and industrialization, closing the gap between energy supply and energy demand in developing countries would require investments of the order of trillions of dollars, even for low-cost options, such as coal, and certainly well in excess of current energy investments in many developing countries.

The bulk of energy infrastructure in developing countries has yet to be built, leaving energy services under-supplied and expensive in several parts of the developing world, where many still rely primarily on traditional biomass fuels, namely, wood, crop wastes and animal dung, for their energy needs.

Under these circumstances, it may be cheaper and easier to switch to a renewable pathway than to retool existing infrastructure. Cost and technical improvements in a wide range of small-scale, decentralized technologies based on renewable forms of energy now offer, in many situations, a cost-effective and sustainable approach to rural electrification. Still, any big push into low-emissions energy sources is likely to be associated with massive investments in developing wind, hydro and other renewable energy sources, interconnecting isolated areas with the main national grid. The rising demand for liquid fuels and gases stemming from accelerated rural development might potentially be met through the development of a modern biomass fuels industry which could simultaneously increase farm and rural industry employment and income. Renewable energies could also generate backward linkages, as the search for inputs that produced a lower level of carbon emissions would provide incentives to innovate and explore new activities. The fact that there are possible alternative strategies for economic and social development, with energy implications, underlines the need to include energy considerations in development planning.

> Any big push into low-emissions energy sources is likely to be associated with massive investments in developing wind, hydro and other renewable energy sources

The energy investment push

Figure II.6 depicts the historical evolution of the energy system and one possible future development path towards decarbonization, as spelled out in the B1 stabilization scenario (see chap. I, note 4). It is an illustration of the needed transformational change of the global energy system. New energy technologies and practices, as well as changes in lifestyles and behaviour, are prerequisites for turning the energy system from its current dependence on fossil energy towards a complete decarbonization by the end of the century. This particular scenario describes a future world that stabilizes concentrations of the greenhouse gases just above the current levels and thereby limits global average temperature change to about 2° C by the end of the century. The climate change posited by such a scenario would be uneven across regions, and in many regions, might significantly exceed the 2° C global average. Hence, even a global temperature increase of 2° C can lead to considerable local vulnerabilities and disruptions in respect of natural ecosystems, water availability and communities in coastal areas (see chap. III). Nevertheless, a 2° C world would be spared the most severe adverse (and perhaps also irreversible) consequences associated with higher rates of climate change. The B1 stabilization scenario can be characterized as a transition towards sustainability that leads to economic convergence and the fulfilment of the Millennium Development Goals in most parts of the world while simultaneously avoiding more drastic climate changes. This is very much in line with the scenario presented in the previous chapter.

> A transformational change of the global energy system is needed

The nature of technological change and the associated deep uncertainties of its impact on the climate challenge require the adoption of innovations as early as possible in order to ensure lower costs and wider diffusion in the following decades. The longer the wait to introduce these advanced technologies, the higher the required emissions reduction will

> The longer we wait to introduce advanced technologies, the higher the required emissions reduction will be

Figure II.6
Historical evolution of, and a possible future for, the global energy system, in the context of the relative shares of the most important energy sources, 1850-2100

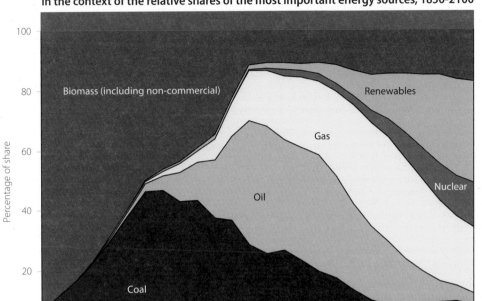

Sources: Grübler, Nakicenovic and Riahi (2007), Nakicenovic and Riahi (2007), and International Institute for Applied Systems Analysis (2007).

eventually be. At the same time, taking the opportunity window for achieving substantial cost buy-downs will require research, development and deployment (RD&D) as well as massive investments to achieve accelerated diffusion and adoption of advanced energy technologies.

It was suggested above that there are significant global mitigation opportunities which correspond to less than €60 per ton of CO_2e. This potential could be larger, especially if the price of carbon increased (Fisher and others, 2007). In mid-2008, for example, the oil price reached almost $140/barrel indicating that the equivalent price of carbon in this range is not outside our recent experience of energy price volatility. However, it is also clear that the spike in oil prices in 2008 was part of a multifaceted development crisis, creating balance-of-payments challenges for energy-importing developing countries, adverse impacts on fiscal solvency, and increases in the costs of a range of basic needs, including food, transportation and energy. Even though the spike was short-lived, a prolonged escalation in energy prices would have been costly in developmental terms for many countries. In this regard, the adoption of a pure carbon market strategy would require the provision of direct subsidies to developing countries in order to offset the adverse impacts of higher energy prices. But these subsidies alone will not suffice: they will need to be supplemented with adequate domestic measures to translate the international subsidies into targeted subsidies aimed at poor and vulnerable groups (see also chap. VI).

Technological learning and the change that it produces are essential for reducing mitigation costs and increasing mitigation potentials (chap. V). It is true that increasing the price of carbon (and other greenhouse gases) could trigger some of the technological, institutional and behavioural changes required for effective emissions reduction. Given the low mitigation costs in developing countries, least-cost mitigation efforts would channel investment to these countries, assuming that appropriate institutional arrangements could

The adoption of a pure carbon market strategy would require the provision of direct subsidies to developing countries

be made. However, these measures would have to be combined with a suite of compensatory policies so as to offset the social and economic costs of the price increase.

To realize the benefits of technological learning, "upfront" investments would need to be made in new and advanced carbon-saving technologies which would, after scale-up and adoption, lower the mitigation costs and increase the mitigation potentials. Chapter I suggests that these will initially have to be public investments.

Energy system investments are shown in figure II.7 for two scenarios, A2 and B1. The former is similar to that depicted in "business-as-usual" scenarios, with a high increase of greenhouse gas emissions leading to a global temperature change of about 4.5° C. B1 corresponds to a more sustainable future with vigorous investment in new technologies and lifestyle changes which result in global temperature change of less than 3° C. The total investments are in the range of $20 trillion by 2030 and are slightly higher for the more sustainable future of B1, owing to the build-up of capital-intensive energy systems. Ensuring that a 2° C target is achieved would imply higher investment still, almost certainly above the trillion dollars-a-year target (see chap. VI). However, in the long term, beyond 2030, the capital costs of ensuring the more sustainable future are significantly lower owing to induced technological change and learning. In other words, early upfront investments would have to be made to enable potential buy-downs along the learning curves. This means that large upfront investments would have to be made in currently developing countries. Indeed, again assuming that they will have the lowest costs and highest mitigation potentials, and largest opportunities for new markets, investments in the energy sector in developing countries should dominate in the coming decades.

Figure II.7
Energy systems investment, 2000-2030

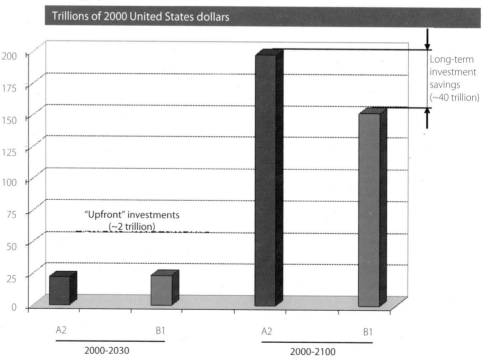

Sources: Grübler, Nakicenovic
and Riahi (2007).

An integrated approach to the mitigation challenge

Energy security[3]

For many advanced countries, the availability of oil in the years ahead has become a matter of some concern and controversy. The United States Department of Energy, in its International Energy Outlook for 2008,[4] predicts that the world energy industry will be capable of supplying 103 million barrels per day of conventional oil in 2030 plus another 10 million barrels in unconventional fluids (biofuels, extra-heavy oil, oil sands, and so on), for a total of 113 million barrels per day. On the other hand, the International Energy Agency (IEA), in its Medium-term oil market report for 2009-2012, released in July 2008, suggests that the industry will be capable of producing 96 million barrels per day by 2013, but expresses considerable doubt about its capacity to raise production much above that level because of declining output at existing fields, a disappointing record of new oilfield discovery, and concerns about the adequacy of future investment.

Many energy experts hope that the supply of other basic fuels—natural gas, coal, nuclear, hydropower and so on—can be expanded even beyond current growth rates in order to compensate for the anticipated shortfall in the availability of oil. Still, without a radical shift in energy strategy, it will be difficult for these sources to fill the gap created by the diminished availability of petroleum. This shift provides the opportunity to meet both climate and energy security goals in advanced countries.

Natural gas is the most attractive of the three fossil fuels because it emits the least amount of climate-altering greenhouse gases. Natural gas was also developed later than oil as a commercial fuel, hence its major reservoirs have not been as fully depleted as those of oil. Nevertheless, gas is a finite commodity like petroleum, and many of the most prolific and easily accessible fields in North America, the North Sea and western Siberia have by now been largely depleted. Although, many new fields in eastern Siberia, the off-shore Islamic Republic of Iran, northern Alaska and Canada, and the Arctic Ocean await exploitation, the costs of developing these reservoirs will be substantially greater than the costs for those now in production, and it is not clear how many of them will attract the high levels of investment needed to bring them online. In sum, while it is reasonable to expect some increase in the availability of natural gas in the years to come, it is unlikely to compensate for the eventual shortfall in petroleum supplies.

Coal is the most abundant of the basic fuels. The technology for using coal to produce electricity is very well developed, and its relatively low cost has made it especially attractive to developing nations like China and India as a source of electric power. With oil and natural gas prices projected to rise in the years ahead as demand outpaces supply, coal is expected to play an ever increasing role in the world's energy mix as a source of fuel for electricity generation. According to the United States Department of Energy, global coal use will rise by 65 per cent between 2005 and 2030, an increase greater than for any other major source of energy. However, when used in a conventional manner, coal releases more CO_2 into the atmosphere per unit of energy produced than the other two fossil fuels, so an increase in coal use of this magnitude will result in a significant worldwide increase in CO_2 emissions, undermining global efforts to slow the rate of climate change. Hence,

Without a radical shift in energy strategy, it will be difficult for other basic fuels to fill the gap created by the diminished availability of petroleum

Natural gas is the most attractive of the fossil fuels because it emits the least amount of climate-altering greenhouse gases

Coal releases more carbon dioxide into the atmosphere per unit of energy produced than do oil and gas

---

3   This section draws extensively on Klare (2008).

4   DOE/EIA-0484 (2008) (Washington, D.C., Energy Information Administration, Office of Integrated Analysis and Forecasting, U.S. Department of Energy, September 2008).

the ability of the international community to make progress in its efforts to stem CO_2 emissions, will preclude a greater reliance on coal-using existing combustion technologies. This reveals the even greater urgency of developing cleaner coal-based technologies and, in particular, carbon capture and sequestration technologies (Ansolabehere and others, 2007); however, without the commitment of much greater resources, the commercial employment of these technologies appears quite some way away.[5]

Another possible substitute for oil is nuclear energy. Because nuclear energy releases no CO_2 emissions, some energy experts see it as an attractive alternative to fossil fuels. Nuclear energy, however, also entails many risks and radioactive waste-related storage problems which have kept costs exceedingly high compared with those of other sources of energy, thereby discouraging Governments and private utilities from building too many reactors. The tempo of reactor construction may pick up in the years ahead in response to rising demand for CO_2-free electrical power, but it is difficult to imagine a scenario entailing enough new plants to raise nuclear power's share of total world energy significantly above its current level of 6 per cent.

From what can be foreseen, therefore, oil will remain the world's leading source of energy for the next quarter-century, even if its share moderately declines from its current level (37 per cent).

Not enough resources are being devoted to ensuring that renewables will replace non-renewable sources of energy within any realistic time frame

The only practical solution to energy insecurity and climate threats is the rapid development of alternatives derived from climate-friendly renewable sources of energy—wind, solar, geothermal, advanced biofuels and so on. This is among the great challenges that will be facing policymakers over the coming century. However, despite the fact that the importance of this task is very widely recognized, not enough resources are being devoted to alternative energy development so as to ensure that renewables will be capable of replacing non-renewable sources of energy within any realistic time frame.

According to the United States Department of Energy, renewable sources of energy will account for only about 8.5 per cent of world energy use in 2030, an insignificant increase above their 7.7 per cent share in 2005.[6] No doubt these projections will be revised upward in response to fresh efforts by the European Union (EU) and the Administration of the new President of the United States, Barack Obama, but it will take a major investment push to lift the share of renewables by more than a few percentage points. After the sharp fall in oil prices between September 2008 and January 2009, many Governments and utilities indicated that they would not be able to proceed with ambitious plans to develop new renewable energy projects because of inadequate funding.[7]

Fully realizing the great potential for renewable sources of energy will require overcoming a number of technological hurdles

Fully realizing the great potential of renewable sources of energy will require overcoming a number of technological hurdles. Before wind and solar power can be used more widely, for example, it will be necessary to devise more efficient electrical storage devices—devices that would be able to store energy when the wind and sun were strong and to release it at night or when the weather was cloudy or windless. More efficient transmission systems are also needed to carry electricity from areas of greatest reliable wind and sunshine to areas of greatest demand. Likewise, new methods are needed to convert waste

---

5   In the United Kingdom for example, the chief executive of Centrica, one of the United Kingdom's largest energy suppliers, has warned that coal plants fitted with carbon capture and storage equipment are unlikely to be ready to make big cuts in the country's emissions for two decades (see "Carbon capture won't work until 2030, says energy boss", *The Guardian*, 26 February 2009).

6   International Energy Outlook for 2008, table A2.

7   See Clifford Kraus, "Alternative energy suddenly faces headwinds", *The New York Times*, 21 October 2008; and Stephen Castle, "European nations seek to revise agreement on emission cuts," *The New York Times*, 17 October 2008.

plant matter into ethanol, so as to spare food crops and other valuable species. Sources of energy like geothermal, tidal power, hydrogen, nuclear fusion and so forth will require a more visionary approach and even greater scientific and technological advancement. These advances, in turn, will require substantial investment which, at present, is not forthcoming from public and private sources on a large enough scale.

As a result of all these challenges, the world is experiencing persistent energy insecurity, which will make it very difficult to overcome recurring economic insecurity. Only by ensuring a reliable, affordable supply of energy will it be possible to chart a stable course for economic recovery and growth. Addressing energy insecurity and transforming the global energy system must therefore constitute a major priority for any long-term programme of economic and climate stabilization in advanced countries.

Without going into detail one can argue that, the ultimate goal of such an effort must be to reduce the world's reliance on fossil fuels, especially oil and coal, and to increase reliance on renewable sources of energy, especially wind, solar and advanced (non-food) biofuels. Such a course will simultaneously address the climate challenge. For advanced countries this, in turn, will require action on:

- *Conservation:* efforts to reduce the consumption of fossil fuels, especially oil. This means, among other things, driving less, driving slower, carpooling more often, trading in gas-guzzling vehicles for fuel-efficient cars, expanding public transportation, and improving the energy efficiency of homes, businesses and electrical appliances of all types.
- *Innovation:* developing ever more fuel-efficient vehicles, factories, appliances, heating systems and so forth; moving from oil-powered cars to gas/electric hybrids, plug-in hybrids and all-electric cars; improving the efficiency and utility of wind and solar power; developing advanced biofuels derived from non-edible plants.
- *Investment:* greatly increased public and private investment in energy alternatives and public transportation. Creative financial inducements for the development and utilization of energy alternatives, including, inter alia, green bonds and a cap-and-trade system for carbon emissions.

Efforts along all fronts must start immediately if real progress is to be made (see box II.1 for an example of possible measures at the regional level in the United States).

Energy access

Given the overall low level of energy consumption in developing countries, the concept of energy security is predictably somewhat different in those countries from that in the more advanced economies. Modern energy services are characterized by inequitability of access, notably between the poor and the affluent, as well as between rural and urban areas. Indeed, about 2 billion people in the world, one third of the world population, are entirely without access to modern energy; and about 1.6 billion are without access to electricity, while 2.4 billion cook with traditional forms of biomass. Limited access to cleaner energy services supplied by modern energy carriers is an important contributor to rising levels of poverty in some sub-Saharan African countries (United Nations Development Programme, 2007a and b). The current investments in the global energy system are estimated at some $500 billion per year (Nakicenovic, Ajanovic and Kimura, 2005). The sustainable scenario depicted in figure II.7 would require at least twice this during the coming decades. In comparison, the share required for ensuring access is relatively small.

Limited access to cleaner energy services supplied by modern energy carriers is an important contributor to rising levels of poverty in some sub-Saharan African countries

Box II.1

Greenhouse gas emissions mitigation in the North-eastern United States of America: the 3 per cent solution

To achieve the necessary reductions required to stabilize concentrations at 450 ppm or less requires a long-term goal of reducing emissions by 80 per cent, and then establishing a strategy for achieving that goal. If reductions begin by 2010, it will be possible to meet reduction goals by reducing emissions by 3 per cent per year over the next 50 years. If this goal is to be reached by 2050 (in 40 years), it will be necessary to cut by 4 per cent per year. For the 3 per cent annual reduction case, emissions will drop in half in 23 years and by 75 per cent in 46 years and will be decreased by 80 per cent by the start of the forty-eighth year. For a 4 per cent annual reduction rate, the 80 per cent reduction will occur in the thirty-seventh year; postponing action will require that we reduce by even greater amounts in later years.

Much of the focus on emissions reductions has, to date, been at the national level. However, local and regional policies will also likely play a critical role in achieving the desired outcome. In the case of the United States, a combination of local and national policies providing incentives and forcing technology to improve by setting strong standards on everything from power plants and buildings industry to transportation are likely to be strongly shaped by actions at the State and local levels.

Policy initiatives in specific sectors will cause transformation to low-carbon infrastructure and reduce the energy and emissions embedded in specific technologies that are part of our day-to-day life. For example, building efficiency standards, appliance efficiency standards, and vehicle emission standards impose a ceiling on inefficiency or emissions and drive the widespread adoption of available efficient technologies. More aggressive mandated efficiency and demand reduction measures for gas and electric utilities, as well as increasing State renewable portfolio standards so that all North-eastern States require at least 20 per cent renewables (as does New Jersey) will further spur the transition to low-emissions energy sources. These policies can be implemented with or without a cap on greenhouse gases, but will be most effective in a strong cap-and-trade environment.

Institutions and small and large commercial customers have multiple options for reducing emissions of greenhouse gases. Through a combination of purchasing energy-efficient equipment (appliances as well as lighting), using green building design concepts, installing renewable energy supplies, using combined heat and power, purchasing fuel-efficient transportation fleets, and purchasing green energy, these entities can significantly reduce their emissions of greenhouse gases, while realizing significant economic savings and improving the quality of their workspace.

Industrial customers can rely on energy-efficient lighting, equipment and energy management principles, as well as on installing renewable energy sources and combined heat and power applications. Many companies have effectively used a combination of efficient technologies, renewable technologies, process redesign, and transportation fleet improvements to realize energy cost savings, reduce their waste stream, and improve their products and services.

State and local governments, in addition to using policy tools to move the North-east on a low-emissions path, can pursue a number of options including direct action to reduce emissions by developing and implementing a climate change action plan, purchasing renewable power, setting and achieving goals for energy efficiency, purchasing efficient equipment for State and municipal use, purchasing efficient vehicles for State and municipal transportation needs, adopting policies to encourage employees to reduce their vehicle miles travelled (for example, encouraging telecommuting and subsidizing use of public transport) and providing incentives for purchase of low-emission vehicles.

There is also the issue of embedded energy in products. For example, the embedded energy in the manufacture and disposal of a vehicle is in the range of 5-10 per cent of the energy that it will consume during its operating life. Ideally, the emissions associated with manufacture and disposal would be taken care of at the auto factory or recycled steel plant. In the absence of such a

Box II.1 (cont'd)

requirement, an individual may choose to offset those emissions through more aggressive reductions in some sector over which he or she has control, or to purchase certified offsets that ensure that a zero-carbon renewable power source will be constructed.

The kind of 50-year schedule for electric power production perceived as being capable of ensuring attainment of the requisite target is set out below:[a]

Near term (1-5 years):

- Manage electric power demand by end-users. This can reduce emissions by the equivalent of 3 per cent per year for 5-20 years. Studies have found that physically equivalent households can range a factor of 2 in their energy used depending on patterns of consumption.
- Replace 12 conventional electric bulbs with compact fluorescent lamps, thereby reducing a typical home electric bill by 3 per cent.

Near to intermediate term (1-15 years):

- Cap emissions on power plants under the Regional Greenhouse Gas Initiative (RGGI), or an economy-wide cap-and-trade programme, and tighten emission limits each decade. Note that a 10 per cent reduction is equivalent to capitalizing the annual 3 per cent reduction for about four years.
- Purchase zero-emissions renewably generated electricity to reduce one's electricity emissions to zero (see below).

Intermediate term (5-25 years):

- Change laws so that distributed clean combined heat and power plants could be built at industrial sites and on university campuses. A combined heat and power plant reduces CO_2 emissions by more than half. This is equivalent to a 3 per cent reduction for 25-30 years.
- Replace a single coal-burning power plant with a natural gas-fired plant, thus reducing emissions in half. These efforts are equivalent to 3 per cent per year reductions for about 25 years.
- Ramp up use of renewable energy including large- and small-scale wind power, individual building solar power and combined heat and power.
- Begin to restructure the power grid to render it more compatible with distributed energy.

Intermediate to long term (10-50 years);

- Replace existing power stations with low- or zero-emissions power plants such as wind, solar or other similar sources. Replacing 18 coal plants per year nationwide is equivalent to approximately a 3 per cent reduction in emissions. The average lifetime of these plants should be 50 years or less so that all coal plants could be replaced in the next half-century if laws required retirement of older, dirtier, less-efficient plants.
- Capture CO_2 and storing it in depleted coal mines, thereby also contributing to emissions reductions.
- Establish a robust "intelligent grid" that has many nodes and multiple distributed energy sources, including, predominantly, renewables and combined heat and power. Structure utility resource planning and cost-recovery policies to achieve this goal.

a This provides examples of the policies and measures needed to deliver such emission reductions. Similar options will need to be exercised in the building, industry and transport sectors in order to meet the targets.

Source: Based on Moomaw and Johnston (2008).

A part of the vast potential future markets for energy are people who are excluded from access either because of the lack of service or because the services are unaffordable. The actual figure for those excluded, which includes the "energy-destitute", varies substantially between 1.6 billion (International Energy Agency, 2005 and 2008b) and 2 billion people (Nakicenovic and others, 2000; and Goldemberg and others, 2000 and 2004). Most of those excluded live in rural areas; about 260 million are estimated to be urban-dwellers (International Energy Agency, 2005). Provision of access over the next two decades would create a huge energy market, increasing the potential benefits from technological learning through much larger scale economies. In addition, this would be equitable and have a highly positive effect in respect of creating new economic activities and development.

An average connection cost for those excluded from energy access of 1,000 dollars per household results in global investment needs of some $25 billion per year

Assuming an average connection cost for those excluded at 1,000 dollars per household (Nakicenovic, 2009) yields global investment needs of some $25 billion per year over the next 20 years. This is a huge sum for the poorest of the developing countries but it is a humble one in comparison with other financial flows. It pales beside the hundreds of billions pledged by many Governments of the countries members of the Organization for Economic Cooperation and Development to rescue the financial sector, automotive industry and many other sectors of the economy. In comparison, the cost of bringing 2 billion into the modern energy service system would appear to be a real bargain. Still, Official Development Assistance (ODA) spent on energy is only about $4 billion annually, which is about 4 per cent of total ODA, estimated at about $100 billion in 2007 (Tirpak and Adams, 2007). Therefore, connecting those excluded exceeds substantially the sums that the developed regions are prepared to invest in energy development in the rest of the world.

Capacity expansion

Going beyond the immediate needs of the energy-destitute in scenarios of future energy development, substantial improvement of energy services is assumed. This renders the developing countries, with their large share of global population, the largest future energy markets. Figure II.8A displays the cumulative installed capacity in the A2r scenario of all power plants in industrialized countries (the North) and the developing countries (the South) from 2010 to 2030 (Grübler, Nakicenovic and Riahi, 2007).

Capacity expansion in the South is expected to be double that in the North over the coming decades

Capacity expansion in the South is expected to be double that in the North over the coming decades, demonstrating how significant growing energy markets will be in the developing parts of the world. Capacity replacement is much larger in the North because of its huge existing stock of power plants and their substantial ageing. In business-as-usual scenarios with continuous reliance on fossil energy, especially coal in the United States, China, India and the Russian Federation among others, the total new capacity to be installed is almost 50 terawatts electric (TWe) or at least 12 times the current global installed capacity. Even under these scenarios, developing parts of the world would expand installed renewable capacity through 2030 equivalent to that of all power plants in the world today and half as much again as that in additional nuclear plants. The potential improvements of this installed capacity are truly huge in the developing countries alone, indicating important investment opportunities for the private sector. However, in this scenario their impact in terms of climate mitigation would be dwarfed by the expansion of traditional fuel sources.

Figure II.8B shows that this picture changes radically in respect of zero-emissions power plants in the stabilization world even if they are based on the fossil-intensive A2r scenario. Stabilization, even with the modest goal of 670 ppm CO_2e by 2100, leads to

Figure II.8
Electrical capacity expansion and capacity replacement by 2030, developing and industrialized countries

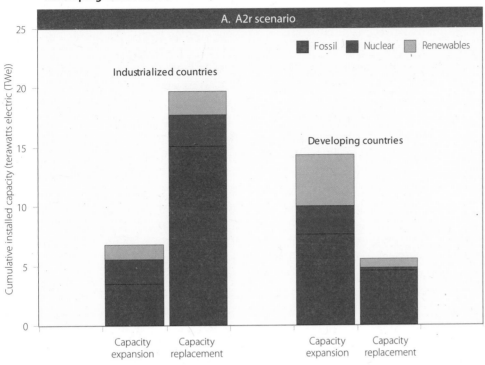

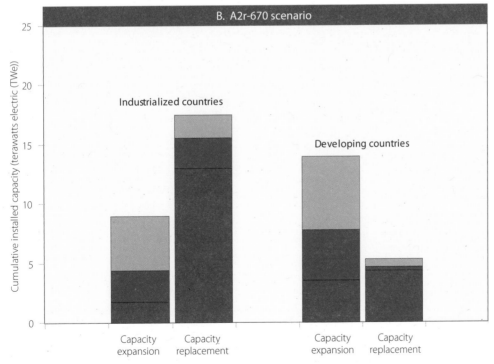

Source: Grübler, Nakicenovic and Riahi (2007).

Notes: The figure illustrates electrical capacity expansion and capacity replacement by 2030 in the developed countries (industrialized) and in developing countries in the reference A2r scenario (panel A) and in stabilization at 670 ppm CO_2-equivalent A2r-670 scenario (panel B). Capacity expansion refers to new power plants, while replacement capacity refers to the power plants that are built in place of those that are to be retired between now and 2030.

substantial restructuring, especially for the new power plants that shift so as to be based predominantly on renewable energy sources and much more nuclear power. Here (and in stabilization versions of the B1 scenario), we assume a universal global mitigation effort. This could be based on minimum costs and free trade in carbon and other goods and services. Alternatively, as discussed in the previous chapter, it could be pursued through a more proactive policy.

The total capacity additions are somewhat lower owing to additional efficiency improvements beyond those in the baseline A2r. Nevertheless, the capacity additions and replacements are huge, especially of renewable and nuclear power plants. About 4TWe of capacity expansion is foreseen in the developed parts of the world, with 2TWe as capacity replacements. In the developing regions, the corresponding installations are about 6TWe of capacity expansion and about 0.5TWe of capacity replacement. Together, over 12TWe of renewable and about 10TWe of nuclear power plants would be installed, or five and half times more than the total installed capacity of all power plants in the world. The interesting feature is that half of all of these plants would be built in the now developing parts of the world and most of them as new capacity expansion and not as replacements of ageing power plants.

This leads to a number of considerations. First, there is a potential risk of lock-in in the traditional technologies if the needed new capacities are not built with the best technologies. In other words, there is a huge incentive for the capital to be attracted to the newest technologies and for there to be free access extended to those in the currently developing parts of the world (for further discussion, see chap. V). Second, there are real possibilities in developing countries of leapfrogging to the most advanced technologies, as the market is huge and would likely lead to large cost reductions and performance improvements (see also chap. IV). Third, there is obvious potential for a virtuous growth circle (which also meets the climate challenge), in which a big public investment push in mitigation action leads to the crowding in of private investment, technological upgrading and productivity growth. This will require strong policy intervention.

Figures II.9 and II.10 illustrate the shift towards decarbonization of electricity generation and primary energy with increasing stringency of climate stabilization goals. Figure II.9 exhibits this trend for A2r and B1 scenarios for electricity generation and figure II.10 does the same for the total primary energy. With increasing stringency of stabilization, there is a significant shift towards decarbonization and increasing investment in carbon-free and carbon-saving technologies. As we have seen above, the largest growing market for these technologies is in the now developing parts of the world (the South). This means not only that increasing financing needs to be secured for these critical investments, but also that most of the induced technological learning, and thus cost reductions, is likely to occur in these regions. In other words, there is a strong potential incentive to invest there, assuming appropriate institutional and financing arrangements.

Feed-in tariffs

A feed-in tariff (FIT) is a policy that obligates utility companies to "feed into" the grid and purchase, at a legally mandated price (or "tariff"), energy generated by any individual or organization from renewable sources. Tariffs are the rates paid per kilowatt-hour for electricity. Thus, feed-in tariffs are the tariffs or rates paid per kilowatt-hour of electricity generation fed into, or sold to, the grid.

FITs constitute one of the array of policy options available to Governments for inducing investments in renewable energy. The other options are (a) renewable portfolio

Figure II.9
**Share of carbon-free in electricity generation
in the A2r scenario (A) and the B1 scenario (B)**

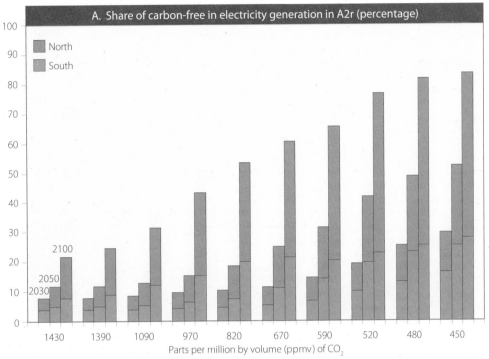

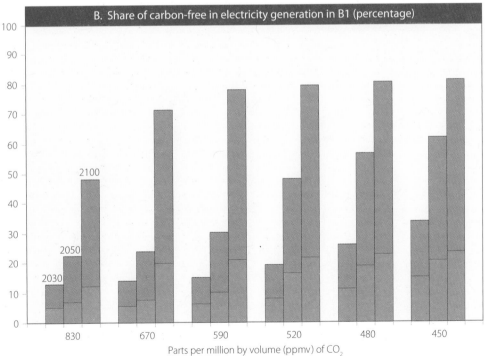

Source: Based on International Institute for Applied Systems Analysis (2007).

Note: These are shares in the developed regions (North) and developing regions (South), with the rest being the global fossil generation. Fossil power plants with carbon capture and storage are included in the carbon-free shares as well as nuclear and all renewable power plants. Shares are for 2030, 2050 and 2100. The bars on the extreme left reflect the reference scenario that leads to CO_2-equivalent atmospheric concentrations of 1430 ppm by 2100, increasing for the A2r scenario (panel A) and 830 ppm for the B1 reference scenario (panel B), while the bars on the extreme right reflect the very low stabilization scenario that leads to 450 ppm concentrations corresponding to about 2° C warming above pre-industrial levels. In between are the intermediate stabilization levels.

Figure II.10
**Share of carbon-free in primary energy mix
in the A2r scenario (A) and the B1 scenario (B)**

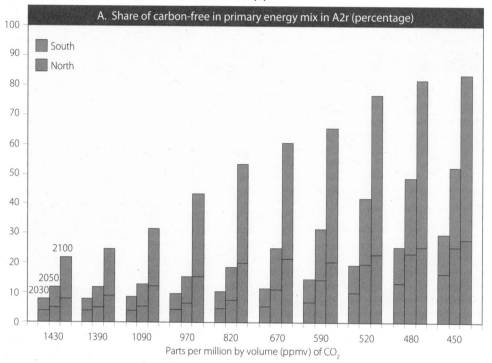

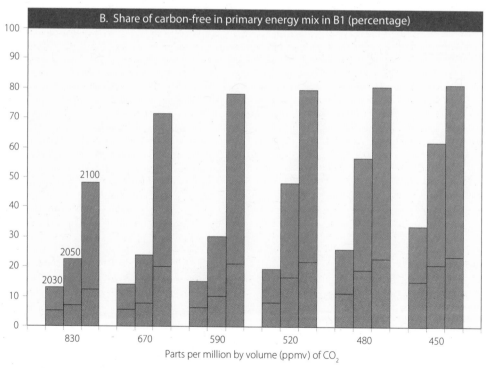

Source: Based on International Institute for Applied Systems Analysis (2007).
Note: See figure II.9.

standards (RFPs), which require utility companies to supply a mandated share of electricity from renewable sources; (b) price-based mechanisms, which raise the price of carbon-based energy, for example, through a carbon tax or a cap-and-trade system; and (c) direct or indirect support for the renewable sector, for example, through allocation of funds for research and development, provision of subsidized credit or land, or even direct public involvement in renewable energy investments.

There is considerable overlap among the various policy options. For example, other forms of support for renewables often accompany FITs. Similarly, cap-and-trade systems are often implemented through RFPs. In some cases, like that of California, FITs were used for implementing a RFP scheme. In practice, FITs have proved to be far more successful at producing verifiable results (Mendonca 2007, Gipe 2009).

FITs have been used for over two decades and are now on the books in at least 45 countries or States across the world. The state of the art has also evolved over time. The one that has received the most favourable attention is the advanced renewable tariff (ART), deployed initially in Germany and now utilized in several other countries and regions.

In terms of history, FITs had first been developed in the United States of America under the aegis of the Public Utility Regulatory Policies Act (PURPA), a part of the National Energy Act of 1978, which allowed connection of renewable generators to the grid and specified that they should be paid for the cost of generation that they avoided. In response, different States developed contractual arrangements, called "standard offer contracts", which were offered to renewable generators. Specifically, in 1984, the California Public Utility Commission instituted Standard Offer No. 4, which fixed the amount to be paid per kilowatt-hour for a long period (generally 10 years, over a 30-year contractual period). This fixed tariff was estimated on the basis of the long-term avoided cost of conventional generation.

For this reason, Standard Offer No. 4 is often perceived as representing the first instance of a successful FIT. It resulted in the establishment of 1,200 megawatts (MW) of new wind generation plants by the mid to late 1980s, which have consistently contributed about 1 per cent of California's consumption for more than two decades. However, Standard Offer contracts were offered only up until 1984 before the collapse of oil prices.

Germany had implemented its Stromeinspeisungsgesetz (StrEG), literally, the law on feeding in electricity to the grid, in 1991. Germany based its tariffs upon a fraction of the retail rate (that is to say, the price at which electricity was sold to consumers), not the wholesale rate (that is to say, the cost at which utilities purchased electricity from other generators). In Germany, consumption taxes constitute a large fraction of the ultimate retail price of electricity. Wind energy and solar energy were paid 90 per cent of the retail rate and hydroelectric plants were paid 80 per cent of the retail rate.

However, these rates too were not sufficiently stable to attract adequate financing. This was corrected in Germany in 2000 by the stipulation that renewable sources of electricity would have priority access to the grid for a host of environmental, social and economic reasons. It also set different tariffs for different technological options (based on the respective cost of generation plus a reasonable profit) and guaranteed them for 20 years. Many developing countries have followed this model, comprising so-called Advanced Renewable Tariffs, since it corresponds with standard practice in respect of other private electricity plants.

In the case of residential rooftop solar photovoltaic (PV), for example Germany's 2004 law offers € 0.57/kWh (~US$ 0.75/kWh), which is a much higher figure than that for other sources. The Canadian Province of Ontario recently revised its laws for the purpose of offering standard contracts differentiated by technology, size and application, including, for example, Can$ 0.80/kWh (US$ 0.62/kWh) for residential rooftop solar PV. In most cases, although tariffs are expressed as a percentage of the retail rate, they are in effect based on the cost of generation plus profit.

In summary, modern policies of Advanced Renewable Tariffs require priority access to the grid, priority purchase of generation from renewable resources, and differentiated tariffs based on the cost of generation plus a reasonable profit.

In developing countries, a major problem stems from the fact that the costs of most renewable options are far higher than the average retail price of electricity, which in turn is held down by reason of the fact that there is a proportion of lower-income groups that can afford electricity only at a cost under $0.06/kWh. This creates a disincentive for producers, who fear future policy changes in case of large-scale uptake of renewable energy generation. In this regard, a FIT option can be successful in developing countries only if it is backed by an international guarantee, and internationally funded subsidies for low-income consumers.

Research and development

The opportunity that crisis gives to fundamental change can be wasted if societies chose instead to subsidize the old systems and perpetuate the old paradigms

The kind of opportunity that a crisis gives to fundamental change can be wasted if societies choose instead to subsidize the old systems and perpetuate the old paradigms, further postponing the embrace of the new and at the same time creating conditions for ever deeper crisis and depression. These risks are probably higher in the developing parts of the world because of their limited financial resources and institutional capabilities for establishing effective policies and measures that lead towards a new phase of growth characterized by pervasive decarbonization.

Research, development and demonstration are vital to the improvement of performance and the lowering of costs in the early stages of technological development

Together, RD&D are vital to the improvement of performance and the lowering of costs in the early stages of technological development. Essentially, the same applies to technology transfer (chap. V). For example, the cost of photovoltaics produced in Japan had halved between 1973 and 1976, but none of this improvement is evident in observed prices because it occurred prior to the installation of any demonstration units, thus cumulative installed capacity was zero. Such RD&D expenditures are a small factor in the cost improvements of technologies that have already advanced to the stage where they have found commercial niche markets and are candidates for pervasive diffusion. However, in the earlier stages, RD&D accounts for a larger share of performance improvements and cost reductions.

Here we affirm that global decarbonization and universal access to energy services are two important opportunities created by the current financial crisis and the ensuing economic depression. While the depression is very disruptive and particularly destructive for the poor, it does at least potentially sow the seeds of renewal, provided that the world is prepared to make the necessary institutional and financial investments.

All of the transformational changes in the energy system need to empowered by vigorous research, development and demonstration efforts, investments, removal of barriers, provision of information and capacity-building

Research and development of innovations that lead to diffusion of new and advanced technologies and practices are a possible solution to the double challenge of providing development opportunities to those who are excluded and allowing for further development opportunities among the more affluent. This needs to occur without risking irreversible changes in ecological, biophysical and biochemical systems. In the energy area, this implies a shift from traditional sources, in the case of those who are excluded from access, to clean fossils and modern renewable energy; and, in the more developed parts of the world, a shift from fossil energy sources to carbon-free and carbon-neutral energy services. In all cases, this means a vigorous improvement of energy efficiencies, from supply to end use, expanding shares of renewables, more natural gas and less coal, vigorous deployment of carbon capture and storage, and—in some cases, where it is socially acceptable and economically viable—also nuclear energy. All of these transformational changes in the energy system need to be empowered by vigorous RD&D efforts, investments, removal of barriers, provision of information and capacity-building (including know-how and know-why).

Current energy RD&D trends are unfortunately moving in the opposite direction. Public expenditures in OECD countries have declined to some $8 billion from about $12 billion two decades ago, while private expenditures have declined to $4.5 billion compared with almost $8 billion a decade ago (International Energy Agency, 2008a). This means that today we are investing barely about $2 per person in the world per year in energy-related RD&D activities. Many studies indicate that this needs to increase by at least a factor of 2–3 in order to enable the transition towards new and advanced technologies in the energy systems (Bierbaum and others, 2007). However, it should be noted that Finland, Japan and Switzerland represent important exceptions, with substantially higher public and private energy RD&D efforts.

All told, RD&D efforts need to be tripled and energy investments at least doubled in order to assure the timely replacement of energy technologies and infrastructures (see chaps. V and VI).

Conclusion

A more sustainable future requires large "upfront" investments. The required investments are likely to exceed a trillion dollars per year from now to 2030, or at least twice the current level of investments, with most of the requirements coming from developing parts of the world. Achieving a transition towards more sustainable development paths will also require substantial and complementary investment in energy RD&D.

The great benefit of these additional investments in a future characterized by carbon-leaner energy systems and a more sustainable development path is that in the long run (to 2050 and beyond), the investments would be substantially lower compared with the business-as-usual alternatives. The reason is that the cumulative nature of technological change translates the early investment in a carbon-leaner future into lower costs of the energy systems in the long run, along with the co-benefits of stabilization.

This all points to the need for radical change in energy policies in order to assure that the investment effort will be adequate in our common future and to promote accelerated technological change in the energy system and end use. The global financial and economic crisis offers a unique opportunity to invest in new technologies and practices that would generate both employment and affluence as well as pave the way for a more sustainable future with lower rates of climate change. The crisis of the "old" offers a historic opportunity to sow the seeds of the "new".

Chapter III
The adaptation challenge

Introduction

The previous chapters have argued that rising living standards in developing countries need not jeopardize efforts to stabilize global emissions, reverse the threat of dangerous global warming or avert catastrophic environmental damage. It is clear, however, that the development path followed by today's rich industrialized countries can no longer serve as a model for catch-up growth. Rather, powering industrial expansion, rapid urbanization and population growth in the developing world will require a big push into cleaner and more efficient technologies, above all in the production and consumption of energy. This will require a transformative public policy agenda and a massive redirection of investment, at both the national and international levels.

But even if policymakers can quickly undertake the transition to a low-emissions growth path, rising global temperatures are unavoidable and will bring serious environmental damage, through spreading drought conditions, a rising sea level, ice-sheet and snow-cover melting, and the occurrence of extreme weather events. These phenomena will, in the coming decades, threaten and destroy economic livelihoods around the globe, in particular of already vulnerable populations, including in developed countries. The scientific community is becoming increasingly alarmed about the potential scale of environmental damage from what it previously considered manageable changes in global temperatures (Adam, 2009a). The threats to livelihoods and security are, correspondingly, likely to be all the greater.

Rising global temperatures will, in the coming decades, threaten and destroy economic livelihoods, in particular of already vulnerable populations

For many developing countries, environmental constraints and shocks are already part of a vicious development cycle, which traps them at a low level of income, undermines their resource base and restricts their capacity to build resilience with respect to future shocks (United Nations, 2008). The constraints and shocks are sure to become even more challenging with global warming. Poor health-care systems, lack of infrastructure, weakly diversified economies, missing institutions and soft governance structures expose poorer countries and communities not just to potentially catastrophic large-scale disasters but also to a more permanent state of economic stress from higher average temperatures, reduced water sources, more frequent flooding and intensified windstorms. These stresses will likely increase the risks of food and income insecurity, further exposing thereby the inadequate levels of health care, sanitation, shelter and social infrastructures.

A warming world is set to become an even more unequal world

Adapting to climate change will have to be a central component of any comprehensive and inclusive climate agenda. Several funds have been set up, at the international level, to finance adaptation measures in developing countries, but these are woefully inadequate for meeting the challenges involved. Scaling up these funds is the first challenge in the adaptation agenda. There is also greater awareness among domestic policymakers of the growing threats from climate change, as well as harder thinking about coping strategies and adaptation programmes. Still, adaptation is seen primarily as an environmental issue and there is a tendency to compartmentalize climate change policies and isolate them in environmental ministries. This constitutes the second big challenge in the adaptation agenda (Ahmad, 2009). Adaptation has to be understood not just as a development challenge, but as one that can be solved only with the full backing of the international community.

Increased investment,
improved access to
finance and strengthened
institutional capacity are
at the heart of confronting
the adaptation challenge in
most developing countries

But even when adaptation measures have been linked to a development strategy, the tendency has been to focus either on poverty alleviation (and thereby view the policy challenge as entailing the promotion of stronger safety nets and innovative insurance mechanisms for vulnerable groups and sectors) or on business opportunities (by strengthening climate-related markets). These actions have a role in a more integrated strategy but they cannot frame it. Rather, the present chapter argues that increased investment, improved access to finance and strengthened regulations and institutional capacity are, as in the case of the mitigation challenge, at the heart of confronting the adaptation challenge in most developing countries. Indeed, synergies between adaptation and mitigation strategies need to be explored much more fully, as an integral part of low-emissions, high-growth development pathways in countries vulnerable to climate change and shocks.

The next section looks at the growing climatic threats that are likely to accompany a warming world, the need to address these threats from a development perspective and the limits of existing approaches. This is followed by a more detailed examination of the threats to rural and urban communities and the more systemic risks associated with health and sanitation, the big challenge for policymakers stemming from the fact that these threats are often interrelated and, more often than not, compound existing vulnerabilities in poorer countries and communities. Some elements of a smarter and more integrated approach to the adaptation challenge are then set out. The final section emphasizes that this challenge will require the full support of the international community—support that, to date, has not been forthcoming on a scale that is anywhere close to being adequate, much less effective.

Adaptation and vulnerability

Mitigation is directed at slowing the growth of future emissions of greenhouse gases and eventually reducing their stock to a level consistent with manageable and stable temperatures. Adaptation is about mobilizing resources and devising policy strategies for building up resilience with respect to the unavoidable negative impacts of higher temperatures and for coping with the consequences. This is not a challenge that is altogether new. Throughout history, human societies have shown an extraordinary capacity for adapting to climatic changes. However, the threats posed to security and livelihoods by anthropogenic global warming, like the appropriate responses, are likely to be unprecedented.[1]

Climate change and vulnerability

Global warming of 4° C or
more is increasingly likely
and Governments need
to be prepared for the
significant impacts on their
economies and populations

Despite considerable variation in scientific estimates of the possible impacts of climate change on environmental stability concern over catastrophic risks to the planet's ecology and life in general continues to grow. For example, Hansen and others (2008) argue that the eventual temperature increase from a doubling of atmospheric carbon dioxide (CO_2) is more likely

---

1   For a discussion of the uneven socio-economic impact of global warming between the years 800 and 1300 and the threats linked to severe aridity in particular, see Fagan (2008). Drawing from the experiences of that period, Fagan concludes:

Drought and water are probably the overwhelming important issues for this and future centuries, times when we will have to be accustomed to making altruistic decisions that will benefit not necessarily ourselves but generations yet unborn. This requires political and social thinking of a kind that barely exists today, where instant gratification and the next election seem more important than acting with a view to the long-term future. And a great deal of long-term thinking will have to involve massive investments in the developing world, for those most at risk (pp. 240-241).

to be 6° C, rather than the 3° C assumed by both the Intergovernmental Panel on Climate Change (2007b) and Stern (2007). Many scientists estimate that global warming of 4° C or more is increasingly likely in this century and that Governments need to be prepared for the significant impacts on their economies and populations (Adam, 2009b).

The damage resulting from climate change will not be felt uniformly across countries and communities (see chap. I). Of the additional 600 million people who could, according to the estimates of the United Nations Development Programme (UNDP) (2007a), become victims of malnutrition by 2080 as a result of climate change, all will be living in what are already the poorest and most vulnerable countries. By contrast, there will be some areas of the world that may experience benefits, for instance, with regard to mortality rates and crop yields, provided that global temperature increases do not greatly exceed 2° C. However, even in developed areas, the proliferation of threats brought about by temperatures rising above 2° C could begin quite rapidly to heighten existing vulnerabilities and to do so with greater severity than expected. Figure III.1 shows, for instance, how various sectors and settlements in the Australasian region are affected by temperature change. Vulnerabilities associated with water security, coastal communities and natural ecosystems will be exposed at smaller temperature rises than will be vulnerabilities associated with infrastructure and food security.

New data on the melting of mountain glaciers and the ice sheets of the Arctic and Antarctic point to an increased likelihood of a significant rise in sea levels, as a result of which several big cities such as New York, London, Tokyo, Dhaka, Shanghai, Mumbai and Rio de Janeiro could be under serious threat. Similarly, in the Andean cordillera, melting of glaciers threatens the water supply and livelihoods of at least 30 million people (see box III.1). The livelihoods of about 500 million people depending on glacier water and approximately 600 million people living in low-level coastal zones are at considerable

The livelihoods of hundreds of millions of people depending on glacier water and living in low-level coastal zones are at considerable risk

Figure III.1
Rising temperatures and vulnerabilities in the Australasian region

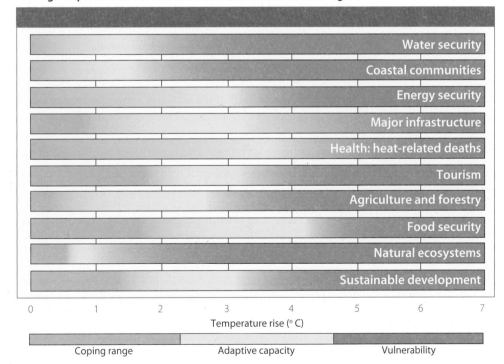

Water security
Coastal communities
Energy security
Major infrastructure
Health: heat-related deaths
Tourism
Agriculture and forestry
Food security
Natural ecosystems
Sustainable development

0   1   2   3   4   5   6   7
Temperature rise (° C)

Coping range   Adaptive capacity   Vulnerability

Source: UN/DESA, based on Intergovernmental Panel on Climate Change (2007c), chap. 11, figure 11.4.

Box III.1

The multiple threats to livelihoods from climate change: the Andean case

The impacts of climate change are cumulative and are closely linked to other vulnerabilities, often in a dangerously reinforcing manner. This is clearly illustrated by the accelerated melting of mountain glaciers, which are a critical source of livelihoods for about 500 million people worldwide and essential contributors to regional and global biodiversity (Intergovernmental Panel on Climate Change, 2007c).

Most of the world's tropical glaciers are located in the Andean mountains of Peru, the Plurinational State of Bolivia and Ecuador, where melting threatens the water supply and livelihoods of at least 30 million people. Over one fifth of the surface of 18 mountain glaciers in Peru has already melted over the past 35 years, while most of the lower-altitude Andean glaciers are expected to diminish substantively during the next 10-20 years.

Direct impacts of this trend are being felt in large cities in the region, which depend on glacial run-offs for their water supply. Quito draws 50 per cent of its water supply from the glacial basin, and La Paz, 30 per cent. The loss in volume of the glacier surface of Peru, equivalent to 7,000 million cubic metres of water (about 10 years of water supply for Lima), has meant a reduction by 12 per cent of the water flow to the country's coastal region, which is home to 60 per cent of the population of Peru.

As glaciers retreat, the capacity to regulate water supply through run-offs during dry and warmer periods and to store water in the form of ice during wet and colder periods is being lost. Notably, with the increasing scarcity of water supply, agriculture and power generation are also at risk. Without sufficient run-offs, pasture land upon which to raise livestock and continue small farming (including, for example, alpaca and sheep herding) will be insufficient. As the cultivation of native tubers and other staples, for example, potatoes and quinoa, is likely to dwindle, farmers may have to resort to planting costly staples that need chemical fertilizers.

Moreover, most Andean countries are also dependent on the glaciers for hydroelectric power generation, which accounts for 50 per cent of the energy supply in the Plurinational State of Bolivia and 70 per cent or more in Colombia, Ecuador and Peru. With rising temperatures, energy generation will be diminished in areas where water basins depend on glaciers. This will, inter alia, increase the need to invest in additional power capacity and explore, as in Peru, thermal-based power options.

Source: "Retracting glacier impacts economic outlook in the tropical Andes", a highlight of the 2007 World Bank report on the impacts of climate change in Latin America, available at http://go.worldbank.org/PVZHO48WT0 (accessed 20 April 2009).

The number of displaced persons in developing countries will be several times higher than the number in developed countries

risk.[2] The extreme case of sea-level rise puts the existence of entire countries, in particular small island developing States, at risk (see box III.2; and Huq and others, 2007).

The same environmental change and shocks will have, of course, different impacts, depending on the level and sophistication of the adaptive capacities that countries and communities can muster.[3] When developed countries are exposed to environmental shocks, they can draw on financial resources and institutional strengths that enable them to bounce back and bolster their resilience with respect to future impacts (Leary and others, 2008a). This is not the case in most developing countries. For instance, the areas of dryland and wetland losses in developing countries resulting from the same sea-level rise could be approximately 1.5 times larger than those in developed countries by 2100, while the number of displaced persons in the former (4 million) will be several times higher than that in the latter, and the protection cost will also be higher in developing countries (see figure III.2).

---

2   Updated information on ice and glacier melting can be obtained from World Meteorological Organization-International Council of Scientific Unions (2009), available at http://216.70.123.96/images/uploads/IPY_State_of_Polar_Research_EN_web.pdf; and at http://news.bbc.co.uk/2/hi/science/nature/7935159.stm.

3   The term "adaptive capacities" covers a range of practices which include, inter alia, *readiness* to deal with climatic changes and shocks, *resilience* in the face of shocks, *responsiveness* to the damages that do occur, and *recovery* once the crisis is over.

Box III.2

In the face of the storm: extreme vulnerability to climate change

Climate change may pose the greatest threat to the world's small island developing States and many of the least developed countries. These countries have contributed the least to overall greenhouse gas emissions.[a] However, owing to low levels of gross national income per capita, low levels of human resource development, severe structural weaknesses and a narrow resource base, they are also the most vulnerable to, and have the least adaptive capacity to deal with, the impact of climate change.

Global warming contributes to a steady rise in sea level: by the end of the twenty-first century, sea levels are expected to have risen by between 0.19 and 0.58 metres (Intergovernmental Panel on Climate Change, 2007c), though a number of climate models indicate that there will be geographical variations. The consequences of such a rise are potentially devastating. Indeed, while sea-level rise poses a real existential threat to many cities and entire countries, which may potentially find large parts of their surface being permanently inundated and submerged, the threat is particularly real to low-lying small island developing States which may be submerged completely. This could result in large-scale migration (see also box III.3).

Climate change is dramatically affecting weather patterns in many areas. Evidence indicates that the number of storms of category 4 or 5 has increased globally since 1970. Among small island developing States, there has already been a noticeable increase in the number of reported natural disasters over the past decades (see figure). In fact, small island developing States are considered to be the country group most vulnerable to the effects of climate change (Heger, Julca and Paddison, 2009).

Another issue requiring urgent attention is the impact of global warming on existing freshwater sources. In many coral atoll countries, freshwater is available from extremely fragile groundwater lenses that are dependent on rainfall; already less than half the population of Kiribati

a For instance, the combined average annual CO_2 emissions of small island developing States and least developed countries amounted to less than 1.3 per cent of the global total for the period 2000-2004, and were exceeded by those of France alone.

Incidence of natural disasters in small island developing States, 1970-2006

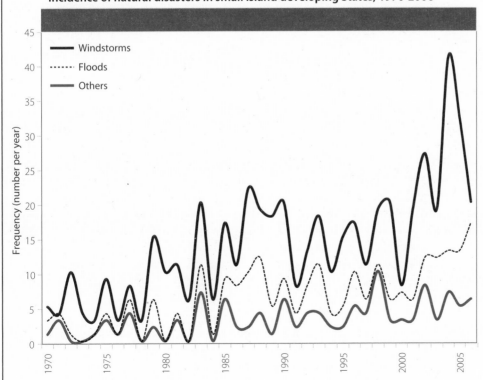

Source: UN/DESA, based on statistics obtained from EM-DAT: Emergency Events Database, available from http://www.emdat.be.

Box III.2 (cont'd)

has access to safe water, while less than 10 per cent of the rural population in Papua New Guinea has access to safe water (Hoegh-Guldberg and others, 2000). Stronger and more frequent storms will lead to contamination of those lenses with seawater, compromising water quality, while more frequent and longer-lasting droughts will reduce the availability of water.

Least developed countries are also extremely vulnerable to the impact of climate change. Projected changes in precipitation will exacerbate a situation already stressed by extreme poverty and other major development challenges. Global warming will primarily affect water resources, agriculture and food security, natural resource management and biodiversity, and human health. Many least developed countries are already experiencing a major deficit in food production; as soil moisture declines and as the risk of water stress and drought increases, the situation will worsen owing to declining crop yields. These impacts will have a significant impact on agricultural trade, economic growth and the achievement of development goals.

Some developed countries are already investing in adaptation; however, developing countries—in particular small island developing States and least developed countries—have limited technical and financial resource capacities and therefore face far greater challenges in implementing adaptation measures. Overcoming those challenges constitutes a critical priority, given the level of exposure and extreme vulnerability within the developing world to the potentially adverse effects of climate change. Developing countries urgently need both to strengthen their capacities to assess their vulnerabilities and deal with the risks of climate change and to develop adaptation strategies that are fully integrated into development planning at the national, regional and international levels.

Many poorer countries and populations will not have the capacities to deal with the damage triggered by warmer temperatures even below the 2º C threshold. Small increases in sea level, the rate of ice-sheet melting, the length of droughts, and the intensity of storms could all prove catastrophic for some countries and communities with limited response capacity. The threats will only further intensify as climate variability becomes the norm and hard-to-predict extreme events become more frequent. For some communities, the climate threat already seems too close and too daunting to allow for measured responses (see box III.3).

In addition to adding new threats and intensifying existing ones, climate change can also be expected to multiply the challenges facing vulnerable communities by compounding interrelated threats (Intergovernmental Panel on Climate Change, 2007c). For instance, the number of outbreaks of tropical diseases is likely to be larger in areas experiencing an increased incidence of heatwaves, leading to the extension of drought-prone areas, while the incidence of water-related diseases is likely to rise in areas with an increased incidence of floods. Increased hurricane activity will also lead to an increase in respiratory diseases (for example, influenza), in particular when emergency shelter is inadequate and in areas with little or no medical assistance. The well-being of people whose main sources of livelihood are lost as a result of these threats, particularly people belonging to vulnerable groups such as children, older persons and women, will be further jeopardized by food insecurity, inadequate shelter and health deterioration.

The recent winter drought in northern China provides an example of the variety of direct and indirect threats to livelihoods and the compounding effects of those threats that can be triggered by climatic shocks. As a consequence of the absence of rain and snow since November 2008, China's Ministry of Water Resources reported in early February 2009 that about 3.7 million people and 1.9 million large animals had limited access to drinking water in northern China, while reduced soil moisture had indirectly affected an estimated 9.7 million hectares of crops, representing 43 per cent of winter wheat

Figure III.2

Differential adaptive capacities to global sea-level rise, developed and developing countries, 2000-2100

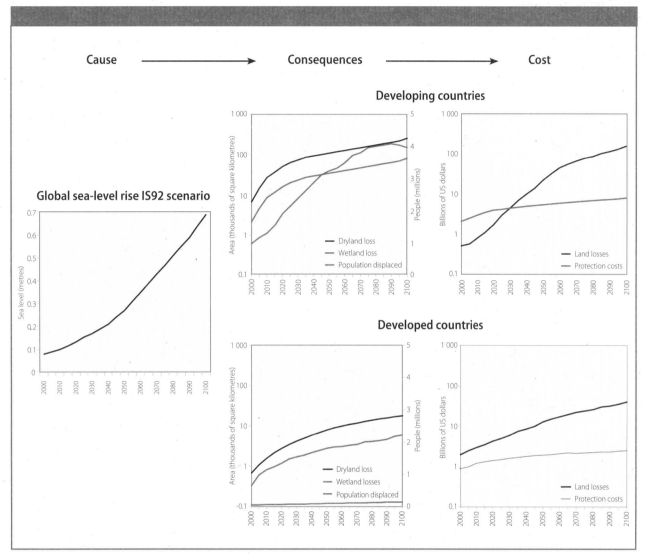

Source: Intergovernmental Panel on Climate Change (2007c).

sources.[4] The scarcity of water resources and the reduction in crop harvesting are likely to increase food insecurity and also add to health risks, including that posed by the greater susceptibility of water-stressed birds to avian flu.[5]

---

4   See   http://pandemicinformationnews.blogspot.com/2009/02/chinas-drought-may-make-birds-more.html.

5   Again, compounding threats will not be limited to poorer countries. The recent collision of economic and environmental risks in California's Central Valley has led to a surge in unemployment rates and food prices and in the number of large areas that are being left fallow. According to McKinley (2009):

(The United States of America's) biggest agricultural engine, California's sprawling Central Valley is being battered by the recession like farmland most everywhere. But in an unlucky strike of nature, the downturn is being deepened by a severe drought that threatens to drive up joblessness, increase food prices and cripple farms and towns. Across the valley, towns are already seeing some of the worst unemployment in the country, with rates three or four times the national average ... With fewer checks to cash, even check-cashing businesses have failed, as have thrift stores, ice cream parlors and hardware stores.

Relocation: desperate measures?

In December 2008, the Executive Secretary of the United Nations Framework Convention on Climate Change said in a press conference that relocation as undertaken by populations of small island developing States was "depressing" and showed that they were "giving up". But is relocation an option only for those who have lost faith, or is it a realistic solution which should have already been considered by now?

At the sixtieth session of the United Nations General Assembly, in 2005, the President of Kiribati mentioned the need for nations to seriously consider the option of relocation: the "ultimate form of adaptation to climate change" (Loughry and McAdam, 2008). In late 2008, the President of Maldives proposed buying land overseas to resettle the population. These small islands are aware of their vulnerability to sea-level rise and are taking their future seriously. Other areas may not perceive the threat as directly, but may be just as vulnerable.

Would it be possible, for instance, to simply move a coastal city inland? What would the implications be for the surrounding communities, the peri-urban landscape and ecosystems? If island residents are considering abandoning their lands, the concept of relocating an entire city is not totally outlandish. However, research on recovery processes following disasters shows that even when new housing settlements are built in new locations, people tend to return to their previous home, even if it is "high risk". There are a number of factors to account for this, but they are usually related to livelihood necessities, mobility and social connections.

How does relocation relate to migration, and how might these processes conflict? Migration requires making decisions that involve risk, because people give up their livelihoods to look for better opportunities. Some specialists predict that the magnitude of the flow of environmental refugees as a consequence of climate change will multiply in the next decades, to as much as 75 million by 2030 (Global Humanitarian Forum, 2009), and in consequence urge nations to take preventive measures and strengthen international cooperation for better management of migration flows. In fact, the Office of the United Nations High Commissioner for Refugees (UNHCR) (2008) noted that little thought had been given to the humanitarian consequences of climate change and cautioned against the possibility of relocation, especially as a result of:

- Hydro-meteorological disasters (flooding, windstorms, mudslides, etc.)
- Zones designated by Governments as being too high-risk and dangerous for human habitation
- Environmental degradation and slow-onset disaster (for example, reduction of water availability, desertification, recurrent flooding, salinization of coastal zones, etc.)
- The case of "sinking" small island States;
- Armed conflict triggered by a decrease in essential resources (for example, water, food) due to climate change.

Guiding Principles on Internal Displacement, which could help facilitate movement, do exist, as well as other frameworks to support the equitable treatment of displaced persons. However, as noted by UNHCR (2008), climate change may put a strain on these frameworks. It may be necessary therefore to reconsider more formally how displaced groups, including cities, would be treated, especially if they were undertaking relocation as a precautionary rather than as a reactive strategy (Schipper, 2009).

Adaptation and development

As discussed in *World Economic and Social Survey 2008* (United Nations, 2008), reduced vulnerability to natural hazards is strongly correlated with income levels, and reflects changes in economic and social structures as countries diversify away from reliance on agricultural activities, establish stronger institutional networks and begin to build more effective welfare States. Adaptation to actual or expected climate change and variations and their effects will inevitably involve large investments to protect existing activities and livelihoods and to facilitate adjustments in respect of livelihoods aimed at limiting the potential damage, coping with the consequences and even exploiting potential opportunities (Intergovernmental Panel on Climate Change, 2007c). Such adjustments can emerge spontaneously as individuals and communities respond to repeated shocks or incremental changes in their surrounding environment. However—and particularly when the changes are on a larger scale—it is deliberate policy decisions and public action, based on research by the scientific community, assessment of previous crisis episodes and consultations with local residents and grass-root groups that have been threatened by environmental changes, that will constitute the basis of lasting solutions.

The burden of adjusting to the growing threats from climate change will be a particularly heavy one for populations that are already challenged by multiple vulnerabilities associated with low levels of economic and human development. Poorer countries and communities with poor health care, lack of infrastructure, weakly diversified economies, missing institutions and soft governance structures may be exposed not just to potentially catastrophic large-scale disasters but also to a more permanent state of economic stress as a result of higher average temperatures, reduced availability of water sources, more frequent flooding and intensified windstorms. These stresses will likely increase the risks of food and income insecurity, further exposing inadequate levels of health care, sanitation, shelter and social infrastructures (Oxfam International, 2007). Thus, countries that are the most vulnerable to climatic shocks often find themselves trapped in a vicious circle of economic insecurity, persistent poverty, vulnerability to shocks and inadequate capacity to cope with those shocks (United Nations, 2008).

Countries that are the most vulnerable to climatic shocks often find themselves trapped in a vicious circle

For many developing countries, breaking this vicious circle is at the heart of the adaptation challenge. The magnitude of the challenge is already familiar from experience with climate-related disasters, as is the difficulty of judging how much of the resulting impacts can be attributed to "normal" economic as opposed to "abnormal" climate factors (Datt and Hoogeveen, 2003). To recognize this difficulty is at the same time to underscore the interrelated nature of climatic and development-related pressures in the adaptation challenge. In addition to the fact that the scale of the damage can often be much larger than that of the resources available to provide suitable protection, what is also clear from the experience with climate-related disasters is that the constraints on mobilizing the resources needed remain binding for poor countries, preventing them from investing in effective adaptation responses.

Constraints on mobilizing the resources needed remain binding for poor countries, preventing them from investing in effective adaptation responses

But even when developing countries have broken this vicious circle and entered a period of more sustained growth, vulnerability to shocks, both internal and external, remains a persistent concern for policymakers. Poor neighbourhoods in growing economies, including in developed countries, are more at risk from shocks, including climatic shocks, because they have fewer coping resources and are inadequately served by day-to-day services, which are taken for granted in areas that are more affluent (Dodman, Ayers and Huq, 2009).[6]

In responding to the adaptation challenge, policymakers can draw usefully on experiences with adjusting to exogenous economic shocks in developing countries. Perhaps the single most important conclusion that emerges from a careful examination of those experiences is that local circumstances and capacities have a profound influence on outcomes and that policy responses should be tailored accordingly. However, some more general lessons can also be drawn of which three, in particular, stand out:

Local circumstances and capacities have a profound influence on outcomes and policy responses should be tailored accordingly

---

6   Vulnerability due to inequalities is a problem not only in developing countries, however, as became apparent from the experience with hurricane Katrina in 2005 (see Guidry and Margolis, 2005).

- If countries are left to make the adjustment themselves, they will likely be forced to squeeze down incomes, which would result in a prolonged and de-stabilizing adjustment process, increasing poverty levels, damaging long-term growth prospects and adding to further vulnerabilities
- Economies that are more diversified (both structurally and spatially) tend to show greater resilience with respect to external shocks and recover more quickly, as do economies that are strongly integrated both internally and externally
- Societies with greater equality are better able to manage shocks by distributing the burden of adjustment and avoiding the possibly dangerous conflicts that adjustment can trigger.

Economic development is the most reliable insurance against the adverse impact of climate change

Adapting to climate change is also very much a *local* challenge which will require strategies and mechanisms that are tailored to differing circumstances and initial adaptive capacity (Yohe and Moss, 2000). There is no one-size-fits-all strategy to deal with the adaptation challenge. Still, in general terms, economic development is the most reliable insurance against the adverse impact of climate change (United Nations, 2008). On the whole, populations that have access to adequate food, clean water, health care and education are better prepared to deal with a variety of shocks, including those arising from climate change. Access to adequate resources with which to invest in adaptive capacity, including human and social capital, determines how resilient countries and communities are likely to be in the face of climate change and variability. In addition, access to technologies and know-how will play an important role in strengthening adaptive capacity. In respect of all these factors, the ability of decision makers to mobilize and manage resources and to engage in difficult trade-offs involving their use will be an essential component of the response to the adaptation challenge.

Food security remains a basic challenge, particularly where agriculture is dominated by smallholder production, productivity is low and support services are poorly developed

There are still many developing countries that, remaining heavily dependent on natural resources-related activities, are likely to be seriously threatened by projected climate changes (Leary and others, 2008b). Communities and countries that primarily produce and export low value added agricultural goods and primary commodities are typically found at the lower end of the development ladder and face some of the greatest development-related risks, including small market size, heavy import dependence, low technological capacity, etc.[7] Food security remains a basic challenge, particularly where agriculture is dominated by smallholder production, productivity is low and support services are poorly developed. The failure to provide more stable livelihoods under these conditions remains a basic policy challenge and one certain to be compounded by climatic changes.

However, many developing countries are undergoing the transition to more urban and economically diversified economies and must often cope with new risks and interrelated shocks, as is apparent in the current economic crisis. By 2030, it is estimated that 60 per cent of the world's population will reside in urban areas, compared with 47 per cent in 2000 (United Nations Human Settlements Programme (UN-Habitat), 2008).[8] Moreover, cities matter now more than ever, as even predominantly rural nations generally derive more than half of their gross domestic product (GDP) from industry and service enterprises, most of which are based in urban areas (Satterthwaite, 2007). Cities also serve as hubs for the stimulation of national and regional growth and are "key nodes of the globalization process"

---

7   Of the estimated 3 billion people living in rural areas in developing countries alone, 2.5 billion are involved in agriculture.

8   Although developing countries are associated with rural landscapes, many actually boast high urbanization rates. For instance, in Africa already two fifths of the continent's inhabitants are urban (United Nations, 2006).

(Sanchez-Rodriguez, Fragkias and Solecki, 2008). The policy challenges accompanying this transition are often compounded by acute levels of insecurity and inequality, as new urban residents oftentimes find themselves forgoing the minimal levels of protection offered in rural communities without adequate (or often any) Government support.

Overall, in the absence of more effective adaptation strategies, the vulnerability differentiating rich and poor countries as well as the rich and poor communities within countries will likely deepen in the face of rising global temperatures. This is a concern for the international community not only in its own right but also because of the fact that, in an increasingly divided and unequal world, agreement on an international framework for tackling climate change is likely to be all the more difficult to achieve.

The limits of existing policy frameworks

As societies begin to seek practical approaches to adaptation, it will be necessary for a more nuanced view to be adopted of the risks arising from a changing climate as they relate to development policy. At the same time, it will also be necessary to adopt a more nuanced view of the development policy challenge itself and, in particular, of the links among investment, diversification and growth. The extent of the building and strengthening of these links will determine how well many poorer countries adapt to warming temperatures.

The economic stabilization and structural adjustment programmes implemented in many developing countries over the past three decades have done little to reduce vulnerability. Those programmes had been adopted in response to a series of large shocks in the late 1970s and early 1980s and the debt crisis that followed. Their aim was to remove structural and institutional impediments to growth and to create more stable and resilient economies. The policies typically allocated a much greater role to market forces in the adjustment process and reduced that of the State, including capacities for providing public services. One prominent aspect of this shifting emphasis was fiscal retrenchment and the accompanying decline in public investment across much of the developing world. As a consequence, even with greater macroeconomic stability, private investment was insufficiently supported through improved infrastructure and basic services, thereby limiting productivity growth and economic diversification. In many instances, income-earning capacities were not improved and sometimes even fell, through premature deindustrialization, wage compression and the informalization of economic activity (United Nations, 2006).

Towards the end of the 1990s, a second generation of adjustment programmes added good governance and poverty reduction to the reform agenda, in part to deal with perceived policy slippages but also in response to the adverse impact of the earlier measures. These efforts have placed a greater emphasis on participation and ownership in the design of programmes, culminating in the preparation of Poverty Reduction Strategy Papers (PRSPs) which have become the main policy vehicle for allocating bilateral grants and concessionary loans and for advancing debt relief. However, the PRSPs have to a very large extent left intact the economic reforms of the first-generation adjustment programmes, have done little to advance serious assessment of the impact of major macroeconomic and structural measures on the poor, and have failed to establish a more integrated approach to economic and social challenges. In particular, they have continued to promote unduly restrictive macroeconomic policies to the detriment of investment-led growth and diversification strategies, have denied the contribution of industrial and technology policies towards supporting such strategies and have adopted a one-size-fits-all approach to integration into the international economy (United Nations Conference on Trade and Development, 2002).

It will be necessary to adopt a more nuanced view of the development policy challenge and of the links among investment, diversification and growth

PRSPs are unlikely to provide the framework for meeting the adaptation challenges facing most developing countries in a warming world. Rather, developing countries have to develop new policies that build robust links among investments, growth and diversification which will allow them to make progressive adjustments to climatic changes and to strengthen national resilience with respect to climatic shocks.

The impacts of climate change

Some forms of damage from climate change will be inflicted gradually, while others will occur suddenly; most of the imminent damages to and adverse impacts on livelihoods are expected to be felt in developing regions

The damage from climate change will not be felt uniformly. Some forms of damage that are due, for instance, to sea-level rise and the spread of drought will be gradual. Other forms of damage will be inflicted suddenly, owing to the greater incidence and intensity of the climatic hazards that result from global warming. Some of the threats will be confined to specific sectors, while others will have a much more systemic impact. Moreover, while the impacts will have ramifications across all countries and regions, their intensity will often be quite localized, with some communities and countries being much more exposed than others. Figure III.3 indicates some of the differential regional impacts, on biodiversity, infrastructure and livelihoods at different degrees of global mean annual temperature change (relative to 1980-1999). In general, most of the imminent damages to and adverse impacts on livelihoods are expected to be felt in developing regions, where drought (Africa) and flooding (parts of Asia) are already a threat in that regard, including at temperatures below 2º C, while heat spells might challenge water security in some developed regions, for instance, in Australia and New Zealand, particularly at temperatures above 2º C.

Agriculture and forestry

Globally, more than one third of households rely on agriculture for their livelihoods; in sub-Saharan Africa, the proportion is over 60 per cent. Moreover, in many poorer countries, primary products are a major source of foreign-exchange earnings and provide important inputs into fledgling manufacturing activities. While the economic weight of this sector is expected to decline further over the coming decades, improving agricultural performance is an essential feature of sustained economic growth, particularly at lower levels of development, and a source of welfare gains through greater food security.

The net impact of climate change on global agricultural production remains uncertain.[9] There are regional variations of global warming, but the agriculture and forestry sectors in developing countries of all regions are particularly vulnerable to climatic shifts, as even small changes in temperatures and precipitation levels as well as climatic shocks can disrupt growth cycles and yields.

Agriculture in rich countries stands to benefit from climate change …

Significant reductions in the average yield of key staples, water and protein sources, and increased flood risks and consequent damage to assets are a few of the most adverse effects of climate change on developing regions and livelihoods. In contrast,

---

9 There is "low to medium confidence" that global agriculture production will increase for temperature increases up to between 1 and 3° C (Intergovernmental Panel on Climate Change, 2007c). More specifically, annual precipitation may increase in East Africa, most of Northern Europe, Canada and the north-eastern United States of America, while seasonal precipitation will increase in, for instance, south-eastern South America, northern Asia, East Asia, South Asia and most of South-East Asia in summer and Central Europe in winter. Seasonal precipitation will decrease in Southern Africa and south-western Australia in winter, while it will decrease all year round in much of the Mediterranean, the northern Sahara and most of Central America (see Intergovernmental Panel on Climate Change, 2007c, for more details).

Figure III.3
Differentiated regional impacts at various degrees of average global temperature rise

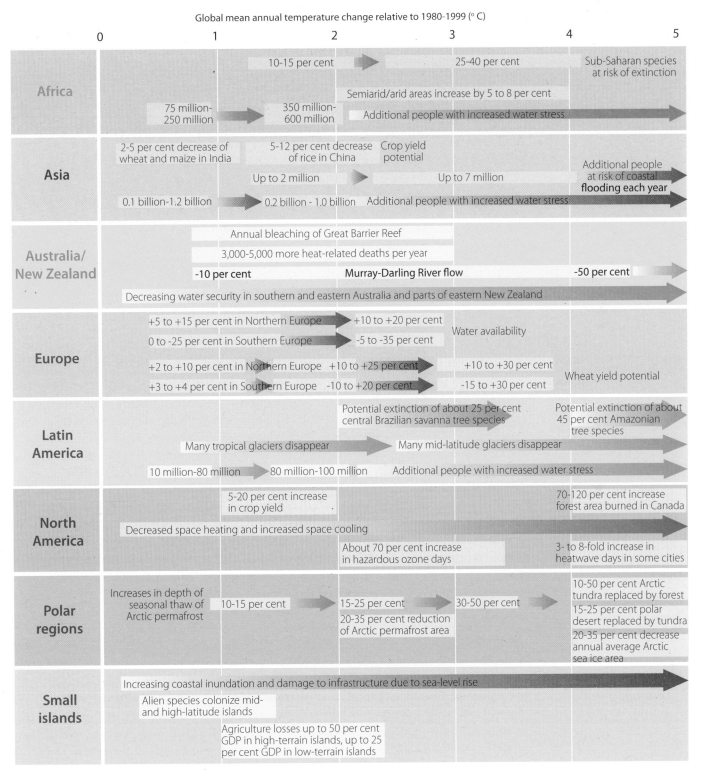

Source: Intergovernmental Panel on Climate Change (2007c).

warming and a general increase in rainfall are likely to lead to increases in crop productivity in Europe, particularly as some crops that are traditionally grown in Southern Europe will become viable further north. Moreover, the area suitable for grain production could potentially increase in Europe by 30–50 per cent by the end of the twenty-first century and aggregate yields of rain-fed agriculture could increase by up to 20 per cent in North America (Intergovernmental Panel on Climate Change, 2007c).[10] However, while agriculture in rich countries stands to benefit from climate change, it is not obvious that the actual gains will be significant as their agricultural sectors continue to shrink and more land is put to non-agricultural use.

… while in developing countries, the impact will be more uniformly negative and in many African countries, yields could drop by up to 50 per cent

Overall, in developing countries, the impact will be more uniformly negative. In addition, the greater reliance on agriculture, and the particular vulnerability of small-scale producers, often occupying marginal lands, limit their ability to deal with even small changes and fluctuations. In many developing regions, growing seasons will shorten, areas suitable for agriculture will decline and land degradation will intensify. This will be the case especially along the margins of semi-arid and arid areas, severely restricting agricultural output (Intergovernmental Panel on Climate Change, 2007c). Moreover, heat-related plant stresses will contribute to reduced yields in key crops, such as wheat, rice, maize and potatoes. It is estimated that basic crop growing capacity will have dropped by 10–20 per cent by 2080 in the 40 poorest countries (predominantly located in tropical Africa) owing to drought alone (Kotschi, 2007), while in many African countries, yields could drop by up to 50 per cent by 2020, with small-scale farmers being the most affected. Likewise, extreme wind and turbulence could, for instance, decrease fish productivity by 50-60 per cent in countries like Angola, the Congo, Côte d'Ivoire, Mali, Mauritania, the Niger, Senegal and Sierra Leone (Alcadi, Mathur and Rémy, 2009).

Scarcity of freshwater already threatens livelihoods linked to agriculture and forestry in an estimated 40 per cent of rural areas worldwide

Food security and rural livelihoods are closely linked to water availability and use (Ludi, 2009). Scarcity of freshwater already threatens livelihoods linked to agriculture and forestry in an estimated 40 per cent of rural areas worldwide and the heightened threat from climate change introduces the risk of far greater damage, thereby increasing the likelihood of social conflict and triggering large-scale migration. There is the likelihood of salinization of rivers caused by rising sea levels which further increases freshwater stress (see annex, for estimated climate change impacts on Africa).

Moreover, where irrigation is to a large degree absent and reliance on rain-fed crops is high, and lack of agricultural inputs such as fertilizers, herbicides and insecticides is present as a factor contributing to low yields, as is the case in many developing economies, climate change can potentially have disastrous consequences in terms of food security. In Mali, for instance, the proportion of the population at risk for hunger could increase from 34 to over 70 per cent by the 2050s (Butt and others, 2005).

Forests cover approximately 30 per cent of the global land surface and are a source of livelihoods for 1.6 billion people (close to 25 per cent of the world's population), providing food, fuel for cooking and heating, medicine, shelter and clothing (Food and Agriculture Organization of the United Nations, 2004). However, only an estimated 5 per cent—largely forest plantations—of the global forest area provides more than one third of commercial global roundwood (Intergovernmental Panel on Climate Change, 2007c), although that share appears set to accelerate over the coming decades. In many rural sub-Saharan African communities, non-timber forest products supply over 50 per cent of a farmer's cash income and provide for the health needs of more than 80 per cent of the population (Food and Agriculture Organization of the United Nations, 2004).

---

10   Provided that temperature changes are not "too" high (see note 9 above).

Rising temperatures, shifting precipitation patterns and increasing emissions are likely to have a significant and largely positive impact on forest growth. However, indirect impacts such as the intensity of forest wildfires, invasions of insects and pathogens, and extreme weather events such as high winds may be less advantageous. Overall, climate change is expected to both increase global timber production and shift supply locations from temperate to tropical zones and from the northern to the southern hemisphere. While this will lead to an increase in the trade in forest products (Hagler, 1998), the benefits are likely to be unevenly distributed. In terms of economic impacts, changes imposed on the structure of forests will likely have a particular adverse impact on many of those persons who depend on forests for their livelihoods, especially as 90 per cent of them are estimated to live in extreme poverty (Food and Agriculture Organization of the United Nations, 2004).

Urban environments

The United Nations estimates that more than half of the world's population already live in urban areas; and it is expected that the proportion of city dwellers in world population will have risen to three quarters by 2050, with almost all of the growth occurring in the developing world. Urbanization is a major driver of climate change and climate change will also have a significant impact on urban environments, adding a dangerous feedback loop to growing urban stresses.

Much of the urbanization in developing countries is unplanned and poses massive challenges, even without taking heightened climatic threats into account. These include health problems linked to air pollution and high population density, problems associated with transportation and inadequate infrastructure, personal safety problems linked to high levels of criminal activity and generally deficient access to and deficient provision of social services. Climate change is likely to exaggerate all these problems. As noted earlier, the most obvious additional threat from climate change, particularly to coastal cities, is posed by sea-level rises (Nicholls and others, 2007). Already, 13 per cent of the world's urban population live in low-elevation coastal zones (defined as being less than 10 metres above sea level) and two thirds of cities with more than 5 million inhabitants are located in such zones; and 21 of the 33 cities that are projected to have a population of 8 million or more by 2015 will be located in vulnerable coastal zones (United Nations Human Settlements Programme (UN-Habitat), 2007).

While the long-run challenge of sea-level rise presents a particular risk to certain areas, coping with an increased incidence of natural hazards poses a more immediate challenge. Tackling this challenge, however, requires greater understanding of what greater climate variability means for existing infrastructure and what sort of new and additional risks it will pose for urban-dwellers. For instance, unplanned urban settlements, in particular slum dwellings, often materialize in high-risk areas, such as river banks and unstable hill slopes. While the dwellers in such slums might manage to cope with occasional shocks, more frequent flooding of greater magnitude would likely bring disruption, pushing them to resettle elsewhere. Given that they were already living in an undesirable location, chances are that they would be pushed further down the poverty ladder and that their exposure to climate change would also likely increase (Schipper, 2009).

In the absence of any forward-planning strategy, an estimated 1 billion inhabitants are already at risk from hydro-meteorological hazards and it is predicted that the figure will have increased to 1.4 billion people by 2020 (United Nations Human Settlements Programme (UN-Habitat), 2007). More frequent and more intense rainfall will, for

The most obvious additional threat from climate change to coastal cities is posed by sea-level rises

An estimated 1 billion urban inhabitants are at risk from hydro-meteorological hazards and the figure will have increased to 1.4 billion by 2020

instance, increase the risk from landslides and the threat from water inundation. In fact, while poor drainage is already a serious issue in many cities, particularly in developing countries (Satterthwaite, 2007), climate change increases the likelihood of flooding and increases the risk of disease.

Interconnected threats are likely to intensify with rapid urbanization. Part of that intensification will reflect increased migration from rural areas, as agricultural liveli-hoods are hit by climate change. Such inflows will increase the pressure on urban services and water resources, infrastructure and urban ecosystems, which will thereby in turn ex-acerbate the vulnerability of urban settlements to direct climate change impacts. Greater levels of inequality often characterize urban societies, which often also have weaker social networks and informal support schemes, making them more vulnerable to shocks than so-cieties in rural areas (Moser, Gauhurts and Gonhan, 1994; Pelling, 2003). Climate change and urban environments are thus intrinsically linked, highlighting the importance of ad-dressing climate change through an integrated approach to adaptation.

Health and water security

The systemic impacts of climate change on health and water security merit particular attention

The need to adapt to difficult environmental conditions has been an omnipresent chal-lenge for human society faced with the interactive threats of disease, water scarcity and food insecurity. Now, with warming on an accelerating trend, addressing the systemic impacts of climate change on *health* and *water security* merits particular attention.

The range of health risks from climate change is likely to be considerable, with all parts of the globe affected as the unprecedented number of deaths in Europe from re-cent heatwaves has demonstrated. However, health vulnerability is very closely linked to other vulnerabilities, with the burden of climate-sensitive diseases overwhelmingly loaded onto the poorest populations who also have the lowest coverage by health services. In fact, the people most vulnerable to climate change are those who have not been well protected by health sector interventions in the past, while the greatest influence on impacts across different regions is not variation in the extent of climate change, but variation in the mag-nitude of pre-existing health problems.

There are 150,000 additional deaths occurring annually in low-income countries from four climate-sensitive health outcomes

A recent assessment by the World Health Organization (2005a) estimates that the burden of disease incurred through the modest warming that has occurred since the 1970s is causing about 150,000 additional deaths annually in low-income countries from four climate-sensitive health outcomes—malnutrition, diarrhoeal disease, malaria and flooding. These additional deaths are concentrated in already vulnerable population groups; for instance, 90 per cent of the burden of malaria and diarrhoea, and almost all of the burden of diseases associated with undernutrition, are borne by children aged 5 years or under (Campbell-Lendrum, 2009). Over the long term, higher temperatures will increase the levels of ozone and other air pollutants that provoke cardiovascular and respi-ratory diseases, and pollen and other aeroallergens that trigger asthma, with the poor and the elderly being hardest hit (Beggs, 2004).

As many of the most important infectious diseases are highly sensitive to both temperature and precipitation conditions, higher temperatures will increase the rates of survival and replication of bacterial contaminants of food and water sources, which con-tribute a large proportion of the burden of diarrhoeal disease, particularly in poor countries. Already, per capita mortality rates from vector-borne diseases are almost 300 times greater in developing regions than in developed ones (World Health Organization, 2006).

Warmer temperatures will also affect diseases transmitted by insects and other vectors as temperature affects their survival and biting rates, and determines the rates of reproduction of parasites within them. Higher temperatures are already increasing the risks of transmission of the most severe forms of malaria among high-altitude populations that lack immunity against such diseases (Bouma, Dye and van der Kaay, 1996; Pascual and others, 2006).

The most immediate effect of climate change on health and well-being is likely to be a function of the availability of water. It is estimated that one quarter of the population in Africa (about 200 million people) experience water stress (Ludi, 2009). Increasing temperatures and more variable precipitation are expected to reduce the availability of freshwater, making it more difficult to fulfil basic needs for drinking, cooking and washing. Meanwhile, a greater incidence of flooding stemming, inter alia, from more intense precipitation and from sea-level rise in lower coastal zones, will cause a further contamination of freshwater supplies, thereby further increasing water scarcity, as well as create opportunities for the breeding of mosquitoes and other disease vectors as people are, for example, forced to store water for longer periods (Nagao and others, 2003). Indeed, water scarcity poses one of the greatest long-term threats linked to climate change: while already more than 2 billion people live in the dry regions of the world and suffer disproportionately from diseases related to contaminated or insufficient water (World Health Organization, 2005b), it is estimated that up to 7 billion people will be at risk from increasing water stress by 2050 (Alcamo, Flörke and Märker, 2007). Moreover, with irrigation water withdrawals accounting for almost 70 per cent of global water withdrawals (Shiklomanov and Rodda, 2003), increased water stress will have a significant impact on health through growing food insecurity.

Higher temperatures and more extreme heatwaves will increase mortality rates; for instance, the effects of a 1° C increase in (average) temperature on ozone and particulate levels may lead to an increase in global deaths from air pollution of over 20,000 per year (Jacobson, 2008). Short-term increases in temperature during summers and hot seasons will also become more frequent and intense. Such short-term fluctuations will particularly affect urban areas owing to the "heat-island effect" resulting from the high absorption of solar radiation in urban environments, as against heat reflection from vegetation. This effect, which can raise temperatures by 5° C–12 °C in urban areas relative to surrounding areas, will heighten the threat of hazards such as heatwaves (Aniello and others, 1995; Patz and others, 2005). The extreme heat of the summer of 2003 provided a stark reminder of the potentially devastating impacts of heatwaves: temperatures that had been up to 30 per cent higher than the seasonal average over large parts of the European continent are estimated to have caused an additional 70,000 deaths (Robine and others, 2008), the majority of which occurred in urban areas.

Thus, overall, a warmer and more variable climate will lead to higher levels of some air pollutants, increase transmission of diseases from poor water, poor sanitation and poor hygiene, increase the hazards of extreme weather, damage agricultural production and lead to severe water stress. While not all of the effects of climate change will be harmful, the overall negative effects of climate change on health are both larger and more strongly supported by evidence than are the possible benefits (World Health Organization, 2002; Intergovernmental Panel on Climate Change, 2007a). Moreover, the health effects of climate change on the poorest populations, in contrast to those of the richer nations, are expected to be overwhelmingly negative and are likely to affect developing countries

Higher temperatures are increasing the risks of malaria among high-altitude populations that lack immunity against such diseases

Higher temperatures and more extreme heatwaves will increase mortality rates

Health effects of climate change on the poorest populations are expected to be overwhelmingly negative

harder and faster than developed ones. In particular, as many developing nations are burdened by high population densities and air pollution and still struggle to supply adequate drainage, running water for basic sanitation and hygiene, and housing, their vulnerability to climate-sensitive infectious diseases and health impacts is likely to continue rising. More importantly, climate variability worsens existing poverty traps, such as those prevailing in rain-fed agricultural sub-Saharan economies, as it will increase the prevalence of malnutrition and infectious diseases.

Meeting the challenge of adaptation

Adaptation to climate change has not been mainstreamed into decision-making processes

Despite the imminent threat, adaptation to climate change in developed and developing countries alike has not been mainstreamed into decision-making processes (Adger and others, 2003; Huq and Reid, 2004). The challenge tends to be addressed by adding an "extra" layer to existing policy designs and implementation mechanisms rather than by adjusting original designs so as to address climate change in a more integral way (O'Brien and others, 2008). Equating adaptation measures with emergency relief and framing the challenge in terms of requests for donor support, which is a frequent approach, has not helped. This has given rise to an often bifurcated approach to adaptation, where efforts either focus on responses to the impacts of climate change (coping measures) or seek to reduce exposure through climate-proofing existing projects and activities, particularly in the context of disaster risk management. Notwithstanding the fact that these two tracks strive for a shared goal, there is a real danger that the underlying philosophies of coping and proofing pull in different policy directions and that fragmented actions will end up, at best, creating partial solution to problems, and, at worst, causing new problems or aggravating existing ones (Sanchez-Rodriguez, Fragkias and Solecki, 2008). As discussed in the *World Economic and Social Survey 2008* (United Nations, 2008), there is indeed a real danger, already apparent in the response to natural disasters, that underlying structural causes of vulnerability and maladaptation will be missed, including a number of closely interlinked and compounding threats to social and economic security.

Large-scale investments and integrated policy efforts are likely to be called for in response to climate-related threats

Recent efforts to forge a more consistent approach to the adaptation challenge stress the central role of market incentives (Organization for Economic Cooperation and Development, 2008). These efforts usefully highlight the methodological challenge inherent in evaluating the costs and benefits of adaptation, point to a role for positive incentives and help expand the scope for more efficient coping and risk-reduction strategies. However, this approach tends to perceive the challenge in terms of a series of discrete and unconnected threats which can be addressed through incremental improvements made to existing arrangements, thereby missing the large-scale investments and integrated policy efforts that are likely to be called for in response to climate-related threats. Moreover, weighing costs and benefits runs the risk of ignoring how vulnerabilities are often deeply embedded in local conditions and histories, sensitivity to which will need to be a central component of effective adaptation strategies.

The alternative approach perceives adaptation in terms of building resilience with respect to climatic shocks and hazards by realizing higher levels of socio-economic development so as to provide threatened communities and countries with the requisite social and economic buffers. Such an approach would contribute to meeting the larger development challenge of overcoming a series of interrelated socio-economic vulnerabilities which can hold back growth prospects and expose communities to unmanageable shocks. These include, inter alia, a narrow economic base, limited access to financial resources, persistent food insecurity, and poor health conditions, which can be addressed only through the mobilization and investment of sizeable resources.

From this perspective, well-designed adaptation measures for addressing climate threats should simultaneously meet other needs, and not be in conflict with development objectives, nor should they produce conditions that increase vulnerability to climate change (Huq, 2002). For example, adaptation to climate change in agriculture should be part of broader agricultural policy efforts to raise productivity and reduce the vulnerability of the sector to outside shocks. Similarly, forest conservation and reforestation policies should be an integral part of broad development and poverty reduction strategies, encompassing investment in economic diversification, human capital and employment creation as well as improvement of land, soil and water management. However, the room for "win-win" (or "no-regrets") solutions should not be exaggerated. The cost of adaptation is likely to be high and a majority of solutions will involve difficult choices and trade-offs which will not be manageable through better project management or calculated technocratic responses but will require enhanced national regulatory authority and strategic planning processes encompassing open discussion within the entire community as well as an acceptance of the fact that negotiating and bargaining will be integral to shaping the final outcome (Someshwar, 2008; Burton, 2008).

> Adaptation measures for addressing climate threats should simultaneously meet other needs and should not be in conflict with development objectives

Such an approach is unlikely, however, to make much progress in the absence of more effective and inclusive institutional responses to the adaptation challenge. This would include closer engagement of policymakers with local communities, where the impact will be most keenly felt and effective investments will have to be made. Still, the scale of resources needed to bolster resilience with respect to climate change will, in most cases, call for national resource mobilization and effective developmental States pursuing an *integrated and strategic approach*. Integration of adaptation measures into their overall planning and budgeting should start with the assessment of local vulnerabilities to existing climate threats, including their variability and extremes, and of the extent to which existing policy and development practice has served to reduce or increase those vulnerabilities. In many cases, such an approach will need to draw lessons from past government failures to build a more integrated approach to the development challenge owing to insufficient dialogue and cooperation among different ministries, as well as investing in new capacities to deal with the specifics of the adaptation challenge. For example, meteorological services in many developing countries, especially least developed economies which to a large extent do not have real agro-meteorological services (Intergovernmental Panel on Climate Change, 2007c), would need to be improved so as to be able to provide agriculture with more reliable forecasts.

> Developmental States pursuing an integrated and strategic approach are needed

An initial step towards achieving a more integrated approach has been taken by some countries through National Adaptation Programmes of Action which were conceived as a means through which least developed countries could secure financial support for adaptation to the averse effects of climate change. The concept was negotiated during the seventh session of the Conference of the Parties to the United Nations Framework Convention on Climate Change,[11] held at Marrakech, Morocco, from 29 October to 10 November 2001. These Programmes of Action, which are structured through a bottom-up approach, are action-oriented and tailored to specific national circumstances; they identify "urgent and immediate" investment projects that could significantly contribute

---

11   United Nations, *Treaty Series*, vol. 1771, No. 30822.

to adaptation and poverty alleviation (see box III.4). Broadly, the participation of Government agencies and civil society, the consistency with national development plans, and the focus on vulnerability assessment have been among the main strengths of National Adaptation Programmes of Action. Yet, difficulties in scaling up projects, and funding and institutional shortcomings (Huq and Osman-Elasha, 2009), as well as the failure to adopt a more broadly developmental approach, need to be overcome.

Box III.4

National Adaptation Programmes of Action: adaptation strategies and mechanisms in least developed countries

In 2001, the Conference of the Parties to the United Nations Framework Convention on Climate Change, at its seventh session, had acknowledged that least developed countries did not have the means to deal with problems associated with adaptation to climate change, including funding investment and the transfer of technology. Recognition of the need to "fast-track" adaptation action in those countries led to the establishment of a work programme on least developed countries, which included the preparation of National Adaptation Programmes of Action to identify "urgent and immediate needs" for adaptation.[a] Each least developed country is granted US$ 200,000 to prepare its National Adaptation Programme of Action. Prioritized activities are identified in project proposals, which are then submitted to the Global Environment Facility (GEF).

a See document FCCC/ CP/2001/13/Add.1 and Corr.1, sect.ll, decision 5/CP.7, paras. 11 and 15.

Although National Adaptation Programme of Action projects tend to bear a strong resemblance to "regular" development projects, each country does in fact propose at least one or two activities that are revealed to be directly related to climate change and variability; sectors involved include food security, infrastructure, coastal zones and marine ecosystems, insurance, early warning and disaster management, terrestrial ecosystems, education and capacity-building, tourism, energy, health and water resources. In general, there is a strong emphasis on poverty reduction and food security.

Currently, 39 National Adaptation Programmes of Action have been completed and an additional 10 are being prepared. As of April 2009, 28 countries had submitted projects for implementation to the Global Environment Facility, of which 23 were approved. Many countries note that barriers to implementing their National Adaptation Programmes of Action are related to many of the problems that each faces in general: insufficient institutions, lack of capacity, policy gaps and insufficient funding. The following cases, on the other hand, highlight how National Adaptation Programme of Action priorities also depend on local characteristics and challenges.

In Cambodia, for instance, National Adaptation Programme of Action priorities concern waterways that are considered essential for flood mitigation and generation of fertile soil. Specifically, Cambodia's coastal area lies in the south-west along the Gulf of Thailand, while the interior of the country contains a large lake, the Tonle Sap, which is seasonally connected to the Mekong River and is extremely important for providing services such as food production and flood protection. As might be expected, one significant project proposed by Cambodia is the rehabilitation of the upper Mekong and provincial waterways for the purpose of addressing frequent flooding. In addition to the importance of these waterways for flood mitigation, they also provide the water used for irrigation, household consumption and transportation. The project therefore aims to clear the waterways, which have become silted, so as to reduce the risk of floods, improve aquatic resources, supply water for irrigation and domestic use, and improve provincial water transportation.

Further, the largest project in Cambodia involves the development and improvement of community irrigation systems to address the risk of drought, which is linked to a prolonged dry season. As very little land in Cambodia is irrigated, this project aims to provide sufficient water for rice farming, reduce the risk of crop failures due to water shortage, and enhance food security and reduce poverty in the rural areas. The project entails rehabilitating 15 existing community irrigation systems as well as constructing 15 new ones, including reservoirs, and is expected to encompass the establishment of water-user associations and the conduct of training on the maintenance and operation of irrigation systems.

In Eritrea sea-level rise is considered one of the main concerns related to climate change owing to the fact that this country has an extensive coastal zone along the Red Sea. Flash floods,

Box III.4 (cont'd)

recurrent drought and an increase in climatic variability are also concerns. Eritrea's National Adaptation Programme of Action process had identified 102 possible projects, of which 5 were ultimately prioritized. The largest project is proposed for the north-western lowland, characterized by low and extremely variable rainfall and a high frequency of droughts, which affect livestock keeping and rain-fed agriculture practices in degraded and arid areas. The focus is on people who had been pastoralists but had to turn to other means of survival when this failed. Now the crops are failing as well. The project aims to reduce vulnerability to climate variability and drought and cope with climate change in the long term through intensification of the agro-pastoralist system. Additional soil moisture will both increase crop productivity and provide fodder for livestock. Thus, the project aims to establish spate-irrigated cereal crop production systems, improve livestock production by improving the rangeland, restock the population of small ruminants, provide machinery and initial agricultural inputs and establish effective community-based institutions.

In Samoa, where nearly three quarters of the population live in the low-lying coastal area, sea-level rise is also a concern. Climate change is expected to reduce overall annual rainfall, but with increased occurrences of high-intensity rainfall, increased average temperature, rising sealevels and increased tropical cyclone frequency and intensity. Development of a climate early warning system is the most important priority project for Samoa; in terms of financing, it accounts for more than one half of the budgeted costs of all nine proposed priority projects. This project seeks to upgrade technical early warning systems and associated technical capabilities to monitor and warn against climate and extreme events; and build sectoral and public capabilities to understand and use climate and early warning hazard information. It is hoped that the project will allow improved local position forecasting and capability; improved warning relay to remote communities, more accurate real-time feedback and relevant local forecasts; improved three-month lead outlooks on drought probabilities and improved input into resource management systems (water, forestry, agriculture, energy); and improved timely warnings, monitoring and identification of flood-prone areas.

Climate-smart development

As noted above, long-term planning and anticipatory action are necessary to prevent increasing vulnerability to climate change in the course of the development process. Tackling only the impacts will fail to address the long-term consequences of climate change: fragmented actions are at best only partial solutions. Moreover, in managing climate change, it is important to avoid considering its impacts in isolation from other processes of change, such as urbanization, economic development, and shifts in land use and resource demands.

Development policy must become climate-smart through its awareness of the range of development risks that will emerge over the coming decades. The commitment of resources to meet these risks should be beneficial if those resources protect the growth path from unforeseen and large-scale shocks. Such a commitment could, however, entail a potential cost to the extent that the resources could have been used directly in financing other productive investments. Policymakers must plan adaptation efforts accordingly, with an eye to boosting broader development efforts. Among such adaptation efforts, special attention could usefully be paid to:

Development must become climate-smart through its awareness of the range of development risks

- *Vulnerable populations,* whose "coping range" with respect to climate shocks is limited. For example, consider food-poor groups in Viet Nam. Groups vulnerable to food poverty are spread throughout the country and encompass different occupations, ethnicities and age groups (Food and Agriculture Organization of the United Nations, 2004). In 2002, 40 per cent of the population belonging to ethnic minorities (mainly located in isolated upland areas of Viet Nam) lived below the food poverty line. The risk of being affected by conditions of destitution was thereby three times higher for these minorities than for the average rural population of the country. In another example, some 28 per cent of people in the Mekong and Red River Deltas (some 8.7 million people) belonging to small farm families, including many female-headed households, are currently estimated to be food-insecure or potentially food-insecure. The populations of both these "groups" are likely to be affected by the adverse consequences of a changing climate. Shifts in rainfall patterns and intensification of extreme events in the uplands, for example, will impact agricultural livelihoods of ethnic minorities. The livelihoods of the already vulnerable landless or small farmers in the Deltas may be subject to additional stress arising from a changing climate, including salinity intrusions in the summer, and potentially higher-than-historic flooding in the monsoon season. Given the already high levels of food poverty and low levels of resilience, the impacts of a changing climate on these groups would be devastating and would require priority considerations in adaptation plans. An exclusive focus on the "poorest of the poor" via programmes of cash transfers, insurance and other safety nets (see United Nations Development Programme, 2007a, chap. 4) can be useful in the short term; but often, for relief purposes, this approach is not likely to be sustainable unless scaled up to include wider rural groups which can often face spells of economic insecurity and poverty.

- *Synergies* in responding to multiple development risks. The failure of key infrastructure systems typically results not from a single factor, but from a combination of risks. For example, a set of factors might comprise declines in the amount and the area of irrigation due to the manifestations of a changing climate (such as higher levels of evapotranspiration induced by higher diurnal temperature) and failures of the socio-polity to ensure employment, food security and, ultimately, a decent standard of living for burgeoning populations. The two processes are apparently disconnected but when they do come together (owing, for example, to a strong El Niño), their combined impacts devastate socio-economic and ecological systems. The interrelation between adaptation and mitigation also provides opportunities for unlocking investment synergies in cases, for example, where irrigation systems expanded to meet adaptation challenges can be used to open up new markets for low-emissions technologies such as those developed to provide renewable energy.

- *Scale economies,* arising from extraordinary opportunities, such as the development of an entire river basin or coastal zone, and long-term development decisions, such as major infrastructure investments in coastal roads, hydropower and irrigation systems. In this regard, the maritime coast of Mozambique, one of the longest in Africa, extends over a distance of 2,400 kilometres, and is home to about 60 per cent of the population. Key economic activities encompassing fisheries, tourism and ports, as well as mining, oil and gas, are of immense economic value today, and will continue to be so in the future, both to local people and at the national level. However, competing claims (from agriculture and manufacturing) for such resources as water and land and waste-water discharge are resulting in a significant reduction in water quality and quantity in the coastal zone, and significant impacts on the delta and mangrove forests. In addition, intense coastal dynamics (for example, wave actions, dispersion of sediments and strong winds and tides), combined with tropical cyclones and heavy rains, are worsening coastal erosion.[12] Current ecological and economic stresses are likely only to increase in the future, owing to increases in population and intensification of development. Climate change is further expected to result in an increased incidence of destructive cyclones, especially in La Niña phases. The Government of Mozambique has drawn up ambitious plans for the sustainable development of the coastal region, including infrastructure (transportation, drainage and water supply), land-use changes, and soft options to manage beach erosion. Such plans, which present unique opportunities for an infusion of massive development, need to deal with climate risks in an integrated manner, across seasonal, inter-annual and multi-decadal time scales.

- *Complementarities,* achieved by piggybacking on efforts already under way, such as the expansion of a metropolitan water supply and sewerage system. The need to investigate and deal with the risks arising from a changing climate to the hydropower project on the Rio Amoya in Colombia has led to the consideration of an adaptation project in the Las Hermosas massif in the central range of the Andes. Design of the 80 megawatt run-of-river generation facility on the Rio Amoya had assumed (as has been the case in many other parts of the world) a climate stationary with regard to stream flows, which continues to be the most common assumption in this location and elsewhere. However, a growing recognition of the potential negative impacts of climate change on the surrounding high-altitude moorland biotope has led to a consideration of the potential risks to biodiversity in the project plans. The Las Hermosas adaptation project now offers an opportunity to reconsider stream flows in the coming decades and formulate plans for dealing with climate-related surprises.

How to apply the integrated approach

To tackle the underlying vulnerabilities that put communities at risk in the face of climate-related threats due to global warming, States must ensure that climate risks are integrated into national and local disaster risk-reduction plans. To be effective, adaptation strategies will have to differentiate among the various dimensions of adaptation at the local, regional, national and international levels as well as within different economic sectors. Table III.1 provides examples of potential adaptation measures for different sectors following the integrated developmental approach suggested above.

Adaptation strategies will have to differentiate among the various dimensions of adaptation both at the local, regional, national and international levels and within different economic sectors

Forestry and agriculture

Adaptation practices in the forestry sector are based in general upon lessons learned from past adaptations to climate variability. Important elements of forest protection encompass not only improved climate forecasting and disease surveillance systems but also strategies for preventing and combating forest fires, including the construction of fire lines, controlled burning and the utilization of drought- and fire-resistant tree species, such as

---

12   Urban and port expansions, along with recent tourism-related development, have increased coastal erosion rates severalfold. At Ponta d'Ouro beach in Southern Mozambique, for instance, the current erosion rate is between 0.95 and 1.75 metres per year, while in other parts of southern Mozambique, the average erosion rate of the coastline between 1971-1975 and 1999-2004 has been 0.11 and 1.10 metres per year in sheltered and exposed beaches, respectively (Government of Mozambique, 2007).

Table III.1
Potential measures of adaptation to climate change for different sectors

Sector	Adaptation measures
Urban planning	Building residences closer to workplaces in order to reduce transportation time and costs, thereby boosting productivity in a service economy
Water	Expanded rainwater harvesting
	Water storage and conservation techniques
	Desalinization
	Increased irrigation efficiency
Agriculture	Adjustment of planting dates and crop diversification
	Crop relocation
	Improved land management, for example, erosion control and soil protection through tree planting
Infrastructure	Improved seawalls and storm surge barriers
	Creation of wetlands as a buffer against sea-level rise and flooding
Settlement	Relocation
Human health	Improved climate-sensitive disease surveillance and control
	Improved water supply and sanitation services
Tourism	Diversification of tourism attractions and revenues
Transport	Realignment and relocation of transportation routes
	Improved standards and planning for infrastructure in order to cope with warming and damage
Energy	Strengthening of generating facilities and grids against floods, windstorms and heavy precipitation

Source: Adapted from table 5-1 in Dodman, Ayers and Huq (2009).

teak, in tropical forest plantations. Moreover, various measures aimed at assisting forests in adapting to climate change are needed to enable sustainable forest management. These would include, for instance, facilitating the adaptive capacity of tree species mainly by maximizing silvicultural genetic variation, but also through management approaches such as minimizing slash, reduced-impact logging and widening buffer strips and firebreaks. In this context, adaptation measures to reduce deforestation would have to entail developing alternative and sustainable economic activities for the communities affected (Phillips, 2009). For instance, in the Brazilian Amazon the livelihoods of approximately 27 million people, many of them poor, mainly depend on activities linked to deforestation such as logging. This ongoing deforestation accounts for about 8 per cent of the world's annual carbon emissions. Measures to be taken to adapt to climate change in both natural and planted forests should enhance forest resilience as well as provide a range of co-benefits, which could include biodiversity conservation, benefits for the hydrologic cycle, soil stabilization and the maintenance of a wide range of livelihood options.

In many poorer countries, increasing productivity of the agriculture sector and reducing its vulnerability to climatic shocks are key to long-term sustainability

In many poorer countries, increasing productivity of the agriculture sector and reducing its vulnerability to climatic shocks are key to long-term sustainability. Maximizing yields over good and bad years, particularly when subsistence farming is involved, by decreasing the chance of crop failure will be an important means of adapting to climate change. This would entail reducing vulnerability as a whole rather than maximizing the yield in an optimum year (Altieri, 1990). Strategies to decrease crop failures will include diversity farming, which is potentially one of the most important strategies for achieving food security in a changing climate, and the utilization of new crop strains—strains that are more weather-resistant and have higher yields. For example, at the Njoro division in Kenya, farmers have been trying to switch from wheat and potatoes to quick-maturing crops such as beans and maize, while planting every time it rains inasmuch as there is no longer a clear-cut growing season (Dodman, Ayers and Huq, 2009). Yet, it is not clear how sustainable this strategy could be, in particular given the multiple vulnerabilities that these types of community often face. Stressed ecosystems and possible reduction of bio-diversity could further weaken livelihoods and multiply the adaptation challenges of the most vulnerable, among them women, children, the sick and older persons.

In Bangladesh, whereas people traditionally grew low-yield deep-water rice during the monsoon season, they now grow, in areas covered by flood management projects, one high-yield rice crop (*aman*) that is planted during the monsoon, another (*boro*) that is planted in the dry season, with irrigation, and a third (*aus*) that is planted in the pre-monsoon season as the predominant crop (Banerjee, 2007). Innovative approaches to protecting agriculture in Bangladesh, which is particularly prone to natural hazards and frequent flooding, also include *dap chas* (floating gardens), where crops are grown on floating rafts to protect them from floods.

The interconnections of the risks arising from development and climate are particularly apparent when considering food security. In the Sudan, persistent and widespread drought is very likely to worsen owing to climate change. On the other hand, a more integrated approach to climate risk and livelihoods has increased resilience in some communities. Water harvesting, new crops and types of livestock, and rehabilitating rangelands, along with access to finance and improving farm skills, all taken together, have enhanced capacity for adaptation and improved food security (Osman-Elasha and others, 2008).

More generally, economic policies to promote agricultural development should focus on extending support services, particularly for smallholders, and improving infrastructure (such as roads and storage facilities as well as irrigation networks). Those policies should address the issue of land reform and build research and technical capabilities. The establishment of strategic food reserves, including at the international level, would allow Governments to reduce price volatility by releasing food in times of emergency and crisis. These reserves would have the potential to benefit poor countries which might not have the capacity to respond quickly to sudden scarcity, while proving more effective than other approaches in controlling international price volatility. The need to adapt to climate change could reinforce strategies to promote adaptive agricultural research and development, particularly in the case of Africa, where there is a large gap between current yields and agricultural potential (Smith, Klein and Huq, 2003). For example, a new rice variety was successfully developed by the Government rice research station in Sierra Leone, with the technology having already been transferred among farmers. The new rice has a higher yield and is more adapted to drier climate conditions (Intergovernmental Panel on Climate Change, 1999).

Urban environments

Urban adaptation requires the adoption of a long-term perspective, one that addresses the factors underlying the vulnerabilities associated with rapid urbanization. The strain on cities in developing countries is already enormous; adding climate change to the picture will perhaps require a paradigm shift in urban planning. Settlements often materialize in

The interconnections of the risks arising from development and climate are particularly apparent when considering food security

Economic policies designed to promote agricultural development should focus on extending support services, particularly for smallholders, and improving infrastructure

high-risk areas, such as river banks or unstable hill slopes, in the absence of any planning strategy or any consideration of future consequences. National policies to identify and influence formal and informal development in these areas are essential, as is the allocation of alternative areas for development in order to anticipate and shape the vision for the city and provide sustainable expansion land for affordable housing. Preventing informal settlements in areas that should not be developed requires governance structures and a solid institutional basis, with city visions and master plans supported by an institutional fabric. Such a fabric is often weak or non-existent in many developing countries.

Disaster risk reduction is an important component of adapting to climate change in the urban sector

Disaster risk reduction is also an important component of adapting to climate change in the urban sector. Institutions established to address disasters are typically weak and need to be strengthened and the traditional focus is on disaster relief. Anticipatory adaptation, in contrast, would encompass preparedness, including relief plans and awareness-raising activities. Thus, abstracting from the emergency dimension of post-disaster response, which consists largely of searching for missing persons and providing short-term shelter and food, anticipatory adaptation in this context will need to focus on infrastructure, land-use planning and regulatory measures. Particular emphasis will need to be placed on temporary dwellings, such as shanty towns and slums, as well as on areas built in vulnerable locations and in high-risk areas, such as river banks or unstable hill slopes, while in many developing countries sewerage and drainage systems would need to be built to reduce the risk resulting from more intense precipitation. Some approaches such as constructing elevated walkways to cope with flooding—an approach adopted, for example, in Bangkok—are mere stopgap measures designed to increase pedestrian mobility in high-traffic areas, rather than to shield people from exposure to stagnant surface water.

The goal should be to reduce vulnerabilities to the impacts that climate change will exert on more extreme weather events and to emphasize thereby the importance of the reduction of sensitivity and exposure to hazards. The urgency of doing this is particularly acute, considering that often 30–50 per cent of the entire population of cities live in settlements that have been developed illegally (Satterthwaite, 2007), many of which are located in vulnerable areas.

Adaptation of urban areas to climate change requires governance that is focused on sustainable development and supported by appropriate institutions

Taking a long-term perspective means that measures must address vulnerability to climate change in the context of rapid urbanization. This would include tackling, for instance, urban legislation that withholds tenure and thus obstructs the consolidation of buildings, thereby contributing to the expansion of areas with shanty towns (Sanderson, 2000). At their best, plans and policies would facilitate urbanization and a process of adaptation. At their worst, they would create perverse incentives which encouraged development in high-risk areas (Satterthwaite, 2007) or activities that increased vulnerability to climate change. In particular, adaptation of urban areas to climate change requires strong governance—governance that is focused on sustainable development and supported by appropriate institutional arrangements (see box III.5 for the case of Durban, South Africa). As things currently stand, most of the risk to urban areas is in fact associated with the incapacity of local governments to, inter alia, ensure provision for infrastructure, for disaster risk reduction and for disaster preparedness.

Health and water security

Protection from and adaptation to climate change risks are part of a basic preventive approach to public health, not a separate or competing demand. However, while the global health community has a wealth of experience in protecting people from climate-related hazards, shortfalls in providing basic public-health services leave much of the global population exposed to climate-related health risks, making it difficult for health services to look beyond the horizon of current urgent health gaps. Thus, there is a need for both additional investment to strengthen key functions, and forward-planning through which to build on these systems, so as to address the changing pattern of the challenges posed by climate change.

This having been said, it should also be noted that adapting to the potential impacts of climate change on health also requires a broader cross-sectoral approach, as the risks that climate change poses to health are very much embedded within the wider challenge of achieving genuinely sustainable development. In particular, the links between poverty and vulnerability to climate change are probably nowhere as evident as in the health sector, highlighting the need for pursuing further development as the overarching strategy for adapting to climate change. Indeed, the largest determinant of vulnerability to climate-related health risks is probably poverty.

There is therefore a general need for more proactive engagement of the health sector with other sectors in adapting to climate change, as health is a cross-cutting issue. For instance, as malnutrition is already the largest single contributor to disease burdens (Ezzati and others, 2004), with the greatest risks in this regard expected to arise in Africa (Parry, Rosenzweig and Livermore, 2005), adapting to climate change-related health risks will entail tackling the impacts of climate change on agricultural yields.

> The links between poverty and vulnerability to climate change are probably nowhere as evident as in the health sector

---

Box III.5

Putting climate change in the agenda: the Durban case

In the wake of the change of Government strategy in South Africa following the fall of the apartheid system in 1994, the Government had on its hands the massive task of including all sectors of society in its development plans. Local government was seen as a key actor in this regard, "given its direct interface with local communities and its pivotal role in service provision" (Roberts, 2008, p. 523).

Because of tensions stemming from differences between the development agenda and the environment agenda, as well as from differences between short- and long-term needs and priorities, the issue of climate change was squeezed between conflicting requirements. Very little internal institutional momentum and knowledge had been developed around the issue of climate change, in part because municipalities did not have an understanding of climate change science nor its local relevance; and "without developing a meaningful understanding of the science, climate change and its significance are unlikely to be effectively understood at the local government level" (ibid., p. 525).

The Durban example illustrates that certain conditions are necessary to ensure institutional and individual ownership of climate change as an important issue. In this regard, the following "institutional markers" have been suggested:

- Emergence of an identifiable political/administrative champion or champions for climate change issues
- Appearance of climate change as a significant issue in mainstream municipal plans
- Allocation of dedicated resources (human and financial) to climate change issues
- Incorporation of climate change considerations into political and administrative decision-making.

Based on how those conditions were met in Durban, it may be concluded that "reasonable progress" has been made in mainstreaming climate change concerns at the local government level. Capacity-building of local government personnel was "key to unlocking this process", which suggests that this can also "unlock endogenous resources and interest in climate change – ultimately making the likelihood of sustainable climate protection interventions greater" (ibid, p. 536).

Source: Roberts (2008).

Improved water management can have a direct impact on development opportunities, because it is primarily poor water management and lack of water entitlements, rather than physical water scarcity, that generate water-related tensions and poverty (Castillo and others, 2007). Along these lines, Bangladesh has begun a pilot project designed to channel the mountains of silt sediment that rivers transport from far away upstream in order to fill in shallow lowlands prone to flooding, or to create new land in order to protect its long, exposed coast against sea-level rise. The silt-trapping experiment has yielded visible gains in small areas such as Beel Bhaina, a low-lying 243-hectare (600-acre) soup bowl of land on the banks of the Hari River, about 55 miles upstream from the Bay of Bengal. United States scientists have recommended a similar silt diversion programme: opening Mississippi River levees south of New Orleans to allow sediment-rich water to flow over the region's marshes—which have been starved of silt since levee-building began in the region hundreds of years ago. An additional advantage of this type of river water-management project is its relative low cost (Sengupta, 2009). These projects serve as illustrations of how to go about improving water and river management in flood-prone areas. Drought-prone areas require parallel kinds of measures.

An even greater threat to existing precarious water management systems is the increased variability in water availability, a consequence of both population increases and a changing climate, which requires increased resilience in water management systems. Although efforts are already under way to strengthen these systems in a number of developing countries (see box III.6), significant public investment will be needed to achieve sustainable results.

The increased variability in water availability is an even greater threat to existing precarious water management systems than poor water management and lack of water entitlements

---

Box III.6

Water and river management in the context of climate change

It is predicted that climate change will have a multiple range of impacts on water resources. Water resources are being eroded, and it is very likely that floods and droughts will become more significant risks in many temperate and humid regions. This will likely affect infrastructures and safety. Approximately 2.3 billion people live in river basins under water stress, where annual per capita water availability is below 1,700 cubic metres. If current consumption patterns continue, at least 3.5 billion people, or about 48 per cent of the world's projected population, will live in water-stressed river basins in 2025.

One example of how building community capacities, applying technologies that are locally available, and undertaking small-scale measures can add up to effective large-scale and pro-poor adaptation is provided by a pilot project undertaken to restore 1,200-year-old village water tank systems (modest earthen dams) in the Godavari River basin in India. Through restoration of 12 tanks serving villages of 42,000 people in the Maner River basin (the Maner is a tributary of the Godavari) for $103,000 in cash and kind, agricultural production and profitability increased owing to more secure access to water; soils enhanced with silt from the tanks; and reduced input costs. In fact, WWF (2008) calculated that the increase in water storage capacity attained by de-silting all the village tanks in the Maner River catchment, at a cost of US$ 635 million, would be similar to that achievable through construction of the proposed Polavaram dam on the Godavari River. While the dam may refill more than once per year, it would cost US$ 4 billion, displace 250,000 people and inundate key habitats, including 60,000 hectares of forest.

Similarly, the restoration of 2,236 square kilometres of floodplains in Eastern Europe, similar in scale to the area inundated in the 2005 and 2006 floods, is providing room to retain and safely release floodwaters along the lower Danube River. International agreements signed between Governments to ensure better water and river management have been a powerful driver of change

Box III.6 (cont'd)

in this project. The cost of the restoration of 37 sites is estimated at €183 million compared with damages of €396 million from the 2005 flood. This will bring in about €112 million per year from ecosystem services, helping to diversify the livelihoods of local peoples. This large-scale adaptation project reveals the value of restoring the natural resilience of the environment with respect to climate events by retaining and releasing peak floods more safely. It will replace vulnerable monocultures with more diverse livelihoods based on natural ecosystems, such as tourism, fishing, grazing and fibre production, which will strengthen local economies.

In the United Republic of Tanzania, following the severe impacts on both people and biodiversity of dry waterways in the headwaters of the Great Ruaha River beginning in the early 1990s, WWF intervened to establish local water users' associations, and assist them in restoring native vegetation in the catchments, protect the river banks, better manage water extractions, and enforce water rules. As a result, better scheduling of water diversions has restored flows in many streams and parts of the Great Ruaha River itself, while a more rigorous environmental flow assessment is under way. The establishment of 20 community conservation banks has also reduced the reliance of many local people on water-related primary industries by facilitating diversification of the local economy and increasing their incomes.

In developing countries, an estimated 90 per cent of waste water is discharged directly into rivers and streams without treatment, and it is expected that climate change will exacerbate the impact of pollutants on livelihoods and further diminish the population of fish and other aquatic wildlife. This has been the case for coastal lagoons in the São João region of Brazil which became polluted with untreated sewage, causing a collapse in the fishing industry and impacting on tourism. However, multi-stakeholder river basin management institutions – the Consórcio Intermunicipal Lagos São João and its companion committee – have progressively fixed the region's environmental problems, facilitating an economic resurgence. A local multi-stakeholder institution approach that practised subsidiarity has engaged a broad spectrum of the local community and empowered them to take action to restore their environment. This has been possible partly owing to effective national and State water laws which gave the basin institutions mandates and access to adequate funding sources. The basin institutions have taken an iterative adaptive management approach to addressing environmental problems and by achieving substantial early successes, have increased community confidence and further support for new interventions. Waste-water discharge has been cut by 75 per cent, reducing the prospect that warmer temperatures will exacerbate pollution impacts. At the same time, wetlands are being restored, thereby increasing the likelihood that species and ecosystems will survive severe climatic events.

By linking local, national and international stakeholders in tackling specific water management-related issues, the adaptation mechanisms used have strengthened the capacities of local people and organizations to improve governance, diversify the local economy, increase resilience and institute adaptive management practices. As mentioned above, these projects tend to be relatively inexpensive, in contrast with some inflexible and large infrastructures which can be costly, displace people, limit villages' self-determination, impose constraints on scaling up implementation, and cause adverse environmental impacts.

Source: Based on information provided and projects supported by WWF, available at http://www.wwf.org.uk/.

International cooperation on adaptation

International cooperation on adaptation is essential for a number of reasons. First, the heaviest impact of human-induced climate change will be on small island developing States and the poorest countries in the world, including many African nations. These are the countries that have contributed least to the problem of global warming. Second, the vulnerability of these, and other developing countries with respect to climate change is reflected in the difficulty experienced by many of them in mobilizing the resources needed to reduce their exposure, to build up resilience and to make a rapid recovery after disasters

A development challenge can be properly met only through large-scale investments and strategic policies that draw on the help of the international community

strike. This is a development challenge that can be properly met only through large-scale investments and strategic policies that strengthen economic and social capacities at the local and national levels and that can draw on the help of the international community in order that those countries may cope and recover when disaster strikes (see box III.7 on international cooperation). Third, finding the right response to adaptation can point the way to developing more integrated responses to other shocks that threaten peace, security and well-being.

Setting aside their responsibility for the heightened threats from climate change, the fact remains that developed countries themselves stand to benefit from helping developing countries adapt. The wider consequences of climate impacts, such as increased destabilization and violence resulting from climate-induced conflict, have the potential to jeopardize national and international security (German Advisory Council on Global Change (WBGU), 2008; Schwartz and Randall, 2003). Moreover, the rising level of global inequality that could result from climatic shocks is in neither the economic interest (given the lost export and investment opportunities that this would entail) nor the political interest (given the threat to global cooperation) of rich countries seeking to forge a global framework for better managing climate change. Developing countries, in turn, should give priority to formulating plans for adaptation and take advantage of expertise made available by adaptation funding to establish more integrated and transparent strategies, which would include close consultation with and the participation of their citizens most immediately affected by rising temperatures and climatic shocks.

Increased destabilization and violence resulting from climate-induced conflict have the potential to jeopardize national and international security

Box III.7

International cooperation and the national adaptation strategy in Bangladesh

The effective early warning system of Bangladesh has already saved tens of thousands of lives. When cyclone Sidr, one of the strongest storms ever to develop in the Bay of Bengal, hit Bangladesh in November 2007, improved early warning technology had already reported the direction and intensity of Sidr 72 hours before. This was made possible by a network headed by the World Meteorological Organization (WMO) global cyclone observatory which fed key data to its regional outpost at India's Meteorological Office in New Delhi.

The message had been relayed to authorities in Dhaka, who passed it on to the local Red Crescent office. Some 40,000 trained volunteers, who then disseminated the information to the 15 districts most likely to be affected, cycled around the country, using megaphones to order residents into the 1,800 cyclone shelters and 440 flood shelters available. When Sidr hit, 2 million were under shelter.

A cyclone of similar magnitude had killed over 190,000 people in 1991; from Sidr, the estimated death toll was in the range of 5,000-10,000.

The system operates in conjunction with a broader action programme supported by donors including the United States of America and the European Union, which since 1991 has supported disaster preparedness and improved post-disaster relief and reconstruction. Under this programme, early warning and evacuation systems are integrated with infrastructure such as cyclone walls to protect Bangladesh from storm surges.

The Bangladesh Centre for Advanced Studies has also been a pioneer in preparing assessments of vulnerability to climate change, while the Bangladesh University of Engineering and Technology has analysed greenhouse gas emissions from different sectors and devised policies and measures designed to ensure better adaptation to climate change in the future.

Yet, Bangladesh has very few financial resources of its own for supporting the required scientific research, with almost the entire budget for the universities and research institutes spent on salaries and running costs, leaving the little, if any, research work to be supported by international donors.

Source: Based on Huq and Ayers (2008); and Huq (2001).

Scientists confirm that the time frame for acting to curb global greenhouse gas emissions and reduce the probability of catastrophic events is no more than decades and possibly years (Pachauri, 2008). Estimates of the cost of adaptation are still quite tentative and incomplete. The risk, however, lies in underestimating the scale of the challenge, which becomes even greater given the slow pace to date of the efforts undertaken to mitigate global warming.

Currently, there are three main flows of adaptation funds (see box III.8): North-South flows, channelled through multilateral adaptation funds and official development assistance (ODA); domestic flows from which developing countries generate and use adaptation funds; and South-South flows. The Global Environment Facility (GEF), an intergovernmental organization launched in 1991, has been entrusted with managing the multilateral adaptation funds sponsored by the United Nations Framework Convention on Climate Change (see also chap. VI). The World Bank has also developed the Climate Investment Funds, which were set up to promote innovative approaches to mitigation and adaptation, including increasing resilience among the most vulnerable communities. Even so, the difference between the sheer size of resources necessary for adaptation, in the range of $50 billion–$100 billion per year and the amount actually mobilized and available (about $154 million) is enormous.

> The gap, in terms of sheer size, between the resources necessary for adaptation and those actually mobilized and available is enormous

A key issue with respect to adaptation funding is its relation to ODA. The difficulty in scaling up aid is a real cause for concern, given the urgency of the adaptation challenge in many countries. The current bilateral instruments are unlikely to match up to the adaptation challenge: more innovative (and predictable) sources of funding will be needed (Müller, 2008). The principles set out in the United Nations Framework Convention on Climate Change, which distinguish between development and adaptation financing, insist on the need for additional funds above the commitments made to meet traditional development challenges. This rightly highlights the responsibility of rich countries for funding adaptation challenges; however, it runs the risk of ignoring the interconnected nature of these two sets of challenges, of sidestepping the long-standing debate on the adverse impact on aid effectiveness of excessive and cross conditionalities, and of leading to a proliferation of funding mechanisms and facilities that would, if history is any guide, likely reduce the effectiveness of international support (see chap. VI for further discussion).

Box III.8

Adaptation funds

A number of funds have so far been established to provide support for the adaptation challenge. They are described directly below:

- The Global Environment Facility (GEF) manages a number of funds: Strategic Priority on Adaptation (SPA)—GEF Trust Fund, Least Developed Countries' Fund (LDCF)—United Nations Framework Convention on Climate Change, and the Special Climate Change Fund (SCCF)—United Nations Framework Convention on Climate Change, with a total pledge of about $320 million, of which about $249 million is in disbursal
- Recently, the World Bank Group, in partnership with the three regional development banks (the Asian Development Bank, the African Development Bank and the Inter-American Development Bank), received pledges of about $6.1 billion for the Climate Investment Funds. Of this amount, less than $1 billion is earmarked for adaptation
- The Cool Earth Partnership of the Government of Japan has committed about $10 bil-

Box III.8 (cont'd)

lion over the next five years to tackle climate change. Although the bulk of assistance ($8 billion) is earmarked for mitigation, adaptation and improved access to clean energy have been allocated $2 billion

- The Environmental Transformation Fund—International Window (ETF-IW) of the United Kingdom of Great Britain and Northern Ireland, which will amount to about 800 million pounds over 2008-2011, has been set up to help developing countries tackle climate change. A large proportion of the proposed funding of ETF-IW has been allocated to the World Bank-administered Climate Investment Funds

- The Global Initiative on Forests and Climate of Australia is a $200 million five-year initiative that aims to facilitate significant and cost-effective reductions in greenhouse gas emissions in developing countries

- The objectives of the European Union Global Climate Change Alliance are to help developing countries integrate development strategies and climate change, help countries participate in global climate change activities that contribute to poverty reduction, and provide technical and financial support that targets five priority areas and related actions: (a) adaptation to climate change, (b) reducing emissions from deforestation, (c) enhancing the participation of poor countries in the Clean Development Mechanism, (d) promoting disaster risk reduction and (e) integrating climate change into poverty reduction efforts. The amounts pledged include €60 million (from the European Commission) for the period 2008–2010, €40 million from the Tenth European Development Fund, intra-ACP (African, Caribbean and Pacific Group of States), for regional action, with an additional €180 million for disaster risk reduction. Sweden pledged an additional €5.5 million in 2008

- The United Nations Development Programme MDG Achievement Fund—Environment and Climate Change thematic window (2007c) has as its objective to help reduce poverty and vulnerability in eligible countries by supporting interventions that improve environmental management and service delivery at the national and local levels, increase access to new financing mechanisms and enhance capacity to adapt to climate change. Spain has pledged US$ 90 million. Almost $86 million has already been committed to date, in 17 programmes with a duration of three years

- The Adaptation Fund was established under the Kyoto Protocol[a] to the United Nations Framework Convention on Climate Change,[b] to be financed mainly with a share of proceeds from Clean Development Mechanism project activities. Convention estimates of potential available funding for the period 2008-2012 are in the range of $80 million-$300 million per year. The Conference of the Parties serving as the meeting of the Parties to the Kyoto Protocol at its third session, held in Bali, Indonesia, from 3 to 15 December 2007, decided that the operating entity of the Adaptation Fund should be the Adaptation Fund Board, comprising 16 members and 16 alternate members, serviced by a Secretariat and a Trustee,[c] and invited the World Bank to serve as the trustee of the Adaptation Fund on an interim basis.[d]

a United Nations, *Treaty Series*, vol. 1771, No. 30822.

b Ibid., vol. 2303, No.30822.

c See FCCC/KP/CMP/ 2007/9/Add.1, decision 1/CMP.3, paras. 3, 6 and 7.

d Ibid., para. 23.

Conclusion

The adaptation challenge from warming temperatures is one that all countries must face in the coming decades, even if rapid progress is made towards a lower-emissions global economy. However, for some, the threat to livelihoods is already very real and, in some extreme cases, approaches catastrophic levels.

The adjustments required to adapt to climate change cannot be assessed in isolation or undertaken incrementally. Rather, they are closely interconnected with other risks and vulnerabilities that accompany the development process and will be heavily constrained by local institutional and technological conditions. Successful adaptation hinges critically on faster and more equitable growth, even as failure to adapt threatens those goals.

This chapter has argued that, in many cases, the response will involve a sizeable investment of resources to make countries and communities more resilient and to address vulnerabilities that can turn even small climatic shocks into long-term development disasters. This excludes a one-size-fits-all policy response. The right approach is an integrated national strategy which will require mobilization of domestic resources and the guidance of an effective developmental State.

Meeting such challenges will require a break with recent policy approaches which have given undue attention to market forces and competition. Adaptation, like mitigation, is a public policy challenge, the complexity of which will require using a broad array of strategies to build resilience.

The chapter has suggested that a smarter approach will build adaptation responses into ongoing development challenges by paying particular attention to vulnerable populations, by making use of large public works and taking advantage of scale economies, by addressing the issue of the thresholds below which current systems consistently fail and by exploiting investment complementarities.

Even so, many countries for whom the challenge is simply too big cannot be expected to meet it by themselves. Hence, it was agreed in Bali that finance and technical assistance would be available to help developing countries meet the adaptation challenge. So far, that assistance has been woefully inadequate and poorly organized. Improvements in this regard are likely to be a prerequisite for making real headway towards putting those countries on more sustainable development paths.

Annex

Sectoral impacts of climate change in Africa

Agro, fisheries, livestock farming and aquaculture	Ecosystems	Water resources	Human health	Settlements, infrastructure, industry
By 2100, Northern African agricultural losses might represent 0.4–1.3 per cent of GDP	Endangered species, including manatees and marine turtles, could be at risk, along with migratory birds (Democratic Republic of the Congo, Ghana and Seychelles)	In Northern Africa, six climate models show a likely increase in the number of people who could experience water stress by 2055	By 2050 and continuing into 2080, a large part of the western Sahel will likely become unsuitable for malaria transmission[a]	In Northern Africa, potential flood risks may arise by 2080 across a range of scenarios of the *Intergovernmental Panel on Climate Change Special Report on Emissions Scenarios* (SRES) (2000)[b] and climate change projections
In Egypt, climate change could decrease production of many crops (ranging from −11 per cent for rice to −28 per cent for soybeans) by 2050, compared with their production under current climate conditions	In Central Africa, mangroves could colonize coastal lagoons because of sea-level rise	In the Ouergha watershed in Morocco and for the period 2000-2020, a 1°C increase in temperature could reduce run-off by 10 per cent, assuming that precipitation levels remain constant	By the 2080s, areas in the Angola highlands currently having low rates of malaria transmission could also become highly suitable for transmission. In general, the highlands of eastern Africa are likely to become more suitable for malaria transmission.	In Western Africa, rise in sea level will significantly impact coastal megacities because of the concentration of the poor in potentially hazardous areas
In the Gulf of Guinea, sea-level rise may breach and destroy low-barrier beaches that limit coastal lagoons, while precipitation changes could affect discharges of the rivers feeding them (affecting lagoonal fisheries and aquaculture)	By 2099, enhanced sand dune activity/mobilization (Angola)	In Egypt, water used in 2000 was estimated at about 70 km3, far in excess of available resources. More than 70 per cent of cultivated area depends on low-efficiency surface irrigation systems, which cause high water losses, decline in land productivity, waterlogging and salinity problems. Unsustainable agricultural practices and improper irrigation management affect the quality of the country's water resources. Reductions in irrigation water quality have, in their turn, harmful effects on irrigated soils and crops	In Central Africa (for example, in the Congo area), places of interest, including wildlife areas and parks, may attract fewer tourists under marked climate changes	In Western Africa, potential flood risks may arise by 2080 across a range of SRES scenarios[b] and climate change projections
Coastal agriculture (palm oil and coconuts in Benin and Côte d'Ivoire; shallots in Ghana) is at risk of inundation and soil salinization	Lake Tanganyika: aquatic losses of about 20 per cent, with 30 per cent decrease in fish yields. Climate change may further reduce lake productivity (Democratic Republic of the Congo)		Based on parasite survey data, it is expected that previously malaria-free highland areas in Ethiopia, Kenya, Rwanda and Burundi could experience modest incursions of the disease by the 2050s, with conditions for transmission becoming highly suitable by the 2080s. By this period, areas currently with low rates of malaria transmission in central Somalia could also become highly suitable	In Western Africa, flood risks and water pollution-related diseases in low-lying regions (coastal areas), as well as coral reef bleaching, could negatively impact tourism
In Guinea, between 130 and 235 square kilometres (km2) of rice fields (17 per cent and 30 per cent of the existing rice field area) could be lost owing to permanent flooding by 2050	There are indications that, by 2020, the ice cap on Mount Kilimanjaro (United Republic of Tanzania) could disappear for the first time in 11,000 years	In Egypt, sea-level rise could impact on the Nile Delta and people living in the Delta and other coastal areas. Temperature rises will likely reduce productivity of major crops and increase water requirements, thereby decreasing crop water-use efficiency. A general increase in irrigation demand is	In Eastern Africa, the probability that sea-level rise could increase flooding, particularly on the coasts of Eastern Africa, may have implications for health	Indian Ocean islands could be endangered by potential changes in location, frequency and intensity of cyclones
By 2100, Western African agricultural losses might represent 2–4 per cent of GDP	Disappearance of low-lying corals and losses of biodiversity are expected (Djibouti)			Eastern African coasts could be affected by potential changes in the frequency and intensity of El Niño-Southern Oscillation events and coral bleaching
With a rise in annual global temperature (for example, 1.5°C–2.0°C), fisheries in north-western Africa will be adversely impacted	In Eastern Africa, proliferation of algae and dinoflagellates could increase the number of people affected by toxins (such as ciguatera) owing to consumption of marine food sources (Comoros)			In Eritrea, a one-metre rise in sea level could cause damage of over US$ 250 million with the submergence of infrastructure and economic installations in Massawa, one of the country's two port cities
	Losses of nyala and zebra (Malawi)			
	By 2099, enhanced sand dune activity/mobilization (Zambia and northern South Africa)			

Table III.1 (cont'd)

Agro, fisheries, livestock farming and aquaculture	Ecosystems	Water resources	Human health	Settlements, infrastructure, industry
In Cameroon, a 15 per cent increase in rainfall by 2100 would likely decrease the penetration of saltwater in Wouri estuary, while an 11 per cent decrease in rainfall would extend the reach of saltwater up to 70 km upstream (affecting lagoonal fisheries and aquaculture)	In Eastern Africa, aquatic losses of about 20 per cent, with 30 per cent decrease in fish yields in Lake Tanganyika. Climate change may further reduce lake productivity (Burundi, United Republic of Tanzania, Zambia)	expected. A projected decline in precipitation and projected population of between 115 million and 179 million by 2050 will increase water stress in all sectors, while a high degree of uncertainty about the flow of the Nile is expected	Rift Valley fever epidemics, evident during the 1997-1998 El Niño event in Eastern Africa and associated with flooding, could increase with a higher frequency of El Niño events	In Eastern Africa, flood risks and water pollution-related diseases in low-lying regions (coastal areas), as well as coral reef bleaching, could negatively impact tourism
In Kenya, losses of mangoes, cashew nuts and coconuts could cost almost US$ 500 million for a sea-level rise of one metre	In South Africa, expected changes in estuaries as a result of reductions in river run-off and inundation of salt marshes following sea-level rise	In Eastern and Western Africa, more people will likely experience a reduction rather than an increase in water stress[a]	Using 16 climate-change scenarios, by 2100, changes in temperature and precipitation could alter the geographical distribution of malaria in Zimbabwe, with previously unsuitable areas of dense human population becoming suitable for transmission. Strong southward expansion of the transmission zone will probably continue into South Africa	Potential flood risks may arise by 2080 across a range of SRES scenarios[b] and climate change projections
Agriculture and the growing seasons in parts of the Ethiopian highlands may lengthen under climate change, owing to a combination of increased temperature and rainfall changes	In South Africa, losses of 51-61 per cent of Fynbos and Succulent Karoo Biomes by 2050	Rainfall is likely to increase in some parts of Eastern Africa, resulting in various hydrologic outcomes	In general, areas of Southern Africa are likely to become more suitable for malaria transmission	
Southern Africa will likely experience notable reductions in maize production under possible increased El Niño-Southern Oscillation conditions	Kruger Park study estimates 66 per cent of nyala and zebra could be lost (South Africa)	In Southern Africa, six climate models show a likely increase in the number of people who could experience water stress by 2055		
In South Africa, crop net revenues will likely fall by as much as 90 per cent by 2100, with small-scale farmers most severely affected	In Southern Africa, projected losses of over 50 per cent of some bird species by 2050. Also, six bird species are estimated to lose substantial portions of their range	In Southern Africa, almost all countries except South Africa will probably experience a significant reduction in stream flow. For South Africa, the stream flow increase under the high-emissions scenarios is modest, at under 10 per cent		
Agriculture and the growing season in parts of Southern Africa, for example, Mozambique, may lengthen under climate change owing to a combination of increased temperature and rainfall changes[a]	In Southern Africa, there would be complex impacts on grasslands, including the role of fire	In terms of precipitation, six General Circulation Models and a composite ensemble of African precipitation models for the period 2070-2099 identify, for example, that parts of Southern Africa would experience significant losses of run-off, with some areas being particularly impacted (for example, parts of South Africa)		

Source: Synthesis based on information provided by Intergovernmental Panel on Climate Change (2007c).

a   Expected benefits.

b   The A1 scenario assumes a world of very rapid economic growth, a global population that peaks in mid-century, and the rapid introduction of new and more efficient technologies; the B1 scenario describes a convergent world, with the same global population as A1, but with more rapid changes in economic structures towards a service and information economy.

Chapter IV
A state of change: development policy and the climate challenge

The previous chapters have suggested that there are alternative climate-friendly development pathways that steer clear of the carbon-intensive technologies that have driven the modern growth process. The present chapter considers the policies that might be necessary at the national level to support what amounts to a new industrial revolution in developing countries.

Economic and technological revolutions that occurred during the course of the last two centuries have opened up opportunities for "latecomers" to kick-start a process of rapid growth and development. However, many countries and communities were unable to utilize, or were prevented from utilizing, those opportunities. At the same time, the economic gains to "first movers" have often been cumulative, resulting in a highly divergent pattern of global economic development characterized by rising gaps in incomes, technological capacity and energy use.

Those precedents are a concern for developing countries which fear being locked out of the latest stage of economic development, while being asked simultaneously to forgo the cheaper technological options that are currently available to them. Moreover, the latest technological revolution is unfolding at a time of profound economic and financial stress in the global economy, which is certain to hit the poorest and most vulnerable countries and communities the hardest, making it all the more difficult for them to adjust to a new economic and technological paradigm.

Recently, the Commission on Growth and Development (World Bank, 2008) argued that a conceptual impasse has been reached in the debate centred around the question "how can we cut carbon emissions to safe levels by midcentury while also accommodating the growth of developing countries?" Removing this impasse is fundamental and urgent. In this chapter, it is argued that implementing a big push, understood as a blend of pro-investment macroeconomic and industrial policies, built around a transformative low-emissions growth path, could be the bridge connecting economic development and reduced emissions. Management of the integrated development strategy needed to achieve this would require, however, the presence of a strong and dynamic developmental State and sufficient policy space to allow that State to adapt climate measures to local needs and sensitivities.

The next section looks at some of the traditional functions of the developmental State and how those relate to the climate challenge. That is followed by a discussion of industrial policy and its role in an investment-led strategy for meeting the climate and development challenges. The final section looks at some specific measures with respect to energy efficiency, cleaner coal and renewables through whose implementation policymakers in developing countries might begin the transition to a low-emissions, high-growth strategy.

Developing countries fear being locked out of the latest stage of economic development, while being asked simultaneously to forgo the cheaper technological options available to them

A big push could be the bridge connecting economic development and reduced emissions but would require the presence of a strong and dynamic developmental State and sufficient policy space

The role of developmental States in a warming world

An investment-led strategy

All economic success stories have enjoyed a sustained burst of growth, allowing them to raise living standards and close the income gap existing between them and more developed countries. Such growth, moreover, is often (though not always) correlated with a broad set of social indicators, including poverty reduction, which together describe a more inclusive development path. This path does not emerge spontaneously, however, and even after a period of rapid growth, countries can get stuck or fall back.

A rapid pace of capital accumulation, accompanied by shifts in the structure of economic activity towards high-productivity sectors, is usually a critical factor behind a sustained acceleration of growth (United Nations, 2006). An important part of the early development policy debate focused on how to quickly raise the share of investment in national income to a level that would trigger a virtuous circle of rising productivity, increasing wages, technological upgrading and social improvements. The required investments are often closely connected, depend on the reaching of a minimum scale to be efficient and may become profitable only over a long period of time. The presence of scale economies, complementarities, threshold effects and other "externalities", as well as the heightened uncertainty they inject into any investment decision, limits the role that market forces by themselves can play in realizing the desired investment path (DeLong, 2005). Infrastructure development, in general, and energy supply, in particular, have always been a critical elements in this story (see chap. II) and, as discussed in previous chapters, the importance of the latter has grown in the context of meeting the climate challenge.

Successful versions of this "big push" concentrated on selective leading sectors whose development would attract a further round of investment through the dynamic cumulative effect of decreasing costs and the expansion of strong backward and forward linkages (Hirschman, 1958). In this regard, the development strategy was less about detailed planning and more about strategic support and coordination, including a significant role for public investment in triggering growth and crowding in private investment along a new development pathway. A given rate of capital accumulation can, of course, depending on its nature and composition, as well as on the efficiency with which production capacity is utilized, generate different rates of output growth. Policies will have a significant bearing on the outcome. The steady rise in the minimum scale of investments needed to launch and maintain an industrialization drive has intensified this challenge over the years.

In most cases, a developmental State helped promote the goals of long-term growth and structural change by increasing the supply of investible resources and socializing long-term investment risk. State-sponsored accumulation involved, variously, the coordinated effort to shift resources into high-productivity activities, the provision of predictable and affordable credit through a managed financial system, and pro-investment macroeconomic policies, as well as direct public investment in some key sectors (Kohli, 2004). The East Asian economies have often been held up as exemplary embodiments of the developmental State (although they have exhibited a good deal of variation), but there are many other such examples (see box IV.1).[1]

> Successful development strategies have been less about detailed planning and more about strategic support and coordination, including a significant role for public investment in triggering growth and crowding in private investment

> A developmental State can promote the goals of long-term growth and structural change by increasing the supply of investible resources and socializing long-term investment risk

---

[1] There is no simple definition of the developmental State. For a useful discussion of contrasting roles of the State in the development process, see Cypher and Dietz (2004), chap. 7. They note (ibid., p. 228) that "development States … have the discretionary power to adopt several roles, depending on the needs and demands of society in general and the specific needs of sectors of the economy. Autonomy allows the developmental state to switch roles in specific sectors, as conditions dictate". (See also Chang and Rowthorn, 1995; Kozul-Wright and Rayment, 2007, pp. 243-252; and World Bank, 1993).

Box IV.1

The Tennessee Valley Authority: a successful big push

The post-war economic rebound of the American South, which followed large public capital investments during the New Deal and the Second World War, is a successful example of a big push. By triggering an increase in the rates of return to private investment, the infusion of public capital through the Tennessee Valley Authority (TVA) provided a major impetus for the rapid post-war industrialization of the Southern economy. Both econometric analysis and survey data from firms that moved South in the years immediately following the War strongly support the notion that big-push dynamics were at work (Bateman, Ros and Taylor, 2008).

TVA had been established on 18 May 1933 by an Act of the United States Congress as part of the New Deal, intended by the President of the United States of America, Franklin D. Roosevelt, to lift the United States out of the depths of the Great Depression. It was conceived both as a development agency, mandated to raise living standards in the Tennessee River Valley, and as a construction and management agency mandated to build and operate dams and structures along the Tennessee River, whose drainage basin over seven States covers some 40,900 square miles (or 105,930 square kilometres). TVA was to function as, in Roosevelt's words, "a corporation clothed with the power of government but possessed of the flexibility and initiative of a private enterprise".

Over the 12-year period spanning its inception in 1933 and the end of the Second World War in 1945, TVA established its institutional framework, built broad-based local support for its programmes, and constructed a physical infrastructure that would serve as the backbone for its accomplishments. This infrastructure included a vast system of multi-purpose dams and reservoirs designed to harness the potential of the Tennessee River and an extensive transmission system created to provide cheap electricity throughout the region. Early and intense efforts to improve agriculture, land use and forestry practices helped to restore and maintain a healthy environmental base, while access to small-scale credit and technical assistance programmes provided the citizens of the Valley with the tools they needed to improve their own lives. It was during those early years that the Tennessee Valley Authority established what may have become its greatest legacy: the integration of a healthy natural resource base, a strong infrastructure, and human capacity to foster the social and economic development of a region.

The need for TVA arose from the dire social and economic conditions in the Tennessee Valley in the 1930s. Although rich in natural resources, the region was largely rural and undeveloped, poverty-stricken and characterized by degraded environmental conditions. Per capita income was one of the lowest in the United States, few people had running water or electricity, and poor sanitary conditions resulted in some of the highest rates of disease and infant mortality in the country. In some areas near the Tennessee River, 1 out of every 3 people had malaria. Illiteracy rates were high and the quality of education was poor. Severe erosion, extensive deforestation and exhausted mines were indicative of a deteriorating environment. Additionally, the navigation potential of the Tennessee River remained untapped owing to hazardous shoals, while the heavy rainfall and steep slopes in the region subjected many areas to repeated and serious flooding. The people of the Tennessee Valley were trapped in a cycle of poverty. The natural resource base of the economy had been deteriorating, which led to widespread poverty and further misuse of the region's resources. The social problems in the Valley could be addressed only by improving the economy, which would depend on a healthy resource base, including land, water and forests.

As the Great Depression of the 1930s deepened and conditions in the Tennessee Valley worsened, Roosevelt sought to create an innovative programme that would revitalize the economy and boost morale. The creation of TVA represented a "bold experiment" aimed at accomplishing the unified development of a river basin. Flood control, navigation and power generation were not ends in themselves, but the means to advance social and economic development.

The vitality of the TVA as an institution was bolstered by its early, tangible and largely positive impact on the lives of the people of the Tennessee Valley. Two major dam construction projects were initiated in the agency's first year of operation. Over the next 12 years, bolstered by the need to support the war effort, progress was remarkable: the navigation channel on the Tennessee

Box IV.1 (cont'd)

Sources: Bateman, Ros and Taylor (2008), and Miller and Reidinger (1998).

River was completed; 26 dams were incorporated into the TVA water control system; and TVA became the largest power producer in the United States. Additionally, farm production levels tripled owing to successful efforts to reduce soil erosion, improve farm practices and introduce fertilizers. Although controversies arose over relocations required during dam building, the Valley residents were put back to work and the overall standard of living improved. TVA won the support of citizens and local governments and gained a national reputation for its work in the area of water resources, land management, forestry, agriculture and energy production.

An investment-led approach to the climate challenge is taking shape in a number of developed countries, and some developing countries, with the inclusion of green investments in stimulus packages designed to create jobs in the face of a severe economic downturn and shift resources into "green jobs" (see box I.4).

> In the developing world, the adjustments accompanying a shift to a low-emissions development pathway are likely to constitute another industrial revolution

However, in the developing world, the adjustments accompanying the shift to a low-emissions development pathway are likely to be much more significant, constituting, in effect, a new industrial revolution. What can, should and almost certainly will make this twenty-first-century revolution different from its predecessors at its core will be its highly efficient use of low-emissions and, in due course, carbon-free energy sources. It is important to see these investments in mitigation as part of a larger shift to a new investment path involving a broad number of sectors and regions and aimed at weakening the climate constraint on global growth. Related investments will be needed to raise agricultural productivity, improve forest management, and ensure a more reliable water supply and a more efficient transport system as well as the steady expansion of green jobs.

From technological learning to technological leapfrogging

> Without constant innovation and learning, the economy remains locked into production methods that use less advanced technology and fails to diversify into more dynamic activities

While economic growth depends on a fast pace of investment accumulation, it is sustained by ongoing structural and technological changes which underpin productivity and income growth. Without constant innovation and learning, the economy remains locked into production methods that use less advanced technology and fails to diversify into more dynamic activities. Given that improved technological knowledge is often embodied in capital goods, a fast pace of capital formation and technological progress are often strongly complementary (Salter, 1969).[2] A pro-investment macroeconomic policy is therefore necessary to strengthen technological development (United Nations, 2006). Still, the tendency of private firms to underinvest in technological knowledge and innovation is a well-established fact, with the danger of locking countries into a weaker growth path. For countries that are not yet at the technological frontier, catching up has involved a

---

2   The complementarities between technological progress and capital accumulation in the case of strong productivity growth in the United States were pointed out by Baumol, Batey Blackman and Wolff (1991), p. 164:

> (E)ven if technological innovation is the undisputed star in the scenario (which is by no means certain), substantial capital accumulation very likely would have been required to put the inventions into practice and to effect their widespread employment. If, moreover, saving and investment play a primary role on their own, it becomes all the more important to explore the nature of that role, recognizing that because of unavoidable interactions between rates of innovation and investment, any attempt to separate the two may prove to be artificial, if not ultimately unworkable.

good deal of active policy support for building technological capacity, including importing technologies from abroad, and learning how to use them most effectively.[3]

Because major innovations involve the co-evolution of technologies and the institutions that support them, there is a tendency to favour incumbents ("lock-in"), making it hard for new technologies to enter ("lock-out"). The removing or reforming of regulatory and institutional barriers that generally favour incumbent technologies aims at creating a level playing field for newcomers. A developmental State can play a directly supportive role by removing barriers and easing entry for a new technology through its procurement policies and its use of subsidies; and it can also provide temporary support to those adversely impacted by the resulting shifts in activity.

Government support for tertiary education, publicly funded research, development and deployment (RD&D) and subsidized research undertaken in the private sector, as well as industry-level training, are instruments that have been extensively used. In recent years, such efforts have been focused on establishing a national system of innovation, including a much stronger partnership between public and private institutions promoting technological development; however, serious financial and institutional obstacles to building such a system have been identified in many developing countries (Nelson, 2007; United Nations Conference on Trade and Development, 2007).

As cleaner technologies and diversification will be a critical part of establishing a new low-emissions growth path, a process of innovation and learning has to be ignited alongside efforts to raise the pace of capital formation. Given the scope of the challenge, this process will have to involve traditional sectors such as agriculture and forestry (box IV.2), as well as more advanced sectors linked to mitigation challenges. This transformation will build, moreover, on the technologies of the previous revolution, namely, information and communications technologies, whose potential to support the smart and efficient production, distribution and use of energy in all its forms is vast and still far from exhausted. Additionally, those technologies offer many organizational, managerial, marketing and research-oriented capabilities which will be particularly useful in fostering productivity growth and finding new markets. If history is any guide, market forces by themselves are unlikely to make the required adjustments.

An attractive concept in the field of sustainable energy development is that of energy leapfrogging (see Gallagher, 2006), whose thrust is that developing countries can avoid the resource-intensive pattern of economic and energy development by "leapfrogging" to the most advanced technologies available, rather than by following the path of conventional energy development that was travelled by industrialized countries. The assumption is that if the advanced, cleaner technologies exist, they can be transferred to, and be widely deployed within, developing countries. The leapfrogging concept has gained ground among policymakers, scholars and students and even, to some extent, in the private sector (see, for example, Goldemberg, 1998; Unruh, 2000; and Murphy, 2001).

The potential for leapfrogging is inherent in both new production processes and new products. Often, there is synergy between the two, as between the use of renewable energy sources and energy-efficient products. For example, switching to a compact fluorescent light bulb makes it economical to supply power from a solar photovoltaic panel. The resulting lighting system is much more satisfactory than its inefficient alternatives: candles, kerosene or the combination of incandescent lights and an unreliable existing electric grid (Goldemberg, 1998).

As cleaner technologies and diversification will be a critical part of establishing a new low-emissions growth path, a process of innovation and learning has to be ignited alongside efforts to raise the pace of capital formation

Developing countries could avoid the resource-intensive pattern of economic and energy development by leapfrogging to the most advanced technologies available

---

3   Learning by doing and using have been highlighted by economists (Rosenberg, 1982).

Box IV.2

Capacity-building for sustainable forestry

During the past several years, efforts have been made to include avoided deforestation and sustainable forestry in international climate change mitigation agreements. (Deforestation alone contributes to about 17 per cent of global CO_2 emissions.) However, inclusion of these activities in emissions accounting requires developing methodologies to monitor, evaluate and verify avoided emissions. Capacity-building needs to include capacity to formulate policies and manage and monitor projects.

Establishing the procedures for designing, reporting and monitoring forestry projects for carbon sequestration that are often complex and require in-depth knowledge constitutes a means of mitigating risks of leakage, non-permanence and uncertainties. Extensive capacity-building is needed if developing countries are to design and implement such projects successfully. The typical ex post approach of payment on delivery of carbon credits may prevent necessary upfront capacity-building measures from being implemented and is a threat to the permanence and quality of forestry projects, which generally require major investments in the planning and implementation phase.

In specific terms, it is likely that a broad implementation of reduced emissions from deforestation and forest degradation (REDD) projects will require training in technical skills such as geographic information system (GIS)-mapping, the use of Global Positioning System (GPS) technology and remote sensing. REDD initiatives aiming at simultaneous sustainable development benefits will require extensive capacity-building on a local level in sustainable forest management, agroforestry, sustainable logging and alternative income-generation.

On a national level, there is a need for assistance in establishing baseline scenarios for deforestation and setting up national systems for monitoring, assessing and verifying emissions (Food and Agriculture Organization of the United Nations, 2008). Many developing countries will also need assistance in strengthening the institutional capacity for planning, creating policy frameworks and enforcing policies and laws. Countries need to create a regulatory framework, to ensure not only climate benefits, but also a fair implementation of REDD practices and sustainable forestry which does not compromise the livelihoods of local and indigenous communities.

Mechanisms and institutional capacity are needed to ensure effective participation in programme planning as well as implementation. Contrary to what is often argued, reducing deforestation and forest degradation does not automatically lead to sustainable development in a broader sense. Sustainable development benefits must be taken into account in the planning and project development phase as well as in the shaping of policy frameworks and mechanisms. Otherwise, there is a risk that REDD initiatives will yield carbon benefits at the expense of local and indigenous communities.

Leapfrogging to new energy technologies has the potential to yield important savings over the long run, but faces significant obstacles

However, leapfrogging to such new energy technologies, while it has the potential to yield important savings over the long run, faces significant obstacles. These might be on the supply side, for instance, owing to the presence of barriers to accessing the required technology, whether because of obstacles to importing the technology from abroad, as is the case for most developing countries (see chap. V), or because of a lack of the technological expertise needed to link technology to local conditions. Obstacles may also exist on the demand side, if a limited market size prevents economies of scale and a rapid running down of costs to make new technologies locally competitive within an acceptable time frame. Thus, there is a role for Governments, including at a local level, to build markets for new technologies, for example, by providing low-cost loans to households and businesses, providing information about new technologies, etc.

The need for a significant scaling up of adaptation capacity in most countries cannot be understated

Still, as noted in chapter II, the need for a significant scaling up of adaptation capacity in most countries cannot be understated. In order to take advantage of these opportunities, it will be necessary to invest in training institutes and schools and expand the availability of basic education, as a foundation for further training, as well as vocational and technical training (United Nations Environment Programme, International Labour Organization, and others, 2008).

The "hardware" training, or training in core skills, may be more important for least developed countries that need to reach the threshold of a skilled labour force in order to be able to absorb technology, whereas higher-income developing countries may be more in need of "software" skills, including in business promotion and networking (United Nations, United Nations Framework Convention on Climate Change, 2003). For small economies, for example the small island developing States, regional cooperation can be crucial as a means to achieve economies of scale in capacity-building. Information technologies also open up new possibilities for remote training.

Managing creative destruction

Development is a continuing process of adjustment and transformation. Changes in the economic system require innovations in the framework of incentives and regulations to ensure that adjustments are smooth. It also requires that institutions be established for purposes of consultation, discussion and participation so as to ensure that those who lose out as a result of such changes do not upset the process. The capacity of the developmental State to provide a coherent vision of the future and to manage the challenges engendered by change, including overcoming vested interests and supporting those losing out, is a key feature of successful development experiences (Evans, 1995).

> The developmental State provides a coherent vision of the future and manages the challenges engendered by change

Meeting the climate challenge will entail significant adjustments, including the phasing out of "dirty" technologies. In particular, it will entail the need not only to find substitutes in the move away from old energy systems, including replacing them with renewable energy sources in many countries, but also to avoid the installation of new facilities that lock industries and countries into high-emitting technologies for years to come, owing to high sunk costs.[4] Managing such adjustments will be critical to achieving the smooth transition to a low-emissions, high-growth development pathway.

The magnitude of the necessary adjustment constitutes a non-marginal change which is unlikely to emerge from the play of market forces alone. Indeed, old technologies are still cheaper and we can expect their price to remain low for the foreseeable future, even if international agreements designed to resolve this issue are put in place as fast as is politically possible. More importantly, old technologies are readily available for replication and installation. While some green technologies are already cost-competitive, others remain costly and still others need to be developed.

Governments can fundamentally shape energy demand through land-use, urban and regional planning, that is to say, through careful spatial planning of different types of economic activities so as to minimize demand for energy, maximize opportunities for cogeneration, and allow for the efficient development of mass transit systems as well as non-motorized forms of transport.

Thus, tackling climate change requires a strong set of legislative/regulatory incentives to prevent the players from becoming directly or indirectly sidetracked by or locked into carbon-intensive options. This necessarily involves a significant degree of coordination among different spheres of government. It also means that an integrated development strategy would have to include a perspective on energy and on the energy-

> Tackling climate change necessarily involves a significant degree of coordination among different spheres of government

---

4   Individuals can also be locked in through consumption of high carbon intensive durable goods.

intensity of the production structure, a vision of urban development and transportation, and a perspective on natural resource use and natural resource intensity of production. This integrated strategy can be launched through a collaborative effort by a developmental State and the private sector to generate a big push that increases the scale of economic activity, thereby eliminating the poverty trap which affects many poor countries, as well as many regions in otherwise prospering developing countries.

Diversification challenges

As discussed in the previous chapter, for many developing countries, adaptation to unavoidable shocks from global warming is the central policy challenge. Some of the smarter policy choices for addressing this challenge were discussed in the previous chapter, including a more integrated approach to adaptation and mitigation issues.

Agriculture, as one of the most climate-sensitive sectors in many developing countries, is in need of such policies. This will require knowledge encompassing new technologies such as sustainable irrigation methods and crop selection and diversification. It is important that a proactive approach be taken in order to prevent production losses and a further aggravation of the food crisis and poverty in rural areas, especially in Africa.[5]

At present, however, agriculture is the main emitter of nitrous oxides and methane (both with high global warming potential) and contributes about 14 per cent of global greenhouse gas emissions (a share roughly comparable to that for the road transport and forestry sectors) (McKinsey & Company, 2009). At the same time, agriculture is an area where emission reductions can be achieved relatively cheaply (Enkvist, Nauclér and Rosander, 2007). The mitigation potential of agriculture is large; on one estimate, by 2030, agricultural emissions at a business-as-usual level could be more than halved through a combination of abatement measures yielding reductions below $10 per ton of CO_2 equivalent (tCO_2e), with many measures having negative costs because of productivity benefits (ibid.). Low-cost measures include improving soil quality (for example, restoring degraded lands) and cropland and grazing land management (for example, reducing fertilizer use, reducing tillage and eliminating burning of crop residues in the field) (Bellarby and others, 2008). Thus, sustainable agriculture can meet climate change mitigation goals as well as the Millennium Development Goals. However, taking advantage of this mitigation and carbon sink potential will require capacity-building programmes, with investments in technical training, provision of extension services, and programmes for sharing good practices.

Like the improvement of land management and agricultural practices, the sustainable production of biofuels from biomass is another important means of mitigating climate change and generating income in the agricultural sector. However, this will require further research on sustainable production methods and the impacts of biofuel production on food production, along with extensive farmer and farm worker training. If the biofuel industry grows, it will require not only a large unskilled labour force, but also skilled labour (Peskett and others, 2007). Consequently, it is important that training be available in the technical and managerial skills needed in the nascent biofuel processing industries, including skills required for the operation and maintenance of biofuel plants.

A combination of large-scale investments, information management and collective action have already been undertaken by countries and communities in the advanced

---

5   On the need for a green revolution in Africa linked to the climate challenge, see Sachs (2008).

For many developing countries, adaptation to unavoidable shocks from global warming is the central policy challenge

Agriculture is an area where emission reductions can be achieved relatively cheaply

The sustainable production of biofuels from biomass can be an important means of mitigating climate change and generating income in the agricultural sector

world to protect themselves against climatic shocks. For many developing countries, on the other hand, the real core of the adaptation challenge is still closely tied up with the need to diversify their economies so as to be able to move away from reliance on a small number of activities, particularly those in the primary sector that are sensitive to climatic shocks and changes, and to shift to new energy sources and to sectors that are less energy-intensive (see box IV.3).

The appropriate strategy is necessarily context-specific. It depends, among other factors, on the level of development, technological capacities, the size of the economy, the natural resource base, government capacities and established State-business relations. It involves not only manufacturing production but also a viable exploitation of the opportunities provided by the resource endowments of a specific country and the development of modern services.

Box IV.3

Diversification of the productive system in South Africa

Historically, low electricity prices have been seen as central to South Africa's competitiveness. The use of cheap and abundant coal in the primary energy mix has provided relatively low-cost electricity, and little incentive for greater energy efficiency. Industrial development has, to a significant extent, been built around energy-intensive sectors. These sectors are sensitive to changes in energy prices, so that particular attention needs to be given to them in the move to a low-emissions economy. While current Government policy has embraced sustainable development goals, the country continues to provide significant incentives for investment in energy-intensive industries. These industries are still an important source of employment, investment and income.

Continuing this approach carries a high risk that the economy will be "locked into" energy-intensive industries, when environmental, economic and social pressures may push South Africa in the opposite direction. Significant investment in energy-intensive industries in the 1990s has had just that effect, and in fact several new megaprojects (including a new aluminium smelter) are now in the planning stage.

An active industrial policy is required to target sectors that are less energy-intensive and enable South Africa's economy to diversify, move away from the country's mineral-energy complex and shift to capital and intermediate goods. This would indeed represent a major shift and could take decades to complete. However, given the lock-in effect, decisions taken today will be critical in changing the trajectory of South Africa's energy development path. "Bending the curve" requires a long-term perspective, but it also involves policy changes in the immediate future.

There is political agreement that, under South Africa's climate policy, emissions will have to peak, plateau and decline. The most effective and affordable short-term strategy for reducing greenhouse gases emissions is an energy-efficiency programme. Multiple studies demonstrate that significant savings can be achieved at no overall cost to the economy and, often, significant benefits can be provided. The next strategy would be to change the fuel mix, notably, to reduce the three-quarters share of coal in the total primary energy supply. In the medium term, reduced-carbon and non-carbon energy supplies, such as natural gas, hydroelectricity (imported from the region) and solar thermal technologies could be introduced into the energy system. These measures can together achieve significant reductions in greenhouse gas emissions in relation to business-as-usual development; but further action will be required to reduce emissions through more aggressive pursuit of the above programmes, possibly with the help of international funding.

Renewable energy options in South Africa have been considered both in terms of electricity-generating renewable technologies (a combination of biomass, solar thermal technologies and wind energy) and a biofuels industry. The electricity target is in line with the State's target

Box IV.3 (cont'd)

of achieving 10,000 gigawatt-hours (GWh) of generated electricity by 2014, but current thinking in Government is that three quarters of this target will eventually be met through biofuels. Investing in more labour-intensive technologies such as renewables would create more "green jobs". Other, more ambitious renewable energy interventions are possible, particularly one involving a massive effort to develop solar energy technologies, since South Africa has excellent solar resources, but this would again depend on the electricity price. Current evidence indicates that solar water heating (for domestic, commercial and potentially industrial applications) is economically viable, even given current low prices. Developing the potential of solar energy in South Africa would probably require a massive State-driven research project and an investment programme similar to the synthetic fuels programme of the 1960s and 1970s. Other supply-side options that require further investigation include new coal technologies and unconventional coal technologies such as fluidized-bed combustion, and others, as well as carbon capture and storage combined with coal gasification. There are currently no reliable estimates for the cost of these programmes, especially given the lack of oil or gas wells in South Africa, a factor that introduces significant technical complications with respect to CO_2 storage. As mentioned above, there are also plans to develop a biofuels industry in South Africa, but on a relatively small scale, leading to the replacement of only about 8 per cent of conventional liquid fuels by 2025, a limit based on the factors of price and available arable land and water resources.

To achieve the desired transformation, five possible components need to be considered. The first is adjustment of State incentives (including industrial incentive programmes and special dispensations on low electricity prices) so as not to attract further energy-intensive investments on terms that would severely restrict future mitigation options, and shift those incentives to lower-emissions industries. Second, South Africa might focus its mitigation efforts on non energy intensive sections of the economy, assuming that their international competitiveness would suffer less. Third, there is an urgent need to tackle the challenge posed by the energy-intensive sectors through a combination of reviewing the existing policy framework, promoting specific energy-intensity targets, conducting international negotiations on the best location for such industries, and carrying out diversification within these sectors. The fourth component is utilization of economic instruments, such as carbon taxes or domestic emissions trading, which would be expected to affect the energy-intensive sectors most strongly. Fifth, the focus of industrial policy and investment strategy could shift to less energy- and emissions-intensive sectors of the economy. The aim of these strategies would be to protect South Africa's competitive advantage in the short and medium terms, while building other competitive advantages in the long term.

Source: Winkler and Marquand (2009).

The revival of industrial policy

There is no "one size fits all" policy solution to the development challenge. This is even more the case when that challenge is combined with the climate challenge

Following a period during which policy options in many developing countries were confined to a narrow band of universal market-friendly measures, there is growing recognition that there is no "one size fits all" policy solution to the development challenge. This is even more the case when that challenge is combined with the climate challenge. Efforts to roll back the State in recent years have seriously debilitated public sector capacity in some countries and left an institutional hiatus which needs, with some urgency, to be filled. The initial level of institutional capacity needed to start raising investment in poor countries is often exaggerated, however (Sachs and others, 2004).

Stronger and more reliable civil service capacities and public institutions will be needed so that more integrated climate and development strategies can be devised and specific policies implemented

Governments have a long history of improving the efficiency of the market system by correcting for market failure, especially in non-competitive markets, and of accelerating growth by providing missing inputs and promoting collaboration among private enterprises and the public sector in the areas of long-term investment, research and development, education and training, etc. Still, government is no less fallible than markets, and the unpredictability of government action can be no less of an obstacle to long-term investment than market failure. More secure property rights are part of ensuring such predictability. However, stronger and more reliable civil service capacities and public institutions will also be needed so that more integrated climate and development strategies can be devised and specific policies implemented (Ahmad, 2009).

As large up-front investments will be needed in both mitigation and adaptation, State-sponsored accumulation will require a coordinated effort to mobilize the required resources, from both domestic and external resources, and to channel them into high-productivity and highly energy-efficient activities. It is essential that the autonomy of financial markets be reduced to the point where macroeconomic policy instruments can be deployed to support a development mandate dedicated to productive investment, structural change and rapid growth.

Fiscal and monetary policies should give priority to increasing public spending, including investments in renewable energy, cleaner energy processes, education, health and infrastructure. This will also entail using subsidized credits, credit guarantees, tax breaks, accelerated depreciation allowances, etc., to boost profits in private firms in the desired sectors. The effects of such policies will be greater if commercial banks make loans more easily available for such investments. However, as discussed in chapter VI, development banks may have a larger role to play in some countries.

As discussed in previous chapters, a big investment push is likely to be aimed at a limited range of industries and sectors and to begin with a prominent role for public investment. There has been much warning of the threat of public investment crowding out private investment. Crowding out, strictly speaking, refers to the variety of channels whereby additional government spending may have little or even a negative effect on total output because of its adverse effects on interest-rate sensitive components of private expenditure. Neither theory nor empirical evidence provides a basis for clear-cut conclusions in these respects. (Everhart and Sumlinski, 2001, table 2.2). Our own big-push scenario allows for considerable crowding in (see box IV.4 and chap. I).

Pro-investment macroeconomic policies are not sufficient by themselves to trigger the shift to a low-emissions, high-growth development pathway, especially one where investment is targeted at specific industries with the greatest potential to advance towards the green economy. Contrary to common perception, many countries, and, notably, the more advanced ones, have maintained industrial policies of some type in recent years. Successful industrial policies have some key ingredients in common: (a) targeted incentives; (b) regulation; (c) coordination of investment decisions; and (d) control mechanisms. These elements can be implemented through diverse instruments, according to the particular characteristics of the sector and country. In many developing countries, these measures have been narrowly targeted at attracting foreign direct investment (FDI).

This implies that many developing countries have the experience and instruments required to target and tailor industrial/productive policies towards a big push in clean energy and towards diversification in support of greater economic resilience. Various factors explain why some countries have been more successful than others in using these policies. In particular, the subsidies and rents that these measures inevitably create are made available on condition of enhanced performance, linked, for example, to technological upgrading, and limits are set for how long they can be used. These and other lessons will certainly need to be absorbed as industrial policies are implemented to meet the climate challenge.[6]

> Contrary to common perception, many countries, and, notably, the more advanced ones, have maintained industrial policies of some type in recent years

> Many developing countries have the experience and instruments required to target and tailor industrial/productive policies towards a big push in clean energy and towards diversification in support of greater economic resilience

---

6   Policymakers in more advanced countries are beginning to rethink these policy options in the context, for example, of the need to transform the automotive sector in light of the climate challenge (see Rothschild, 2009).

Box IV.4

Crowding in of private investments in a low-emissions, high-growth development path

As demonstrated by the analysis provided in chapter I, simple continuation of past growth patterns would fail to generate sustained high growth for developing countries and would also fail to generate the energy saving and emission reduction needed to avert potentially catastrophic consequences for the world as a whole. To effect a change in course towards a low-emissions, catch-up development pathway, high, upfront public investments are needed. A big push of public investment, along with other measures, is expected to "crowd in" the private investments that are also needed to achieve the desired structural change. However, as the mobilization of large amounts of public resources would be needed, it could well be that the measures would induce some private investors to direct their spending towards the greening of the economy, while discouraging others from investing, inasmuch as interest rates might rise and available savings in financial markets might be "crowded out" by public sector demand for such resources. The prospect of possibly substantial increases in public debts could further erode private investor confidence in respect of making long-term investments.

Existing global models used for the economic analysis of climate change typically do not capture these financial dimensions. The greatest difficulty lies in modelling investment and financial behaviour adequately in a context of great uncertainty and over long periods of time, as required by climate change analysis. The United Nations Global Policy Model (GPM) has been designed to analyse global macroeconomic interactions, but inasmuch as it encompasses the global production and use of different sources of energy, it contains the elements needed to analyse the global financial implications of a big energy and technology push aimed at addressing climate change. The Global Policy Model considers the channels through which a public investment push could crowd in private investment (namely, growth and targeted incentives) and crowd out private resources (namely, interest rates and changes in market confidence and expectations along with shifts in levels of public debt, inflation, the value of private assets and other financial variables).

The figure shows the results of simulations with the Global Policy Model in a scenario with three types of policy adjustment: (a) one where countries worldwide are assumed to increase public spending levels by between 1 and 5 per cent of GDP;[a] (b) one where high-emission energy demand is constrained (reflecting, for instance, a cap-and-trade mechanism) to yield lower emissions and greater energy efficiency;[b] and (c) one where economic resilience of developing countries is strengthened by providing them, especially the poorest countries, with full and duty-free market access to developed-country markets, leading to greater economic diversification.[c]

The policy changes would yield faster growth (2.5 per cent per year in developed countries and 6 per cent per year in developing countries), allowing for growth in private incomes and consumption spending and promoting private investments. By the model's parameter estimates,[d] these positive effects of the public investment-led strategy towards achieving low-emissions economies outweigh the crowding out effects through the financial channels. By 2030, the level of private investment would be 1-4 per cent higher than in the business-as-usual scenario. The crowding-in effect would be stronger in the least developed countries, where the fiscal stimuli are greater. Rising private incomes would also help increase the tax base, but not enough to prevent public debt ratios from increasing to relatively high levels. Over the longer run, public indebtedness would stabilize in the developed countries, but at levels of over 100 per cent of gross domestic product (GDP) (see the three right-hand graphs), which many Governments may consider too high for comfort. By 2030, public indebtedness in developing countries would also have risen significantly (by 26 percentage points of GDP over the baseline scenario). In virtue of the assumed international coordination of these strategies, the model suggests that, even at these levels of public indebtedness, continued economic growth, energy saving and trade impulses would continue to crowd in private investment. Nonetheless, public debts cannot rise infinitely. Complementary measures will need to be considered to prevent public indebtedness from becoming explosive. For developed countries, these would need to be sought in the form of new taxes (such as a carbon tax), while developing countries might utilize both fiscal measures and alternative non-debt creating financing support (for example, through a foreign direct investment stimulus in some cases or foreign aid in the case of the poorest countries). The various financing options are discussed further in chapter VI.

a In the model, aggregate public expenditures are adjusted, but—in conjunction with the second policy component—these may be seen to have been allocated for achieving greater energy efficiency and low-emissions energy production in the developed countries and for a combination of public investment projects for low-emissions energy, adaptation and general developmental infrastructure in the developing countries. The size of the fiscal stimulus varies by needs, with greater spending increases for the poorer countries, especially the least developed countries, which have greater infrastructural deficits and adaptation needs.

b The constraint is set to induce a reduction in the use of fossil-fuel energy by at least 4 per cent per year.

c The first policy component (public investments in infrastructure, energy and human capital) is also expected to support trading capacity and economic diversification. In addition, greater commodity price stability would support long-term investments towards diversification. In the model, this is achieved by triggering supply and demand adjustments under international trade agreements.

d Please note that all behavioural relations of the model were estimated econometrically, yielding robust and plausible parameter values (see Cripps, Izurieta and Vos (forthcoming)).

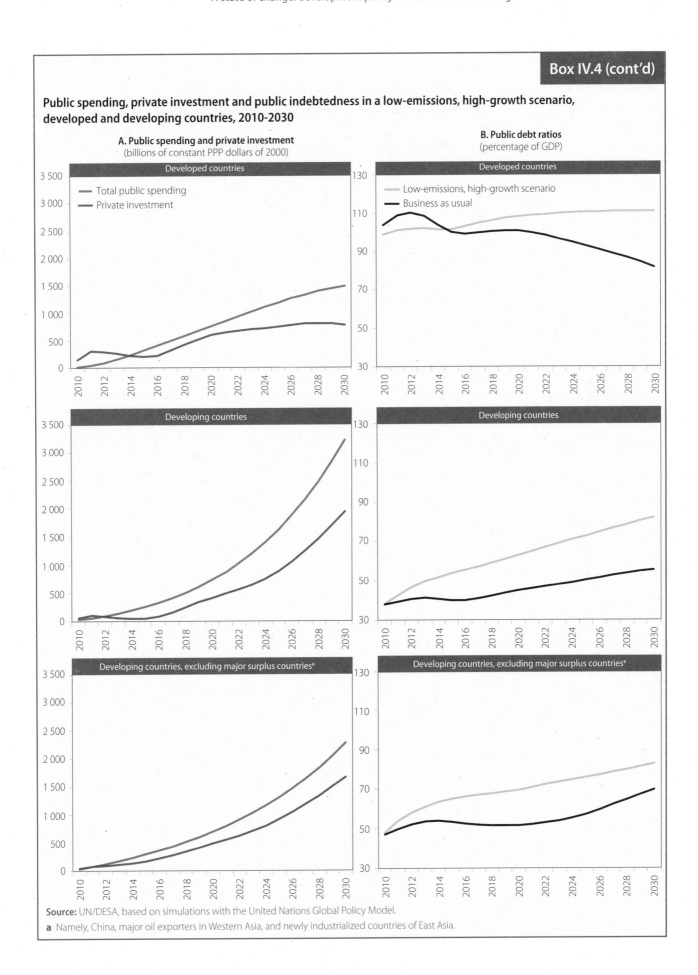

Public spending, private investment and public indebtedness in a low-emissions, high-growth scenario, developed and developing countries, 2010-2030

A. Public spending and private investment
(billions of constant PPP dollars of 2000)

B. Public debt ratios
(percentage of GDP)

Box IV.4 (cont'd)

Developed countries
— Total public spending
— Private investment

Developed countries
— Low-emissions, high-growth scenario
— Business as usual

Developing countries

Developing countries

Developing countries, excluding major surplus countries[a]

Developing countries, excluding major surplus countries[a]

Source: UN/DESA, based on simulations with the United Nations Global Policy Model.

a Namely, China, major oil exporters in Western Asia, and newly industrialized countries of East Asia.

Table IV.1 presents a selection of policies focused on specific sectors such as energy, transport and extractive industries. Currently, many countries still have policies favouring high-emissions sectors like hydrocarbons. A logical, though not easy, first step would be to reorient support from these sectors towards renewable and/or cleaner energy sources.

Developing countries operate today in a global policy environment that is quite different from the one of two or three decades ago.[7] In particular, there has been a tendency to discipline national economic policies through multilateral, regional or bilateral agreements. These disciplines impose restrictions on the ability of developing countries to conduct certain types of industrial policies. Rodrik (2007) presents a comprehensive

Table IV.1
Illustrative list of industrial policies in support of production and investment, with a special focus on energy, transport and extractive sectors

	Loans for working capital	Loans for fixed assets and/or investment projects	Equity investment	Loans to specific sectors	Credit programmes for particular regions	Horizontal tax incentives	Tax incentives to specifc sectors	Tax incentives to particular regions
Argentina	X	X		X	X		Mining, forestry	
Brazil	X	X	X	Oil, gas, shipping, power	X			X
Chile	X	X			X	X	Forestry, oil, nuclear	X
China	X	X		X	X		X	X
Colombia	X	X	X	X	X			X
Ecuador	X	X	X				Mining	
El Salvador	X	X		Mining				
Ghana	X	X		X			X	X
Honduras	X	X		Transport				
India	X	X		X	X	X	Infrastructure, power, transport	X
Malaysia	X	X		Shipping			X	X
Mexico	X	X	X	X	X	X	Forestry, transportation	
Nicaragua	X	X						
Nigeria	X	X		X	X		Oil, gas, energy	X
Panama	X	X					Forestry	
Paraguay	X	X				X		X
Peru	X	X					Mining, oil	X
Thailand	X	X	X				Utilities, infrastructure, environment	X
Uganda	X	X		Forestry			X	X
Uruguay	X	X				X	Hydrocarbons, shipping, forestry	
Venezuela (Bolivarian Republic of)	X	X				X	Hydrocarbons	

Source: Rodrik (2007), table 4.2.

---

7   Adapted from Rodrik (2007), p. 122. Chapter V widens the analysis of trade rules pertinent to climate change.

summary of the specific rules under the different international agreements.[8] Direct export subsidies[9] are now illegal (for all but least developed countries), as are domestic content requirements on enterprises that are linked to trade, quantitative restrictions on imports, and patent laws that fall short of international standards. However, there remains much scope for coherent industrial policies, especially if countries do not give up their policy autonomy any further by signing bilateral agreements or adhering to restrictive international codes (see box IV. 5).

There remains much scope for coherent industrial policies, especially if countries do not give up their policy autonomy any further by signing bilateral agreements or adhering to restrictive international codes

---

Box IV.5

A big energy push in India: the role of renewables

Continued catch-up growth in India will depend, in no small part, on large-scale investments in its energy sector. With economic growth targeted at 7-8 per cent, energy requirements are expected to grow at 5.6-6.4 per cent annually, representing a fourfold increase over the next 25 years. Electricity generation, heavily dependent on coal, will be the primary source of emissions growth.

As part of its efforts to address high energy demand and the potentially adverse environmental effects of intense energy use, India has enacted legislation and pursued policies to improve the availability of alternative energy sources. Laws and policies aimed at promoting renewable energy in the electricity sectors include:

- The Electricity Act of 2003, which mandates the promotion of cogeneration and generation of electricity through renewable sources of energy. This is achieved by providing suitable measures for connectivity with the grid, for the sale of electricity, and for purchase of electricity from these sources, specifying a percentage of total consumption of electricity in the area of a distribution licensee. The Act mandates that newly created State electricity regulatory commissions fix a minimum percentage of power procurement from renewable energy. Already, about half of the States of India have set, or are in the process of setting, renewable power obligations. The State electricity regulatory commissions have also provided preferential tariffs and energy transmission regulations for renewable power generators

- The National Electricity Policy of 2005, through which authority is granted to each State legislator to create a renewable energy portfolio standard for transmission and distribution companies serving their jurisdictions

- The Renewable Energy Plan 2012, which targets achieving a 10 per cent share for renewable energy in incremental power capacity. This should lead to an additional grid-connected 10,000 megawatts (MW) of renewable energy.

Other initiatives include the installment of 1 million household solar water heating systems; electrification by renewable mini-grids for 24,000 villages that are currently without electricity; the deployment of 5 million solar lanterns and 2 million solar home lighting systems; and the establishment of an additional 3 million small biogas plants.

The central Government also provides financial and fiscal incentives to allow renewable energy to become competitive with other sources of conventional energy in India. These policies feature, inter alia, income tax holidays, accelerated depreciation of investments in renewable energy technologies, duty-free import of renewable energy equipment, concessional rates on customs and excise duties on the import of capital equipment, capital subsidies and concessionary financing from India's Renewable Energy Development Agency, requirements for energy purchases by distribution companies, and exemptions from electricity taxes and sales taxes.

---

8   Table 4.3 of Rodrik (2007) shows how restrictions are defined under each institution or agreement and under what conditions they apply.

9   Least developed countries and developing countries with less than US$ 1,000 per capita gross national product (GNP) are exempted from rules on subsidies under the Agreement on Subsidies and Countervailing Measures.

Box IV.5 (cont'd)

These initiatives have helped India become the country with the most developed and diversified renewable energy market in South Asia. The annual turnover of the renewable energy industry in India is approximately $500 million, with a total renewable energy investment of about $1 billion. India uses up 3,500 MW of total installed capacity from renewable sources. This is just a fraction of the estimated total economic potential of 100,000 MW.

Nonetheless, renewables still account for only less than 1 per cent of all electricity currently produced in the country. This is because many renewable technologies, such as wind turbines, operate intermittently and cannot function at 100 per cent capacity. The wind-energy industry has been booming in India over the past few years. According to the World Market Update 2006, India had the third largest increase in annual capacity in the world, with 1,840 MW in new capacity. The cumulative installed MW capacity for wind power in India is projected to grow from 6,228 MW in 2006 to 18,028 MW in 2011, which reflects a compound annual growth rate of approximately 25 per cent. In order to support the growth of the domestic wind industry, the Ministry of New and Renewable Energy of the Government of India has encouraged State Governments to implement national policy guidelines for wind development. In addition, new initiatives are being undertaken by the Ministry to reassess India's wind power potential, which is currently estimated to be 45,000 MW, or one third of total energy consumption.

While India has made much progress in developing its production of renewable energy, there are several causes for concern regarding factors that may limit the full use of the country's renewable energy potential. A first concern is whether the growth of the sector will be lasting under the present policy framework. The currently generous Government subsidies provide a windfall to producers, but such subsidies may be difficult to sustain over time as the market for renewables expands. Second, there are constraints on the technologies that are being applied. The production of wind energy is already hitting capacity constraints, as existing turbines have limited potential. In some cases, there is no incentive to replace them with more efficient turbines as producers have been guaranteed a pre-established return, requiring taxpayers to make up the difference if actual returns fall short. Third, State-administered auctions have stalled the development of the country's potential to generate hydroelectric power, as they have given rise to speculative purchases of rights to a site by developers, rather than purchases for long-term investment. Finally, considerable confusion persists at the State level regarding how to implement the renewable energy portfolio standard, as required by the Electricity Act. As a consequence, different standards apply across States. In some States, the renewable energy portfolio standard is comparatively higher; in other States, there are carve-outs for specific types of renewable energy; and in most States, there are price differentials in respect of the power purchase tariffs that each distribution licensee must adhere to when meeting its renewable energy portfolio standard.

All of these factors lead to confusion and sometimes to litigation, as some distributors are balking at the power purchase tariff terms and price levels. Although State-to-State differentials in power policy and renewable energy potential are important, some standardization, at least in respect of setting the power purchase price, would be helpful (United States Agency for International Development, 2007).

Sources: Gibbs (2008); and Tufts University, Fletcher School (2008).

The example of the ethanol industry in Brazil demonstrates how critical Government support can be, particularly during the early phase of development and deployment of a new technology, and how it may need to be sustained until it has taken firm root in the marketplace (box IV.6). The Government of Brazil, at both the federal and the State levels, had an essential role to play in providing incentives to scale up production and in setting up a clear institutional framework. This role included setting technical standards, supporting the technologies involved in ethanol production and use, providing financial advantages, and ensuring appropriate market conditions.

The introduction of renewable sources entails the challenge of making complementary investments along the supply chain

Replacing old technologies, like gasoline in the case of Brazil, with renewable sources entails the challenge of making complementary investments along the supply chain. In the particular case of gasoline, consumers are reluctant to buy cars using a new fuel that may be difficult to find. Service station owners are not interested in investing in a parallel fuel distribution system, since the number of potential users is usually very

Box IV.6

Brazil's sugar cane-based ethanol industry

Brazil's ethanol industry was established in the 1930s. With more sugar than it could use, the Government determined that sugar cane should be utilized for ethanol production and made ethanol, added to gasoline, a mandatory automobile fuel. Following the international oil crisis in 1973, the industry made significant progress. The Government launched the National Alcohol Programme (Pro-Álcool) in 1975 to increase production yields, modernize and expand distilleries, and establish new production plants. Although ethanol production initially had been heavily subsidized,[a] over time all subsidies were eliminated. In 2008, ethanol was sold roughly at between 50 and 60 per cent of the price of gasoline at the pump, owing to sharp reductions in production costs.

Policies that were key to Brazil's success in substituting fossil fuel consumption for ethanol use include the following: (a) obligating the State-owned oil company, Petrobras, to purchase a guaranteed amount of ethanol; (b) providing economic incentives to agro-industrial enterprises to produce ethanol, including loans with low, subsidized interest rates (this policy applied from 1980 to 1985); (c) incentives to consumers by guaranteeing a price of ethanol at the pump at 59 per cent of the price of gasoline;[b] (d) requiring the automobile industry to produce cars able to run partially or totally on biofuels; (e) allowing renewable energy-based independent producers of electric power to compete with traditional public utility firms in the electricity market at large; (f) stimulating and supporting private ownership of sugar mills, which helped increase competition and efficiency; and (g) stimulating rural activities based on biomass energy to increase employment in rural areas.

The Sugar cane Technology Centre, a privately funded research institute in São Paulo, was key to improving ethanol production technology, having invested about $20 million per year in research at the peak of the programme. Researchers at the Centre and other institutions also found ways to use sugar cane fibre residue, known as bagasse, to produce energy, building on existing methods of burning bagasse to power steam turbines for electricity generation and using the remaining heat from the turbines for the distillation process. They developed cauldrons operating at greater pressure so that more energy could be produced, allowing many ethanol plants to become self-powered. This contributed significantly to keeping ethanol production costs low.

Thanks to steady productivity improvements, the cost of producing ethanol declined by an annual average of 3.8 per cent from 1980 to 1985 and of 5.7 per cent from 1985 to 2005. As cumulative experience increased, the cost per unit of energy declined and is now one third of its initial value (see figure).

a The price paid to producers in 1980 was $700 for 1,000 litres. By 2004, it had reached $200 per 1,000 litres, becoming economically competitive with gasoline based on international prices for oil (equivalent to US$ 40 per barrel).

b This was possible because the Government had been in charge of setting the gasoline price at that time.

Producers' price of ethanol compared with gasoline prices in Brazil

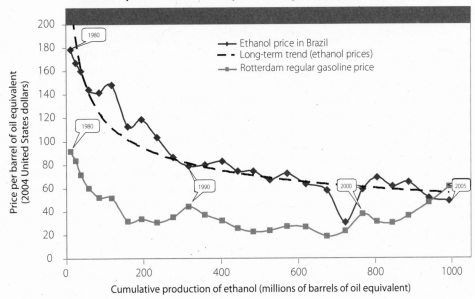

Source: Nakicenovic (2009).

Box IV.6 (cont'd)

c The 2008/09 harvest year saw a record crop estimated at 562 million tons of sugar cane and nearly 27 billion litres of ethanol processed in 400 plants nationwide (Brazilian Sugar Cane Industry Association (UNICA) and Institute for International Trade Negotiations of Brazil (ICONE), 2009).

Sources: Goldemberg (2008); Goldemberg and others (2004); Moreira (2006); Almeida (2007); Food and Agriculture Organization of the United Nations (2008); Nakicenovic (2009); United Nations, Department of Economic and Social Affairs (2008); and Brazilian Sugar Cane Industry Association (UNICA) and Institute for International Trade Negotiations of Brazil (ICONE), 2009.

In 2009, Brazil has been the second biggest producer of ethanol in the world (20 billion litres) after the United States (24 billion litres).c Close to 80 per cent of this is for the domestic market; the fuel used in 45 per cent of vehicles in Brazil is ethanol. Part of the demand is due to the success of flex-fuel vehicles (FFV) released in 2003, which can run on gasoline, ethanol or a mixture of both. Flex-fuel cars renewed consumer interest in ethanol and intensified demand for this biofuel. Flex-fuel vehicles accounted for 26 per cent of the light vehicle fleet in 2008, and the figure is estimated to reach 50 per cent by 2012. According to Brazil's National Association of Automotive Vehicle Manufacturers (ANFAVEA), 85 per cent of cars—some 4 million vehicles—sold in Brazil today are flex-fuel. Researchers at the Delphi Technology Centre in São Paulo have developed a fuel system for motorcycles that can also use ethanol–gasoline blends in any proportion. The first ethanol-powered bus, developed at the University of São Paulo, has been undergoing road tests since December 2007 to assess its economic viability. Brazil's aviation company, EmBRAER, has had an ethanol-fuelled agriculture monoplane in use since 2004.

The Government's reasons for supporting biofuels have expanded to include concerns about greenhouse gas emissions and climate change, rural employment and equity issues, and local air pollution. The use of ethanol as a replacement for gasoline has led to an overall reduction of 9.2 million tons of carbon per year in carbon emissions in Brazil (10 per cent of the total). Evaluations of ethanol's impact on air quality found that E-10 (gasohol, a fuel mixture of 10 per cent ethanol and 90 per cent gasoline) reduced carbon monoxide, a precursor for ozone formation, by more than 25 per cent. When used as an additive, ethanol also displaces highly toxic and volatile components of gasoline (such as lead, benzene, toluene and xylene).

Brazil is now offering its expertise to other countries, especially developing countries that could produce biofuels but still depend on oil. In 2008, Brazil signed agreements with countries in Africa, the Caribbean and other parts of Latin America. Most of these agreements involve the transfer of Brazil's ethanol production technology.

small. This is why government policies to spur investment and drive demand for selected technologies are so important (Goldemberg, 1998).

Additionally, in most countries, government is the single largest individual consumer (see Bhandarkar and Alvarez-Rivero (2008), p. 391). Thus, government procurement policies, including methods such as tendering and holding of reverse auctions, can constitute an important instrument. As a major purchaser of electricity and vehicles, Governments could provide a significant boost to low-emissions options through the appropriate procurement bidding specifications. Such green procurement could extend as well to new construction of government buildings, ranging from offices to schools and hospitals.

The balance between acquiring technologies from abroad and developing local technology may well shift over time

Specific industrial policies will vary depending on the particular country, with some placing a greater reliance on technologies acquired from abroad through trade and foreign investment, and others exerting greater effort on behalf of local technology development. The balance between the two types of policies may well shift over time as a country familiarizes itself with imported technologies and acquires the capability to replicate, adapt and improve them.

For some developing countries with strong technological capabilities there may be even scope for pushing the technological frontier outwards. Thus far, there are relatively few examples of developing countries that have established and maintained a strong lead in technologies of global significance, with large markets even in developed countries. This is changing, however, as a number of middle-income developing countries acquire stronger technological capabilities and establish innovation systems.

Some policy steps towards a low-emissions future

In developing countries, there is a need for policies that foster "strategic deployment" of new technologies, in view of the advantages to be gained by building up new industries and accelerating movement down the learning (hence, cost) curves (Grubb, 2004). Strategic deployment generally requires a range of incentives, regulation and direct public investment.

Figure IV.1 presents some of the major technologies involved and how soon they might be ready for large-scale deployment. These technologies include:

- Advanced technologies (such as gasification) for generating electricity from coal and biomass: a suite of technologies whose accelerated deployment will bring higher efficiency, reduced emissions and compatibility with carbon dioxide capture and storage technologies

- Advanced low-energy building technologies, for markets that are impeded by numerous barriers associated with the construction industry and rental markets

- More advanced primary renewables, notably solar PV, for which potential scale economies remain large, and wind energy, which is a significant contributor to emission reductions, and for which onshore deployment involves local learning and, requires related industrial innovation.

A range of government subsidies to producers or users of new technology can be so designed as to speed technology deployment through the offer of financial rewards in contrast with the regulatory sanctions typically associated with enforcing standards (see chap. II). Subsidies can take a variety of forms. More specifically:

> A range of government subsidies to producers or users of new technology can be so designed as to speed technology deployment through the offer of financial rewards in contrast with the regulatory sanctions typically associated with enforcing standards

Figure IV.1
Technology development and CO$_2$ mitigation for power generation

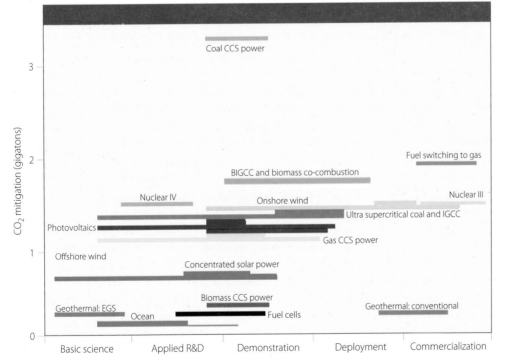

Source: International Energy Agency (2008a).
Abbreviations: CCS, carbon capture and sequestration; IGCC, integrated gasification combined cycle; BIGCC, biomass integrated gasification combined cycle; EGS, enhanced geothermal systems.

- Investment tax credits to firms that bring a new technology to market can lower the upfront investment costs of producing a new type of equipment, and can be tied either to costs or to the production level. These policies work to increase the supply of a new technology on the market

- Production tax credits are subsidies granted for a particular type of electricity generation on a per-unit-of-production basis, making renewables such as wind more competitive with respect to higher-emissions production methods

- To increase demand for a new technology, tax credits or rebates can be granted to purchasers as well as producers, reducing the cost differences between old and new technologies and making the lower-emitting or more efficient new products relatively more attractive. For example, many States offer tax rebates to consumers who purchase high-efficiency appliances

- Loan guarantees also subsidize industry by shifting the risk of failure or default to the government and lowering the costs of capital for private firms below what would be available on the open market for an unproved but promising technology

- Limiting legal liability to the users of a new technology constitutes another implicit subsidy from government, insulating parties from possible economic damages. This approach may be relevant for carbon-capture-and-sequestration technology, where a release of geologically sequestered CO_2 could potentially undo climate benefits and cause additional harm, giving rise to litigation against the technology developer.

Energy efficiency

There is a potential for considerable emissions gains from improving energy efficiency at the industry and household levels

As discussed elsewhere in the *Survey*, there is a potential for emissions gains from improving energy efficiency at the industry and household levels. The building sector, transport and industry appear to offer sizeable opportunities for low-cost improvements; but there are also potential, if less well researched, gains to be reaped in agriculture (Ürge-Vorsatz and Metz, 2009). There are also other potential benefits to be derived from creating jobs in new business activities.

In South Africa, for example, interventions consist primarily of improved building design and improved heating, ventilating and air conditioning (HVAC) efficiency (Winkler, 2006, pp. 161–163 and 176). A "cleaner and more efficient residential energy scenario" involves energy-efficient housing shells, efficiency interventions such as deployment of compact fluorescent lamps (CFLs) and geyser insulation blankets, and a number of fuel-switching options, including installation of solar water heating, replacement of other fuels with liquefied petroleum gas (LPG) for cooking, and replacement of paraffin with electricity for lighting, linked to substantial increases in the residential electrification rate. Despite the promotion of win-win gains, however, widespread implementation requires some initial investments and efforts to overcome key informational, institutional, social, financial and technical barriers through "significant policy intervention" (Winkler, 2006, p. 160).

There are a range of incentive measures that aim at reducing initial costs associated with increasing energy efficiency, including subsidies or grants for energy efficiency investments, tax relief for purchase of energy-efficient equipment, subsidies for energy audits, and loans or guarantee funds for energy efficiency projects (Peck and Chipman, 2008). Tax incentives, guarantees and other financing measures can help investors overcome the possible constraints on paying the upfront cost of efficiency improvements (Tufts University, Fletcher School, 2008).

Cleaner coal[10]

Coal is an abundant, low-cost energy resource, but it is also carbon-intensive and polluting. Coal meets just over one quarter of the world's demand for primary energy. In terms of its consumption, coal, instead of being replaced by other sources, is expected to expand rapidly in the years to come. Coal emissions are projected to grow worldwide by 65 per cent from 2005 to 2030 (see chap. II).

Globally, two market imperfections currently limit the uptake of cleaner coal technologies: it costs less to pollute than to control pollution; and barriers such as high development costs slow technological change. Accelerating deployment will require changes at the national and international levels. Commercial deployment of cleaner coal technologies requires investment certainty through stable policies which recognize the costs and risks of long-term capital investment in pollution control, ultra-supercritical, integrated gasification combined cycle (IGCC) and carbon capture and sequestration (CCS) technologies.

Globally, it costs less to pollute than to control pollution; and barriers such as high development costs slow technological change

Experience worldwide shows that deployment of clean coal technologies must encompass the entire coal supply chain, and that parallel progress is needed in technical and non-technical areas for coal to remain an acceptable component in a country's energy mix. A modern coal-fired power plant cannot be considered in isolation from the coal mines, transport infrastructure and coal markets that supply it. This again underscores the importance of integrated policy responses.

Deployment of clean coal technologies must encompass the entire coal supply chain

One major challenge will be to develop and deploy systems for CO_2 capture and storage, a critical technology for coal's long-term future, but one that has not yet been demonstrated on a commercial scale at any coal-fired power plant. Such demonstrations are 5-10 years away in advanced economies. However, this may be an opportunity for some developing countries, and China is already participating in R&D initiatives that aim at accelerating progress.

More broadly, China has an unprecedented opportunity to become a major player in the global market for cleaner, more efficient coal technologies. It has already developed some unique technologies, which it would be sensible for other countries to adopt, and it will certainly create more. It should work with other Governments to create a global market for clean energy technologies, and allow its manufacturing industry to respond with commercially relevant products, for local markets and for export.

China has an unprecedented opportunity to become a major player in the global market for cleaner, more efficient coal technologies

China will need to decide for itself how to proceed, but its actions, more than those of any other country, will shape the global approach to the cleaner use of coal which is urgently needed in order to avert the worst effects of climate change. Hence, the three priorities for international engagement with China are:

- Government-industry partnerships to develop and demonstrate low-emissions, cleaner coal technologies
- Technology transfer and deployment of cleaner coal technologies through commercial arrangements that respond to the market demand created in China and elsewhere
- Negotiations leading to successful international accords which create national, regional and global markets for clean, low-emissions technologies.

New technologies such as direct coal liquefaction, in whose development China is already a pioneer, and algae-based technologies for reducing emissions will require greater research efforts.

---

10   The present section is based on International Energy Agency (2009).

Greater efforts in R&D are needed globally; however additional spending alone simply is not an adequate response to the challenges faced by the energy industry as a whole. China has shown a willingness to participate in international partnerships and joint ventures in many fields aimed at researching, developing and demonstrating new technologies. In the case of cleaner coal, such active participation can speed progress towards those technologies that are most appropriate for commercial markets within China and elsewhere.

Renewables

Strategic deployment of new technologies brings advantages by building up new industries and accelerating movement down experience curves. Strategic deployment policies build market scale and thereby bring down the cost of technologies (Grubb, 2004). At the same time, strategic deployment generally requires regulation which fosters adoption of technologies that would otherwise be uneconomical; in this way, the benefits of learning by doing and other scale economies are secured.

Even with the expansion of coal consumption in China and India, its growth does not match that of renewables which is doubling every two to five years. For example, India, where wind capacity is twice as large as nuclear capacity, is now the fourth largest windmill installer in the world. Hence, perhaps coal is the fuel of the past and the present, and alternatives and efficiency are the fuels of the future.

What form is ideal for incentives depends on the technology being deployed. The market for solar energy products such as photovoltaic panels, solar water heating, and solar power concentrators encompasses a spectrum of scales ranging from industrial power generation to smaller commercial-scale and domestic installations. Wind power, on the other hand, is almost entirely produced at industrial scale by large companies. Because wind farms are financed by large corporations with access to financial markets, the wind industry has preferred the long-term payback of production tax credits, which provide a return on every kilowatt produced, as a means of making their power more competitive on the market. The biggest concern for smaller-scale solar installations, however, is not the long-term return to the power generated (much of the return is in reduced bills for small producers, not in profits from selling the produced energy), but rather the initial high cost of installing a system. In this case, an investment tax credit is a better instrument for the industry, allowing for a lowering of the price that producers of solar products have to charge their customers for the equipment. To make a subsidy programme cost-effective, care should be given to eliminating free riders (those companies that would have upgraded their equipment even without a subsidy) and reducing transaction costs.

Other policies that have been used to promote renewables include:

- Feed-in tariffs, as adopted particularly in continental Europe but also in parts of North America and China (see box IV.7 and chap. II), which mandate a specific (premium) price to be paid for electricity generated from renewable sources such as wind and solar energy

- Renewable obligations, known in North America as portfolio standards, which require utilities to source a certain percentage of their electricity from renewable sources generally through systems of tradable certificates (see box II.1)

- Other technology or fuel mandates, such as Brazil's long-standing requirement that cars run entirely or partly on ethanol (see box IV.6), a requirement that has also been established in China (see box IV.7).

> To make a subsidy programme cost-effective, care should be given to eliminating free riders and reducing transaction costs

China now ranks among the top countries in respect of the number of its patents for renewable energy technologies. The Government of China had to implement diverse policies to overcome such barriers to renewable energy development as: (a) the high cost of developing renewable energy; (b) the difficulty of connecting renewable energy to the grid; (c) institutional impediments; (d) the lack of international investment; (e) a weak legal and regulatory framework; and (f) an uncertain level of future demand and thus of prices for renewable energy.

Box IV.7

Renewable energy in China

China's power supply has not kept pace with energy demand, despite an annual growth rate of 8 per cent in installed capacity over the last two decades. When energy shortages in 1986 reached 17 per cent of annual power consumption, China had begun instituting reforms in its energy sector, focusing on reducing energy intensity and developing renewable energy. Since the drafting of China's version of Agenda 21 in 1994, renewable energy technologies have received increased attention. Guidelines on renewable energy development were included in the eleventh Five-year Plan (2006-2010). China's Renewable Energy Industries Association, established through the United Nations Development Programme (UNDP) and the Global Environment Facility (GEF), brought together national and international investors in this field. Despite legal and structural reforms in the energy industry undertaken over two decades, it is estimated that environmental pollution still costs China as much as $64 billion or 3 per cent of gross domestic product (GDP), in 2004, according to the Green GDP Accounting research project (Zhang, 2007).

The new Renewable Energy Promotion Law (the Renewables Law) became effective from January 2006. It entails the first comprehensive policy to promote renewable energy in China and provides the legal basis for all activities related to renewable energy. The law targets a substantial increase in the share of renewables in total energy consumption.

The relevant provisions of the Renewables Law are: (a) a mandated market share: the aim is to raise the share of renewable energy goals in gross energy consumption to 5 per cent by 2010 and to 10 per cent by 2020; (b) a competitive bidding process on the basis of Government-approved concessions; (c) the stipulation that power grids must purchase electricity from qualified grid-connected renewable facilities; (d) application of a feed-in tariff entailing fixed-term, differential but favourable pricing for grid-connected renewable energy; and (e) price setting in the renewable energy sector based on what is required for both the development and utilization of required technologies and the provision of an economical and reasonable service.

The Government of China has implemented supplementary policy initiatives to support the implementation of the law. These include, among others, subsidies to assist renewable energy research and development; favourable accounting rules for capitalization of research and development costs within high-tech institutions; use of income tax revenues to support the local development of renewable energy development; and grants and preferential loans for small and medium-sized technical enterprises supporting energy efficiency and renewable energy. Furthermore, through the National Township Electrification Programme, 20 megawatts (MW) of solar photovoltaic (PV) energy sources, 840 kilowatts (kW) from wind sources and 200 MW from small hydropower plants were installed to power 1,000 villages through renewable energy. The Sunlight Programme, which is to be completed in 2010, implements large-scale grid-connected PV projects, PV/hybrid village power demonstration systems, and home-PV projects for remote areas. The Brightness Programme was instituted with the support of multilateral assistance to install several solar and wind systems in north-western China. In addition, the "Ride the Wind" Programme, a bilateral cooperation programme established to install wind turbines in various parts of China, involves joint ventures of Chinese and international renewable technology manufacturers aimed at aiding the development of renewable energy for use by local manufacturing industries. Finally, the Government has issued mandates for blending biofuels with vehicle fuels. In addition, China's eleventh Five-year Plan targets the reduction of energy intensity by 20 per cent between 2006 and 2010.

Source: Tufts University, Fletcher School (2008).

Conclusion.

Most developing countries are reluctant to accept binding emissions targets. Their concerns are rooted in fundamental development challenges and reflected in the United Nations Framework Convention on Climate Change.[11] Under the Convention, countries are recognized to have "common but differentiated responsibilities" (sixth preambular para.). While developed countries are to "take the lead in combating climate change" (article 3, para. 1), for developing countries, "economic and social development and poverty eradication are the first and overriding priorities" (article 4, para. 7). Developing countries believe that developed countries have yet to demonstrate their leadership in tackling the climate challenge and that being held to specific emission levels regardless of the economic consequences would be tantamount to putting a cap on their growth and fostering the perpetuation of unacceptable levels of poverty and inequality.

Establishing low-emissions, high-growth development pathways will be key to meeting the climate challenge, reducing global inequality and tackling extreme poverty. If history is any guide, it is unlikely that market forces, by themselves, would be able to establish such pathways and serve as guides through the transition. This chapter has argued that developing countries require the presence of strong and dynamic developmental States capable of providing a coherent vision of the future, of managing the conflicts that arise from change and of establishing the kind of integrated strategy that will be needed. Such States have managed successful transitions in the past by mobilizing resources and providing missing inputs for productive activities, socializing investment risk, removing barriers, and providing temporary support to those adversely impacted by the shifts in activities. This has involved a blend of pro-investment macroeconomic and industrial policies. Fiscal and monetary policies have given priority to increasing public spending, including investments in energy, education, health and infrastructure. Subsidized credits, credit guarantees, tax breaks, accelerated depreciation allowances, etc., have been used to boost profits in private firms in targeted sectors.

All these elements will certainly be needed if the new generation of development strategies aimed at low emissions and high growth are to be successful. Such strategies would have to develop a clear vision for energy production and for the energy-intensity of the production structure, for urban development and transportation, and for natural resource use and natural resource intensity of production.

An integrated strategy will involve a collaborative effort between a developmental State and the private sector. This will necessarily be context-specific. It will depend, among other factors, on the level of development, technological capacities, the size of the economy, the natural resource base, government capacities and established State-business relations. Initial steps can be taken through fostering energy efficiency, implementing cleaner coal processes and developing renewable energy sources. Yet, mitigation efforts, no matter how necessary, will not be sufficient to protect developing countries from the threats posed by climate change. The best defence against such threats remains the diversification of economic structures to enable them to shift from a reliance on a small number of activities, particularly those in the primary sector that are sensitive to climatic shocks and changes.

> Developing countries require the presence of strong and dynamic developmental States capable of providing a coherent vision of the future, of managing the conflicts that arise from change and of drawing up the kind of integrated strategy that will be needed

> A new generation of development strategies requires a vision for energy production, for the energy-intensity of the production structure, for urban development and transportation, and for natural resource use and natural resource intensity of production

---

11   United Nations, *Treaty Series*, vol. 1771, No. 30822.

Chapter V
Technology transfer and the climate challenge

Introduction

In previous chapters, it has been argued that a big investment push to transform energy production and use and to diversify into activities less vulnerable to climatic shocks is the basis for an integrated response to climate and development challenges. That push is to be spearheaded by public investments but it will be sustained only by crowding private investors into an expanding green economy. It must also be accompanied by the technological advances needed to meet mitigation and adaptation challenges. Those advances will entail diffusing existing low-emissions technologies, scaling up new, commercially ready technologies and advancing new breakthrough technologies.

A rapid pace of capital formation is often accompanied by an accelerated pace of technological upgrading and learning. However, noting the familiar market failures which tend to slow or halt technological progress, chapter IV suggested that a strong public policy agenda mixing price incentives, regulation and interventionist measures, particularly within industrial policy, would also be required to ensure a continuous process of technological learning and upgrading. It also suggested that a developmental State would be needed to promote such an agenda in most developing countries. When the required technologies are not available domestically but have to be imported from abroad and adapted to local circumstances and conditions, that agenda becomes more complicated, in large part because the balance between owners and users of technology is tilted even more in favour of the former.

Technology flows through several well-known channels, the most important being trade, foreign direct investment (FDI) and cross-border technology licensing. Scientific and technical knowledge also flows internationally through research publications, research collaboration and the movement of skilled personnel. Acceleration of the flows of climate-friendly technology raises many of the same issues and challenges facing any other sort of technology. What differentiates those technologies from many—but not all—others is the urgency and scale of the transfers likely to be needed to meet the climate challenge. But there is also an underlying ethical challenge posed by climate-friendly technologies, given that the countries most responsible for climate change, or at least their corporations, are set to profit through the transfer of technologies to countries that bear little or no responsibility for the problem.

> The countries most responsible for climate change, or at least their corporations, are set to profit further through the transfer of technologies to countries that bear little or no responsibility for the problem

Implementation of the appropriate measures for facilitating the transfer of clean technologies and building the local capacity to use them effectively in developing countries will require much greater collaboration among countries. Such collaboration could help bring technologies more quickly to their commercialization stage and encourage further breakthroughs in cutting-edge low-emissions technologies. However, in many developing countries where the key challenge is diffusing existing low-emissions technologies, international support is needed for research, development and deployment (RD&D), the removal of trade barriers, access to affordable financing, and effective capacity-building. Any concerted international effort to promote access to low-emissions technologies should not, moreover, suppress the ability of the developing countries themselves to produce such technologies and to become competitive on international markets.

> The transfer of clean technologies and building the local capacity to use them effectively in developing countries will require much greater collaboration among countries

South-South climate technology flows could play a significant role in that transition, given the advances that have been made in some developing countries in areas such as biofuels and renewable energy

The present chapter is concerned with the international transfer and diffusion of technologies for climate change mitigation and adaptation.[1] The focus is on the "North-South" transfer of technologies, which would allow developing countries to undertake cost-effective actions consistent with and capable, ideally, of reinforcing their wider economic and social development. It identifies some of the main barriers obstructing such transfer and diffusion and proposes measures for removing or overcoming them. In response to the limited technological flows to date, resulting partly from the slow pace in blazing low-emissions development pathways and partly from the failure to fulfil promises made in international agreements, the chapter is largely concerned with how to anticipate possible future challenges. It suggests, given the scale and urgency of the climate challenge, that the international community must give much more serious attention to the kind of architecture needed to ensure greater transfers of technology so as to speed the transition to low-emissions development pathways. South-South climate technology flows could also play a significant role in that transition given the advances that have been made in some developing countries in areas such as biofuels and renewable energy. How to facilitate such flows will also require greater consideration in subsequent discussions of the technology transfer challenge.

Technology transfer for climate change: a global public policy challenge

There is agreement that technology transfer will be fundamental to enabling an effective implementation of the United Nations Framework Convention on Climate Change[2] beyond 2012. As early as 1972, the United Nations Conference on the Human Environment in 1972 (United Nations, 1972) had included explicit language emphasizing the importance of technology transfer for the achievement of environmental and developmental goals. Language that referred to technology transfer also appeared in the 1987 Montreal Protocol on Substances that Deplete the Ozone Layer[3] (see box V.1) and the Basel Convention on the Control of Transboundary Movements of Hazardous Wastes and their Disposal.[4]

The United Nations Conference on Environment and Development, held in Rio de Janeiro in 1992, gave a new urgency to the transfer of environmentally sound technologies (ESTs) for climate change mitigation. Developments subsequent to the adoption of the United Nations Framework Convention on Climate Change related to technology transfer have included the adoption of the Buenos Aires Plan of Action by the Conference of the Parties to the United Nations Framework Convention on Climate Change at its fourth session, held at Buenos Aires from 2 to 14 November 1998.[5] The Conference of the Parties requested that developed countries "take all practicable steps to promote, facilitate and finance" the transfer of environmentally sound technologies to developing countries and their access thereto.[6] In particular, the Plan of Action envisions an "enabling environment … to stimulate private sector investment" in the transfer of environmentally sound technologies.[7]

---

1   These are a subset of environmentally sound technologies (ESTs) that are climate-related.

2   United Nations, *Treaty Series*, vol. 1771, No. 30822.

3   Ibid., vol. 1552, No. 26369.

4   Ibid., vol. 1673, No. 28911.

5   FCCC/CP/1998/16/Add.1, sect. I, decision 1/CP.4. The Plan of Action was adopted as specified in decisions 2/CP. 4-8/CP.4.

6   Ibid., decision 4/CP.4, para. 3 (a).

7   Ibid., para. 7 (d).

Box V.1

Lessons learned from the implementation of the Montreal Protocol

The Montreal Protocol on Substances that Deplete the Ozone Layer[a] was agreed in 1987 and entered into force on 1 January 1989. The Protocol was a response to the fact that scientists had showed that some man-made substances were contributing to the depletion of the Earth's ozone layer, which protects life from damaging ultraviolet radiation. The Protocol is considered one of the most successful global environmental agreements and stimulated the development and worldwide transfer of technologies to protect the stratospheric ozone layer.

The Protocol requires that Parties eliminate emissions of most ozone depleting substances. Environmentally safe substitutes and related technologies have been used to achieve this objective. Since many of these technologies are widely available only in a relatively few countries and since the global market has been slow to bring these technologies to some parts of the world, deliberated and active international technology transfer programmes have been needed to eliminate emissions of ozone depleting substances (Strelneck and Linquiti, 1995).

The Multilateral Fund for the implementation of the Montreal Protocol was established by the London Amendment to the Montreal Protocol in 1990 to assist developing-country parties to the Protocol, whose annual per capita consumption and production of ozone depleting substances is less than 0.3 kilogram (kg), in complying with the control measures of the Protocol. The Fund covers the incremental costs associated with technology transfer, including the costs of on-site engineering, equipment purchase and installation, training, and start-up. Capacity-building projects, such as the establishment of national ozone offices and regional ozone network offices, are also eligible for funding (Andersen, Madhava Sarma and Taddonio, 2007). As of April 2008, the contributions made to the Multilateral Fund by some 49 developed countries (including countries with economies in transition) totalled over US$ 2.3 billion.

Lessons have been derived from implementation of the Montreal Protocol which may be of interest to those involved in the climate change process (Andersen, Madhava Sarma and Taddonio, 2007). The lessons relevant to technology transfer include: the need for developing visionary technology assessments; empowering the financial mechanism to be a proactive instrument for technology transfer; developing and implementing training programmes; and using regulations and policies to promote technology transfer.

[a] United Nations, *Treaty Series*, vol. 1552, No. 26369.

In order to operationalize the relevant provisions of the Framework Convention on technology, the intergovernmental process, through the Conference of the Parties to the United Nations Framework Convention on Climate Change at its seventh session, held at Marrakech, Morocco, from 29 October to 10 November 2001, agreed on a technology transfer framework,[8] comprising the following set of key themes and areas for meaningful and effective actions:

- *Technology needs and needs assessment*: a set of country-driven activities that identify and determine the mitigation and adaptation technology priorities, particularly of developing countries

- *Technology information*: this component defines the means, including hardware, software and networking, to facilitate the flow of information between different stakeholders to enhance the development and transfer of environmentally sound technologies

- *Enabling environments*: this component focuses on government actions, inter alia, fair trade policies, removal of technical, legal and administrative barriers to technology transfer, sound economic policy, regulatory frameworks and

---

8   FCCC/CP/2001/13/Add. 1 and Corr. 1, decision 4/CP.7, annex.

transparency, all of which are essential to creating an enabling environment conducive to public and private sector technology transfer

- *Capacity-building*: a process that seeks to build, develop, strengthen, enhance and improve existing scientific and technical skills, capabilities and institutions, particularly in developing countries, to enable them to access, adapt, manage and develop environmentally sound technologies

- *Mechanisms for technology transfer*: facilitators of the support of financial, institutional and methodological activities: (a) to enhance the coordination of the full range of stakeholders in different countries and regions; (b) to engage them in cooperative efforts through technology cooperation and partnerships (public/public, private/public and private/private); and (c) to facilitate the development of projects and programmes to support such ends.

An expert group on technology transfer was subsequently established as an institutional arrangement to facilitate the implementation of the technology transfer framework,[9] and enhanced action was agreed on technology development and transfer to support action on mitigation and adaptation under the Bali Action Plan.[10]

The discussion on promoting technology transfer to tackle the climate challenge has evolved in parallel with, but somewhat independently from, the recent discussion on the best ways to transfer technology to meet development goals. Essentially, the former focuses on how quickly the technological knowledge required to tackle the climate challenge can be put to widespread use in the economy, whether in that of developed or of developing countries, through learning and adaptation. The resulting agenda implicitly acknowledges the need to address various market failures that can hamper the spread of technological knowledge. In recent years, the development challenge has focused unduly on protecting the international position of the creators and owners of technology by linking intellectual property rights to multilateral trade rules such as the Agreement on Trade-related Aspects of Intellectual Property Rights (TRIPS) (World Trade Organization, 1994), and the Agreement on Trade-related Investment Measures, (ibid.), and through bilateral negotiations.[11] This puts greater emphasis on the importance of innovation. Protecting the owners of knowledge is also often taken as a measure of how committed countries are to good governance and an indication of whether or not their investment climate might be attractive to foreign firms, whose presence is seen as the surest guarantor of ways to access more advanced technologies (Maskus, 2000).

However, neither perspective appears to comprehend the urgency of the technological challenge or its links to the idea of a big push onto a new low-emissions growth path, particularly by developing countries. In fact, as discussed in chapter II, RD&D spending on some of the key technologies needed to support this transition appears to be moving in the wrong direction. Reversing this trend will be essential for building momentum towards a low-emissions future. Such action will likely have to draw on a variety of mechanisms at the international level and will ultimately require determined leadership that puts collective security before narrow commercial interest.

---

9   Ibid., decision 4/CP.7, para. 2.

10   FCCC/CP/2007/6/Add. 1, decision 1/CP.13, para. 1 (d).

11   See Littleton (2008) for a complete review.

Intellectual property rights

Incentives or obstacles

The obligation to respect intellectual property rights raises the cost of accessing technology. Whether this will constitute an important barrier to technology transfer will depend, inter alia, on whether the particular technology that is patented has cost-effective substitutes or alternatives, and on the degree of competition in the industry, which can affect the price of and the terms for licensing. Moreover, the technology covered by an individual patent may provide only a partial capability for exploiting an innovation; total capability might in fact depend on technologies protected by multiple patents or a combination of patented technologies and other forms of knowledge. Forms of legal protection of property rights such as patents and copyrights constitute only one means of protecting a technological advantage. Trade secrets and firm-specific know-how, including knowledge embodied in skilled personnel, can also be important.

There is vigorous debate over whether intellectual property rights, on balance, help or hinder technology transfer. The evidence is inconclusive and there is also variation by industry, where characteristics like market dynamism, technological sophistication, importance of RD&D, and ease of imitation and market entry come into play. There is also variation according to level of economic development. In high-income countries, stronger patent rights have been associated with higher levels of productivity, RD&D expenditures, trade flows, FDI and sophistication of the technologies transferred. However, even among these countries, there is considerable variation, and it is unclear if intellectual property rights are a cause or an effect of these outcomes. On the other hand, weak intellectual property rights in the least developed countries tend to be associated with low levels of RD&D, FDI inflows, etc. (Blyde and Acea, 2003; Smith, 2001).[12] However, cause and effect are again difficult to distinguish and even when technology is transferred to the least developed countries, the principal constraint on its wider use tends to be limited absorption capacity (United Nations Conference on Trade and Development, 2007).

Given that stronger protection of intellectual property rights raises the costs of obtaining technologies, it has generally been accepted that low-income developing countries should be exempt from strong intellectual property rights-related obligations and that the strength of those obligations should only rise with levels of development (Hoekman, Maskus and Saggi, 2004). However, given that the current regime is unduly biased towards the owners rather than towards the users of technology, a more graduated approach is likely to be supportive of large-scale technology transfer only if it is accompanied by complementary measures with respect to financing, RD&D and technical cooperation, which has not been the case in recent years.

The potential trade-off between intellectual property right protection and technology development and transfer is a very important issue in the context of climate change. As is clear from figure V.1, the distribution of patent ownership of climate-related technologies is very heavily skewed in favour of advanced economies. However, to date, Barton (2007) finds mixed evidence of the importance of intellectual property rights in technology transfer. Based on the examination of three sectors (photovoltaics (PV), wind and biofuels), he concludes that, rather than basic technologies, what are usually patented are specific improvements or features. What matters more are other market distortions.

A more graduated approach is likely to be supportive of large-scale technology transfer only if it is accompanied by complementary measures with respect to financing, RD&D and technical cooperation

---

12   However, at least one investigator finds positive correlations between strong protection of intellectual property rights and economic growth—among low- but not among middle-income countries (Falvey, Foster and Greenaway, 2006).

Figure V.1
**Share of patent ownership in the areas of renewable energy
and motor vehicles abatement among selected countries, 2000-2004**

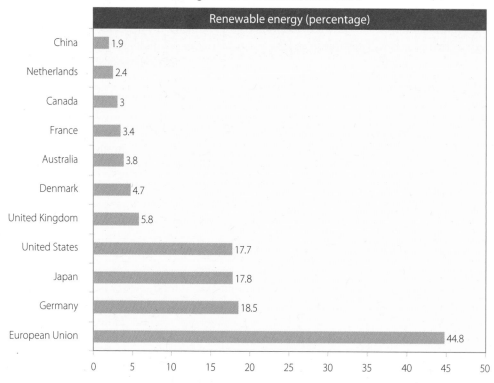

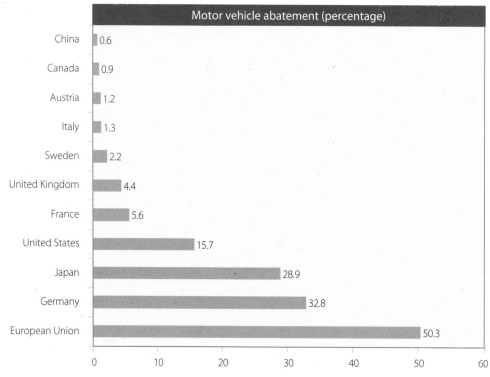

Source: Organization for
Economic Cooperation and
Development (2007).

In the photovoltaics sector, the developing nations are facing a loose oligopoly with many entrants. Thus, developing countries like India and China, for example, have been able to enter and compete in the industry. In respect of biofuel technologies, intellectual property rights do not appear to be barring developing countries from accessing the current-generation technologies, as shown by the developments in many countries, including Brazil, Malaysia, South Africa and Thailand.

A much harder question to answer is what lies ahead. To the extent that developing countries make a big investment push to establish a low-emissions development pathway, the market for new technologies can be expected to expand rapidly. Unanticipated obstacles to the transfer of technologies could slow that transition, particularly the emergence of new sectors linked to these technologies, or necessitate large shifts of resources to already advanced economies through technology payments.

The most significant barriers and distortions are likely to be associated with the market power of a small number of producers located in advanced economies. The wind sector appears to be the most concentrated of the three renewable energy sectors examined in the Barton study and a tight control over intellectual property may act to deter technology transfer. Even so, some developing nations have been able to build wind farms with equipment from the global market without incurring unduly steep intellectual property costs. The challenge for these developing countries is to enter the global market for wind turbines. The existing industry leaders are strong and they are hesitant to share cutting-edge technology out of fear of creating new competitors (see box V.2). Two developing

---

Box V.2

Foreign direct investment (FDI) and technology transfer in the wind sector

A recent study of wind power in China examined foreign and domestic companies involved in China's wind turbine industry and compared the extent of technology transfer in four case studies. These four cases exhibited three types of ownership models, which greatly impacted the extent of technology transfer: (a) limited joint ventures, where all materials and technology are developed and owned by the foreign company but manufactured with Chinese labour and materials (for example, NEG Micon/Vestas and GE Wind); (b) joint ventures, where a foreign company develops the technology, which is then owned by a Chinese company and components are made with Chinese labour and materials (for example, Xi'an-Nordex); and (c) Chinese-owned, where a Chinese company develops and owns the technology and oversees the production of the materials (for example, Goldwind-China).

The study found that, regardless of the ownership model, very few foreign companies have transferred wind power technology. Foreign-owned companies have not challenged the local content requirement because they have been able to do well in the market and retain control of their intellectual property.

In response, the Government of China is considering the implementation of local intellectual property requirements for wind power in an attempt to push international companies to transfer more technology. Such stipulations on intellectual property requirements could be contested by international companies under the rules of the World Trade Organization or by simply limiting new FDI in this sector.

The Government has also been trying, with some success, to promote strong independent Chinese wind power companies. Among Chinese wind power enterprises, several manufacturers produce equipment that is up to 30 per cent cheaper than that produced by their foreign counterparts, but generally such equipment is not as advanced in design. For example, Chinese firms rely on 600-750-kilowatt (KW) capacity turbines, while General Electric offers 1.5-megawatts (MW) and Vestas provides 2-MW turbines. The manufacturing capacity of China is changing fast, with the nation on track to exceed the 30-gigawatt (GW) target by 2020.

Source: Lewis, 2006.

nations with significant bargaining advantages in their own right, namely, China and India, have succeeded in building important firms over the past decade. Whether other developing countries will be able to replicate that success is uncertain.

Multilateral actions to accelerate technology transfer among countries can be of several sorts: those that exploit existing flexibilities of the Agreement on Trade-related Aspects of Intellectual Property Rights, those that require a modification of that Agreement and other disciplines in the framework of the World Trade Organization, and those that are not necessarily linked to the multilateral trade framework, including initiatives to foster technology-related absorptive capacity and innovation in developing countries through international cooperation.

Taking advantage of flexibilities of the Agreement on Trade-related Aspects of Intellectual Property Rights

Several flexibilities within the TRIPS Agreement could be exploited, ranging from limiting patentability to making use of compulsory licensing or even expanding its use with a view to serving regional markets.

Limiting patentability

Patentability refers to the boundaries established to determine what inventions can be patented. Article 27 of the Agreement on Trade-related Aspects of Intellectual Property Rights states that "patents shall be available for any inventions … in all fields of technology, provided that they are new, involve an inventive step and are capable of industrial application". These relatively loose criteria for patentability leave some space for the formulation by the individual country of its own policy, including limiting patentability. Further defining the criteria and thereby limiting patentability can have a positive impact on technology transfer and innovation by reducing possible conflict with existing patents (Oliva, 2008).

Certain technologies could be excluded from patentability, especially those that are deemed necessary to tackle climate change and/or are subject to anti-competitive measures

Based on the stated goals and guiding principles of the Agreement on Trade-related Aspects of Intellectual Property Rights regarding technology transfer, certain technologies could be excluded from patentability, especially those that are deemed necessary to tackle climate change and/or are subject to anti-competitive measures, while remaining consistent with the principles of the Agreement (Littleton, 2008). Examples of such exclusion already exist within the Convention on Biological Diversity[13] and the International Treaty on Plant Genetic Resources for Food and Agriculture[14] (Littleton, 2008). As the ongoing negotiations within the World Intellectual Property Organization (WIPO) of a substantive patent law treaty would eliminate this opportunity (World Intellectual Property Organization, 2008), its impact on climate-related technology transfer should be carefully examined before those negotiations are completed.

Exempting climate-friendly technologies from patenting is one way to reduce costs. The rationale for such a proposal lies in the seriousness of the climate change issue and the threat that it poses, particularly to developing countries. Variants of the proposal include: exemption of climate-friendly technologies and products from patenting;

---

13   United Nations, *Treaty Series*, vol. 1760, No. 30619.

14   Food and Agriculture Organization of the United Nations, *Report of the Conference of FAO, Thirty-first Session, Rome, 2-13 November 2001* (C 2001/REP), appendix D.

exemption from patenting in developing countries only; allowing developing countries to exclude patents for climate-friendly technologies and products, if they so choose; granting of voluntary licenses on request, free of royalty; and of granting of voluntary licences automatically, with compensation given to the owner of the technology.[15]

These options could perhaps be applied on a graduated basis to countries at different levels of development, the first three to low-income developing countries and the last two to middle- and high-income developing countries. The size of the country could be another criterion for choosing the appropriate type of flexibility.[16] For small a country, acquiring a licence for climate-related technology may not be profitable even if it is a middle- or high-income developing country, unless it is able to use the licence to tap export markets. In that case, the royalty could be reduced or eliminated and/or the exhaustion of patent rights could be extended from a domestic to a whole region.

Compulsory licensing

Even when a technology has been patented, articles 30 and 31 of the Agreement on Trade-related Aspects of Intellectual Property Rights offer opportunities for allowing unauthorized, automatic use of a patented technology without the consent of the patent-holder through compulsory licensing under certain circumstances. For article 30 to be used to obtain compulsory licensing, countries would have to claim that mitigating or adapting to climate change qualified as entailing the "legitimate interests of third parties", as required by the article. A second exception allows unauthorized use by a country when "necessary for the protection of its essential security interests" (article 73 (b)) or "the maintenance of international peace and security" (article 73 (c)). Whether this condition could be invoked would depend on the existence of a threat of climate catastrophe.

Article 31 of the Agreement sets out the other conditions for allowing compulsory licensing of a patented product. There are two major criteria to be met by a member of the World Trade Organization in order for it to qualify for an exception under article 31. First, reasonable efforts must be made to gain appropriate authorization from the holder of the intellectual property rights in question (article 31 (b)). This negotiation requirement may be waived when the member determines (using its own judgement) that a "national emergency" or "other circumstances of extreme urgency" demand unauthorized use without delay. The holder of the intellectual property rights must still be notified "as soon as reasonably practicable".

Discussions leading to the recognition of public health related exceptions showed some flexibility in interpreting what constitutes "exigent circumstances",[17] opening the door to potential use of these exceptions in the climate change context.[18] Climate change is increasingly perceived as a public-health "emergency" which would justify compulsory licensing exceptions under article 31 (Third World Network, 2008). Indeed, the United States Environmental Protection Agency (EPA) had been ordered by the Supreme Court to rule if carbon dioxide (CO_2) was a pollutant that endangered public health and

---

15   The last two options entail exceptions to patent rights rather than limiting of patentability.

16   However, all developing countries rightly point out that the new technologies are needed to counter a global threat that was created by today's advanced countries.

17   Defined as an emergency situation requiring swift action to prevent imminent danger to life or serious damage to property, or to forestall the imminent escape of a suspect, or destruction of evidence.

18   See, for example, the Declaration on the TRIPS Agreement and public health (World Trade Organization, 2001), para. 5 (c).

welfare, in which case it would be obligated to regulate it under the 1990 Clean Air Act. On 20 March 2009, the Agency issued an "endangerment finding".[19]

Second, sales of protected assets must be predominantly in the domestic market for the entity granted the exception (article 31 (f)). Thus, exceptions related to climate change would have to be sought by firms in various developing countries to ensure an effective and rapid diffusion of the technology. Limiting the technology to one (small or poor) country, however, might prevent the capture of economies of scale which would make the technology cost-effective. Recognition of this fact in the case of the public-health exception was reflected in the temporary waiving of the domestic market requirement in countries with insufficient domestic production.[20]

The General Council of the World Trade Organization has adopted an amendment of the TRIPS Agreement[21] by which the above-mentioned domestic-market restriction would be waived for developing countries for certain pharmaceuticals so as to enable the export of those products to regional markets.[22] (As the amendment has not yet been ratified by two thirds of the membership, it has not entered into force.) This waiver could conceivably be extended to climate-friendly technologies, particularly in light of what is stated in paragraph 5 (b) of the Declaration on the TRIPS Agreement and public health, namely, that "(e) each member has the right to grant compulsory licences and the freedom to determine the grounds upon which such licences are granted". Such an amendment would certainly meet with strong resistance from owners of technologies in countries members of the Organization for Economic Cooperation and Development (OECD), who could lose potential rents. However, and even ignoring the health parallel, it can be argued that if such technologies do not currently reach developing countries, then the loss of rent occasioned by giving them compulsory access would be limited (Hoekman, Maskus and Saggi, 2004).

A regional approach can also be beneficial in respect of the rules of exhaustion, which refers to the expiration of patent protection of a specific item once it has been sold (Littleton, 2008). Article 6 of the Agreement on Trade-related Aspects of Intellectual Property Rights leaves the determination of these rules to each member. In general, exhaustion can be universal or territorial. According to the rule of universal exhaustion, the patent-holder cannot limit the distribution of the item once it has been sold. This opens the way for parallel importing and the possibility for others to compete with the patent-holder in other countries. The rule of territorial exhaustion, usually preferred by patent-holders, limits the right to sell the item without authorization from the patent-holder and thus no parallel importing can take place without the patent-holder's consent. These different systems provide different incentives for technology transfer and innovation. While parallel imports increase competition and can lead to lower prices and greater accessibility of technology, they may discourage innovation by limiting patent-holders' profits. Regional exhaustion could be an attractive compromise solution. Here, parallel importing would be allowed only when the product was sold within the region at issue. By creating geographical buffer zones for patent protection, yet at the same time allowing for parallel importing, regional exhaustion might properly balance technology transfer with incentives to innovate (Littleton, 2008).

19 Bryan Walsh, "EPA calls CO_2 a danger—at last", *Time*, 23 March 2009.
20 See the decision of the General Council of the World Trade Organization of 30 August 2003 on the implementation of paragraph 6 of the Doha Declaration on the TRIPS Agreement and public health (World Trade Organization, 2003), para. 2 (a) (ii).
21 See the decision of the General Council of 6 December 2005 on the amendment of the TRIPS Agreement (WT/L/641).
22 Ibid., attachment, annex, para. 3.

Modifying the Agreement on Trade-related Aspects of Intellectual Property Rights[23]

Climate-related technology exceptions could be sought along the lines established to secure exceptions for essential medicines, as described above. A new "Declaration on TRIPS and climate change" might clarify existing flexibilities and offer new incentives for transfer of environmentally sound technologies. In particular, exceptions for least developed countries and small island developing States could be pursued, given that, in these countries, trade and investment flows appear to be not as responsive to protection of intellectual property rights and the dangers posed by climate change are particularly acute.[24] As suggested earlier, such a modification would have to take into account the uncertain and ever changing nature of the climate change problem and address adaptation as well as mitigation technologies.

Strong, integrated pro-competition provisions would also promote technology transfer. The class of restrictive business conditions considered in article 40 of the Agreement on Trade-related Aspects of Intellectual Property Rights could be expanded, and compulsory licensing under article 31 could be facilitated for environmentally sound technologies. As noted by Matsushita, Schönbaum and Mavroidis (2006), "many developing countries take the view that compulsory licensing should be required if the public interest is injured due to an abuse of patent monopoly". With their growing clout in the World Trade Organization, these members could redefine and expand the concept of "abuse" in this context beyond licensing restrictions to include other intellectual property rights-related practices which erect barriers to climate-friendly technology transfer (Hutchison, forthcoming).[25] Developed countries could also take the lead here by mandating compulsory licensing for climate-related intellectual property rights held domestically, a strategy that has yet to be tried out.[26] Pro-competition provisions would, however, meet with strong resistance from intellectual property right holders who exert great influence with several members of the World Trade Organization.

Procedures for challenging patents could be made less cumbersome so as to lower costs for developing countries (Stiglitz, 2008). Creation of a straightforward pre-patent opposition process could further reduce costs and prevent abuses.

Licensing guidelines might be promulgated that provide for fixed, moderate fees for environmentally sound technology patent licensees. In cases where the protected asset clearly has environmental benefits, the intellectual property right holder would bear the burden of proof in demonstrating why compulsory licensing would be unwarranted (Scherer, 1984; Stiglitz, 2008). A tiered application fee system for intellectual property rights could waive payments for patent-holders who authorize transfer of climate-friendly technologies to developing countries (Barton and Maskus, 2006; Maskus, 2004).

If the granting of full licences is an unrealistic option, then temporary licences could be granted along the lines established for conferral of plant breeders' exemptions and farmers' privileges under the International Treaty on Plant Genetic Resources for

Climate-related technology exceptions could be sought along the lines established to secure exceptions for essential medicines

---

23   The present section draws on Littleton (2008).

24   However, many developing countries insist that the issue is, again, not their ability to pay, but ensuring that those responsible for the climate problem carry the burden.

25   On the other hand, excessive fear of increased competition might, on balance, hinder technology transfer.

26   For example, the United States of America could mandate that climate-friendly technology patent-holders license their technologies abroad under specified terms. Admittedly, agreement on this proposal would be quite difficult to achieve, for political reasons.

Food and Agriculture.[27] For example, intellectual property right holders could provide developing-country users with technologies for a limited period, with the expectation of receiving payment once the technology was "tropicalized", that is to say, adapted to local requirements. This proposal would work with climate-change adaptation technologies as well as with mitigation technologies.

Mechanisms through which to evaluate progress on technology transfer could benefit from being strengthened

Mechanisms through which to evaluate progress on technology transfer could benefit from being strengthened. Such mechanisms might be TRIPS Agreement-based or might involve multiple World Trade Organization Agreements (Maskus, 2004). The problems with current evaluation are the result of both: non-transparency and lack of a viable enforcement mechanism. In the absence of formal enforcement, "naming and shaming" would at least provide some measure of accountability.

There are, of course, great political difficulties involved in modifying any World Trade Organization Agreement. Technology transfer measures can often disadvantage intellectual property right holders, who have great political influence in developed countries. Moreover, despite the acknowledgment of development goals, it is equal treatment of nations that is at the heart of the TRIPS Agreement. However, equal treatment of technologies may not be as crucial, as evidenced by the progress in respect of essential medicines. Global action to address climate change is certainly not a zero-sum game, and any World Trade Organization member hoping for modification of the TRIPS Agreement in this area will need to stress common interests in advancing the global public good of a stable climate. Still, issues of fairness will also need to be addressed in any reform effort.

Further options for addressing intellectual property rights-related issues and innovation incentives

The institutional role of the World Trade Organization in the area of climate change has "barely begun to be thought through" (Evans and Steven, 2009, p. 32). However, mixing trade disciplines with climate concerns raises serious issues, particularly for developing countries. A few other proposals for facilitating technology access and diffusion, which may or may not be integrated in a World Trade Organization framework, are provided here:

Open-source information access and increased sharing of public RD&D results

Difficulty of access to information on available technologies is a constraint on technology transfer and adoption. One proposed solution is to establish an information access agreement. As far back as 1992, there were calls for an information clearing house of climate-friendly technologies (see, for example, chap. 34 of Agenda 21 (United Nations, 1992)). Some efforts have been made by UNFCCC in supporting its technology transfer framework and in undertaking technology needs assessments. However, such efforts need to be expanded and better integrated with wider development challenges.

The Multilateral System of Access and Benefit-Sharing of the International Treaty on Plant Genetic Resources for Food and Agriculture could be a model for an agreement on access to climate-friendly technologies (Halewood and Nnadozie, 2008). Along these lines, Barton and Maskus (2006) have proposed a formal agreement on access

---

27 Breeders' exemptions allow breeders to use protected varieties of plants to create new varieties through experimentation. Farmers' privileges permit farmers to save and reuse protected seed varieties for subsequent harvests.

to basic science and technology "to ensure widespread access to essential scientific results and to enhance the transfer of basic technological information to the developing world at reasonable cost". As a World Trade Organization agreement, this instrument could take advantage of the dispute settlement mechanisms and other institutional structures.

Establishing such an agreement would encounter some difficulties. For one thing, drawing an acceptable line between "basic" and "applied" research would be a challenge. So as to favour climate-friendly technologies, the notion of what is "basic" could be construed more broadly in the context of global public goods (Barton and Maskus, 2006). In borderline cases, guidelines concerning which research results were confidential and which could be made public would need to be established.

Dedicated funding mechanisms

Governments can subsidize technology development and transfer, either individually or in concert. Subsidies, tax breaks and other fiscal incentives of individual countries constitute the most straightforward method of funding. They can direct the focus of private firms towards particular sectors like those encompassing climate change-related technologies by reducing the risk level of RD&D projects (Stiglitz, 2008). However, the financial impact of individual Governments is limited. Moreover, such expenditures are exploitable by "free riders" on the global level (Barton and Maskus, 2006).

A coordinated international funding mechanism would help solve the free-rider problem. Possibilities in this regard include a trust fund encouraging RD&D directly in developing countries (Roffe, 2002), a patent acquisition fund established to buy intellectual property rights from patent-holders (United Nations, Department of Economic and Social Affairs, 2008) and a fund that covers the difference in cost between the environmentally sound technologies and the business-as-usual technology for developing-country firms (like the Multilateral Fund for the Implementation of the Montreal Protocol, see box V.I).

A technology prize system could circumvent intellectual property rights-related problems. Within such a system, the performance characteristics of a desired technology would be defined, a contest would be announced for its development, and a prize would be awarded to the successful innovator in exchange for the intellectual property rights. Prizes help to both reduce wasteful spending on marketing and lower incentives for anti-competitive behaviour (Stiglitz, 2008). Prizes, like advance purchase funds/agreements, work best with a specific, clearly-defined objective (such as a vaccine for a specific disease).

Technology development and transfer mechanisms

At the international level, such a mechanism could be established under the auspices of the Conference of the Parties to the United Nations Framework Convention on Climate Change, supported by a secretariat and various expert panels set up to examine the various dimensions of the technology challenge in developing countries and, where appropriate, to provide technical assistance on the range of technology options available for mitigating and adapting to climate change. This model has been successfully employed within the institutional structure of the Montreal Protocol on Substances that Deplete the Ozone Layer and could be adapted to the climate change context.

At regional and national levels, centres dedicated to low-emissions technology innovation and diffusion could be created and linked to and through the international

Governments can subsidize technology development and transfer, either individually or in concert

A coordinated international funding mechanism would help solve the free-rider problem

At the international level, a technology transfer mechanism could be established under the auspices of the Conference of the Parties to the United Nations Framework Convention on Climate Change mechanism. They would have an important role to play in making technologies accessible and affordable in developing countries. At least in the initial stages, these centres are likely to be publicly funded, though the precise mix of donor, public and private funding would vary across countries and over time. What particular mixture of basic research, field trials, business incubator services, venture capital funding, technical advice and support, and policy and market analysis is adopted will be very much contingent on local conditions and challenges.

Technology transfer through investment

Accessing clean technologies through foreign direct investment

Many descriptions of foreign direct investment (FDI) emphasize that it is the exploitation of firm-specific advantages, including intellectual property and leading technologies, that allows large corporations to undertake risky and costly activities outside their immediate domestic and regional locations. Hosting such firms has been seen as one way for developing countries to close the technological gap between them and more advanced countries. In recent years, the policies devised by developing countries to attract those firms have undergone a shift from providing the firm with a protected local market to liberalizing country rules on FDI and trade, including through the creation of export processing zones. The expectation was that this would help break not only the technological constraint but also the foreign-exchange constraint on growth. The results have often been disappointing, particularly in cases where FDI has been a substitute for local domestic capacity-building efforts (United Nations, 2006).

FDI tends to be a lag variable in the growth process: even when it does materialize, active policies are needed to ensure that there are valuable spillovers into the local economy

While technology may be physically transferred from the home to the host country through FDI, the question remains what sort of linkages the transfer creates with the rest of the host economy. How large are the technology spillovers and do they, as Hirschman (1971) asked almost 40 years ago, act as "a spur to the expansion of missing local inputs" or do they actually "harm the quality of local factors of production"? Answering these questions in greater detail would require a long detour extending beyond the remit of this *Survey*. However, worth noting in what is an already extensive literature are two broad findings which will have a bearing on the role of FDI along any new low-emissions pathway. First, FDI tends to be a lag variable in the growth process; that is to say, it is attracted by various factors such as market size, presence of suppliers, human capital, etc., which are the result of a successful development push. Second, even when it does materialize, active policies are needed to ensure that there are valuable spillovers into the local economy.[28]

Those spillovers can occur in a number of ways: through the movement of skilled personnel between a multinational subsidiary or joint venture and other firms, through technology imitation by competitors, and through technology sharing with suppliers, customers or business partners.

Strong intellectual property right protection is not necessary for extensive foreign investment to occur, as the case of China clearly demonstrates. The country's large market and rapid growth have compelled foreign companies to invest, even at the risk of losing control of proprietary technologies. Countries with "weak" intellectual property right regimes, for example, the Republic of Korea, Taiwan Province of China and Brazil in the pre-TRIPS Agreement era have been among the major technology borrowers (Correa, 2005, p. 228).

---

28   On the links between FDI and development, see Kozul-Wright and Rayment (2007, chap.4).

Recent research on FDI as a vehicle for technology transfer (Todo and Miyamoto, 2006; O'Connor and Lunati, 2008) has pointed to a few conditions that influence the extent of technology, or knowledge, spillovers. Todo and Miyamoto used industry panel data from Indonesia to examine knowledge spillovers between subsidiaries of Japanese multinational corporations and Indonesian firms. They concluded that the spillovers were significant only when the Japanese subsidiaries had invested in RD&D themselves; otherwise, the spillovers were negligible. Other studies found that the RD&D undertaken by local firms also affected the extent to which knowledge spillovers from foreign-invested firms occurred. Miyamoto (2008) found a significant positive relationship in Indonesia between the training investments of local firms and the extent of knowledge spillovers from foreign ones. All of these findings lead to the conclusion that technology or knowledge transfer through FDI is not automatic, but depends on complementary investments by both foreign and local firms.

There has been little research undertaken to date on the role of FDI spillovers in supporting a transformative low-emissions growth path. However, the case of wind technology in China suggests that hosting FDI is, by itself, no guarantee (see box V.2). A recent study of China's automotive industry (Gallagher, 2006) is also instructive in this regard. The transportation sector is part of an interconnected bloc of related sectors that are expected to lead China to the next stage of industrial development. The sector has grown particularly rapidly since the early 1980s, thanks in part to joint ventures with foreign automobile companies producing largely for the growing domestic market. This growth has, in turn, contributed in recent years to China's very rapid growth in oil imports. Until 2000, the sector had been subject to few regulations and standards on emissions. Since then, stricter regulations have been introduced in an effort to force foreign firms to transfer cleaner technologies. However, the evidence suggests that, while these firms have introduced more modern pollution control technologies, they have been reluctant to introduce cutting-edge technology and the overall impact of their efforts has been dwarfed by the scale effect of rising car ownership. The study concludes that market incentives are, by themselves, unlikely to help China jump to the next stage in terms of cleaner vehicles, such as fuel-cell vehicles, given prohibitive prices and the control exerted over intellectual property by foreign firms. The study showed that the current producers of hybrid vehicles, for example, have been unwilling to transfer hybrid-vehicle technologies for production inside China. Rather, the Government will need to consider a more comprehensive and integrated policy approach, one that seeks to bolster local learning in the automotive sector through support for RD&D and engineering training, including through overseas study, and efforts to foster demand for cleaner automobiles in response to higher prices and tighter regulations. While these measures can provide clear signals to private investors, both domestic and foreign, to move towards cleaner technologies, wider national planning initiatives to improve and expand public infrastructure will also be needed to ensure that the transportation system evolves in line with climate objectives.

> Technology or knowledge transfer through FDI is not automatic, but depends on complementary investments by both foreign and local firms

> The Government of China will need to consider a more comprehensive and integrated policy approach, one that seeks to bolster local learning

CDM and technology transfer

The market-driven Clean Development Mechanism (CDM) was established under the Kyoto Protocol to the United Nations Framework Convention on Climate Change[29] to help developed countries meet their emission targets, by encouraging firms in the private sector to contribute to emission reduction efforts and through investments in developing countries. Although they do not necessarily entail FDI, many of these projects involve

---

29   United Nations, *Treaty Series*, vol. 2303, No. 30822.

transnational corporations from the advanced countries. It was expected that such private sector transfers would assist in the transfer of environmentally sound technologies to developing countries.

A few studies have tried to determine to what extent technology transfer is actually occurring through the Clean Development Mechanism process. Most recently, the United Nations Framework Convention on Climate Change Registration and Issuance Unit CDM/SDM (Seres and Haites, 2008) issued its own report on the Clean Development Mechanism and technology transfer. Based on documentation for 3,296 registered and proposed CDM projects, it found that roughly 36 per cent of the projects, which accounted for 59 per cent of the estimated annual emission reductions, claimed to involve technology transfer, indicating that projects claiming technology transfer were, on average, substantially larger than those that made no technology transfer claim. It also found that about 30 per cent of unilateral projects, 40 per cent of projects with foreign participants and 30 per cent of small-scale projects claimed technology transfer, as compared with 36 per cent of all projects. The study found that the technology transferred originated mainly from Japan, Germany, the United States of America, France, and the United Kingdom of Great Britain and Northern Ireland, which accounted for over 70 per cent.

Studies find wide variation across countries in the reported technology transfer associated with CDM projects. Dechezleprêtre, Glachant and Ménière (2009) focused on four countries accounting for about three fourths of all CDM projects: Brazil, China, India and Mexico. While 68 per cent of projects in Mexico included an international transfer of technology, the rates for India, Brazil and China were 12 per cent, 40 per cent and 59 per cent, respectively. One reason for the high rates of technology transfer in Mexico and Brazil is that in those countries foreign companies have a significant involvement in CDM projects, which is less the case in China and India. Seres and Haites (2008) observed that such cross-country variation could also be attributable to trade policy, with some countries imposing significantly higher tariffs on imported equipment than others. This factor's being a handicap to technology deployment clearly depends on whether domestic technological capabilities are effective substitutes. Technology transfer in a specific type of CDM project generally declines over time, suggesting a progressively greater reliance on local knowledge and equipment.

So far, the operation of the Clean Development Mechanism has been on much too limited a scale and has been too heavily concentrated in a few developing countries to allow it to initiate and sustain the kind of big push towards cleaner technologies recommended in this *Survey*. Moves towards the creation of a simplified Clean Development Mechanism, including sectoral or technological benchmarks, might make it more effective in raising technological standards in the longer run. However, this is likely to take time.

One reason for the high rates of technology transfer in Mexico and Brazil is that in those countries, foreign companies have a significant involvement in CDM projects, which is less the case in China and India

Trade and climate-related technology transfer

As a consequence of the fact that Governments are becoming more serious about addressing climate change, there has been a revival of the North-South trade and environment debates on how to distinguish between legitimate environmental and health protection measures, as allowed in the World Trade Organization, and disguised trade protectionism measures. Despite the establishment of a World Trade Organization Committee on Trade and Environment in 1994 to address contentious trade and environment issues, such as how to speed up the transfer of environmentally sound technologies while remaining World Trade

Organization-compliant, not much progress has been made. The few clarifications provided have emerged instead from World Trade Organization dispute panels considering whether importing countries could ban import of tuna and shrimps from countries that did not use devices to avoid by-catches of dolphins and endangered turtles. More of these trade disputes are to be expected, given the absence of prior agreements on how to handle the measures being proposed to account for the carbon-intensity of traded goods and on subsidies to encourage the development of lower-carbon energy sources.

We review these issues below as well as some proposals that have been put forth with regard to speeding up the transfer of climate-related technologies in ways that take into account the principle of common and differentiated responsibilities as embodied in the United Nations Framework Convention on Climate Change and its equivalent within the framework of the World Trade Organization, namely, the principle of special and differentiated treatment for developing countries. Nations agreed upon these principles based on the understanding that they reflected the differences in capabilities and in the responsibility for the cumulative greenhouse gas emissions causing climate change. There was also recognition of the fact that developing countries aspired to attain higher levels of economic development and social well-being for their citizens.

For instance, under the Kyoto Protocol, developing countries do not have binding greenhouse gas reduction commitments although they must collect data and undertake mitigation and adaptation measures. The level and extent of developing countries' mitigation actions will depend in turn on promised financial, technological and capacity-building support from developed countries.

Trade-related actions that have been proposed include faster liberalization of trade in climate-related environmental goods and services, making the intellectual property rights regime more lenient with respect to climate-related environmental goods and services, and revisiting the Agreements on Subsidies and Countervailing Measures, contained in the Marrakesh Agreement (World Trade Organization, 1994), to allow subsidies that foster investments in low-emissions technologies.

The potential benefits of trade liberalization to the environment, including climate change, and development have been highlighted since the adoption of Agenda 21 (United Nations, 1992). Principle 12 of the Rio Declaration on Environment and Development (ibid.) states that Governments should "promote a supportive and open international economic system that would lead to economic growth and sustainable development in all countries, to better address the problems of environmental degradation". Trade is important because imported capital goods and services provide an additional channel to access environmental technologies and know-how generated in developed countries, other than FDI or licensing.

Trade liberalization on its own is not sufficient, however, for effective technology transfer. Indeed, despite unprecedented market liberalization, and several commitments to the transfer of technology in both the United Nations Framework Convention on Climate Change and the Kyoto Protocol thereto, as well as within the World Trade Organization, evidence of technology transfer is slim. It was thought that early liberalization of environmental goods and services would contribute to environmental goals by lowering prices of environmental goods and services relative to their non-environmental or mainstream counterparts, thus facilitating and promoting more environmentally sustainable production and consumption. To support climate actions, the World Bank (2008a) proposed accelerated liberalization of products, technologies and services used in Clean Development Mechanism projects to reduce equipment and other

The level and extent of developing countries' mitigation actions will depend in turn on promised financial, technological and capacity-building support from developed countries

Trade liberalization on its own is not sufficient, however, for effective technology transfer

costs. Liberalization of environmental goods and services has been slowed owing not only to the failure to conclude the Doha Round but also to the lack of a definition of what constitutes environmental goods and services and the different views held by the North and the South regarding which tariffs should be lowered more quickly.

Liberalization of trade in climate-related environmental goods and services

As a general rule, developing countries rely much more on tariffs to generate revenues than do developed countries, which have the institutions in place to collect income and sales, or value-added, taxes. Significant reduction of these tariffs means lower revenues for investment in social and infrastructure development.

With respect to liberalization of environmental goods and services, the goals are different for developing and developed countries. The former want access to adaptation technologies while protecting their nascent environmental goods and services industries so as to eventually become competitors in these emerging industries. Developed countries that have comparative advantages in capital- and technology-intensive environmental goods and services propose early liberalization of those goods. Another obstacle to agreeing on a definition of a list of "eligible" environmental goods and services or climate-related technologies hinges on the lack of specificity with which goods and services are tracked for customs and duty purposes. They are tracked through the World Customs Organization Harmonized Commodity Description and Coding System (HS) and have been harmonized to only a six-digit level. Because the six-digit level is still highly aggregated, it lumps together goods that serve for both environmental and non-environmental use, such as "pumps for liquid", which are often used in manufacturing wind turbines but also in other industrial processes. Liberalizing these goods under this HS code would result in a relinquishment of tariff revenues from all such pumps as well as expose local enterprises, often small and medium-sized, to international competition.

Thus, developing countries fear that the negotiations on environmental goods and services are yet another attempt at prying open their markets. Meanwhile, they observe that developed countries have been slow to meet their obligations in respect of the technology transfer, capacity-building and financial assistance required to allow developing countries to acquire needed climate-related technologies.

Developing countries would certainly retain more policy space if they were not required to lower the tariffs on "environmental goods" to low levels or zero in compliance with binding World Trade Organization commitments. They would then have the option to develop their own industries and products while maintaining tariffs that were appropriate to this objective, or to liberalize the applied tariffs on certain environment-related products. This is important because, increasingly, World Trade Organization tariffs reductions are bound; in other words, they cannot be raised again once lowered.[30] Without proper safeguards, the acceleration of liberalization of tariffs on environmental goods and services would reduce the policy options available to developing countries for promoting local production along their low-emissions development pathway (Khor, forthcoming).

> With respect to liberalization of environmental goods and services, the goals are different for developing and developed countries

> Developed countries have been slow to meet their obligations in respect of the technology transfer, capacity-building, and financial assistance required to allow developing countries to acquire needed climate-related technologies

> Developing countries would have more policy space if they were not required to lower the tariffs on "environmental goods" to low levels or zero

---

30 During the Uruguay Round of multilateral trade negotiations, developing countries increased the proportion of imports whose tariff rates were "bound" (committed and difficult to increase) from 21 per cent to 73 per cent. Data available at the World Trade Organization website, http://www.wto.org/english/theWTO_e/whatis_e/tif_e/agrm2_e.htm (accessed 13 May 2009).

The second definitional issue concerns traditional environmental goods and services such as water treatment, waste collection technologies, etc., versus environmentally preferable products (EPPs). The initial list of environmental goods and services proposed by the developed countries mirrored the list of Asia-Pacific Economic Cooperation (APEC) and included typically capital- and technology-intensive products. Environmentally preferable products, instead of providing an end-of-pipe solution to pollution, reduce pollution during the production process or during the use phase of a product. Well-known examples are organic foods and coffee, and goods whose manufacture emits less or which are more energy-efficient in use, such as hybrid cars. The debate over environmentally preferable products in the World Trade Organization is at heart a debate about whether (and how) the World Trade Organization can distinguish between otherwise similar products based on their processes or production methods (PPMs).

The most favoured nation and national treatment principles now embodied in the World Trade Organization prevent discrimination among "like products" originating from different trading partners, as well as between a country's own and like foreign products. Developing countries, fearing that developed nations could use processes or production methods as the basis for non-tariff barriers (by imposing high process-related environmental standards hard to achieve by developing countries), have always taken the position that if the end products have the same physical characteristics, then they are "like products" regardless of how they were produced. However, recent dispute panel findings over the shrimp import and turtle by-catch issue mentioned above seem to indicate that, as long as measures to protect the environment (the endangered turtle species in this case) are non-discriminatory between domestic and international producers, or among international producers, they are World Trade Organization-compliant under article XX of the General Agreement on Tariffs and Trade (GATT), which allows exceptions to World Trade Organization trade rules to protect human, animal or plant life or health. Latin American countries recently proposed including sustainable agricultural products on the list of environmental goods and services, clearly an opening towards environmentally preferable products.[31]

Given the lack of progress at the multilateral level, the International Institute for Sustainable Development (Cosbey, 2008) has suggested that efforts might be pursued in bilateral and regional trade agreements and/or through plurilateral agreements similar to the World Trade Organization procurement agreements, whereby members could opt for voluntary agreements which come into effect only when enough countries have joined. Other proposals have insisted that the technologies be demand-driven, whereby developing countries would assess their adaptation and mitigation needs and/or development goals and put the technologies concerned on the list.

Embodied carbon

The contentious environmentally preferable products, or processes and production method-related, issue has been revived in the talks on border adjustments which would apply different tariffs to goods entering a country or bloc based on the carbon emitted in their production processes, or the carbon embodied in them. Lawyers disagree among themselves over the details, but they all seem to conclude that most border carbon adjustments would be hard to implement in such a way as to be compliant with current World Trade Organization rules.

---

31   This proposal, as well as the proposal of Brazil to include bioethanol, was resisted by the OECD countries.

As developed countries are putting in place policies to tackle climate change, their energy- and carbon-intensive industries fear having to compete with producers that do not face higher energy prices in non-Annex I countries. Developed-country Governments may also fear so-called carbon leakage—the relocation of such industries to non-regulated countries, with associated economic costs and no environmental benefit. A number of developed countries are thus proposing border adjustments that would "correct" for the differential in carbon emitted in the production of imported goods. If all developed countries join a regime of binding quantitative emission targets, then these measures would be directed largely at developing countries, notably the major emitters. The intention is to encourage them to become part of a regime of binding targets as well.

Developing countries will eventually have in any case to make significant cuts in their emissions from business-as-usual trajectories if the probability of catastrophic climate change is to be limited. However, for reasons outlined in earlier chapters, they cannot be expected to do so on the same terms or in the same time frame as developed countries, or without financial and technological support from developed countries.

Using stronger measures as a stick to induce developing countries to take on binding commitments is likely only to erode trust between North and South

Using stronger measures as a stick to induce developing countries to take on binding commitments is likely only to erode trust between North and South, especially as developed countries have yet to make the firm offer of a carrot of substantial financial and technological support to developing countries.

Not only may border adjustments be unnecessary, they are also unlikely to achieve their goal

Not only may border adjustments be unnecessary, they are also unlikely to achieve their goal (Cosbey, 2008). They may not be necessary because only a few energy-intensive sectors (steel, aluminium, paper, chemicals and cement) would be affected, and these are only responsible for a small proportion of economic activity in the developed world. In the United Kingdom, for example, their share of gross domestic product (GDP) is only 0.5 per cent (ibid.). Border adjustments may not reach their goal because they are likely only to reroute trade through countries with strong climate measures. China's export of carbon-intensive goods to the United States, as a proportion of China's GDP, for instance, is not getting close to even 1 per cent. Also, if the border measures cover only basic materials (such as aluminium), they hurt the domestic producers that use this input in their processes. If they covered manufactured goods (such as aluminium-frame bicycles), it would become very difficult to estimate border adjustments. As described above, if they are to be in compliance with the non-discrimination principle of the World Trade Organization and the principle of common and differentiated responsibilities under the United Nations Framework Convention on Climate Change, they will be extremely difficult to design.

Without the appropriate incentives and support, lower fossil fuel prices are likely to increase consumption of these carbon-intensive fuels in developing countries without comparable domestic policies

The need for financial and technological support to developing countries is made even more urgent inasmuch as, when developed countries put in place measures to discourage the use of fossil fuels, their decreased demand for those fuels will exert downward pressure on world coal and oil prices. Without the appropriate incentives and support, lower fossil fuel prices are likely to increase consumption of these carbon-intensive fuels in developing countries without comparable domestic policies (Fortunato, 2009; Cosbey, 2008).

Low-emissions energy subsidies

The push to decarbonize economies will require Government incentives (as well as regulations)

In addition to the issue of embodied carbon, subsidies to support lower-carbon energy sources may also raise questions of World Trade Organization compliance. The energy sector produces two thirds of the greenhouse gas emissions that cause climate change. Policies to curb climate change focus on taxing or capping CO_2 emissions from fossil fuels and/

or on providing subsidies to alternative energy sources. However, the push to decarbonize economies will require Government incentives (as well as regulations) and it is therefore imperative that countries clarify which subsidies would be World Trade Organization-compliant. This issue may be easier to resolve than the above issues of environmentally preferable products and liberalization of environmental goods and services because there is a precedent: There had been an exception for environmental subsidies under the Agreement on Subsidies and Countervailing Measures which lapsed in 1999 and could be revived to allow climate-related subsidies that do not injure competitors in other countries.

If the non-actionability of these subsidies could be renewed, both developed and developing countries would be allowed to subsidize general research (assistance for research activities by firms or higher education or research establishments on a contract basis with firms) on climate mitigation and adaptation, without fear of trade sanctions (Hoekman, Maskus and Saggi, 2004).

With regard to carbon trading systems, it is unclear whether free allocation of emissions allowances would be considered subsidies under the Agreement on Subsidies and Countervailing Measures, as there is no body of jurisprudence on this point (Hufbauer and Kim, 2009). It is worth noting that under the Agreement on Subsidies and Countervailing Measures, countervailing duties could not be applied on countries that failed to take actions on climate change. A lack of action does not constitute "a subsidy" under the Agreement.[32]

The multilateral investment agreement, the Agreement on Trade-related Investment Measures, has few obligations. However, the 2,500 bilateral investment agreements and the bilateral investment chapters in regional trade agreements contain strong measures. In the North American Free Trade Agreement (NAFTA), the expropriation was so broad and led to so many arbitrations that the United States, Canada and Mexico agreed to clarify and limit the definition of which investors could claim expropriation under the Chapter concerned. These arbitrations have, in some cases, had a chilling effect on countries considering stronger regulations. The fear is that investors could claim that the new regulations constituted unfair and inequitable treatment. Clarification on which climate-related investments could constitute indirect expropriation would be warranted in order to give countries the policy space within which to put in place appropriate regulations without the fear of having to pay excessive compensation to foreign companies.

International policies and measures to build capacity in developing countries

Technology absorption requires investment in both physical and human capital. The faster the pace of capital formation, the greater the likelihood of such absorption. However, as discussed in chapter IV, promoting local technological learning and capacities will be critical to the successful use of technological knowledge in meeting the climate challenge. As figure V.2 suggests, technology needs will differ from region to region. But, in all cases, active government policy will be a component of successful outcomes (see chap. IV). Moreover, the global nature and urgency of the climate challenge imply that the rapid dissemination of appropriate technological options will require international collaboration.

The global nature and urgency of the climate challenge imply that the rapid dissemination of appropriate technological options will require international collaboration

---

32 Previous experience indicates that successful efficiency efforts can lead to the "rebound effect" whereby overall consumption increases. Measures will have to address the absolute consumption of energy.

Figure V.2

Commonly identified renewable energy technology needs and energy efficiency technology needs in the building and residential subsectors, selected regions

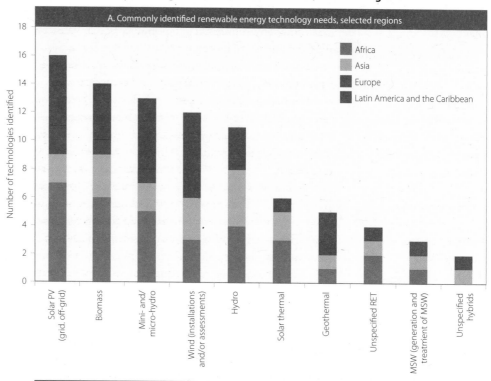

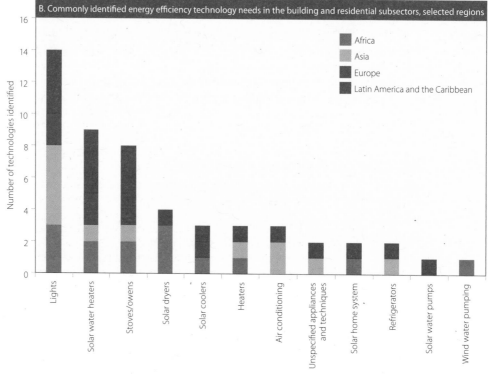

Source: United Nations, United Nations Framework Convention on Climate Change (2006).

Abbreviations: PV, photovoltaic; MSW, municipal solid waste; RET, renewable energy technology.

This is particularly true in the area of RD&D, where developing countries lag significantly and risk falling further behind as new technologies emerge. Important examples of technologies that will be critical to a new development pathway include carbon capture and sequestration (CCS), low-emissions biofuels, and breakthroughs in renewable energy sources such as solar panels. Moreover, developing countries also need access to best practices with respect to adaptation technologies, in the areas of agriculture, disaster management and urban planning. These technologies are often closely interrelated and link the climate threat to other threats, such as food and energy security. Consequently, developments in all these areas are best addressed through a structured global programme and funding (Stern, 2009, p. 173). Publicly funded research holds out the best hope of developing greater coordination among the myriad research institutions, in the private sector, the non-profit sector and academia, that are already working to meet these challenges and is moreover more likely to ensure the widest dissemination of the results (box V.3). Transparent and readily accessible research is all the more important because regulatory and legal frameworks, such as standard-setting, are likely to emerge on the basis of these results.

Particularly with respect to cutting-edge technologies, well-educated engineers and managers are essential.[33] Enhanced education and sustained training programmes are needed in the areas of technical, administrative, financial, regulatory and legal skills (United Nations, United Nations Framework Convention on Climate Change, 2003). In addition to making improvements in domestic education, developing countries, in order to

> Publicly funded research holds out the best hope of developing greater coordination among the myriad research institutions, in the private sector, the non-profit sector and academia

> Mechanisms to retain and bring back trained labour include wage flexibility, repatriation grants, and incentives to start technology firms

---

Box V.3

Intellectual property rights and publicly funded technologies

The issue of publicly owned technology transfer was addressed at the United Nations Conference on Environmental Development, held in Rio de Janeiro in 1992. Agenda 21[a] (chap. 34, para. 34.18 (a)) states that Governments and international organizations should promote the "Formulation of policies and programmes for the effective transfer of environmentally sound technologies that are publicly owned or in the public domain". Implementation of this provision has been very weak.

Developed-country Governments sponsor a range of research and development (R&D) activities geared towards developing climate technologies. For example, in 2001 Governments within the European Union (EU) spent almost 350 million euros for R&D in renewable energy, more than half of the total expenditure (EU Directorate-General for Research, 2006). Public sector spending is equally important in the United States of America. For example, for the wind, biofuels and photovoltaic sector, the United States Department of Energy spent approximately USA 356 million (2008 budget) (Barton, 2007, p. 7).

Sathaye, Jolt and De La Rue du Can (2005) surveyed Government-sponsored R&D in the United States, Canada, the United Kingdom of Great Britain and Northern Ireland, the Republic of Korea and other countries members of the Organization for Economic Cooperation and Development (OECD) and found that it is a common practice for Governments to grant ownership of intellectual property rights (patents, copyrights, trademarks, etc.) to the recipient research institutions. In the United States, for example, Government-sponsored research usually ends up being patented (Barton, 2007, p. 8).

Given the role that Governments play as the main driver of R&D for climate technologies, it will be necessary for modalities for the transfer of publicly funded climate technologies to developing countries to be explored. OECD countries, which tend to hold ownership of most of the technology needed for mitigation and abatement, are in a strategic position to influence technology flows directly through their influence on the private sector or on public institutes which receive funding for their R&D and thus should be more active in transferring technologies to developing countries.

a United Nations (1992)

---

[33] One advantage of traditional knowledge and technology, on the other hand, stems from the fact that sufficient human capital is probably already in place in developing countries.

guard against a "brain drain", can offer incentives to students. Mechanisms to retain and bring back trained labour include wage flexibility, repatriation grants, and incentives to start technology firms. Developed countries, for their part, should subsidize offshore training, conference attendance and, in some cases, temporary employment for graduates from developing countries. Grant proposals for research on environmentally sound technologies involving developing-country teams could also receive special consideration (Maskus, 2004). Capacity-building might also be pursued through cooperation agreements that increasingly accompany regional trade agreements among OECD countries. These would help developing countries conduct an assessment of the obstacles to their low-emissions energy development. Aid-for-trade programmes should also be tapped in this regard.

What is clearly required is a massive international effort (United Nations, Department of Economic and Social Affairs, 2009). Table V.1 presents various innovative mechanisms to promote technology development and transfer. Three closely related initiatives could plant the seeds of greater international collaboration in developing the skills and technologies needed to tackle climate change:

Table V.1
Innovative mechanisms to promote technology development and transfer

Mechanism	Rationale	Issues to consider
Publicly supported centres for technology development and transfer	Green revolution model of technology diffusion: makes technologies available to developing countries without intellectual property right protection	Suitable for mitigation or only for adaptation technologies
Technology funding mechanism to enable participation of developing countries in international R&D projects	Resultant intellectual property rights could be shared; patent buyouts could make privately owned technologies available to developing countries	Is there sufficient incentive for participation by developed-country private sector technology leaders?
Patent pools to streamline licensing of inventions needed to exploit a given technology	Developing-country licensees will not have to deal with multiple patent-holders	What are the incentives to patent-holders? Would government regulation be needed?
Global R&D alliance for research on key adaptation technologies	Model of research on neglected tropical diseases	Is such an approach suited to mitigation technologies?
Global clean technology venture capital fund	Fund located with a multilateral financing institution which will also have the rights to intellectual property	Will new technology ventures be viable commercially if they do not own intellectual property?
Eco-Patent Commons for environmentally sustainable technologies	Approach initiated by the private sector to make certain environmentally sound technologies available royalty-free on a "give-one, take-one" model	Voluntary, private incentives appear weak. What about those companies without a patent to contribute?
Blue Skies proposal of European Patent Office: differentiated patent system with climate change technologies based on a licensing of rights	Complex new technologies based on cumulative innovation processes need to be treated differently from, for example, pharmaceuticals	Appears to address concerns similar to those addressed by the patent pools proposal: more specifics needed on implications for technology access
More favourable tax treatment in developed countries for private sector R&D performed in developing countries	More proactive, technology-push approach by developed-country Governments	May face domestic political constraints
Technology prizes	Reward innovation without awarding intellectual property rights to innovators	Requires a well-specified research objective

Source: United Nations, Department of Economic and Social Affairs (2008).

- *A multilateral technology fund* to support an international programme on the diffusion of climate technology and to strengthen and coordinate regional and national RD&D efforts in developing countries. Such a fund could be housed in the secretariat of the United Nations Framework Convention on Climate Change and draw on the existing network of scholars and scientists within the Intergovernmental Panel on Climate Change (IPCC) in the design of its programmes. Financing such a programme can draw lessons from the experience with the Global Environment Facility (GEF) (see box V.4 and chapter VI). The steady decline in public RD&D in the energy sector is an indication of the urgency of establishing such a fund. A comprehensive programme would need to focus on the full range of technological challenges at the basic science, applied RD&D, demonstration, deployment and commercialization stages of developing cleaner technologies. However, coordinated funding for the development, demonstration and deployment of critical technologies such as carbon capture and sequestration and the next generation of biofuels, in which developing countries have a particular interest, would have to be high up in the agenda. Given the public nature of RD&D, it would be essential to ensure dedicated and predictable financing for such a fund, using the kinds of instruments discussed in the chapter VI. Such a fund could act as a focal point for the coordination of ongoing research in climate technologies at the international and national levels and among public, private and non-profit organizations, while ensuring open access to all available research in line with the urgency of the challenge.

- *A human skills transfer programme.* A scaled-up human capacity development effort could complement the fund and would consist of a temporary (perhaps only a virtual) movement of skilled unemployed/underemployed workers from developed countries (engineers, technicians, primary education teachers, experts in sustainable agriculture, and qualified blue- and white-collar workers) into developing countries to provide workforce and vocational "train the trainers"-type training. An innovative means of accomplishing this would be "reverse outsourcing", that is to say, programmes utilizing the Internet and other communications technologies, through which long-distance training services in critical areas would be provided by developed countries to developing ones. During a recession, many highly skilled technicians, teachers and professionals are laid off. Even if only 5 or 10 per cent of them participated in a technology transfer corps organized through the development cooperation agencies for periods ranging from six months to two years, significant skills and know-how transfer could be effected. This would be a win-win solution for developing countries requiring more help and for cash-constrained developed countries obliged, nonetheless, to pay unemployment insurance.

- *A public technology pool.* The results of fully funded public research on climate technologies should not be the basis of private patents: it should be made available at low or no cost to all countries. A technical secretariat would be needed to monitor, collect and disseminate such research, to act as a clearing house for existing publicly funded technologies and to actively promote access to those technologies, particularly for developing countries. Such a body could work alongside the Global Technology Fund to ensure the widest dissemination of future research sponsored by that Fund.

Box V.4

The Global Environment Facility

Technology transfer is seen as playing a critical role in the global response to the challenges of climate change. Indeed, promotion of and cooperation in the transfer of environmentally sound technologies derive from a commitment embodied in the United Nations Framework Convention on Climate Change. In order to pursue these goals, the Convention proposed the creation of a financial mechanism. The Global Environment Facility (GEF) serves as that mechanism for the Convention.

Over the past 17 years, the Global Environment Facility has been financing projects to promote the transfer of environmentally sound technologies under the guidance of the Conference of the Parties to the Convention. During this period, about $2.5 billion for climate change projects has been allocated, which leveraged approximately $15 billion in co-financing. Most financing is in the form of grants to developing countries and countries with economies in transition. Through its Small Grants Programme, the Facility has also made more than 10,000 small grants directly to non-governmental and community organizations.

Some examples of environmentally sound technologies supported by the Global Environment Facility are described below.

Energy-efficient lighting and appliances

The Global Environment Facility has built a portfolio promoting energy-efficient appliances and technologies in developing countries. GEF-supported interventions typically focus on instituting energy-efficiency standards and labels, consumer education, and testing and certification of appliances. In countries where there is substantial manufacturing capacity, the Facility has also supported enterprises in developing new energy-efficient appliance models and in acquiring technical information and knowledge from more advanced countries.

In Tunisia, for example, 10 out of 12 local appliance manufacturers are offering more energy-efficient models. In China, the GEF project to promote energy-efficient refrigerators adopted a two-pronged approach comprising technology push and market pull. Technology push is achieved through technical assistance to refrigerator and compressor manufacturers, technology upgrades, and designer training programmes, while market pull is achieved through the promulgation of energy-efficiency standards.

Since the mid-1990s, the Global Environment Facility has supported the dissemination of efficient lighting technologies in more than two dozen countries. The Facility has also launched a global efficient lighting initiative, approved by the GEF Council in 2007, to accelerate the phase-out of inefficient lighting through the United Nations Environment Programme (UNEP) and the United Nations Development Programme (UNDP); at the same time, support is being extended to more countries and programmes at the national level.

Industrial energy-efficiency technologies

The Global Environment Facility has funded more than 30 projects in the industrial sector to promote technology upgrading and the adoption and diffusion of energy-efficient technologies. Some projects focus on the development of market mechanisms such as energy service companies, the creation of dedicated financing instruments, and technical assistance to stimulate investments in new technologies. Other projects are designed to identify one or more subsectors where specific technologies can be promoted. The range of industries includes construction materials (brick, cement and glass), steel, coke-making, foundry, paper, ceramics, textiles, food and beverage, tea, rubber and wood. A number of projects also promote energy-efficient equipment such as boilers, motors and pumps, as well as cogeneration in the industrial sector. In some projects, the Facility has promoted South-South technology transfer; one such project has entailed the transfer of energy-efficient brick kiln technology from China to Bangladesh.

Box V.4 (cont'd)

High-efficiency boilers

The China Efficient Industrial Boilers project had received a $32.8 million grant from the Global Environment Facility to (a) upgrade existing boiler models by introducing advanced combustion systems and auxiliary equipment from developed countries; (b) adopt new high-efficiency boiler models by introducing modern manufacturing techniques and boiler designs; and (c) provide technical assistance and training for boiler producers and consumers. Completed in 2004, the project successfully supported international technology transfer of boiler technologies which benefited nine boiler manufacturers and nine boiler auxiliary equipment makers. With GEF support, the manufacturers in China acquired advanced efficient boiler technologies, built prototypes, and began commercial production. Through technical assistance, the project also led to the revision and formulation of national and sector standards, while strengthening the technical capacity of China's boiler sector.

Solar water heaters

Although solar water heater technology is sometimes perceived to be simple, such a perception can in fact be misleading. The quality of the fittings, of the solar collectors and of the installation has substantial impact on satisfactory operation. Accordingly, inexpensive materials, poor workmanship and shoddy installation have often resulted in non-functional units and abandonment of installations. GEF experience has shown that knowledgeable staff and the observance of high standards are critical to the successful dissemination of this technology.

In Morocco, for example, early solar water heaters had tended to be of low quality. As a result, they fell into disuse and the market languished. Through a Global Environment Facility project, the older non-functioning installations were repaired, new higher-quality standards were adopted, and technicians and staff were trained to ensure that future installations would be of satisfactory quality. In addition, to encourage production and sale of the higher-quality units, a subsidy was offered to early adopters of water heaters who met the new standard. These initiatives revived the market, which is now growing rapidly, along with the industry as a whole.

Waste to energy

A number of projects have supported utilization of methane from municipal waste, in the form of either solid wastes in landfills or liquid biological wastes. Many of these projects have qualified for Global Environment Facility support as both renewable energy projects and short-term response measures because of their cost-effectiveness. The Facility played a role in helping increase the uptake of these technologies; now its support is no longer needed, as the projects are eligible for funding and highly profitable when implemented under the Clean Development Mechanism.

The India biomethanation project, whose implementation had been proposed in the early 1990s, was designed to exploit India's endogenous capacity to adapt and replicate biogas technology for industrial wastes. A pre-existing challenge had arisen from the fact that biological waste from agroprocessing and related industries deposited substantial quantities of methane and other pollutants into nearby waters. The intent of the project was to produce the methane in a controlled environment, and then capture and use it to produce energy.

Concentrating solar power

The Global Environment Facility, together with India, Mexico, Morocco and Egypt, developed a portfolio of four concentrating solar power demonstration plants. The projects built (typically 30 megawatt) solar fields as part of hybrid gas-turbine plants. Successful hybridization of the gas-turbine and solar power plants would enable the projects to dispatch power at will, thereby making them more economically attractive.

Conclusion

A rapid pace of investment will not be sufficient to meet the climate challenge unless it is accompanied by a technological transformation, with increased capacity to produce, operate and deploy climate-friendly technologies. However, for many developing countries, the cost of accessing those technologies could prove prohibitive. Although developed countries have committed themselves to leading the change towards cleaner technologies and ensuring that developing countries are not left behind, neither commitment has been fulfilled. Innovative transfer of both technologies and know-how will be required to meet climate change objectives in the context of both mitigation and adaptation.

This chapter has identified possible obstacles to the transfer of technology that could arise internationally with respect to intellectual property rights, corporate behaviour and trading rules. To date, these factors have not proved prohibitive. However, they are likely to take on greater significance if developing countries embark on a big push towards a low-emissions, high-growth development pathway. Anticipating those obstacles and devising ways around them constitute an urgent task of the international community. This would require consensus, since it might entail the amendment of World Trade Organization rules and special climate waivers based on the urgency of the rapidly evolving climate situation. It will also require careful attention to the implications of the World Trade Organization principles of non-discrimination and United Nations Framework Convention on Climate Change principles, especially that of common and differentiated responsibilities and capabilities. This has to be based on ability and historical obligations. Since any post-2012 agreement is likely to retain these principles, the challenge will be to ensure the coherence and compatibility of their applications.

Chapter VI
Financing the development response to climate change

Introduction

There is no way round the need for large-scale investments to meet the climate challenge, in both developed and developing countries. Developed countries have begun to make the required adjustments focusing, in particular, on energy efficiency. However, and despite their expressions of concern and commitment, the pace has been slow. In 2008 and 2009, the inclusion of green investments in stimulus packages in response to the global financial crisis has raised expectations that a more sustained effort is now under way in those countries. Still, their policymakers need to think on a much larger scale when it comes to emission cuts.

Developing countries can be expected to follow the lead of the developed countries only if the latter's response is consistent with long-standing growth and development objectives. The present *Survey* has suggested that the key to its being so lies in the adoption of an investment-led and integrated approach. In particular, large-scale investments will need to be front-loaded to ensure the achievement of a "big push" into the generation of low-emissions energy sources and the mitigation of and adaptation to climatic threats and shocks. These investments, however, will involve significant initial costs and carry a high degree of uncertainty.

The economic debate within the global discussion of climate policy has been dominated by assessments of market-based mechanisms such as cap and trade and carbon taxation, both aiming at changing price incentives so that investments in energy efficiency and renewables become more attractive. Private investment will, of course, have a predominant role in any low-emissions economic future and there is little doubt that establishing a realistic price for carbon will have to be part of any policy agenda. The question, however, is whether such mechanisms can induce the required shifts in production and consumption patterns and mobilize the large-scale investments needed to avert the catastrophic risk that climate change poses, as well as ensure that the adjustments take place in a fair and orderly manner. This seems doubtful. It is generally recognized that price mechanisms are an unreliable guide in cases where the investments to be undertaken are on a very large scale and where returns are not immediately visible, are unpredictable and are dependent on a series of complementary investment efforts and policy initiatives (DeLong, 2005). This is all the more true today, where the marriage of the climate and development challenges is taking place against the backdrop of systemic financial market failure and where carbon markets are exhibiting a degree of price volatility which is not compatible with long-term investment planning (Nell, Semmler and Rezai, 2009).

While market mechanisms should be assigned their role in a more comprehensive package of measures, the kind of investment path to be followed to meet the climate challenge will require heavy reliance on regulation and large-scale public investments in order for the necessary transformative shift to take place.

Historically, public investment, financed both by tax revenues and by long-term borrowing, has played a transformative role in shaping development pathways,

Large-scale investments will need to be front-loaded

The kind of investment path to be followed to meet the climate challenge will require heavy reliance on regulation and large-scale public investments in order for the necessary transformative shift to take place including in today's most advanced economies (Rohatyn, 2009). In many cases, external financial support has been critical. Achievement of the transition to a low-emissions, high-growth path in developing countries will also require massive public investment in most cases, funded to a large extent through external resources, particularly in the early stages. Together with achievement of non-marginal changes in the cost of carbon emissions, the aim of such investments will be to crowd in profitable investment opportunities for the private sector along the new development pathway.

Given the great uncertainties regarding the precise costs and the effectiveness of the types of measures mentioned so far, it is not easy to define an appropriate financing framework for climate change. Depending on what target is used for stabilizing green-house gas (GHG) concentrations and what assumptions are made about the effectiveness of the measures, estimates of the annual cost of mitigation range from as little as 0.2 per cent to as much as 2 per cent of world gross product (WGP) by 2030. In all cases, however, doing nothing would lead to much higher economic losses. Adaptation costs are particularly uncertain, with upper-bound estimates for additional annual investments set at about $170 billion by 2030. On this order of magnitude, addressing climate change seems quite affordable. However, most of these estimates seem to understate the scale of adjustments that will need to be taken. They appear to have taken into account neither the larger global macroeconomic setting in which it is presumed that a new investment path will take shape and, in particular, the constraints many developing countries face in raising investment levels, nor whether those investments have the potential to trigger a high-growth pathway along which countries can meet long-standing development goals.

The key issues with regard to finding the right financing framework are, first, what measures will be most effective in both mobilizing the required amount of resources and steering investments in the desired direction; and second, how the costs should be distributed across nations and population groups. The first issue may be framed along the lines suggested by figure VI.1, which depicts various mechanisms for covering the estimated costs of the climate challenge and their evolution over time. Figure VI.I.A, derived from a World Bank study (World Bank, 2009), depicts a rapidly growing role, albeit tentative for market-based mechanisms, complemented by a more measured increase in multilateral funding. Together, market-based mechanisms and multilateral funding would quickly establish the right climate for private investment. Based on the analysis in the previous chapters, this *Survey* would suggest a somewhat different structure. As depicted in figure VI.1.B, the required reductions in greenhouse gas emissions will require large-scale upfront investments to generate a non-marginal push in the desired direction, led by public investments and strong shifts in incentives to crowd in private investments.

The present chapter begins by assessing the likely scale of resources needed to achieve low-emissions, high-growth pathways, and to make vulnerable countries and communities more resilient with respect to climate change and shocks. It then considers how those resources could be mobilized and, in particular, both the advantages and the limitations of cap-and-trade mechanisms and carbon taxes as financing vehicles in the initial stages of shifting to the new pathway. A wide mix of financial mechanisms will likely be required, including through domestic resource mobilization. The chapter concludes with a consideration of the elements of an alternative global investment regime, initially dependent on significant public sector involvement and a prominent role for a multilateral financing mechanism.

The key issues with regard to finding the right financing framework are, first, what measures will be most effective in both mobilizing the required amount of resources and steering investments in the desired direction; and second, how the costs should be distributed

Figure VI.1
Strategic investment and financing mechanisms for developing countries

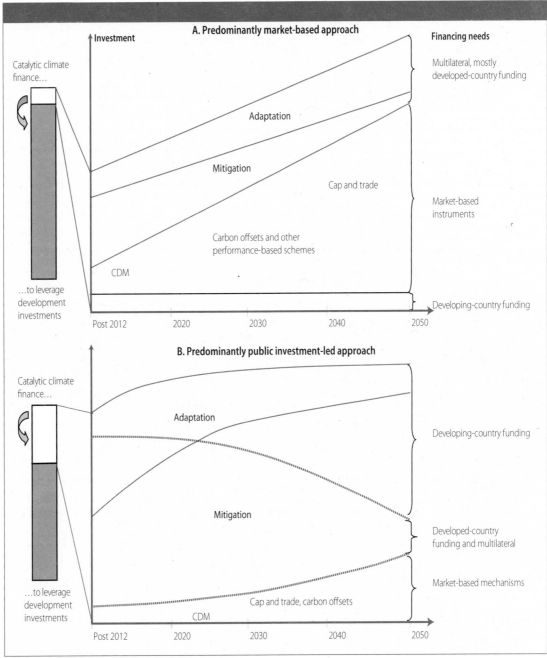

Sources: World Bank (2009), for figure VI.1A; and United Nations, Department of Economic and Social Affairs, for figure VI.1B.

Estimating financing requirements

The parties to the United Nations Framework Convention on Climate Change[1] agreed (article 4.3) that developed countries would have to provide financial resources to developing countries to meet "agreed full incremental costs" of implementing mitigation and adaptation activities as well as related activities encompassing, inter alia, climate research, training and management of sinks. These, it should be noted, are not voluntary commitments but treaty obligations. However, estimates of those global costs vary widely depending upon the assumptions made about the required emissions target, and the complex feedback linkages between economic and climatic conditions, among other factors (see chap. I). What is certain is that the longer the response to climate change is delayed, the more damaging will be the threats to lives and livelihoods, and the greater will be the resources required to respond to those threats. In this respect, Stern (2009, p. 12) correctly argues that the "ratchet effect" linked to the growing stock of greenhouse gases in the atmosphere, coupled with long investment lifetimes, implies that "decisions, plans and incentive structures we make and create in the coming months and years will have a profound effect on the future of the planet" (see also chap. II). It is also important to recognize that there will not be a single mix of decisions, plans and incentives across all countries and, in particular, there will likely be some sharp differences between developed and developing economies, given the higher mitigation and adaptation costs facing the latter.

Mitigation costs

Figure VI.2 and table VI.1 present some recent estimates of mitigation costs. Given the uncertainties and unknowns in these costing exercises, it is not surprising to find the range varying from as little as 0.2 to about 2 per cent of WGP, or between $180 billion and $1.2 trillion per annum (by 2030). The range of estimates depends on methodologies used as well as on whether the target of stabilization of greenhouse gas concentrations is set at 450 parts per million (ppm) or 550 ppm. In all cases, the costs are considerably higher under a business-as-usual scenario, in which case permanent losses of projected WGP could be as high as 20 percent.

United Nations, United Nations Framework Convention on Climate Change (2008, table 4) provides a near lower-bound estimate of $200 billion-$210 billion in additional investment and financial flows globally in 2030 for mitigation efforts that cut CO_2 emissions by 25 per cent below 2000 levels by 2030. The McKinsey study estimates that the figure could rise to as high as $800 billion for the 450 ppm target, more than half of which would be in developing countries.[2] Stern's latest estimate calls for an even bigger push, as he puts the additional cost at between $600 billion and $1.2 trillion depending on whether the target is, respectively, 550 ppm or 450 ppm (figure VI.2 and Stern 2009).

More than half of the incremental costs of greenhouse gas abatement are expected to fall on developing countries, whose energy investments over the coming decades are projected to grow much faster than those of developed countries (see chap. II). Among the incremental costs are those associated with investments in: renewable energy, which at

---

1   United Nations, *Treaty Series*, vol. 1771, No. 30822.

2   However, operating and maintenance costs are not included in these figures. Actual costs for mitigation efforts might therefore be even higher. The International Energy Agency (2008b) has, for example, estimated that owing to higher capital costs for energy supply facilities, total additional investment needed in 2030 to reduce energy-related CO_2 emissions alone would be about 170 per cent higher than in earlier estimates.

Figure VI.2

Range of estimates of annual additional cost of mitigation strategies, 550 ppm and 450 ppm scenarios, world and developing countries

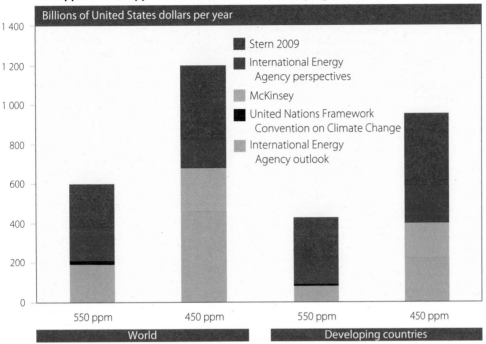

Sources: Stern (2009); International Energy Agency (2008a and b); United Nations, United Nations Framework Convention on Climate Change (2008); and McKinsey & Company (2009).

current prices remains a more costly source of electricity than coal or other fossil-fuel alternatives; more efficient and other lower-emitting coal-based power plants, including integrated gasification combined cycles and supercritical coal power plants; carbon capture and storage; and more energy-efficient boilers, furnaces and other industrial equipment. However, from a development perspective, it is very difficult to separate these incremental investments from the bigger investment challenge of meeting growing energy demand in developing countries, as well as interrelated demands on the transportation system and in urban expansion, improved irrigation and water management to strengthen the productivity of the rural economy, and so forth.

Adaptation costs

Estimates of adaptation costs have focused on the additional amount of investment needed to reduce the impact of anticipated future damages caused by weather events, in terms mainly of measures to increase resilience and reduce the impact of disasters. In addition, adaptation costs may also include coping and relief expenditures when damages actually occur. However, because these costs depend on the probability and severity of climatic threats, whose impact is closely linked to other vulnerabilities, it can be difficult to determine where traditional development expenditures end and new adaptation expenditures begin (see chap. IV; McGray and others, 2007; and Bapna and McGray, 2009).

Estimating the costs of adaptation with precision is even more difficult, not only because adaptation measures will be widespread and heterogeneous, but also because these measures need to be embedded in broader development strategies, as discussed in chapter III. The United Nations Framework Convention on Climate Change secretariat estimates that additional annual investment and financial flows needed worldwide would be in the

Table VI.1
Range of estimates of global mitigation costs according to various studies

Study	Estimate (percentage of WGP)	Estimate (US dollars)	Main characteristics
Intergovernmental Panel on Climate Change (2007d)	0.2-0.6 per cent (median of WGP reduction); 0.6-3 per cent (minimum and maximum estimate of WGP reduction)		• Estimates the global macroeconomic cost n 2030 for least-cost trajectories towards given long-term stabilization levels • Lower stabilization levels imply higher GDP reductions
Stern (2006 and 2009)	Annual investment costs: 1 per cent of WGP, revised upwards to 2 per cent; costs of inaction: 5-20 per cent of WGP reduction by 2050	• 500 ppm: 1,200 billion/year • 500 ppm: 600 billion/year	• Compares investment costs of mitigation with the cost of inaction in order to assess the cost-benefit of acting against climate change • Aggregates several previous studies in a model to estimate the costs; does not provide new estimates • Methodology and model assumptions are the target of criticisms
Vattenfall (2007)	0.6-1.4 per cent of WGP by 2030		• More accurate methodology for assessing the cost-benefit of a group of policies and interventions to mitigate climate change
McKinsey (2009)	Annual investment costs: 1.3 per cent of forecasted WGP in 2030	• 450 ppm: 680 billion/year	• Disaggregates the abatement potential and costs by economic sector and geographical region • Presents accurate sensitivity analysis with respect to different core parameters • Presents different abatement opportunities and assesses the potential contribution of each one

Sources: United Nations Development Programme (2007a); United Nations, United Nations Framework Convention on Climate Change (2008); Intergovernmental Panel on Climate Change (2007d); Stern (2006); Vattenfall (2007); and McKinsey & Company (2009).

order of $49 billion-$171 billion by 2030 (see table VI.2). Its adaptation scenario covers five sectors, with the largest element of uncertainty in this estimate lying in the cost of adapting infrastructure, which may range between $8 billion and $130 billion. Other sources have produced similar estimates for adaptation. *Human Development Report 2007/2008* (United Nations Development Programme, 2007a) estimates that annual adaptation investment needs would reach $86 billion by 2015, while recent calculations of the World Bank (2009) put annual adaptation costs in the range of $10 billion-$40 billion by 2030.

Table VI.2.
Additional investment and financial flows needed for adaptation in 2030, by sector

Sector	Areas/adaptation measures considered	Global cost (billions of 2005 United States dollars)	Proportion needed in developing countries (percentage)
Agriculture, forestry and fisheries	Production and processing, research and development, extension activities	14	50
Water supply	Water supply infrastructure	11	80
Human health	Treating increased cases of diarrhoeal disease, malnutrition and malaria	5	100
Coastal zones	Beach nourishment and dykes	11	45
Infrastructure	New infrastructure	8–130	25
Total		**49–171**	**34–57**

Source: United Nations, United Nations Framework Convention on Climate Change (2008, table 5).

The financing challenge

The estimated additional investments needed for adaptation and mitigation to address climate change are large in absolute terms. Still, it is often pointed out that these are only a small fraction of world output (in the order of 1 and 2 per cent of WGP) and of estimated total global investment (2.5-5.0 per cent) in 2030. There is, however, a growing recognition that many of these investments need to be front-loaded, both to effectuate the urgent shift to a low-emissions economy and to minimize the damage from unavoidable changes in the climate. Front-loading implies much more pressure on the financial system in mobilizing the required resources. Moreover, as suggested in earlier chapters, these additional investments in adaptation and mitigation are often closely interrelated and will make sense only in combination with complementary investments designed to meet wider development objectives, such as developing infrastructure, raising agricultural productivity and diversifying economic activity.

Investments in adaptation and mitigation are often closely interrelated

Despite the recent proliferation of climate-related funds, the amount currently promised and expected to be available for meeting the climate challenge in the near term, from bilateral and multilateral sources, is woefully inadequate. Current dedicated climate resources have been estimated at about $21 billion and are very heavily skewed towards mitigation (table VI.3). The total amount of climate financing will be a large multiple of that figure, and on some estimates could be 9-10 times the 2008 levels of official development assistance (ODA).

The amount available for meeting the climate challenge, from bilateral and multilateral sources, is woefully inadequate

The difficulty involved in reaching even those levels of ODA suggests that global financing for climate change will require a much more determined effort on the part of advanced countries to provide bold leadership on the climate issue and bolster international cooperation. But it will also require an effort on the part of developing countries to mobilize a larger share of their resources for cleaner investments along a new, sustainable growth path.

Table VI.3.
Bilateral and multilateral financing mechanisms for mitigation and adaptation in developing countries

Name	Total (millions of United States dollars: exchange rates of November 2008)	Use	Details
Under the United Nations Framework Convention on Climate Change			
GEF-4[a]	1 030	M	Time frame: 2006-2010; $352 million already committed as of December 2008
Sustainable Forest Management	154	M	Special programme under GEF-4 for land use, land-use change and forestry
Strategic Priority on Adaptation (SPA)	50	A	Pilot programme on adaptation of the GEF Trust Fund; all resources have been allocated
Special Climate Change Fund (SCCF Adaptation)	90	A	Include pledges as of December 2008; $68 million has been allocated to 15 projects as of November 2008; operated by GEF
Least Developed Countries' Fund	172	A	Include pledges as of December 2008; $91.8 million has been received as of November 2008; operated by GEF
Adaptation Fund	400-1 500	A	Time frame: 2008-2012; as of October 2008, $91.3 million was available (4 million certified emission reductions (CERs) at €17.5 per CER)
Bilateral			
Cool Earth Partnership (Japan)	10 000	A, M	Provides grants and loans; time frame: 2008-2012; up to $2 billion to improve access to clean energy, and US$ 8 billion for preferential interest rate loans for mitigation projects
Climate and Forest Initiative (CFI) (Norway)	2 250	M	Provides grants; time frame: 2008-2012; pledged US$ 102 million to the Amazon Fund
International Window of the Environmental Transformation Fund (ETF-IW) (United Kingdom)	1 182	A, M	Provides grants and loans; time frame: 2008-2010; most of the funds will be allocated trough the World Bank Climate Investment Funds
Amazon Fund (Brazil)	1 000	M	So far, only Norway has pledged, in the amount of US$ 102; donations to be administered by the National Development Bank of Brazil
International Climate Initiative (ICI) (Germany)	764	A, M	Provides grants; funding for the initiative will be generated from auctioning 10 per cent of its allowances from the Emission Trading Scheme of the European Union (EU ETS); it has earmarked up to €120 million for the next five years
International Forest Carbon Initiative (IFCI) (Australia)	129	M	Provides grants; time frame 2007-2011; as of November 2008, US$ 50 million was allocated
United Nations Development Programme-Spain MDG Achievement Fund - Environment and Climate Change thematic window	90	A, M	Provides grants; time frame: 2007-2010; Spain has pledged €528 to the Fund and US$ 90 million has been allocated for the Environment and Climate Change thematic window
Global Climate Change Alliance (GCCA) (European Commission)	76	A, M	Provides grants; time frame: 2007-2011; targets most vulnerable countries (least developed countries and small islands)

Table VI.3 (cont'd)			
Name	Total (millions of United States dollars: exchange rates of November 2008)	Use	Details
Multilateral			
Forest Carbon Partnership Facility (World Bank)	300	M	Provides grants and loans; time frame 2008-2020
Global Facility for Disaster Reduction and Recovery (GFDRR)	84	A	Provides grants; time frame 2007-2010; targets high-risk low- and middle-income countries to mainstream disaster reduction in development strategies
United Nations Collaborative Programme on Reducing Emissions from Deforestation and Forest Degradation in Developing Countries (UN-REDD)	35	M	Provides grants; administered by the UNDP; Norway, through its Climate and Forest Initiative, is the first donor, with US$ 12 million
Climate Investment Funds:	6 340		Time frame: 2009-2012; administered by the World Bank
• Clean Technology Fund	4 334	M	Provides grants and loans; funded by the United States, to be administered by the World Bank ($2 billion); the United Kingdom and Japan have pledged the additional resources
• Strategic Climate Fund	2 006	A, M	Provides grants and loans, including the Forest Investment Programme ($58 million) and the Scaling up Renewable Energy in Low Income Countries Programme ($70 million), for mitigation; and the Pilot Programme for Climate Resilience ($240 million), for adaptation
Sustainable Energy and Climate Change Initiative (SECCI)	29	A, M	Provides grants and loans; the fund backs major investments in the development of biofuels, renewable energy, energy efficiency, and a wide range of sustainable energy options

Sources: Adapted and updated from Porter and others (2008); and United Nations, United Nations Framework Convention on Climate Change (2008).
Abbreviations: A, Adaptation; M, Mitigation.
a   Fourth replenishment of the Global Environment Facility.

The purpose of a sustained injection of external financing in amounts large enough to give a big push onto a low-emissions development path is to simultaneously accelerate and sustain growth in developing countries at levels higher than in the past. As discussed in earlier chapters, this initial big push from official sources of finance, in combination with various policy mixes, including price incentives, regulation and targeted industrial policies, would begin to raise domestic sources of finance for investment in both the public and the private sectors. The evolving mix of public and private investment will no doubt vary among countries, but for many developing countries, and possibly for some developed countries, public investment will have to take the lead, along with stronger regulations, before large-scale private investment begins to materialize.

A big push from official sources of finance would begin to raise domestic sources of finance for investment in both the public and private sectors

Crowding in private sector resources

A clear-cut objective for policymakers addressing the climate challenge is to reveal the hidden costs in choosing high-emissions over low-emissions technology. In the case of adaptation, incentives will likely involve the sharing of costs among consumers, private operators and Governments (Organization for Economic Cooperation and Development, 2008, p. 124).

Insurance markets offer a possible option and various innovative instruments have been introduced in recent years. However, these instruments still operate on a very limited scale, even in more advanced countries, and tend to be a particularly expensive option in developing countries where coverage is very limited (Barnett and Mahul, 2007; United Nations, 2008).

Voluntary standards do not bite unless accompanied by regulation

Some companies have started to implement voluntary emission caps and a growing number of consumers are adjusting their consumption patterns in order to lower footprint levels. Absent more aggressive government intervention, it is unlikely that these trends will be quantitatively sufficient and timely enough to make a significant impact on greenhouse gas emissions. Voluntary emissions standards may hurt relative competitiveness and increase production costs in the short term, reducing incentives to adopt more stringent standards. The experience of the State of California is perhaps the exception to the rule that voluntary standards will not bite. California's emission standards and reduction targets, obtained by negotiating with private companies, have raised awareness among consumers and producers: average per capita consumption of energy in California is 50 per cent of the United States average. In cooperation with 20 other States, California has also established targets for the use of alternative energy. The California Renewables Portfolio Standard requires the use of 20 per cent renewable energy by 2010. However, these voluntary efforts are in the context of a State with a strong regulatory record on environmental standards.

The present section reviews a range of mechanisms considered thus far that fall broadly in the category of market-based measures, as their main focus is on changing the price of carbon to draw resource allocation away from emission-intensive forms of energy. Several of these mechanisms are also expected to mobilize resources necessary for financing other investments in greater energy efficiency and use of renewable energy, including related public investments.

Market-based incentives for scaling up investment in developing countries

Mitigating climate change using prices is focused on creating economic incentives for consumers and producers to drive greenhouse gas emission reductions

Much of the economic policy debate on climate change has been dominated by the search for market-based solutions to problems of acknowledged market failure. Mitigating climate change using prices is focused on creating economic incentives for consumers and producers to drive greenhouse gas emission reductions, by internalizing externalities so that agents account and pay for their level of emissions, and to do so as efficiently as possible, assuming that all investment opportunities for cutting emissions that cost less than the established price for carbon will be seized.

There are two main groups of instruments for achieving this aim: (a) establishing a price of greenhouse gas emissions, using capital markets to value specific activities and, for adaptation purposes, to price risks through insurance premiums; and (b) imposing taxes, fees and levies on inputs, final products or activities/services. These instruments will no doubt have a role to play in any mix of policy initiatives created to meet the climate challenge. The real question is whether they can acquire the kind of global reach that appears to be necessary if they are to play a lead role in meeting that challenge.

Cap and trade

Pricing greenhouse gas emissions as a pillar of mitigation policy emerged in the early 1990s with the United Nations Framework Convention on Climate Change and took on greater prominence with the legally binding targets to reduce greenhouse emissions set by the Kyoto Protocol to the United Nations Framework Convention on Climate Change.[3] The Protocol (adopted by the Conference of the Parties to the Convention in December 1997) set differentiated targets for industrialized countries, while setting up an emissions trading scheme to meet those targets. A financing mechanism for projects in developing countries, the Clean Development Mechanism (CDM), was launched at the same time.

These mechanisms are essentially designed around a cap-and-trade programme, where Governments set an overall emissions cap and then issue tradable permits to firms which allow them to emit a specified quantity of greenhouse gases. Those that can reduce their emissions more cheaply can sell their allowances. Doing so is expected to promote competition, thereby reducing long-term costs. While the current volume of carbon trading at a little over $100 billion is still quite small, compared, for instance, with that on financial derivatives markets, according to some it could become the "world's biggest commodity market" and prospectively the world's biggest market overall within a decade (Lohmann, 2008). The trading of emission certificates as financial assets and speculative investments can generate a high volatility in the price of carbon. A recent assessment of the European Union (EU) experience with emissions trading found that (between September 2005 and March 2008) the price of carbon was more volatile than stock market indices, with a standard deviation on the return on the emissions price 10 times higher than the return on equity (Nell, Semmler and Rezai, 2009). Volume instability and price volatility may not provide adequate incentives for long-term investment decisions as a response to climate change on the part of market participants.

On some counts, trading is necessary to advance the serious regulation needed to establish a price for carbon. It is also recognized that the cap-and-trade scheme cannot begin on a global scale, as the trading of permits will initially be confined to developed countries, with developing countries pulled in indirectly through the Clean Development Mechanism by the funding of emissions-reducing projects prior to their participation.

Between 2004 and 2007, the Clean Development Mechanism implemented 700 projects with a total value of $6 billion for developing countries, albeit with almost 4 out of 5 projects concentrated in just four countries: Brazil, China, India and Mexico (United Nations, United Nations Framework Convention on Climate Change, 2007b, and chap. V). The United Nations Framework Convention on Climate Change secretariat, (United Nations, United Nations Framework Convention on Climate Change, 2008) has estimated that the mitigation potential in 2020 in developing countries will be approximately 7 gigatons of CO_2 equivalent (Gt CO_2e) and that most of the potential projects will be available at a cost of less than $25 per ton of CO_2e. Total demand for credits for certified emission reductions (CERs) in 2020 is estimated at between 0.5 and 1.7 Gt CO_2e, which could represent $10 billion-$34 billion in additional investments in developing countries (New Carbon Finance, 2008; IDE-ACarbon, 2008; Point Carbon, 2008). Moreover, if permits for developed countries are auctioned, this will provide additional financing for mitigation efforts in developing countries.

However, there are serious limitations to the scaling up of this mechanism to generate in a timely manner the required resources for developing countries (Griffith-Jones and others, 2009). The need for effective regulation and monitoring of innovative financial instruments may raise administrative costs and act to deter some, particularly developing, countries. Significantly, the largest carbon market, the Emission Trading Scheme (EU ETS) of the EU, was created by government regulation. Significant investments in training and education are also likely to be required. The success of the sulphur trading scheme in the United States of America certainly appears to have depended on these supportive conditions being in place (see box VI.1).

---

3   United Nations, *Treaty Series*, vol. 2303, No. 30822.

Box VI.1

Sulphur trading and why it worked

Market mechanisms do not work in a vacuum: they are shaped by many factors. The United States system of sulphur emissions trading, the inspiration for many cap-and-trade proposals, is often credited with having triggered a dramatic reduction in the costs of pollution control. The Clean Air Act Amendments of 1990 had established the system, setting a cap on sulphur emissions at about half of the 1980 emissions and distributing allowances to businesses, roughly in proportion to past emissions. All large stationary sources of sulphur emissions, primarily coal-burning power plants, were included. The trading system was phased in from 1995 to 2000, with costs of controlling sulphur far below the levels that had been anticipated in advance.

However, this result cannot be attributed to trading alone: the low cost made itself apparent quite early, at a time when the volume of emissions trading was quite small. Several other events also played important parts in driving down the costs. Just before trading began, a sharp reduction in railroad freight rates made it affordable to bring low-sulphur coal from Wyoming, replacing high-sulphur coal from the closer Appalachian coalfields, to Midwestern power plants. Some State regulations required even greater sulphur reduction than that stipulated by the national law, so it took no extra effort for power plants in those States to comply with the new national standard. At the same time, prices were declining for scrubbers, the pollution control devices that remove sulphur emissions. In this context, the emissions trading system may have made some contribution to lowering costs, but it operated on a field tilted in its favour. Without all the helpful coincidences, sulphur emissions trading would have looked much less successful.

If the United States sulphur emissions trading experience is the model for the carbon market mechanism, then the most important question about market incentives may be, What other initiatives are needed to complement the market and again tilt the field in favour of success? It is not hard to identify the areas—energy efficiency, and low-carbon and no-carbon energy sources—where investment in research and development are needed. This is not just a matter of costs, but also of opportunities—to create new industries and jobs and to launch a promising new path of technological development.

Source: Ackerman (2009).

While in theory carbon trading sets an absolute limit on a pollutant, the Kyoto Protocol permits developed countries to substitute reductions in their own greenhouse gas emissions by financing projects that reduce emissions in other countries.

From a development perspective, the danger of cap and trade is that it allows richer countries to continue their emitting according to unchanged patterns of consumption and production. This approach arguably takes the attention of these countries away from the more urgent efforts of tackling climate mitigation at home, even as it closes developing countries off from relatively cheap options of future emissions reductions (Banuri and Opschoor, 2007). In this respect, it is important to recognize that the cap-and-trade system has been designed to conform to the policy experience, institutional capacity and economic conditions of rich countries. By default, this provides significant advantages to them, as the essential baseline is the current emissions of the high-emitting countries.

International negotiations are likely to address some of the weaknesses of cap and trade as an approach to climate financing and will probably establish targets by sectors with standardized benchmarks (see, for example, the Harvard Project on International Climate Agreements (2008)). However, even though financial flows and participation levels have grown since their inception, emissions trading and the Clean Development Mechanism have not been particularly effective in encouraging a transition away from fossil energy. To date, the EU scheme has not been effective in reducing emissions among the main traders (Capoor and Ambrosi, 2008; WWF, 2007). Moreover, advocates of cap and trade tend to ignore the long history of successful State regulation of environmental issues

The cap-and-trade system has been designed to conform to the policy experience, institutional capacity and economic conditions of rich countries

Emissions trading and the Clean Development Mechanism have not been particularly effective in encouraging a transition away from fossil energy

which unfolded in the absence of trading schemes, including contemporary successes in conventional pollution regulation (Lohmann, 2006).

Perhaps the more sensible, forward-looking view is to recognize that carbon markets will continue to expand but that the pace and scale will not be sufficient to help developing countries break the financial constraint on proceeding along a low-emissions development pathway.

Carbon taxes

By increasing the cost of emissions to private parties in a more predictable manner than cap and trade, carbon taxes provide the opportunity to both raise public revenues and mitigate climate damage by increasing the cost of emissions to private parties. Their possible advantage lies in the more predictable price impact and the ease of design and administration. On the other hand, they can provoke political resistance.[4] In mature economies, properly designed carbon taxes could play an important role. In developing countries, their role is likely to be more limited. Hence, proposals by, for example, the International Monetary Fund (IMF) (2008b), for a global tax on carbon as the best means of mitigating climate externalities need to be treated with caution.

Estimates by the United Nations Development Programme (2007a) put the potential revenue at $265 billion if a $20 tax per ton of CO_2 is charged in countries members of the Organization for Economic Cooperation and Development (OECD) at current emission levels. Many OECD countries already have carbon taxes aimed mainly at financing their domestic budgets (Organization for Economic Cooperation and Development, 1997), rather than at financing low-emissions development or other public goods. EU also applies differential taxes on energy to products, such as natural gas compared with diesel or petrol, when they are used as motor or heating fuel. It is worth noting that, while these taxes appear to have contributed to energy efficiency, they have hardly been sufficient to counter the threat of warming temperatures.

While carbon taxes appear to have contributed to energy efficiency, they have hardly been sufficient to counter the threat of warming temperatures

Other schemes have been proposed to specifically finance climate change activities. A proposal similar to France's solidarity tax, which is intended to finance access to HIV/AIDS treatment in low-income countries, maintains that a $7 levy per passenger on international flights could result in $14 billion per year (United Nations Development Programme, 2007a; UNITAID, 2007). Because air fuel is often tax-exempt, such a levy actually reduces the implicit subsidy for air travel relative to other modes of transportation. Reducing subsidies to fossil fuels could help lower emissions and provide incentives for the transition towards a low-emissions economy. Subsidies to oil fuels—the difference between the end-user price and the price in a competitive market—have been estimated at $300 billion per year or 0.7 per cent of WGP (United Nations Environment Programme, International Labour Organization, and others, 2008). But, particularly in developing countries, raising the price of essential goods (energy as well as food and water) could render them unaffordable by lower income groups. Not only would this be regressive, it would also be socially unacceptable and environmentally unpredictable.

A related mechanism entails imposing fees and levies for activities/services whose benefits are not adequately captured by market prices. Owing to their specificity, ecosystem services cannot be traded as easily as liquid financial assets. As an alternative, several methodologies have been created to assess market value of these services and charge

---

4   On the political resistance to both cap-and-trade and carbon tax proposals in the United States, see John M. Broder "From a theory to a consensus on emissions", *The New York Times*, 16 May 2009.

the potential beneficiaries, using a "pay as you use the service" approach involving using shadow prices (Costanza and others, 1997). The idea of preserving ecosystems through the use of the services they provide is at the core of the strategies to reduce emissions from deforestation (see box VI.2).

Box VI.2

Financing forests and the reduction of emissions from deforestation and forest degradation (REDD)

In addition to providing multiple services and goods, forests can play a key role in tackling climate change. Forestry, as defined by the Intergovernmental Panel on Climate Change, accounts for about 17.4 per cent of global greenhouse gas emissions, and is therefore the third largest source of anthropogenic greenhouse gas emissions after energy supply and industrial activity. Loss of tropical forest results annually in emissions that are comparable to the total annual CO_2 emissions from the United States of America or China. Emissions from deforestation alone could increase atmospheric carbon stock by about 30 parts per million (ppm) by 2100. In order to stabilize the current CO_2e level of 433 ppm at a targeted 445-490 ppm, forests will need to form a central part of any global climate change deal.

The Stern Review, among other studies, considers curbing deforestation a highly cost-effective and relatively quick way of reducing greenhouse gas emissions. The resources required to halve emissions from the forest sector by 2030 could lie between $17 billion and $33 billion per year if forests are included in global carbon trading. If the international community does nothing to bring deforestation to a halt, the global economic cost of climate change caused by the degradation and losses of forests could reach $1 trillion per year by 2100. This is additional to the cost of the impact of industrial emissions.

At present, only a very small share of the existing investment in the forest sector is allocated to addressing climate change and less than 25 per cent of that share is invested in developing countries and economies in transition. Fortunately, the importance of limiting deforestation and forest degradation has been recognized by climate change negotiators, as reflected in the final outcome of the thirteen session of the Conference of the Parties to the United Nations Framework Convention on Climate Change, held in Bali, Indonesia, from 3-15 December 2007.[a]

a See, for example, FCCC/CP/2007/6/Add.1, decision 2/CP.13.

To fully realize the potential of reducing emissions from deforestation and forest degradation (REDD), several new financing initiatives have been launched. By far the most significant is Norway's commitment to provide $600 million annually towards efforts to reduce carbon emissions from deforestation and forest degradation in developing countries. Other donors, including Australia, Finland, Spain, Japan, Switzerland, the United Kingdom of Great Britain and Northern Ireland and the United States of America, have contributed or have signalled their intent to contribute funds to climate change and forests programmes.

The World Bank has established the Forest Carbon Partnership Facility to help reduce emissions from deforestation and degradation and to help build capacity for REDD activities in 25 pilot developing countries. The target capitalization is at least $300 million. The World Bank is also currently developing the Forest Investment Programme to support REDD-related efforts of developing countries, providing upfront bridge financing for readiness reforms and investments identified through national REDD strategies. The targeted level of funding for the proposed Forest Investment Programme is $500 million.

The Food and Agriculture Organization of the United Nations, the United Nations Development Programme and the United Nations Environment Programme have jointly launched the Collaborative Programme on Reducing Emissions from Deforestation and Forest Degradation in Developing Countries (UN-REDD), including a portfolio of $52 million (to be financed by Norway), to provide assistance in REDD capacity-building to pilot developing countries. The immediate goal is to assess whether carefully designed payment structures and capacity support can create incentives for emission reductions while maintaining and improving the other ecosystem services that forests provide. To be successful, this initiative warrants the wider participation of United Nations bodies involved in climate change and forests.

Box VI.2 (cont'd)

Development of a REDD mechanism must be based on sound methodologies for estimating and monitoring changes in forest cover and associated carbon stocks and greenhouse gas emissions, incremental changes due to sustainable management of forests, and reduction of emissions due to deforestation and forest degradation. The methodological challenge has proved to be much more difficult for emissions due to forest degradation than for emissions due to deforestation. There are also policy issues that have to be taken into account in the REDD negotiations such as the rights of stakeholders, in particular indigenous peoples, and the opportunity costs of other land uses and forest management systems (see box IV.2).

REDD negotiators should also ensure that the final outcome does not disadvantage countries that have already taken steps to eliminate or reduce deforestation and to manage their forests sustainably, or countries where forests are sustainably managed. The final outcome of the REDD programme should ensure that forest-related climate change options support sustainable development in both forest-rich and forest-poor countries. It should tackle drivers of deforestation that lie outside the forest sector, and support transparent, inclusive and accountable forest governance. It is also crucial to recognize the comprehensiveness of sustainable forest management, which goes beyond emissions and carbon potentials of forests.

Source: UN/DESA, United Nations Forum on Forests Secretariat.

However, the level both of the knowledge required to set an efficient tax and of the capacity needed to administer it are generally quite high and may not yet be achievable by many developing countries. Moreover, as indicated, estimates of damages caused by carbon emissions vary hugely, because of the different assumptions made in order to value inter-temporal trade-offs or non-monetary damages, or to account for incomplete information and uncertainty (Schroeder, 2008).

Any global carbon tax would require multilateral cooperation to harmonize tax systems so as to facilitate a joint decision on the level and incidence of the tax and on how to allocate the revenues. Without a robust international framework, differentiated taxes may serve discriminatory political or trade objectives instead of furthering climate change mitigation (as in the case, for example, of United States subsidies to ethanol and barriers to Brazil's ethanol exports). The idea, moreover, of stripping national authorities of their powers in this regard has met with stubborn resistance in a number of countries.

An unavoidable feature of a uniform global carbon tax, even if it were to be introduced gradually, would be the taxation of developing countries at several times the rate of industrialized countries, measured as a proportion of GDP. This would impose a disproportionate burden of adjustment on developing countries, although per capita emissions in developing countries are low compared with those in industrialized ones.

Moreover, carbon pricing will affect the level and distribution of real household income, both directly through a household's use of fossil fuels and indirectly through the prices of other commodities. A carbon tax has been found to place a disproportionately heavy burden on low-income groups in some contexts, by raising not only the direct cost of energy but all final prices for goods in which that energy has been used. In such cases, lower-income households would pay disproportionately more in environmental compliance costs. In order to avoid undesired distributional effects, one option would be to introduce differentiated pricing (and hence taxation) by, for example, increasing prices commensurate with the amount of energy used; alternatively, compensatory mechanisms in the form of subsidies for lower-income groups could be put in place.

Carbon taxation would therefore need to be in the first instance an instrument for providing incentives towards mitigation in advanced countries and a source of financing of climate-related programmes of action, including in developing countries. Potentially, this could yield significant resources to cover international funding requirements.

Carbon taxation would therefore in the first instance need to be an instrument for providing incentives towards mitigation in advanced countries and a source of financing of climate-related programmes of action, including in developing countries

With a carbon price of $50 per ton of CO_2, renewable energy like onshore wind would be roughly competitive with dirty coal; and with oil prices at $150 a barrel, wind would be competitive with coal and gas, in the absence of a carbon price (Stern, 2009, p. 43). Even without a market-determined carbon price, taxing greenhouse gas emitting sources of energy would help make renewable sources economically more attractive. A tax of $50 per ton, through which many renewables would become economically viable, could mobilize $500 billion in resources annually and suffice to cover part of the mitigation costs according to the higher estimates reported in figure VI.2.[5] Carbon taxes will not provide an unlimited source of funding and will drop off as greenhouse gas emissions are effectively reduced to low levels, but in the initial stages, they may play an important role in sourcing a substantial part of the investment costs of the big push that needs to be accomplished in the coming decades.

Sources of "green" investment

Foreign direct investment, portfolio investment, microfinance and public-private partnerships could be promoted to scale up private financing for climate change mitigation and adaptation

Equity markets could provide another mechanism for mobilizing private financing for investments in green technologies and low-emissions energy sources and infrastructure and for transfers of resources to developing countries. Incentives structures would need to shift so as to favour such investments, which could be achieved if reduction targets are clear and sufficiently aggressive to produce a price of carbon high enough to raise the profitability of alternative, low-emissions investments or if there were fiscal incentives and public investments to raise the rate of return on "green" investments equally. Foreign direct investment (FDI), portfolio investment, microfinance and public-private partnerships could be promoted to scale up private financing for climate change mitigation and adaptation.

Foreign direct investment can be a relatively stable source of financing, with advantages in terms of transferring technology and standards which could allow for leapfrogging into some cleaner sectors such as renewable energy. Some of the big emitting sectors, such as road transport, metals, mining chemical, timber, cement, etc., are dominated by large international firms. Their investments and practices will likely have a big influence on the timing of alternative development pathways (Goldman Sachs, 2008). Moreover, given the advances in clean technologies made by some developing countries in, for example, wind technology, South-South FDI may be an important component of a new development pathway. However, given that FDI tends to lag rather than lead economic growth, it is unlikely to play a significant role in the early stages of a shift onto such a development pathway, particularly given the initial high degree of uncertainty and the absence of the domestic inputs and complementary investments that large international firms, particularly in high-technology activities, need in order to operate efficiently. Moreover, as discussed in the previous chapters, its contribution will depend on effective policy action by the Government of the host country.

Portfolio investments may be mobilized through venture capital funds as well as "green" funds and stocks and could appeal to those investors willing to allocate their investments to options that might generate less return but would have potential in terms of mitigation and socially responsible business practices. However, the funds made available through this channel to developing countries so far have been both limited and skewed in favour of one or two countries. Without other conditioning factors, the amount of resources that can be raised is likely to remain quite small. First, without a sufficient rise in

---

5   As there is a strong likelihood, of course, that developed countries would need some of the revenues to offset the costs of their own adjustment to a low emissions future, the idea that all the revenue raised would go to investment in mitigation, let alone to developing countries, needs to be qualified.

the price of carbon and government intervention through regulatory measures and fiscal incentives, the private sector will not find these instruments sufficiently attractive based on the standard risk-return calculus. For example, the value of equity investments in biofuels has recently fallen as a result of lower energy demand and oil prices. Second, in order for this to become an important vehicle for investment in developing countries, the supply of climate-accountable financial instruments has to increase significantly. Currently, almost all investment opportunities are concentrated in developed countries.

Nonetheless, some private equity investment firms that are focused on climate change mitigation are beginning to perceive clean infrastructure, primarily renewable energy, as offering viable financing opportunities.[6] This is taking place on a limited scale, however, even in fast-growing developing countries (like China, India and Brazil), as they are all still faced with deficiencies in terms of an infrastructure adequate enough to support production and distribution of renewable energy. Although China is likely the largest market for this type of private financial flow, there remain challenges to private investment because of national policies requiring links with firms based in China. Nevertheless, an increasing number of investment banks are beginning to see increasing opportunities, most likely because of renewable energy quotas and feed-in tariffs rewarding investment in this area, and investors are beginning to act on these prospects. Again, this trend underscores the need for rapid action in policy creation; private investors, particularly in this market, may take significant time to respond to incentives.

Microfinance could be another vehicle for mobilizing local private resources for investments in sustainable development. Over the past three decades, microfinance has grown dramatically. According to recent estimates, there were more than 7,000 microcredit institutions in 2006, serving about 80 million people in about 65 countries, including some developed ones. Microfinance has expanded beyond merely encompassing programmes of credit provisioning so as to now include schemes of microsavings and microinsurance. Some of these schemes already have a climate dimension. Given the close links between poverty reduction and climate vulnerability, scaling up microfinance has been considered a possible source of finance for climate adaptation (Hammill, Matthew and McCarter, 2008). The Grameen Bank has already begun to extend loans for clean energy products, such as solar home systems, with spin-offs to microenterprises, while further opportunites exist in cleaner cooking products, biofuels and low-emissions agriculture (Rippey, 2009). However, scaling up microfinance for long-term investment in productive activities and sustainable development will require support through a broader development strategy, including investments in infrastructure and human capital (United Nations, 2008).

Public-private partnerships and guarantees can provide meaningful support to stimulating private financing in projects for increasing energy efficiency and renewable energy in developing countries. Partnerships have assumed growing importance in recent years as a vehicle for infrastructure projects and delivery of health services (Nikolic and Maikisch, 2006). They have also been used to bolster technological development, including in the field of clean energy (Sagar, Bremner and Grubb, 2008). However, there are doubts about their cost-effectiveness and whether they represent the best way to deliver at scale.

Guarantees can take various forms. A consumer financing programme for solar photovoltaic systems in southern India is a good example of a case where Government-guaranteed credits helped overcome lack of access of consumers to what was needed to allow them to make the necessary upfront investments for using the solar energy (see box VI.3). Lack of knowledge or experience may also create barriers to investments in

Some private equity investment firms that are focused on climate change mitigation are beginning to perceive clean infrastructure, primarily renewable energy, as offering viable financing opportunities

Scaling up microfinance for long-term investment in productive activities and sustainable development will require support through a broader development strategy

---

6 For example, Climate Change Capital, a London-based investment private equity firm, is currently working on launching a China-based clean infrastructure fund.

Establishing a consumer financing programme for solar photovoltaic (PV) systems in southern India

The low rate of access to electricity, and shortages even when electricity is available, have led households of India to look to alternative power supply systems such as inverters, diesel generators and, in some rare cases, solar photovoltaic (PV) systems. Though India has one of the most comprehensive renewable energy development programmes among the developing countries (see chap. IV), several barriers have prevented the wider adoption of solar home systems which could provide clean energy for lighting. In particular, a combination of insufficient credit and lack of awareness about solar home systems among potential customers has restricted market development. The United Nations Environment Programme (UNEP) in collaboration with local stakeholders has established a programme to increase access by rural households to credit to allow them to buy solar home systems. The objective was to help India's banking partners develop lending portfolios specifically targeted at financing solar home systems in poorly served regions of southern India, including, in particular, poor households in rural and semi-urban areas, which bear the brunt of power shortages and have limited access to expensive alternatives. The project was initiated in 2002 and completed in 2007.

An important step in the course of the project was consultation with stakeholders, particularly potential bank partners and vendors. After consultations, an interest rate subsidy was decided on as the financial mechanism of the project. By providing loans with an interest rate buy-down, the project addressed the "high upfront cost" and the high credit cost, which were the barriers identified by stakeholders. The project was also expected to help increase awareness and confidence in solar home systems technology, bring down the financing costs of the technology in India, and widen the market.

The project was formally launched by the partner banks in 2003: in April by the Canara Bank and in June by the Syndicate Bank. Four solar vendors had met the qualification criteria and could send their customers either to Canara or to Syndicate Bank branches for solar home systems financing. Prior to the launching of the project, only about 1,400 solar home systems had been financed in Karnataka. The project plan had set an ambitious target of 18,000 over the project lifetime. By the time the project ended in May 2007, more than 19,000 loans had been financed, through more than 2,000 participating bank branches, the fastest growth having been in rural areas, in part owing to the increasing participation of the nine Grameen banks.

A properly designed programme, involving stakeholders both during the design and execution stages, can help develop markets for renewable energy, as is evident from the success of India's solar project. Continuous monitoring and involvement of stakeholders at all stages of execution were the key to the success of the programme. The longer-term success of any such programme is dependent, however, on in its ability to transit smoothly to the commercial market.

Source: UNEP, Risø Centre.

renewable energy. The International Finance Corporation (IFC), the private sector arm of the World Bank Group has been particularly innovative in this area. By establishing partnerships with banks in developing countries, IFC helps local financial institutions identify which of their clients could implement energy efficiency programmes. When a loan is given, training is provided on how to structure those programmes to further encourage investments, IFC also issues a partial risk guarantee against default. In practice, default rates are significantly lower for energy efficiency projects than for those in other sectors.[7] The guarantees and training thus seem to have been conducive to an efficient use of IFC resources, helping the private sector overcome its initial reluctance to invest in energy efficiency and renewable energy sectors in developing countries.

---

7   Information based on consultations with IFC staff.

Public sector financing

As noted elsewhere (United Nations, 2006, chap. IV), in many developing countries the markets for long-term financing, such as bond markets, are weakly developed. This typically limits both Governments and private investors with respect to mobilizing enough long-term finance to be able to undertake the large-scale investments necessary for economic and social development. Such investment costs may be too large for Governments to finance from yearly tax revenue, while the lack of a bond market limits the capacity for domestic public borrowing for these purposes. Private investors, in turn, will anticipate returns below social returns in the investments concerned (Stiglitz, 1994).

Economy-wide externalities are particularly prominent in certain key sectors, such as infrastructure, which are characterized by lumpy investments, long gestation lags, higher risks and lower profits. In any economy where private businesses have a predominant role, market signals and private financial institutions can result in the avoidance of these sectors by investors, thereby slowing long-term growth and development. Correcting this kind of market failure provides a role for policymakers in ensuring an adequate flow of credit at favourable costs to frontline technologies and sectors with potentially large social returns (Chandrasekar, 2008). The investment challenge associated with climate change is no different. To accelerate private investment in mitigation, policymakers and public authorities will need to apply incentives through regulatory frameworks, subsidies, guarantees, and financing of the incremental costs of switching technology, among other policy instruments.

Still, large upfront investment costs pose a significant obstacle for many developing countries. The resources committed to date to meet the climate challenge, and the limits of relying on market mechanisms, suggest that the developed countries have yet to take seriously the kind of adjustment that they are expecting from developing countries.

Domestic resource mobilization

According to the logic of a big push, increased public investment creates a matching increased amount of *new* saving, instead of drawing on *existing* saving. At the same time, that higher level of saving creates demand for new financial instruments, including the funding of public sector investments. However, this does not occur automatically and financing gaps have to be filled. Governments must, at the same time, consider how their fiscal space can be expanded and refocused in order to meet their climate objectives without jeopardizing other goals. This is true of developed and developing countries alike, but the challenge is particularly significant in the latter.

In developing countries, on average, the tax revenue collected as a proportion of GDP is only two thirds of the proportion in richer countries, and the larger share is in the form of indirect taxes, as opposed to direct taxes on incomes, profit and capital gains. Tax administration is often weak and subject to evasion and abuse.[8] In identifying the resources needed to move towards a low-emissions growth pattern, developing countries, in particular, should undertake fiscal reforms that enable a shift away from a reliance on trade, and other indirect taxes, with a view to increasing progressivity and expanding the fiscal space.

On the expenditure side, many Governments are being advised, on climate change-related grounds, to reconsider energy subsidies for low-income households. While the fiscal benefit of removing energy subsidies for low-income households clearly exists,

To accelerate private investment in mitigation, policymakers and public authorities will need to apply incentives through regulatory frameworks, subsidies, guarantees and financing of the incremental costs of switching technology, among other policy instruments

According to the logic of a big push, increased public investment creates a matching increased amount of new saving, instead of drawing on existing saving

---

8   For a further discussion of these issues, see Spiegel (2008) and di John (2007).

both the climate impact and the single-minded focus on this subsidy are questionable. Faced with higher energy prices, low-income households have been known to substitute unpriced energy sources, such as firewood, which has a negative impact on the environment and their own productivity and standard of living.

In the designing of a low-emissions financing strategy, there will have to be deployed a vector of subsidies, tariffs and taxes, of which energy subsidies for the poor should constitute only a part. Simply emphasizing the removal of energy subsidies could undermine equity objectives and thus set back structural transformation and development. On the revenue side, equity considerations will also have to play a key role in generating the needed financing for low-emissions energy investment, and progressive approaches to taxation and fees will need to be a key element in the climate financing strategy.

A number of developing countries have witnessed the growth of markets for Government bonds in recent years. In light of the financial crisis and the calls for reforming the financial system, issuance of "green bonds" to fund the climate challenge could be an additional financing tool, along the lines of war bonds, in some emerging economies and a safer haven for the rising level of personal savings in a more regulated financial system (see box VI.4 and New Economics Foundation, 2008). Government guarantees and tax breaks could also be used to channel savings into investments that reduce carbon use, including infrastructural investment, as is the case in the United States municipal bonds market.

A vector of subsidies, tariffs and taxes will have to be deployed, of which energy subsidies for the poor should constitute only a part

The issuance of "green bonds" to fund the climate challenge, could be an additional financing tool, along the lines of war bonds, in some emerging economies

---

Box VI.4

Green bonds

The need for capital to finance projects targeted at either mitigation of or adaptation to climate change is immense. Securing finance for investments in such areas which have the inherent characteristics of public goods is less clearcut, however. In particular, given the volume of funds required, as well as the need for sustaining such investments over longer periods of time, relying on public coffers may not be a sufficient or feasible option if this implies either a diversion of expenditure from other items or a significant increase in taxation. An obvious solution is to tap capital markets and to entice members of the private sector into willingly investing their savings in such projects by issuing debt securities that are backed by a larger public entity.

Demand for securities that specifically support low-carbon activities or foster adaptation to climate change is likely to be significant; in contrast to common debt securities, such *green bonds* (also called "climate bonds" or "environment bonds") could also yield a feel-good dividend generated by the support of environmentally friendly projects. Interest in green bonds appears to be increasing at all levels.

While still small compared with that of the United States of America, the international market for sub-sovereign bond issuances has deepened over the last decade, with greater overall volume, larger issues and longer maturities (Platz, 2009). Several municipalities and cities have already issued green bonds on a small scale and Governments have now sprung on board. For instance, $2 billion worth of AAA-rated bonds were issued in the United States in 2004 to finance reclaiming of contaminated industrial and commercial land, to encourage energy conservation and to promote use of renewable energy sources. Similarly, a bond issue worth $530 million was approved in Malaysia in 2006 to finance planting of trees on 375,000 hectares of land.

International institutions have also recognized the merits of green bonds: the European Investment Bank issued *climate awareness bonds* worth more than €1 billion in 2007 to fund renewable energy projects; and the World Bank, in partnership with Skandinaviska Enskilda Banken (SEB) in Sweden, issued green bonds worth $300 million (SEK 2.325 billion) in 2008.

The idea of offering debt securities that appeal to an investor's conscience is not a new one: a number of countries issued *war bonds* to finance military operations during the Second World War. Moreover, history shows that such instruments are able to leverage significant amounts of

Box VI.4 (cont'd)

private finance: at the end of the War, *war bonds* had, for instance, been purchased by every second American; they were responsible for the raising of more than $185 billion at the time, equivalent in inflation-adjusted terms to more than $2 trillion today. For many countries, including the United States and Germany, municipal bonds have played an important role in financing essential services, in particular water supply systems. Historical experience suggests that certain supply (issuer)-side and demand (investor)-side factors are critical for the development of the sub-sovereign debt market. On the demand side, these factors include the presence of financial intermediaries and investors with suitable long-term portfolio needs, issuer familiarity and confidence with respect to similar securities, the ability to trade debt issuances on secondary markets and low credit and market risk. Supply-side features comprise improved capacity of municipalities to manage and support debt, low issuance costs, suitable regulatory and legal environments and, in some cases, credit enhancements such as guarantees or pooled financing schemes. Thus, in countries that fulfil most of these conditions, green bonds would appear to be a potential source of significant funding for public entities engaged in tackling the global warming challenge.

The scale on which "green" debt instruments can be issued depends in part on the sophistication of domestic financial markets and the overall debt burden of the country. Expansion of a market for such funds is ultimately contingent on the national Government's ability to raise tax revenues and to set the rate of return on domestic investment. Equity and development considerations are important in respect of relaxing constraints on both. Progressive taxation will ensure greater government revenues as income grows, including from the growing class of bond owners, who are likely to be in upper income brackets. State intervention in establishing rates of return on domestic investment involves capping income from capital in exchange for less risky and less volatile income streams. The capacity of national Governments to influence average domestic returns on investments critically depends on their ability and willingness to manage capital flows. By imposing taxes and restrictions on capital and controlling flows in and out of their borders, Governments will restore their ability to exercise an independent monetary policy, and to influence interest rates in a manner appropriate for stimulating long-term investment.

Public sector development banks provide an alternative funding channel for long-term investment in many developing countries. The record of these institutions in generating long-term financing is uneven, although they have had a particularly important role to play in infrastructure development. Success stories suggest that these banks are most successful when they also encourage the development of complementary private financial institutions, are assiduous in monitoring the recipients of their own funds and avoid excessive public sector risks and badly targeted interest-rate subsidies (United Nations, 2005, pp. 24-25). These institutions have been neglected in recent years in favour of private capital markets and public-private partnerships. However, in the absence of effective regulatory, policy and institutional frameworks, the record of the private sector when it was left with providing the required financing, particularly to essential utilities and services such as energy, has not been a satisfactory one. In many cases, reforming and recapitalizing development banks will be important for a successful transition to low-emission development pathways. Brazil, China and India have gained some experience in using both development banks and special lending windows of commercial banks underwritten by Government guarantees (see box VI.5).

In the absence of effective regulatory, policy and institutional frameworks, the record of the private sector when it was left with providing the required financing, particularly to essential utilities and services such as energy, has not been a satisfactory one

Box VI.5

Developing financial intermediation mechanisms for energy efficiency projects in Brazil, China and India

The potential high returns accruing from energy efficiency projects have been demonstrated; and if the proper delivery mechanisms can be developed, large profit-making investment should become available. However, the sustainable mechanisms that can help overcome many of the barriers inhibiting investment in energy efficiency are still in their infancy and their effectiveness has not been proved. The objective of the Three-Country Energy Efficiency Project (the 3CEE project) was to achieve major increases in energy efficiency investments by the domestic financial sectors in Brazil, China and India by addressing those barriers through a set of activities, and to identify viable financial mechanisms targeting the banking sector and energy service companies in each country. Initiated in November 2002, the project was completed in May 2007.

The activities included technical assistance, training, and applied research covering the following four areas of country interest: development of commercial banking windows for energy efficiency projects; support for energy service companies; guarantee funds for energy efficiency; and equity funding for energy service companies/energy efficiency projects.

Other important project activities included multiple international cross-country exchange workshops and dissemination to allow practitioners from each of the three countries to learn from each other and to tackle jointly the practical problems that each faced in overcoming barriers to increased efficiency investment.

Technical analysis was one of the major activities across various components and significant work was completed in all three countries in this area. In Brazil, venture capital, private equity capital, and shared risk in energy efficiency project work finally led to approval by the Brazilian Development Bank (BNDES) of a new risk-sharing credit line for energy efficiency projects in May 2006, with the participation of several local banks. Support to energy service companies through the project increased their capacity to implement energy efficiency projects through performance contracting. The Energy Sector Management Assistance Programme is providing support for the implementation of the scheme.

In India, new appraisal methodologies and financial structures for energy efficiency projects were developed and training programmes for bankers were conducted. Five of India's banks (the State Bank of India, Canara Bank, Union Bank, the Bank of Baroda and the Bank of India) had launched new schemes for energy efficiency lending by the time the project was completed in 2007.

In China, emphasis was given to developing larger energy efficiency schemes at individual banks which have received strong support from Chinese stakeholders. A large World Bank pipeline project was developed, focusing on promoting the direct bank financing of medium and large-sized energy efficiency projects, whose chief goal is to establish sustainable energy efficiency lending businesses in China's banks. Two of China's domestic banks were selected to act as financial institutions. Capacity-building of energy service companies was carried out through training programmes conducted by the China Energy Management Company Association, the association of energy service companies. The project also catalysed the outreach to local banks and financial stakeholders, supplementing the efforts under the World Bank/Global Environment Facility Energy Conservation II Project guarantee fund in China.

Source: UNEP, Risø Centre.

International financing

International support is indispensable for effective financing of public investment to meet mitigation and adaptation goals

International support is indispensable for effective financing of public investment to meet mitigation and adaptation goals. The urgency of increased support arises against a backdrop of persistent weaknesses in the architecture of development finance at both the bilateral and multilateral levels. The financial mechanisms uniquely designed to manage the climate challenge under the United Nations Framework Convention on Climate Change include a number of grant-based adaptation funds operating under the administrative auspices of the Global Environment Facility (GEF). These rely on a mixture of voluntary contributions and resources from a 2 per cent levy on transactions under the Clean Development Mechanism. The Global Environment Facility is particularly important because it is able to fund more risky projects and has demonstrated its competence in working in countries that may not attract foreign investors either through the Clean Development Mechanism or directly. Since its inception in 1991, the Facility has allocated more than $3 billion for projects and has co-financed an additional $14 billion. A second channel encompasses funds and programmes arising from the loans and grants of bilateral agencies, the largest of which is Japan's Cool Earth Partnership, established in 2008, which aims to allocate $10 billion in funds over five years. The third channel comprises existing multilateral development institutions, which not only include a variety of mechanisms with a climate-related component but have also set up several specific funds to provide loans, grants and concessional funding, the largest of which are the recently established Climate Investment Funds of the World Bank, a $6 billion multilateral initiative announced at the July 2008 G8 meeting.

As summarized in table VI.3, this emerging climate architecture is as unnecessarily complex as it is massively underfunded. The array of funds and funding mechanisms lack adequate coordination, leaving many gaps and overlaps. Even though there is still great uncertainty about the level of required transfers for developing countries, there is little doubt that the funding gap is the single largest constraint on progress in climate negotiations. Moreover, even assuming that donor countries met the target of 0.7 per cent of gross national product (GNP) for ODA, and developing countries agreed that the additional resources, of between $160 billion-$200 billion, could be used for climate purposes, the funding shortfall from ODA would still be in the order of hundreds of billions of dollars per year (Müller, 2008, p. 7).

The key to any scaling-up exercise resides in finding more predictable multilateral sources of finance. These could come, in part, from the sale of emissions permits or increased carbon taxes in donor countries; more innovative sources of finance, however, will likely be needed. An innovative source of finance framework is a wide-ranging initiative to pilot and implement a variety of new and predictable financing mechanisms and to mobilize countries of widely varying situations for the common purpose of achieving internationally agreed development goals. A hallmark of this approach is global solidarity, with sources of finance coordinated internationally but implemented at a national level. Unlike traditional development financing approaches, which still depend on the political goodwill of rich countries, albeit with a greater emphasis in recent years on "partnerships" in the use of resources, the innovative sources of finance framework entails joint design and decision-making by developing and developed countries for the purpose of raising the resources required to meet a common goal.

The amounts raised to date have not been significant in comparison with ODA flows and so far have been mainly directed at meeting global health objectives. However, a number of proposals raise the possibility of much larger funding possibilities (see box VI.6). Starting with the proposal to use special drawing rights (SDRs) for development purposes, as contained in paragraph 44 of the 2002 Monterrey Consensus of the International Conference on Financing for Development, there have been a wide range of creative ideas emerging. The proposal on special drawing rights already embeds the feature of cooperation on the revenue-raising side of development finance, since all member countries of IMF would have to contribute their currencies under this mechanism.

The emerging climate architecture is as unnecessarily complex as it is massively underfunded

The key to any scaling-up exercise resides in finding more predictable multilateral sources of finance; a hallmark of this approach is global solidarity

Box VI.6

Proposals for mobilizing new, additional and significant financial resources

Between the thirteenth session of the Conference of the Parties to the United Nations Framework Convention on Climate Change, held in Bali, Indonesia, from 3 to 15 December 2007, and the fourteenth session of the Conference of the Parties, held in Poznan, Poland, from 1 to 12 December 2008, a number of financing proposals have been advanced by the parties. The major ones are briefly summarized below, along with some others not advanced by the parties themselves. They relate principally to the means of mobilization of financial resources, but some of them also address the issue of the institutional architecture and governance structure of a financing mechanism.

Developing countries emphasize the central role of public finances and the importance of predictability of resource flows. Developed countries generally support the use of existing institutions to channel any additional funds and stress the important role to be played by the private sector in financing through foreign direct investment (FDI) (Santarius and others, 2009). Some of the main alternative proposals for financial resource mobilization are:

- *Enhanced Clean Development Mechanism (offsetting)*. The deficiencies of the Clean Development Mechanism at present for facilitating large-scale resource transfers are widely acknowledged. Much attention has been focused on reforming the Clean Development Mechanism so as to replace its project focus with a programmatic and/or policy focus, with the expectation of larger impacts, shorter funding cycles and lower transaction costs. The United Nations Framework Convention on Climate Change secretariat estimates that, by 2020, offsetting could yield up to $40.8 billion per year, still only a fraction of estimated incremental costs in developing countries

- *Compulsory leveraged offsetting*. One proposal (Pendleton and Retallack, 2009) suggests that the Annex I emissions to be covered by developing-country Clean Development Mechanism projects should be offset not ton for ton but in a ratio, for example, of 2:1 or higher.[a] Thus, a developed-country emitter wishing to use the Clean Development Mechanism to cover one ton of its own unmitigated emissions would need to invest in two or more tons of emission reductions in developing countries. This proposal has the virtue of simplicity, essentially utilizing the existing Clean Development Mechanism framework but applying a compulsory leverage ratio to the Mechanism's transactions. Also, depending on the leverage ratio chosen, the proposal could generate significant financial transfers. Thus, an Annex I reduction target of 40 per cent below 1990 levels by 2020 and a 2:1 leverage ratio could generate $130 billion per year in Clean Development Mechanism financing

- *Mandatory assessment*. The Group of 77 and China have proposed that Annex I parties contribute from 0.5 to 1.0 per cent of their gross national income to climate change financing in non-Annex I countries, to be channelled through a multilateral climate technology fund under the authority of the United Nations Framework Convention on Climate Change. This would generate approximately $150 billion-$300 billion per year at pre-crisis income levels of major Organization for Economic Cooperation and Development (OECD) economies

- *Assessed contributions based on the criterion of fairness and the polluter pays principle*. Mexico has proposed the creation of a multilateral climate change fund, to which all countries would contribute, on the basis of greenhouse gas emissions,

a The American Clean Energy and Security Act of 2009 contains a provision of this sort, whereby a ton of domestic CO_2 emissions could be offset against only four fifths of a ton of developing-country emissions. This means that to cover the full ton, a United States emitter would need to buy 1.25 tons of credit from the Clean Development Mechanism, representing a leverage of 1.25:1.

Box VI.6 (cont'd)

population and gross domestic product, in accordance with the principle of common but differentiated responsibilities and respective capabilities. The fund would be used to finance both mitigation and adaptation

- **Revenue from a global auction of a portion of assigned amount units (AAUs)**. Norway has proposed withholding 2 per cent of permits from national quota allocations (assigned amount units (AAUs)) of all parties and auctioning them directly, or raising revenue through a tax on the issuance of assigned amount units. The portion to be auctioned could be adjusted to achieve a revenue target. By Norway's estimate, given recent carbon market prices and price expectations, a 2 per cent auction could generate revenues of $15 billion-$25 billion per year

- **Crediting nationally appropriate mitigation actions (NAMAs)**. The Republic of Korea has proposed a system of credits for nationally appropriate mitigation actions, so that developing countries could borrow against anticipated future carbon credit sales in order to finance early action. Crediting nationally appropriate mitigation actions would help finance already planned low-carbon strategies in developing countries (Pendleton and Retallack, 2009)

- **Global carbon levy**: Switzerland has proposed a $2 per ton global carbon dioxide levy on all fossil fuel emissions, with exemptions for least developed countries, with a portion of revenues allocated to a multilateral adaptation fund and another portion channelled into each country's national climate change fund. The estimated revenue raised would be $48.5 billion, dependent on the price of fossil fuels. The incidence of such a levy needs to be carefully considered, as it could well be regressive

- **Other levy-based proposals**. Brazil has advanced a proposal with some similarity to Switzerland's, with a 10 per cent petroleum and coal tax used to finance a global fund to be used for technology transfer, adaptation and compensation for forest preservation. Such a tax, at current prices, would generate an estimated $130 billion in revenue. The least developed countries have proposed an international levy on aviation to the tune of $4 billion-$10 billion and a levy on bunker fuels for shipping and aviation to the tune of $4 billion-15 billion (Pendleton and Redallack, 2009)

- **Unrelated levies**. Various proposals have been made for raising revenues for climate change action from sources not closely linked to greenhouse gas emissions, for example, financial transactions, assets in tax havens, etc. These proposals are marred by what is perceived to be the arbitrariness of their choice of source and by the fact that the worthy competing causes that could benefit from such financing are indeed numerous.

Subsequent proposals have explored the possibility of using special drawing rights for development financing as well as liquidity provisioning (Aryeetey, 2003; Soros, 2002). International levies collected on air travel or financial transactions also overcome the traditional dependence of multilateral resources on the outcomes of political processes in the donor countries. One mechanism already being discussed within this framework is the currency transaction tax, which could raise at least $50 billion per year at a rate of 0.5 per cent; a tax on carbon market transactions has also been considered as a possible source of multilateral finance.

Towards a global investment regime to address the climate challenge

While market-based approaches will need to be part of the solution, as argued throughout this *Survey*, the key focus of a wider approach should be on meeting the major investment challenge of simultaneously addressing climate change, sustainability and economic development. Without significant financial transfers from wealthy countries, any expectation that poorer countries will move onto a low-emissions growth path is almost certain to be disappointed.

This investment-led approach seeks to bring about a change in the development trajectory so as to meet the growth and development goals of developing countries consistent with reducing their carbon dependence. At the national level, and as part of a long-term industrial development strategy, public investment in mitigation and adaptation activities needs to be scaled up. Energy provision is a central component of this strategy but it is interlinked with transportation, water security and economic diversification (chaps. II and III). Industrial policy—understood not only as targeting and coordinating specific sectoral support measures undertaken by Governments, but also as entailing the socialization of investment risks, the removal of barriers to adopting otherwise profitable technologies and support for technological learning and upgrading—has a key role to play both domestically (chap. IV) and internationally (chap. V). A successful investment push along these lines would in turn increase productivity and reduce the costs of using new technologies, thereby opening up further investment opportunities.

In comparison with market-based mechanisms which would likely be accompanied by adjustments, a globally funded public investment programme would promote equity by enabling the developing world to sustain catch-up growth through the mobilization of resources domestically, while making significant cuts in emissions (chap. I). Such an investment programme would utilize market mechanisms insofar as government policy provided clear and unequivocal signals to private enterprises about the next wave of investment opportunities, without being based on a single price-based intervention.

Efforts to develop an investment programme that combines development and environmental goals on the scale that has been discussed in the present *Survey* have been few and far between. This, of course, is why we are now facing the challenge before us. However, the establishment by Brazil of a sugar cane-based ethanol energy and transport system is one recent example of the success of such efforts, even more telling since it has been achieved by a developing country. A historical example concerns an underappreciated component of New Deal policies in the United States of the 1930s, namely, the Tennessee Valley Authority (see chap. IV, box IV.1). With support at the federal level from the Rural Electrification Administration and the Reconstruction Finance Corporation, the Authority combined development, energy and environmental objectives into a concerted and coordinated effort to transform the economic potential of the Southern States by lowering transport costs, reducing the risk of flooding and creating a low-cost source of power that not only directly raised living standards but also helped the region crowd in substantial private investment and create new jobs. The big difference this time around is that the new investment deal that is needed to meet the climate challenge must be recognized as a truly global project.

> A globally funded public investment programme would promote equity by enabling the developing world to sustain catch-up growth through the mobilization of resources domestically, while making significant cuts in emissions

Elements of a global programme

The review of available estimates of mitigation and adaptation costs suggests that additional annual total investments in developing countries could be upwards of one trillion dollars per year. The breakdown between the public and private sector will no doubt vary considerably across time and among countries. However, according to the suggested scenario in part B of figure VI.1, the initial push would be strongly biased towards the public sector and marked by the need to front-load much of the required investment in the early stages of a new development path. It seems likely, as a consequence, that even the highest estimates underestimate the scale of the immediate challenge facing many developing countries if they are to establish a new low-emissions, high-growth development pathway.

The present *Survey* does not attempt a detailed breakdown of the big push but, as highlighted in the preceding sections, it is clear that there needs to be a radical shift in the existing system of funding for mitigation and adaptation efforts. A central message is that, to bring about changes, a mix of financing mechanisms will be needed—a mix that will vary across countries and over time. In the present section, we focus on the public investment aspect of the pathway in developing countries.

A global approach to a publicly funded investment programme is based on three elements:

- A development accord that recognizes equity as an integral part of a global response to climate change
- Additional and substantially scaled-up financing to allow for climate action with greater urgency: the case for a big push
- Independent and participatory governance structures along the lines of the Marshall Plan.

> There needs to be a radical shift in the existing system of funding for mitigation and adaptation efforts

A development accord

Equity is an essential ingredient of an effective global climate change policy, as reflected in the principle of "common but differentiated responsibilities and respective capabilities", as set forth in paragraph 1, article 3, of the United Nations Framework Convention on Climate Change. Not only have today's high-income economies generated about 80 per cent of past fossil fuel-based emissions, but those same emissions have helped carry them to high levels of social and economic well-being. These countries carry the responsibility for the bulk of climate damage but they also have the capacity to repair it (Müller, 2008). However, from a long-term perspective, limiting further damage also requires that developing countries shift their energy and land use and their consumption needs towards low-emissions options.

Compelling developing countries to cut emissions at this stage of their development constitutes an inappropriate—and unworkable—approach to facilitating progress. Such an approach would almost certainly freeze a pattern of income inequality that already exhibits intolerable income gaps within and, in particular, across countries. Catch-up growth and convergence remain fundamental policy priorities. Reconciling this with climate objectives can be achieved only if the investments needed to drive growth assume a technological profile different from the one that drove the historically unprecedented growth performance of today's advanced economies.

> Equity is an essential ingredient of an effective global climate change policy

It is important to acknowledge that developing countries have already begun to take significant steps towards developing energy efficiency and cleaner energy sources and building multilateral support to finance further emissions reductions at an accelerated pace (Pendleton and Retallack, 2009). However, much higher initial investment costs will need to be incurred if the adjustment to a low-emissions economy is to take place at a faster pace and on the requisite scale to meet climate goals while at the same time ensuring the achievement of development goals.

This will require additional multilateral financing, on an adequate and predictable scale, comprising grants, concessional loans and compensatory payments. In the context of the ongoing United Nations Framework Convention on Climate Change negotiations, developing countries have insisted on the fact that article 4, paragraph 3, of the Framework Convention implies that Annex II countries have a clear-cut responsibility for providing new and additional financial resources to meet the agreed full costs incurred by developing-country parties in complying with their obligations. Translating such responsibilities into tangible resources is still a major stumbling block, depending on how much weight is given to responsibility and capability. Placing this challenge in the context of an evolving investment programme is to recognize that developing countries will themselves be responsible for mobilizing resources on an increasing scale over time, as well as for insisting on the responsibility of developed countries for meeting the additional costs of undertaking such investments in the initial stages of the transition.

Additional and substantially scaled-up financing

The existing ODA model is not up to the task of funding the climate challenge

In light of previous discussions, it becomes clear that the existing ODA model is not up to the task of funding the climate challenge. More substantial and more predictable forms of financing will most certainly have to be found and new mechanisms of resource mobilization will have to be considered, such as those suggested in box VI.6.

Yet, the obvious starting point for the scaling up resources would be to insist that advanced countries meet their existing commitment to a target a 0.7 per cent of GNP for ODA. Developing countries have rightly expressed both their reservations about treating climate commitments simply as aid and their concerns, also justified, that additional expenditures linked to climate change could "crowd out" assistance for development goals. However, climate vulnerability is closely linked to interlocking stresses related to other development challenges which in turn reinforce climatic vulnerabilities (chap. III). These close links between adaptation and development should provide extensive scope for synergies if developed countries remain faithful to their ODA commitments (Levina, 2007). It will be imperative, however, to recognize that financing for adaptation is not aid as such but is much closer to a form of compensation paid by high-emitting countries for the damage they are inflicting. There is no shortage of institutions available to channel such funding. However, new funding mechanisms may still be needed, in the area, for example, of disaster management (United Nations, 2008). The bigger challenge is likely to be one of coordinating the required expansion of ODA, ensuring consistency across funding sources, and reducing duplication and waste. This may require the establishment of a central agency to collect international adaptation funding and to provide some degree of coherence across programmes (Müller, 2008).

The "bilateralization" of multilateral aid should be minimized by imposing coordination between funds and integrating resources

That said, criticisms of the governance of the aid architecture will need to be urgently addressed as funding is scaled up. In the first place, the lack of transparency in the donor-dependent approach to the design of specific-purpose funds, as is particularly apparent with respect to the current pattern of adaptation funding, will need to be corrected. International cooperation should assist the integration of mitigation and adaptation in the national policies of developing countries under the "country-led and country-owned" principle. Second, there will be an urgent need to rationalize and minimize proliferation of funding mechanisms. There has been a proliferation of specific funds administered by bilateral agencies, which differ widely in terms of purposes, amount mobilized, time-horizons and mechanisms for channelling resources to developing countries. The "bilateralization" of multilateral aid should be minimized by imposing coordination between funds and integrating resources; for example, funding for reducing emissions from deforestation and forest degradation could expand by combining resources and approaches from different institutions (such as the forestry funds of Norway and Australia, and the Amazon Fund).

That the capacity to scale up multilateral financing exists has been revealed by the financial crisis and this bodes well for climate financing. However, with the attention of the international community focused on the deepening global economic crisis, there is the danger that efforts to finance an effective response to climate change will be delayed. Delaying investments in a new energy, transportation and health infrastructure, bolstering the productivity of the rural economy and making it less susceptible to climatic shocks, is as unnecessary as it is self-defeating (Stern and Kuroda, 2009). Making up for the loss of private demand from the ongoing economic crisis will require vigorous counter-cyclical fiscal policies for which a truly global coordinated response is appropriate (United Nations, 2009). In this context, increased public investment to meet climate as well as development objectives will bring short-term benefits through a demand impulse while aiding the transition towards low-emissions economies.

However, developing countries are concerned that a dominant role for existing multilateral institutions in future climate-related financing will perpetuate the unsatisfactory practices associated with past development finance. The kinds of conditionalities attached to that financing are seen as particularly unacceptable given that climate finance, even more than development finance, is required to make adjustments to the past actions of richer countries. Moreover, developing countries insist that decision-making should be based on the one-country, one-vote principle (as under the framework of the United Nations Framework Convention on Climate Change) and not on the amount of money contributed, as is still the case in the international financial institutions. In these respects, many of the recently established climate funds appear to represent, on one recent assessment, "a distinct step back from the GEF compromise" and "are almost certain to create a new level of North-South political discord over the funding for global environmental action at a historical juncture, when the world can ill afford it" (Porter and others, 2008, p. 47).

As suggested earlier, the initial responsibility for ensuring adequate multilateral funding lies with Annex II countries. Using the Greenhouse Development Rights (GDR) methodology discussed in chapter I, a possible breakdown of their contribution is given in table VI.4. For every 100 billion dollars of climate financing, EU would contribute 32.9 billion, the United States 47.7 billion and Japan 11.2 billion. The Commission of Experts of the President of the General Assembly (the Stiglitz Commission) (United Nations, 2009) has recently proposed that industrialized countries dedicate 1 per cent of their national stimulus packages, in addition to traditional ODA commitments, to help address the strains imposed by the global economic downturn on the poorest citizens. In respect of the OECD countries, the average weighted stimulus package will account for about the 3.4 per cent of GDP over the period 2008-2010 (Organization for Economic Cooperation and Development, 2009). That would generate additional ODA of over 1.3 billion dollars over two years. As such, this represents a symbolic acceptance of the global nature of the challenge.

The initial responsibility for ensuring adequate multilateral funding lies with Annex II countries

Table VI.4.
Possible breakdown of climate-related ODA flows for Annex II countries to 2020

	Population (percentage of world total)	GDP per capita (United States dollars purchasing power parity)	Climate-related ODA (percentage of flows)	Share of ODA by Annex II countries as of 2008 (percentage)
EU-15[a]	5.80	33 754	32.9	28.3
of which:				
Germany	1.20	34 812	7.8	11.6
United Kingdom	0.90	34 953	5.3	9.5
France	0.91	33 953	4.6	9.1
United States	4.50	45 640	47.7	21.7
Japan	1.90	33 422	11.2	7.8
Others	1.00	38 149	8.2	11.9
Total Annex II countries	**13.20**	**30 924**	**100.0**	**100.0**

Source: Pendleton and Retallack (2009).

a   The 12 accession countries of the European Union (EU) are not listed in Annex II but are probably exposed to article 4.3 obligations as a result of their EU membership. However, because of their relatively marginal impact on the big picture as presented in this table, they are not included in the calculation.

The steady increase in the finance, on a scale that is commensurate with the projected scale of public investment that is required in order to shift to a low-emissions development pathway will need new international funding instruments of the kind suggested earlier. These will have to be considered in an open and dispassionate manner if real and timely progress is to be made.

Independent and participatory governance structures

Donor Governments seem to have opted for a disjointed approach which encourages fragmentation of the global response to climate change, to the great detriment of efforts to achieve effectiveness, efficiency and equity

At a time when the international community needs to bring together myriad elements, mechanisms and agreements into a strategic framework, donor Governments seem to have opted for a disjointed approach which encourages fragmentation of the global response to climate change, to the great detriment of efforts to achieve effectiveness, efficiency and equity. A global investment programme aimed at effectuating the shift to low-emissions, high-growth development pathways requires a governance structure that is able to pursue a much more focused and coherent agenda, prevents dominance by donor countries and provides for participatory decision-making on financial contributions and disbursements. Stern (2009, pp. 200-202) has recently argued, on these grounds, that the climate challenge probably needs a new institutional architecture.

Certainly, in dealing with the large scale of the financial transfers required for mitigation and adaptation in developing countries, there is a clear need for an enhanced financial mechanism, building on article 11 of the United Nations Framework Convention on Climate Change. As a minimum, against the backdrop of the proliferation of multilateral and bilateral financing mechanisms, such a body is needed for measuring, reporting and verifying financial flows from a variety of developed-country sources and for ensuring that greater coherence in the emerging system of climate financing is achieved (Pendleton and Retallack, 2009).

The bigger question concerns the management and allocation of financial resources. It is often argued that the World Bank and other multilateral development banks might be better positioned to scale up financing than a fund under the authority of the United Nations Framework Convention on Climate Change. However, these institutions have major limitations in the context of global environmental finance (Porter and others, 2008). For instance, the newly established Climate Investment Funds that are administered by the World Bank have been criticized not only for their governance structure, which replicates the existing asymmetries of the Executive Board of the World Bank, but also for undermining the United Nations Framework Convention on Climate Change and for not being truly additional to existing ODA commitments (Tan, 2008). Indeed, on their own assessment, multilateral development banks still do not seem to be systematically factoring climate change into their investment choices and need to do more to ensure that all of their investments and lending operations take climate change into account (World Bank, 2008b; Ballesteros, 2008). Moreover, the bias in the lending activities of multilateral development banks since the mid-1990s raises questions about the suitability of these institutions for administering a publicly led global investment programme. The largest decline in World Bank lending for infrastructure projects since the mid-1990s has occurred in the electricity sector, triggered by the expectation that the private sector would take up the slack (Platz and Schroeder, 2007). While the direction of the trend has been reversed since 2002, new commitments on average have not yet reached the levels of the mid-1990s.

Developing countries have also pointed out that additional financing, even on concessionary terms, to help them switch to cleaner energy sources will likely mean their acquiring additional debt to address a problem to which they contributed relatively little. This raises long-standing concerns for many developing countries about the role of development finance, including the privileged position of creditors in international financial negotiations, and the use of adjustment lending, through attached conditionalities, to shape their policy options across a broad range of economic and social issues. They are concerned that housing any new financing mechanisms in the international financial institutions would subject them to the same governance arrangements and conditionalities as were imposed on previous loans from these institutions. The Group of 77 and China have expressed their preference for a global fund to be governed, not by the international financial institutions or the Global Environmental Facility,[9] but by the Parties to the United Nations Framework Convention on Climate Change, following the model of the Multilateral Fund for the Implementation of the Montreal Protocol and of the Adaptation Fund under the Kyoto Protocol. On the other hand, a number of Annex I countries have reservations about following the Montreal Protocol model for climate change financing.

Entrusting a Conference of the Parties-accountable body with the mandate for a global investment programme could be an important first step towards the development of a broader institutional structure on global climate change financing. However, such a response could introduce the danger of locking new financing into an environmental project-based approach, which would run counter to the arguments presented in this chapter.

Entrusting a Conference of the Parties-accountable body with the mandate for a global investment programme could be an important first step towards the development of a broader institutional structure on global climate change financing

---

The Global Environment Facility has indicated its intention to review and reshape its governance structure in response to developing-country concerns over representation.

Living up to the challenge: lessons from the Marshall Plan

Whatever the institutional details finally agreed to, the right model for meeting shared global challenges is still the Marshall Plan, as also noted by Al Gore in his Nobel Lecture in 2007. On many counts, the scale and urgency of the climate and development challenges need an integrated emergency response of the kind that informed the Marshall Plan. Moreover, part of the success of the Plan was due to the fact that it bypassed the fledgling Bretton Woods institutions which had not appeared to be up to the job of fashioning policies and supporting institutional reforms attuned to local conditions. Many might see this as the principal lesson to be applied to the current challenge.

However, as noted in the *World Economic and Social Survey 2008* (United Nations, 2008), the Marshall Plan is not a blueprint which can simply be rolled out to meet contemporary challenges. Rather, it encompasses a set of broad principles which can be tailored to contemporary challenges and sensitivities.

Despite the demonstrated success of the Marshall Plan framework in Europe in the 1940s, "aid" has developed over the years into a mixture of assistance for an assortment of specific projects and ad hoc responses to unexpected shocks with little apparent coherence, in respect either of the countries that receive it or of its global distribution. Donor conferences are driven more by what donors want to promote than by the desire to support specific multi-year national programmes. It is difficult to see how aid can ever be really effective without an articulation of macroeconomic objectives and detailed programmes for infrastructure investment, etc., and without a coherent account of priorities—what should be done and in what order—and a sense of the necessary complementarities among different investments and projects.

National development programmes along the lines of the Marshall Plan would make it easier to provide general, non-project assistance to Government budgets or for financing the balance of payments, as was the case for a number of European countries under Marshall Aid. The structural changes implied by the shift to a low-emissions development pathway will surely bring with them fiscal and current-account pressures even as long-run adjustments are realized. The need to provide financial assistance to deal with long-term imbalances is usually seen by the international financial institutions as evidence of a weak commitment to reform and as encouraging a slackening of discipline by postponing necessary adjustment. This was not the view of the Marshall Planners, who regarded such assistance as an investment in structural change and as providing Governments with the breathing space required to ensure the success of difficult and often painful policies. Nor can it be the view if the climate and development challenges are to be met.

Another major attraction of a Marshall Plan framework is that it can serve an important political function. A multi-year programme for achieving economic and environmental objectives, setting out their interrelationships, the means to achieve them and their dependence on outside assistance, effectively embodies a Government's vision of the kind of societal structure at which it is aiming. Obviously of a highly political nature, the proposed programme provides the basis for democratic discussion and for the kind of negotiations among competing views that should take place. The task is not an easy one, as is shown by the history of indicative planning in France (Cohen, 1977), but obtaining popular support for such a programme can be a major stimulus for change. This will not always result in what the international financial institutions regard as the "best" policies, but the advantage of democratic processes is that they generate pressures to correct mistakes.

The creation of a "new Marshall Plan" could thus be the means of providing a concrete operational basis for such ideas as "ownership" and "partnership", which otherwise risk degenerating into empty slogans. Moreover, a coherent national programme bolstered by popular support, indicating where outside assistance could be most effective, ipso facto becomes a powerful vehicle for persuading potential donors to respond to national priorities instead of following their own preferences with regard to what might be available in a basket of seemingly unrelated projects.

Conclusion

In terms of the need to secure international cooperation, the climate financing challenge is substantial and daunting. It is clear that, while market-based and voluntary approaches will have an important role to play over time, they are inadequate for meeting the immediate financing requirements. The shift to a low-emissions, high-growth development pathway in the developing world is unlikely to be led by private sector investment and risk-taking. Thus, more binding modalities of international cooperation must be pursued at the same time that countries are dealing with the financial crisis. The same limitations that dog international cooperation in respect of financing development apply to the response to climate change. In the face of this predicament, it is important to realize, however, that the international community can overcome the two sets of limitations simultaneously by recognizing that a global investment programme directed towards climate change objectives represents a key intervention in favour of development.

Bibliography

Ackerman, Frank (2007). Debating climate economics: the Stern Review vs. its critics. Report to Friends of the Earth-UK. Medford, Massachusetts: Global Development and Environment Institute, Tufts University. July.

_____ (2009). *Can We Afford the Future: The Economics of a Warming World.* London: ZED Books.

_____, and Elizabeth Stanton (2009). Projections Regarding Climate Change and Development. Background paper prepared for *World Economic and Social Survey 2009.*

_____, and others (2008). Did the Stern Review underestimate U.S. and global climate damages? Background paper prepared for *World Economic and Social Survey 2009.*

Adam, David (2009a). Amazon could shrink by 85% due to climate change, scientists say. 11 March. Available at http://www.guardian.co.uk/environment/2009/mar/11/amazon-global-warming-trees.

_____ (2009b). Global warming "will be worse than expected" warns Stern. 12 March. Available at http://www.guardian.co.uk/environment/2009/mar/12/climate-change-scienceofclimatechange.

Adger, W. N., and others (2003). Adaptation to climate change in the developing world. *Progress in Development Studies*, vol. 3, No. 3, pp. 179-195.

Agarwal, Anil, and Sunita Narain (1991). *Global Warming in an Unequal World: A Case of Environmental Colonialism.* New Delhi: Centre for Science and the Environment.

Ahmad, Imran Habib (2009). Climate policy integration: towards operationalization. DESA Working Paper, No. 73. ST/ESA/2009/DWP/73. New York: Department of Economic and Social Affairs of the United Nations Secretariat. March.

Alcadi, R., S. Mathur and P. Rémy (2009). Research and innovation for smallholder farmers in the context of climate change. Discussion paper prepared for round table 3 organized during the thirty-second session of the Governing Council of the International Fund for Agricultural Development, 18 February. Available at http://www.ifad.org/events/gc/32/roundtables/3.pdf.

Alcamo, Joseph, Martina Flörke and Michael Märker (2007). Future long-term changes in global water resources driven by socio-economic and climatic change. *Hydrological Sciences Journal*, vol. 52, No. 2 (April), pp. 247-275.

Almeida, Carla (2007). Sugarcane ethanol: Brazil's biofuel success. Science and Development Network. December.

Altieri, Miguel Angel (1990). Agroecology. In *Agroecology*, C. Ronald Carrol, John H. Vandermeer and Peter M. Rosset, eds. New York: McGraw-Hill, pp. 551-564.

Andersen, Stephen O., K. Madhava Sarma and Kristen Taddonio (2007). *Technology Transfer for the Ozone Layer: Lessons for Climate Change.* London: Earthscan.

Aniello, Cathy, and others (1995). Mapping micro-urban heat islands using LANDSAT TM and a GIS. *Computers & Geosciences*, vol. 21, No. 8 (October), pp. 965-967.

Ansolabehere, Stephen, and others (2007). *The Future of Coal: An Interdisciplinary MIT Study*. Cambridge, Massachusetts: Massachusetts Institute of Technology. Available at http://web.mit.edu/coal.

Argote, Linda, and Dennis Epple (1990). Learning curves in manufacturing. *Science*, vol. 247, No. 4945 (23 February), pp. 920-924.

Arrow, Kenneth J. (1962). The economic implications of learning by doing. *Review of Economic Studies*, vol. 29, No. 3, pp. 155-173.

Aryeetey, Ernest (2004). *A Development-focused Allocation of the Special Drawing Rights, United Nations University World Institute for Development Economics Research Discussion Paper*, No. 2003/3. Helsinki, Finland: UNU-WIDER.

Ausubel, J. H., and A. Gruebler (1995). Working less and living longer: long-term trends in working time and time budgets. *Technological Forecasting and Social Change*, vol. 50, No. 3, pp. 195-213. Available as International Institute for Applied Systems Analysis reprint, No. RP-96-004, Laxenburg, Austria.

Baer, Paul, Tom Athanasiou and Sivan Kartha (2007). *The Right to Development in a Climate Constrained World: The Greenhouse Development Rights Framework*. Publication series on Ecology, vol. I. Berlin: Heinrich-Böll-Stiftung, Christian Aid, EcoEquity and the Stockholm Environment Institute. November. Available at http://www.boell.de/downloads/gdr_klein_en.pdf.

_____, and others (2008). *The Greenhouse Development Rights Framework: The Right to Development in a Climate Constrained World*, revised 2nd ed. Berlin: Heinrich Böll Foundation. November.

Ballesteros, Maria Athena (2008). Unfinished business on climate change investment funds. Washington, D. C.: World Resources Institute. 8 October.

Banerjee, L. (2007). Effects of flood on agricultural productivity in Bangladesh. Mimeo.

Banuri, Tariq (2007). A development round of climate negotiations. Paper prepared for the Stockholm Environment Institute. March.

_____, and Hans Opschoor (2007). Climate change and sustainable development. DESA Working Paper, No. 56. ST/ESA/2007/DWP/56. New York: Department of Economic and Social Affairs of the United Nations Secretariat.

Bapna, Manish, and Heather McGray (2009). Financing adaptation: opportunities for innovation and experimentation. In *Climate Change and Global Poverty: A Billion Lives in the Balance*, Lael Brainard, Abigail Jones and Nigel Purvis, eds. Washington, D. C.: The Brookings Institution.

Barker, Terry, Athanasios Dagoumas and Jonathan Rubin (2009). The macroeconomic rebound effect and the world economy. *Energy Efficiency*, pp. 1570-6478. Published online 28 May.

Barnett, B. J., and O. Mahul (2007). Weather index insurance for agriculture. *American Journal of Agricultural Economics*, vol. 89, No. 5, pp. 1241-1247.

Barton, John H. (2007). Intellectual property and access to clean energy technologies in developing countries: an analysis of solar photovoltaic, biofuel and wind technologies. *ICTSD Trade and Sustainable Energy Series Issue Paper*, No. 2. Geneva: International Centre for Trade and Sustainable Development Programme on Trade and Environment. December.

_____, and Keith E. Maskus (2006). Economic perspectives on a multilateral agreement on open access to basic science and technology. In *Economic Development and Multilateral Trade Cooperation*, Simon J. Evenett and Bernard M. Hoekman, eds. Basingstoke, United Kingdom: World Bank and Palgrave MacMillan.

Bateman, Fred, Jaime Ros and Jason E. Taylor (2008). Did New Deal and World War II public capital investments facilitate a "big push" in the American South? Unpublished manuscript. May.

Baumol, William J., Sue Anne Batey Blackman and Edward N. Wolff (1991). *Productivity and American Leadership*. Cambridge, Massachusetts: The MIT Press.

Beggs, P. J. (2004). Impacts of climate change on aeroallergens: past and future. *Clinical and Experimental Allergy*, vol. 34, No. 10, pp. 1507-1513.

Bellarby, Jessica, and others (2008). Cool farming: climate impacts of agriculture and mitigation potential. Amsterdam: Greenpeace International.

Bhandarkar, Malika, and Tarcisio Alvarez-Rivero (2008). From supply chains to value chains: a spotlight on CSR. In *Industrial Development for the 21st Century*, David O'Connor and Monica Kjollerstrom, eds. London: Zed Books.

Bierbaum, R., and others (2007). Confronting climate change: avoiding the unmanageable and managing the unavoidable. Report prepared for the Commission on Sustainable Development by the Scientific Expert Group on Climate Change. Washington, D. C.: United Nations Foundation; and Research Triangle Park, North Carolina: Sigma Xi, The Scientific Research Society.

Bindra, S. P., and Rajab Hokoma (2009). Meeting the energy challenge for sustainable development of developing countries. *Proceedings of the International Conference on Energy and Environment*, 19-21 March.

Blair, Dennis (2009). Comments at the Hearing of the House Permanent Select Committee on Intelligence Annual threat assessment, House of Representatives, Washington, D. C., 25 February.

Blyde, Juan S., and Christina Acea (2003). How does intellectual property affect foreign direct investment in Latin America? *Integration and Trade Journal*, vol. 7, No. 19 (July-December), pp. 135-152.

Bouma, M. J., C. Dye, H. J. van der Kaay (1996). Falciparum malaria and climate change in the Northwest Frontier Province of Pakistan. *The American Journal of Tropical Medicine and Hygiene*, vol. 55, No. 2, pp. 131-137.

Brazilian Sugar Cane Industry Association (UNICA) and Institute for International Trade Negotiations of Brazil (ICONE) (2009). Sustainable production and use of sugarcane ethanol in Brazil. Document submitted to the Convention on Biological Diversity secretariat.

Burton, Ian (2008). Beyond borders: the need for strategic global adaptation. International Institute for Environment and Development, Sustainable Development opinion paper. December. Available at http://www.iied.org/pubs/display.php?o=17046IIED.

Butt, T. A., and others (2005). The economic and food security implications of climate change in Mali. *Climatic Change*, vol. 68, No. 3, pp. 355-378.

Calderón, César, and Luis Servén (2003). The output cost of Latin America's infrastructure gap. In *The Limits of Stabilization: Infrastructure, Public Deficits and Growth in Latin America*, William Easterly and Luis Servén, eds. Palo Alto, California, and Washington, D. C.: Stanford University Press and World Bank.

Campbell-Lendrum, D. (2009). Saving lives while saving the planet: protecting health from climate change. Background paper prepared for *World Economic and Social Survey 2009*.

Canning, David (1998). A data base of world infrastructure stocks, 1950-1995. World Bank Policy Research Working Paper, No. 1929. Washington, D. C.: World Bank.

Cantley, Mark F. and Devendra Sahal (1980). Who learns what? a conceptual description of capability and learning in technological systems. Research report RR-80-42. Laxenburg, Austria: International Institute for Applied Systems Analysis. December.

Capoor, Karan, and Phillipe Ambrosi (2008). *States and Trends of the Carbon Market 2008*. Washington, D. C.: World Bank Institute.

Castillo, G. E., and others (2007). Reversing the flow: agricultural water management pathways for poverty reduction. In *Water for food, Water for life: A Comprehensive Assessment of Water Management in Agriculture*, David Molden, ed. London: Earthscan, pp. 149-191.

Chakravarty, Soibal, and others (2008). Climate policy based on individual emissions. Princeton, New Jersey: Princeton Environmental Center, Princeton University.

Chandrasekar, C. P. (2008). Financial Policies. In *National Development Strategies: Policy Notes*. Sales No. E.08.II.A.4. New York: Department of Economic and Social Affairs of the United Nations Secretariat.

Chang, Ha-Joon, and Bob Rowthorn, eds. (1995). *The Role of the State in Economic Change*. WIDER Studies in Development Economics. Oxford, United Kingdom: Clarendon Press.

Chen, S., and M. Ravallion (2008). The developing world is poorer than we thought, but no less successful in the fight against poverty. *World Bank Policy Research Working Paper*, No. 4703. Washington, D. C.: World Bank.

Cohen, S. (1977). *Modern Capitalist Planning: The French Model*. Berkeley, California: University of California Press.

Coldham and Hartman Architects (2009). Coldham and Hartman Architects. Amherst, Massachusetts. Available at http://www.coldhamandhartman.com/.

Correa, Carlos (2005). Can the TRIPS Agreement foster technology transfer to developing countries? In *International Public Goods and Transfer of Technology: Under a Globalized Intellectual Property Regime*, Keith E. Maskus and Jerome H. Reichman, eds. Cambridge, United Kingdom: Cambridge University Press.

Cosbey, Aaron, ed. (2008). *Trade and Climate Change: Issues in Perspective*. Final Report and Synthesis of Discussions, Trade and Climate Change Seminar, Copenhagen, 18-20 June 2008. Winnipeg, Canada: International Institute for Sustainable Development.

Costanza, Robert, and others (1997). The value of the world's ecosystem services and natural capital, *Nature*, vol. 387 (15 May), pp. 253-260.

Cripps, Francis, Alex Izurieta and Rob Vos (forthcoming). Gains from international policy coordination: simulations with the UN Global Policy Model. DESA Working Paper, forthcoming. New York: Department of Economic and Social Affairs of the United Nations Secretariat.

Crutzen, P. J., and T. E. Graedel (1986). The role of atmospheric chemistry in environment-development interactions. In *Sustainable Development of the Biosphere*, W. C. Clark and R. E. Munn, eds. Cambridge, United Kingdom: Cambridge University Press.

Cypher, James M., and James L. Dietz (2004). *The Process of Economic Development*. London: Routledge.

Das, Keshab (2006). *Electricity and Rural Development Linkage*. Working Paper, No. 172. Ahmedabad, India: Gujarat Institute of Development Research. August.

Dasgupta, Partha (2008). Creative accounting. *Nature*, vol. 456 (30 October), p. 44.

Datt, G., and H. Hoogeveen (2003). El Niño or el peso? crisis, poverty and income distribution in the Philippines. *World Development*, vol. 31, No. 7, pp. 1103-1124.

Dechezleprêtre, Antoine, Matthieu Glachant and Yann Ménière (2009). Technology transfer by CDM projects: a comparison of Brazil, China, India and Mexico. *Energy Policy*, vol. 37, No. 2 (February), pp. 703-711.

Dell, Melissa, Benjamin F. Jones and Benjamin A. Olken (2008). Climate change and economic growth: Evidence from the last half century. *NBER Working Paper*, No. W14132. Cambridge, Massachusetts: National Bureau of Economic Research. June.

DeLong, J. Bradford (2005). Adding to the Marshallian toolkit: big push and nonlinearity in history and theory. Draft of paper prepared for the International Food Policy Research Institute (IFPRI)/Cornell Conference on Threshold Effects and Non-linearities in Growth and Development, held at IFPRI, Washington, D. C., 11-13 May 2005.

Di John, Jonathan (2007). The political economy of taxation and tax reform in developing countries. In *Institutional Change and Economic Development*, H. J. Chang, ed. New York: Anthem Press and United Nations University Press.

Dodman, David, Jessica Ayers and Saleemul Huq (2009). Building resilience. In The Worldwatch Institute, *State of the World 2009: Into a Warming World*. New York: W.W. Norton and Company.

Elliot, D. (2005). Employment, Income and the MDGs: critical linkages and guiding actions. Durham, United Kingdom: Springfield Centre for Business in Development.

Enkvist, Per-Anders, Tomas Nauclér and Jerker Rosander (2007). A cost curve for greenhouse gas reduction. *The McKinsey Quarterly*, No. 1, pp. 35-45.

EU Directorate-General for Research (2006). Sustainable Energy Systems. Brussels: European Commission.

European Commission and European Union Energy Initiative for Poverty Eradication and Sustainable Development (2006). The EU Energy Initiative: increasing access to energy for poverty eradication and sustainable development. Belgium. Available at http://www.pedz.uni-mannheim.de/daten/edz-k/dev/06/euei_en.pdf.

European Parliament (2007). Resolution of 29 November 2007 on trade and climate change. 2007/2003(INI). Brussels.

Evans, Alex, and David Steven (2009). An institutional architecture for climate change. Concept paper commissioned by the Department for International Development, Center on International Cooperation, New York.

Evans, David (2009). Equity, efficiency and compensation in the climate change challenge: analyzing the distribution of costs and benefits. Background paper prepared for *World Economic and Social Survey 2009*.

Evans, Peter (1995). *Embedded Autonomy: States and Industrial Transformation*. Princeton, New Jersey: Princeton University Press.

Everhart, Stephen S., and Mariusz A. Sumlinski (2001). Trends in private investment in developing countries: statistics for 1970-2000 and the impact on private investment of corruption and the quality of public investment. International Finance Corporation Discussion Paper, No. 44. Washington, D. C.: World Bank. September.

Ezzati, M., and others, eds. (2004). *Comparative Quantification of Health Risks: Global and Regional Burden of Disease Attributable to Selected Major Risk Factors*, vols. 1-3. Geneva: World Health Organization.

Fagan, Brian (2008). *The Great Warming: Climate Change and the Rise and Fall of Civilizations*. New York: Bloomsbury Press.

Falvey, Rod, Neil Foster and David Greenaway (2006). Intellectual property rights and economic growth. *Review of Development Economics*, vol. 10, No. 4, pp. 700-719.

Fan, Gang, and others (2008). Toward a low carbon economy: China and the world. Beijing, China: Economics of Climate Change. Draft paper.

Fisher, Brian, and others (2007). Issues related to mitigation in the long-term context. In *Climate Change 2007: Mitigation. Contribution of Working Group III to the Fourth Assessment Report of the Intergovernmental Panel on Climate Change*, B. Metz and others, eds. Cambridge, United Kingdom: Cambridge University Press, Cambridge, chap. 3, pp. 169-250.

Food and Agriculture Organization of the United Nations (FAO) (2004). Trade and sustainable forest management: impacts and interactions. Analytic study of the global project GCP/INT/775/JPN. Impact assessment of forests products trade in the promotion of sustainable forest management. Rome: FAO, Forestry Department.

_____ (2008). *The State of Food and Agriculture, 2008*. Rome: FAO.

Foray, Dominique (2008). Technology transfer in the TRIPS age: the need for new types of partnerships between the least developed and most advanced economies. Available at http://www.iprsonline.org/ictsd/Dialogues/2008-06-16/Technology_transfer_in-the%20_TRIPS_age%20_abstract_ofpaper.pdf (accessed 15 December 2008). Prepared for the International Centre for Trade and Sustainable Development.

Fortunato, Piergiuseppe (2009). An overview of the linkages between greenhouse gas emissions and international trade. Background paper prepared for *World Economic and Social Survey 2009*.

Freeman, C. (1989). The third Kondratieff wave: age of steel, electrification and imperialism. Research Memorandum, No. 89-032. Maastricht, Netherlands: Maastricht Economic Research Institute on Innovation and Technology.

Gallagher, Kelly Sims (2006). Limits to leapfrogging in energy technologies? evidence from the Chinese automobile industry. *Energy Policy*, vol. 34, No. 4 (March), pp. 383-394.

Gao, Guangsheng (2007). Carbon emission right allocation under climate change. *Advances in Climate Change Research*, vol. 3 (Supplement), pp. 87-91.

German Advisory Council on Global Change (WBGU) (2008). *Climate Change as a Security Risk*. London: Earthscan. Available in English at http://www.wbgu. de/wbgu_jg2007_engl.pdf.

German Technical Cooperation (GTZ) (2005). Liquid biofuels for transportation in Tanzania: potential and implications for sustainable agriculture and energy in the 21st century. Eschborn, Germany: Bundeministerium für Ernährung, Landwirtschaft und Verbraucherschutz (BMELV), Fachagentur Nachwachsende Rohstoffe (FNR) and GTZ. August.

Gibbs, Tim (2008). Switched-on India: how can India address climate change and meet its energy needs? London: Institute for Public Policy Research. January.

Gipe, Paul (2009). Innovation and Ontario's feed-in tariff program. Presentation given at the 8th Annual Ontario Power Summit, Toronto, Ontario, 26 May. Available at http://www.wind-works.org/FeedLaws/Canada/Gipe%20Third%20 Industrial%20Revolution%20May%2028%202009.pdf.

Global Commons Institute (2008). Contraction and convergence: a global solution to a global problem. Available at http://www.gci.org.uk/contconv/cc.html.

Global Humanitarian Forum (2009). *Human Impact Report. Climate Change: The Anatomy of a Silent Crisis*. Geneva: Global Humanitarian Forum.

Goldemberg, José (1998). Leapfrogging energy technologies. *Energy Policy*, vol. 2, No. 10, pp. 729-741.

_____ (2007). Ethanol for a sustainable energy future. *Science*, vol. 315, No. 5813 (9 February), pp. 808-810.

_____ (2008). The Brazilian biofuels industry. *Biotechnology for Biofuels*, vol. 1, No. 6.

_____, and others (2004). Ethanol learning curve: the Brazilian experience. *Biomass and Bioenergy*, vol. 26, No. 3 (March), pp. 301-304.

_____, eds. (2000). *World Energy Assessment Report: Energy and the Challenge of Sustainability*. New York: United Nations Development Programme. Sales No. E.00.III.B.5.

_____ (2004). *World Energy Assessment Overview: 2004 Update*. New York: United Nations Development Programme, Department of Economic and Social Affairs of the United Nations Secretariat and World Energy Council.

Goldman Sachs (2008). A warming investment climate. GS Sustain, Goldman Investment Research. 17 October.

Gore, Al (2007). Nobel Lecture. Oslo, 10 December.

Government of Mozambique (2007). National Adaptation Programme of Action. Maputo: Ministry for the Coordination of Environmental Affairs.

Griffith-Jones, Stephanie, and others (2009). The role of private investment in increasing climate-friendly technologies in developing countries. Background paper prepared for *World Economic and Social Survey 2009*.

Gritsevskyi, A., and N. Nakicenovic (2000). Modeling uncertainty of induced technological change. *Energy Policy*, vol. 28, No. 13, pp. 907-921. Also in A. Grübler, N. Nakicenovic and W. D. Nordhaus, eds., *Technological Change and the Environment* (Washington, D. C., Resources for the Future Press, 2002) pp. 251-279. Also available as International Institute for Applied Systems Analysis reprint, No. RR-00-24, Laxenburg, Austria.

Grubb, M. (2004). Technology innovation and climate change policy: an overview of issues and options. *Keio Economic Studies* (Japan), vol. 41, No. 2, pp. 103-132.

Grübler, A. (1998). *Technology and Global Change.* Cambridge, United Kingdom: Cambridge University Press.

_____, N. Nakicenovic and K. Riahi (2007). Scenarios of long-term socio-economic and environmental development under climate stabilization. *Technological Forecasting and Social Change*, vol. 74, No. 7 (Special Issue: September), pp. 887-935.

_____, N. Nakicenovic and D. G. Victor (1999a). Modeling technological change: implications for the global environment. *Annual Review of Energy and the Environment*, vol. 24, No. 1, pp. 545-569. Also available as International Institute for Applied Systems Analysis reprint, No. RR-00-03, Laxenburg, Austria.

_____ (1999b). Dynamics of energy technologies and global change. Energy Policy, vol. 27, No. 5 (May), pp. 247-280. Also available as International Institute for Applied Systems Analysis reprint, No. RR-99-7, Laxenburg, Austria.

Guidry, Virginia Thompson, and Lewis H. Margolis (2005). Unequal respiratory health risk: using GIS to explore hurricane-related flooding in eastern North Carolina. *Environmental Research*, vol. 98, No. 3 (July), pp. 383-389.

Hagler, R. W. (1998). The global timber supply/demand balance to 2030: has the equation changed? Multi-Client Study by Wood Resources International, Reston, Virginia.

Halewood, Michael, and Kent Nnadozie (2008). Giving priority to the commons: the International Treaty on Plant Genetic Resources for Food and Agriculture (ITPGRFA). In *The Future Control of Food: A Guide to International Negotiations and Rules on Intellectual Property, Biodiversity and Food Security*, Geoff Tansey and Tamsin Rajotte, eds. London: Earthscan, pp. 115-140.

Hammill, Anne, Richard Matthew and Elissa McCarter (2008). Microfinance and climate change adaptation. *IDS Bulletin*, vol. 39, No. 4 (September). Sussex, United Kingdom: Institute of Development Studies.

Hansen, James, and others (2008). Target atmospheric CO_2: where should humanity aim? *The Open Atmospheric Science Journal* (Goddard Institute for Space Studies, New York, New York), vol. 2, pp. 217-231.

Harvard Project on International Climate Agreements (2008). Designing the post-Kyoto climate regime: lessons from the Harvard Project on International Climate Agreements. An interim progress report for the 14th Conference of the Parties, Framework Convention on Climate Change, Poznan, Poland, December 2008.

Hazell, Peter, and R. K. Pachauri (2006). Overview. In Bioenergy and agriculture: promises and challenges, Peter Hazell and R. K. Pachauri, eds. 2020 Focus, No. 14. Washington, D. C.: International Food Policy Research Institute.

Heger, Martin, Alex Julca and Oliver Paddison (2009). *Analysing the Impact of Natural Disasters in Small Economies: The Caribbean Case. UNU-WIDER Research Paper*, No. 2008/25. Helsinki: United Nations University World Institute for Development Economics Research (UNU-WIDER). Forthcoming in 2009 in *Dimensions of Vulnerability: Risk and Poverty in Developing Countries*, W. Naudé, A. Santos-Paulino and M. McGillivray, eds. Helsinki: UNU-WIDER.

Helm, Dieter (2008). Climate-change policy: why has so little been achieved? *Oxford Review of Economic Policy*, vol. 24, No. 2, pp. 211-238.

Hirschman, Albert O. (1958). *The Strategy of Economic Development*. New Haven, Connecticut: Yale University Press.

Hirschman, Albert O. (1971). *Bias for Hope: Essays on Development and Latin America*. New Haven Connecticut: Yale University Press.

Hoegh-Guldberg, O., and others (2000). *Pacific in Peril: Biological, Economic and Social Impacts of Climate Change on Pacific Coral Reefs*. Sydney, Australia: Greenpeace, p. 36.

Hoekman, Bernard M., Keith E. Maskus and Kamal Saggi (2004). Transfer of technology to developing countries: unilateral and multilateral policy options. World Bank Policy Research Working Paper No. 3332. Washington, D. C.: World Bank.

Hufbauer, Gary Clyde, and Jisun Kim (2009). Climate policy options and the World Trade Organization. Economics: The Open-Access, Open-Assessment E-Journal. Discussion paper, No. 2009-20. 25 March.

Huq, Saleemul (2001). Climate change and Bangladesh. *Science*, vol. 294, No. 5547 (23 November), p. 1617.

_____ (2002). Lessons learned from adaptation to climate change in Bangladesh. Climate Change Discussion Paper. Washington, D. C.: World Bank Environment Department. October.

_____, and Jessica Ayers (2008). Taking steps: mainstreaming national adaptation. International Institute for Environment and Development briefing. November. Available at http://www.iied.org/pubs/display.php?o=1704011ED.

Huq, Saleemul, and Balgis Osman-Elasha (2009). The status of the LDCF and NAPAs. Power point presentation at the International Scientific Congress on Climate Change: Climate Change: Global Risks, Challenges and Decisions (Copenhagen, 10-12 March 2009), session 41 entitled "Adaptation to climate change in least developed countries: challenges, experiences and ways forward", part I.

Huq, Saleemul, and Hannah Reid (2004). Mainstreaming adaptation in development. *IDS Bulletin*, vol. 35, No. 3, pp. 15-21.

Huq, Saleemul, and others (2007). Editorial: reducing risks to cities from disasters and climate change. *Environment and Urbanization* (International Institute for Environment and Development), vol. 19, No. 1, pp. 3-15.

Hutchison, Cameron J. (forthcoming). Over 5 billion not served: the TRIPS compulsory licensing export restriction. *University of Ottawa Law and Technology Journal*. Available at http://ssrn.com/abstract=1012625 (accessed 31 July 2008).

IDEACarbon (2008). The long-term potential of the carbon market. Press release, 29 February.

Ingram, Gregory K., and Marianne Fay (2008). Physical infrastructure. In *International Handbook of Development Economics*, vol. I, Amitava Krishna Dutt and Jaime Ros, eds. Cheltenham, United Kingdom: Edward Elgar Publishing.

Inter-American Development Bank (IADB) (2005). The Millennium Development Goals in Latin America and the Caribbean. Available at http://www.iadb.org/sds/mdg/file/Cover,%20Foreword%20and%20Introduction.pdf.

Intergovernmental Panel on Climate Change (IPCC) (1999). *Methodological and Technological Issues in Technology Transfer*. Cambridge, United Kingdom: Cambridge University Press, chap. 16 ("Case studies"), case study 29, entitled "ROK-5 mangrove rice variety in Sierra Leone". Available at http://www.grida.no/publications/other/ipcc_sr/.

_____ (2000). *Methodological and Technological Issues in Technology Transfer*, Bert Metz and others. Cambridge, United Kingdom: Cambridge University Press.

_____ (2007a). *Climate Change 2007: Synthesis Report*. Geneva: Intergovernmental Panel on Climate Change.

_____ (2007b). *Climate Change 2007: The Physical Science Basis. Contribution of Working Group I to the Fourth Assessment Report of the Intergovernmental Panel on Climate Change*, S. Solomon and others, eds. Cambridge, United Kingdom: Cambridge University Press.

_____ (2007c). *Climate Change 2007: Impacts, Adaptation and Vulnerability. Contribution of Working Group II to the Fourth Assessment Report of the Intergovernmental Panel on Climate Change*, M. L. Parry and others, eds. Cambridge, United Kingdom: Cambridge University Press.

_____ (2007d). *Climate Change 2007: Mitigation. Contribution of Working Group III to the Fourth Assessment Report of the Intergovernmental Panel on Climate Change*, B. Metz and others, eds. Cambridge, United Kingdom: Cambridge University Press.

International Centre for Trade and Sustainable Development (2007). Climate change, technology transfer and intellectual property rights. Background paper for the Trade and Climate Change Seminar, 18-20 June 2008, Copenhagen, Denmark. Geneva: International Centre for Trade and Sustainable Development.

International Energy Agency (IEA) (2004). Prospects for CO_2 capture and storage: energy technology analysis. Paris: International Energy Agency and Organization for Economic Cooperation and Development. Available at http://www.iea.org/textbase/nppdf/free/2004/prospects.pdf.

_____ (2005). *World Energy Outlook*. Paris: Organization for Economic Cooperation and Development and International Energy Agency.

_____ (2008a). *Energy Technology Perspectives 2008: Scenarios and Strategies to 2050*. Paris: Organization for Economic Cooperation and Development and International Energy Agency.

_____ (2008b). *World Energy Outlook*. Paris: Organization for Economic Cooperation and Development and International Energy Agency.

_____ (2009). *Cleaner Coal in China*. Paris: Organization for Economic Cooperation and Development.

International Institute for Applied Systems Analysis (IIASA) (2007). Greenhouse Gas Initiative (GGI) Scenario Database. Available at http://www.iiasa.ac.at/web-apps/ggi/GgiDb/dsd?Action=htmlpage&page=series.

International Labour Organization (ILO) (2007). Decent work for sustainable development: the challenge of climate change. GB.300/WP/SDG/1. Geneva: Governing Body of the International Labour Office (300th Session), Working Party on the Social Dimension of Globalization. November.

_____ (2008). *Skills for Improved Productivity, Employment Growth and Development*. Report V submitted to the International Labour Conference, 97th Session, 28 May-13 June 2008. Geneva: International Labour Office.

International Monetary Fund (IMF) (2008a). Climate change and the global economy. In *World Economic Outlook: April 2008*. Washington, D. C.: International Monetary Fund.

_____ (2008b). *World Economic Outlook, October 2008: Financial Stress, Downturns, and Recoveries*. Washington, D. C.: IMF.

Jacobson, M. Z. (2008). On the causal link between carbon dioxide and air pollution mortality. *Geophysical Research Letters*, vol. 35, No. 3.

Kathuria, Vinish (2002). Technology transfer for GHG reduction: a framework with application to India. *Technological Forecasting and Social Change*, vol. 69, No. 4, pp. 405-430.

Karekezi, S., and A. Sihag (2004). "Energy Access" Working Group Global Network on Energy for Sustainable Development synthesis/compilation report. Roskilde, Denmark: Risø National Laboratory.

Keppo, I, and S. Rao (2007). International climate regimes: effects of delayed participation. *Technological Forecasting and Social Change*, vol. 74, No. 7 (Special Issue: September), pp. 962-979.

Khor, Martin (forthcoming). The Climate and Trade relations: Some Issues. New York: United Nations Development Programme.

Kindleberger, Charles (1986). International public goods without international government. *American Economic Review*, vol. 76, No. 1 (March), pp. 1-13.

Klare, Michael (2008). Persistent energy insecurity and the global economic crisis. Paper presented at the panel discussion on "Overcoming economic insecurity", Second Committee, United Nations General Assembly, 11 November.

Kohli, Atul (2004). *State Directed Development: Political Power and Industrialization in the Global Periphery*. Cambridge, United Kingdom: Cambridge University Press.

Kotschi, J. (2007). Agricultural biodiversity is essential for adapting to climate change. *GAIA - Ecological Perspectives for Science and Society*, vol. 16, No. 2 (June), pp. 98-101.

Kozul-Wright, Richard, and Paul Rayment (2007). *The Resistible Rise of Market Fundamentalism: Rethinking Development Policy in an Unbalanced World*. Penang, Malaysia: Zed Books and Third World Network.

Leary, Neil, and others, eds. (2008a). *Climate Change and Vulnerability*. London: Earthscan.

_____ (2008b). *Climate Change and Adaptation*. London: Earthscan.

Levina, Ellina (2007). Adaptation to climate change: International agreements for local needs. COM/ENV/EPOC/IEA/SLT(2007)6. Paris: Organization for Economic Cooperation and Development and International Energy Agency. Available at http://www.oecd.org/dataoecd/15/11/39725521.pdf.

Lewis, Joanna (2006). International technology transfer experiences in China's electricity and transport sectors. Arlington, Virginia: Pew Center on Global Climate Change.

Littleton, Matthew (2008). The TRIPS Agreement and transfer of climate-change-related technologies to developing countries. DESA Working Paper, No. 71. ST/ESA/2008/DWP/71. New York: Department of Economic and Social Affairs of the United Nations Secretariat. October.

Lohmann, Larry (2006). Carbon trading: a critical conversation on climate change, privatisation and power. *Development Dialogue*, No. 48. Uppsala, Sweden: Dag Hammarskjöld Centre.

_____ (2008). Financialization, quantism and carbon markets: variations on Polanyian themes. Dorset, United Kingdom: The Corner House. 24 January.

Loughry, Maryanne, and Jane McAdam (2008). Kiribati: relocation and adaptation. *Forced Migration Review*, vol. 31, pp. 51-52.

Ludi, Eva (2009). Climate change, water and food security. *Overseas Development Institute Background Note*. London: ODI. March.

Maddison, Angus (2006). *The World Economy: Volume 1: A Millennial Perspective; and Volume 2: Historical Statistics*. OECD Development Centre Studies. Paris: Organization for Economic Cooperation and Development. December.

Marland, Gregg, Tom Boden and Robert J. Andres (2008). Carbon Dioxide Information Analysis Center (CDIAC) database. Oak Ridge, Tennessee: Oak Ridge National Laboratory. Available at http://cdiac.ornl.gov.

Maskus, Keith E. (2000). Intellectual property rights and foreign direct investment. Centre for International Economic Studies Working Paper, No. 22. Boulder, Colorado: University of Colorado at Boulder, Department of Economics. May.

_____ (2003). Transfer of technology and technological capacity building. Paper presented at the ICTSD-UNCTAD Dialogue, 2nd Bellagio Series on Development and Intellectual Property, 18-21 September 2003. Available at http://www.iprsonline.org/unctadictsd/bellagio/docs/Maskus_Bellagio2.pdf (accessed 15 December 2008).

_____ (2004). Encouraging international technology transfer. UNCTAD-ICTSD Project on IPRs and Sustainable Development, Issue Paper, No. 7 (May). Geneva: United Nations Conference on Trade and Development and International Centre for Trade and Sustainable Development.

Matsushita, Mitsuo, Thomas J. Schönbaum and Petros C. Mavroidis (2006). *The World Trade Organization: Law, Practice, and Policy*, 2nd ed. Oxford, United Kingdom: Oxford University Press.

McGray, H., and others (2007). *Weathering the Storm: Options for Framing Adaptation and Development*. Washington, D. C.: World Resources Institute.

McKinley, Jesse (2009). Drought adds to hardships in California. *The New York Times*. 21 February. Available at http://www.nytimes.com/2009/02/22/us/22mendota.html.

McKinsey & Company (2009). Pathways to a low-carbon economy: version 2 of the global greenhouse gas abatement cost curve. January.

Mendonca, Miguel (2007). *Feed-in Tariffs: Accelerating the Deployment of Renewable Energy*. London: Earthscan.

Meinshausen, Malte and others (2009). Greenhouse-gas emission targets for limiting global warming to 2°C. *Nature*, vol. 458 (30 April), pp. 1158-1162.

Miller, Barbara A., and Richard B. Reidinger (1998). *Comprehensive River Basin Development: The Tennessee Valley Authority*. World Bank Technical Paper, No. 416. Washington, D. C.: World Bank.

Mills, Evan (2005). Insurance in a climate of change. *Science*, vol. 309, No. 5737 (12 August), pp. 1040-1044.

Müller, Benito (2008). International adaptation finance: the need for an innovative and strategic approach. Oxford, United Kingdom: Oxford Institute for Energy Studies. June.

_____, and Cameron Hepburn (2006). *IATAL: an outline proposal for an International Air Travel Adaptation Levy*. EV36. Oxford, United Kingdom: Oxford Institute for Energy Studies. October. Available at http://www.oxfordenergy.org/pdfs/EV36.pdf.

Müller, Benito, and Harald Winkler (2008). *One step forward, two steps back? the governance of the World Bank Climate Investment Funds*. Oxford Energy and Environment Comment. Oxford, United Kingdom: Oxford Institute for Energy Studies. February.

Miyamoto, Koji (2008). Human capital formation and foreign direct investment in developing countries. In *Foreign Direct Investment, Technology and Skills in Developing Countries*, A. Mercado, K. Miyamoto and D. O'Connor, eds. *OECD Journal*, vol. 2008/1. Paris: Organization for Economic Cooperation and Development. August.

Moomaw, William, and Lucy Johnston (2008). Emissions mitigation opportunities and practice in Northeastern United States. *Mitigation and Adaptation Strategies for Global Change*, vol. 13, No. 5, pp. 615-642.

Moreira, Jose Roberto (2006). Brazil's experience with bioenergy. In *Bioenergy and Agriculture: Promises and Challenges*, Peter Hazell and R. K. Pachauri, eds. Washington, D. C.: International Food Policy Research Institute.

Moser, C., M. Gauhurts and H. Gonhan (1994). *Urban Poverty Research Sourcebook: Sub-City Level Research*. Washington, D. C.: World Bank.

Murphy, James T. (2001). Making the energy transition in rural East Africa: is leapfrogging an alternative? *Technological Forecasting and Social Change*, vol. 68, No. 2, pp. 173-193.

Murphy, J. M., and others (2004). Quantification of modeling uncertainties in a large ensemble of climate change simulations. *Nature*, vol. 430, No. 7001 (12 August), pp. 768-772.

Nagao, Y., and others (2003). Climatic and social risk factors for Aedes infestation in rural Thailand. *Tropical Medicine and International Health*, vol. 8, No. 7 (July), pp. 650-659.

Nakicenovic, Nebojsa (2009). Supportive policies for developing countries: a paradigm shift. Background paper prepared for *World Economic and Social Survey 2009*.

_____, A. Ajanovic and O. Kimura (2005). Global scenarios for the energy infrastructure development. Interim report, No. IR-05-028. Laxenburg, Austria: International Institute for Applied Systems Analysis.

Nakicenovic, N., and K. Riahi, eds. (2007). *Technological Forecasting and Social Change*, vol. 74, No. 7 (September). Special issue on Integrated assessment of uncertainties in greenhouse gas emissions and their mitigation.

Nakicenovic, N., and others (2000). IPCC Special Report on Emissions Scenarios. Special Report of IPCC Working Group III. Cambridge, United Kingdom: Cambridge University Press. Also available at http://www.grida.no/climate/ ipcc/emission/index.htm.

Narain, Sunita, and Matthew Riddle (2007). Greenhouse justice: an entitlement framework for managing the global atmospheric commons. In *Reclaiming Nature: Environmental Justice and Ecological Restoration*, J. K. Boyce and E. A. Stanton, eds. London: Anthem Press, pp. 401-414.

Nell, Edward, Willi Semmler and Armon Rezai (2009). Economic growth and climate change: cap-and-trade or emissions tax? SCEPA Working Paper, No. 2009-4. New York, New York: Schwartz Center of Economic Policy Analysis, The New School for Social Research.

Nelson, Richard R. (2007). Economic development from the perspective of evolutionary economic theory. Draft paper prepared for the Meeting of Experts on FDI, Technology and Competitiveness, United Nations Conference on Trade and Development, Geneva, 8 and 9 March.

New Carbon Finance (2008). With an international agreement on climate change, the carbon market could be two to three times as large as today. Press release, 28 January.

New Economics Foundation (2008). *A Green New Deal: Joined-up Policies to Solve the Triple Crunch of the Credit Crisis, Climate Change and High Oil Prices*. London: Green New Deal Group.

Nicholls, R., and others (2007). Ranking of the world's cities most exposed to coastal flooding today and in the future: executive summary. Paris: Organization for Economic Cooperation and Development. Extract from OECD Working Paper, No. 1 (ENV/WKP(2007)1).

Nikolic, Irina A., and Harand Maikisch (2006). Public-private partnerships and collaboration in the health sector: an overview with case studies from recent European experience. *Health Nutrition and Population (HNP) Discussion Paper*. Washington, D. C.: World Bank, Human Development Network.

O'Brien, Karen, and others (2008). Disaster risk reduction, climate change adaptation and human security. Report prepared for the Royal Norwegian Ministry of Foreign Affairs by the Global Environmental Change and Human Security (GECHS) Project. *GECHS Report* 2008: 3. Oslo: University of Oslo, GECHS International Project Office, Department of Sociology and Human Geography.

O'Connor, D., and M. Lunati (2008). Economic opening and the demand for skills in developing countries. In *Foreign Direct Investment, Technology and Skills in Developing Countries*, A. Mercado, K. Miyamoto and D. O'Connor, eds. *OECD Journal*, vol. 2008/1. Paris: Organization for Economic Cooperation and Development. August.

Oliva, Maria Julia (2008). Climate change, technology transfer and intellectual property rights: key issues (chap. 4). In *Trade and Climate Change: Issues in Perspective*, Aaron Cosbey, ed. Final Report and Synthesis of Discussions, Trade and Climate Change Seminar, Copenhagen, 18-20 June 2008. Winnipeg, Canada: International Institute for Sustainable Development.

Organization for Economic Cooperation and Development (OECD) (1997). Economic fiscal instruments: taxation (i.e. carbon/energy). Working Paper, No. 4. OECD/GD(97)188. Paris: OECD Annex I Expert Group on the United Nations, United Nations Framework Convention on Climate Change.

_____ (2007). Patent Database. Paris: Organization for Economic Cooperation and Development.

_____ (2008). *Economic Aspects of Adaptation to Climate Change: Costs, Benefits and Policy Instruments*. Paris: Organization for Economic Cooperation and Development.

_____ (2009). Economic Outlook. Interim report. March. Available at http://www.oecd.org/dataoecd/18/1/42443150.pdf.

Osman-Elasha, Balgis, and others (2008). Community development and coping with drought in rural Sudan. In *Climate Change and Adaptation*, Neil Leary and others, eds. London: Earthscan.

Oxfam International (2007). Adapting to climate change: what's needed in poor countries, and who should pay. Oxfam briefing paper, No. 104. London. 29 May.

Pacala, S. and R. Socolow (2004). Stabilization wedges: solving the climate problem for the next 50 years with current technologies. *Science*, vol. 305, No. 5686 (13 August), pp. 968-972.

Pachauri, R. K. (2008). Climate change: key findings from the IPCC Fourth Assessment Report. Sacramento, California Air Resources Board. 27 June. World Meteorological Organization and United Nations Environment Programme.

Parra, Mariangela (2009). Bringing back the developmental State in the context of climate change. Background paper prepared for *World Economic and Social Survey 2009*.

Parry, Martin, Cynthia Rosenzweig and Matthew Livermore (2005). Climate change, global food supply and risk of hunger. *Philosophical Transactions of the Royal Society* (London), vol. 360, No. 1463, pp. 2125-2138.

Pascual, M., and others (2006). Malaria resurgence in the East African highlands: temperature trends revisited. *Proceedings of the National Academy of Sciences of the United States of America*, vol. 103, No. 15 (11 April), pp. 5829-5834.

Patz, Jonathan A., and others (2005). Impact of regional climate change on human health. *Nature*, vol. 438, No. 7066 (17 November), pp. 310-317.

Peck, Mohan, and Ralph Chipman (2008). Industrial energy and material efficiency: what role for policies? In *Industrial Development for the 21ˢᵗ Century*, David O'Connor and Monica Kjollerstrom, eds. London: Zed Books.

Pelling, M., ed. (2003). *Natural Disasters and Development in a Globalising World*. London: Routledge.

Pendleton, Andrew, and Simon Retallack (2009). Fairness in global climate change finance. London: Institute for Public Policy Research. March. Available at http://www.indiaenvironmentportal.org.in/files/Mar09-fairness_global_finance.pdf.

Peskett, Leo, and others (2007). Biofuels, agriculture and poverty reduction. *Natural Resource Perspectives*, No. 107. London: Overseas Development Institute. June.

_____ (2008). Making REDD work for the poor. Poverty Environment Partnership. September.

Phillips, Tom (2008). Brazil announces plan to slash rainforest destruction. 2 December. Available at http://www.guardian.co.uk/environment/2008/dec/02/forests-brazil.

_____ (2009). Poor Brazilians rejoice as loggers return to pillage the rainforest. 15 February. Available at http://www.guardian.co.uk/environment/2009/feb/15/amazon-deforestation-brazil.

Platz, Daniel (2009). Infrastructure finance in developing countries: the potential of sub-sovereign bonds. DESA Working Paper, No. 74. ST/ESA/2009/DWP/74. New York: Department of Economic and Social Affairs of the United Nations Secretariat.

_____, and Frank Schroeder (2007). *Moving Beyond the Privatization Debate: Different Approaches to Water and Electricity in Developing Countries, Dialogue on Globalization Occasional Paper*, No. 34 (September). New York: Friedrich Ebert Foundation.

Point Carbon (2008). Carbon market transactions: dominated by financials? Carbon Market Analyst, 21 May.

Pollin, Robert, and Jeannette Wicks-Lim (2008). Job opportunities for the green economy: a state-by-state picture of occupation that gain from green investments. Amherst, Massachusetts: Political Economy Research Institute. June.

Porter, Gareth, and others (2008). New finance for climate change and the environment. Washington, D. C.: WWF Macroeconomics Program Office.

Raupach, Michael, and others (2007). Global and regional drivers of accelerating CO_2 emissions. *Proceedings of the National Academy of Sciences*, vol. 104, No. 24 (June).

Rippey, Paul (2009). Microfinance and climate change: threats and opportunities. CGAP Focus Note, No.53. Washington, D. C.: Consultative Group to Assist the Poor.

Roberts, Debra (2008). Thinking globally, acting locally: institutionalizing climate change at the local government level in Durban, South Africa. *Environment and Urbanization*, vol. 20, No. 2, pp. 521-537.

Robine, J. M., and others (2008). Death toll exceeded 70,000 in Europe during the summer of 2003. *Comptes rendus biologies*, vol. 331, No. 2 (February), pp. 171-178.

Rodríguez, Francisco (2007). Growth empirics in a complex world: a guide for applied economists and policy makers. In *Growth Divergences: Explaining Differences in Economic Performance*, José Antonio Ocampo, Jomo K. S. and Rob Vos, eds. Penang, Malaysia: Orient Longman, Zed Books and Third World Network, in cooperation with the United Nations.

Rodrik, Dani (2007). *One Economics, Many Recipes: Globalization, Institutions, and Economic Growth.* Princeton, New Jersey: Princeton University Press.

Roffe, Pedro (2002). Preliminary note on the WTO Working Group on Trade and Transfer of Technology. Geneva: United Nations Conference on Trade and Development.

Rohatyn, Felix (2009). *Bold Endeavors: How our Government Built America and Why It Must Rebuild Now.* New York, New York: Simon and Schuster.

Rosenberg, N. (1982). *Inside the Black Box: Technology and Economics.* Cambridge, United Kingdom: Cambridge University Press.

Rothschild, Emma (2009). Can we transform the auto-industrial society? *The New York Review of Books*, vol. 56, No. 3 (26 February).

Rudd, Kevin (2009). The global financial crisis. *The Australian*, No. 42 (February).

Sachs, Jeffrey (2008). The American green revolution. *Scientific American*. May.

_____, and others (2004). Ending Africa's poverty trap. *Brookings Papers on Economic Activity*, No. 1 (2004). Washington, D. C.: The Brookings Institution Press.

Sagar, Ambuj, Cath Bremner and Michael Grubb (2008). Public-private roles and partnerships for innovation and technology transfer. Presentation to the Carbon Trust. 7 November. Available at http://www.un.org/esa/sustdev/sdissues/energy/op/beijing_hlccc_nov08/TrackC_7Nov_C.Bremner.pdf.

Salter, Wilfred (1969). *Productivity and Technological Change.* Cambridge, United Kingdom: Cambridge University Press.

Sanchez-Rodriguez, Roberto, Michail Fragkias and William Solecki (2008). Urban responses to climate change: a focus on the Americas. A workshop report: Urbanization and Global Environmental Change, an International Human Dimensions Programme on Global Environmental Change core project.

Sanderson, D. (2000). Cities, livelihoods and disasters. *Environment and Urbanization*, vol. 12, No. 2, pp. 93-102.

Santarius, T., and others (2009). Pit stop Poznan: an analysis of negotiations on the Bali Action Plan at the stopover to Copenhagen. Berlin: Wuppertal Institute for Climate, Environment and Energy.

Satterthwaite, David (2007). Climate change and urbanization: effects and implications for urban governance. UN/POP/EGM-URB/2008/16. 27 December. Paper presented at the United Nations Expert Group Meeting on Population Distribution, Urbanization, Internal Migration and Development, New York, 21-23 January 2008.

Sathaye, J., E. Jolt, and S. De La Rue du Can (2005). Overview of IPR practices for publicly-funded technologies. Paper prepared for the United Nations, United Nations Framework Convention on Climate Change Expert Group on Technology Transfer. Available at http://unfccc.int/ttclear/pdf/EGTT/11%20 Bonn%202005/IPRandOtherIssuesAssociatedwithPublicly-FundedTech.pdf.

Scherer, F. M. (1984). *Innovation and Growth: Schumpeterian Perspectives*. Cambridge, Massachusetts: The MIT Press.

Schipper, Lisa F. (2009). Adapting to climate change in developing countries: institutional and policy responses for urbanizing societies. Background paper prepared for *World Economic and Social Survey 2009*.

Schmidt, Gavin (2009). *Climate Change*. New York, New York: W.W. Norton and Company.

Schroeder, Frank (2008). Carbon taxes for managing climate change. G-24 Policy Brief, No. 27. Washington, D. C.

Schumpeter, J. A. (1942). *Capitalism, Socialism and Democracy*. New York: Harper and Brothers.

Schwartz, Peter and Doug Randall (2003). An abrupt climate change scenario and its implications for United States national security. Report prepared by Global Business Network for the Department of Defense. October. Available at http://www.gbn.com/consulting/article_details.php?id=53.

Sengupta, Somini (2009). Bangladesh tries using silt to protect against sea levels. *International Herald Tribune*. 20 March. Available at http://www.iht.com/ articles/2009/03/20/asia/bangla.php?page=1.

Seres, Stephen, and Eric Haites (2008). Analysis of technology transfer in CDM projects. Report prepared for the United Nations Framework Convention on Climate Change Registration and Issuance Unit. December.

Shiklomanov, I. A., and J. C. Rodda, eds. (2003). *World Water Resources at the Beginning of the 21st Century*. Cambridge, United Kingdom: Cambridge University Press.

Smith, Joel B., Richard J. T. Klein and Saleemul Huq, eds. (2003). *Climate Change, Adaptive Capacity and Development*. London: Imperial College Press.

Smith, Pamela J. (2001). How do foreign patent rights affect U.S. exports, affiliate sales, and licenses? *Journal of International Economics*, vol. 55, No. 2 (December), pp. 411-439.

Someshwar, Shiv (2008). Adaptation as "climate-smart" development. *Development*, vol. 51, No. 3 (September), pp. 366-374.

Soros, George (2002). *On Globalization*. Cambridge, Massachusetts: The Perseus Books Group.

_____ (2008). *The New Paradigm for Financial Markets: The Credit Crisis of 2008 and What It Means*. New York, New York: Public Affairs.

Spiegel, Shari (2008). Macroeconomic and growth policies. In *National Development Strategies: Policy Notes*. Sales No. E.08.II.A.4. New York: Department of Economic and Social Affairs of the United Nations Secretariat.

Stern, Nicholas (2006). *The Stern Review on the Economics of Climate Change*. Cambridge, United Kingdom: Cambridge University Press.

_____ (2007). *The Economics of Climate Change: The Review*. Cambridge, United Kingdom: Cambridge University Press.

_____ (2009). *A Blueprint for a Safer Planet: How to Manage Climate Change and Create a New Era of Prosperity*. London: The Bodley Head.

_____, and Haruhiko Kuroda (2009). Why global warming could make or break south-east Asia. *The Guardian*, 5 May.

Stiglitz, Joseph (1994). The role of the state in financial markets. In *Proceedings of the World Bank Annual Conference on Development Economics 1993: Supplement to the Bank Economic Review and World Bank Research Observer*. Washington, D. C.: World Bank.

_____ (2008). Economic foundations of intellectual property rights. *Duke Law Journal*, vol. 57, No. 6 (April), pp. 1693-1724. Available at http://www.law.duke.edu/shell/cite.pl?57+Duke+L.+J.+1693.

Stockholm Environment Institute (2008). International climate policy. Stockholm Environment Institute policy brief for the Commission on Climate Change and Development. Stockholm.

Strelneck, David, and Peter Linquiti (1995). Environmental technology transfer to developing countries: practical lessons learned during implementation of the Montreal Protocol. Paper prepared for presentation at the 17th Annual Research Conference of the Association for Public Policy and Management. Fairfax, Virginia: ICF Consulting.

Takada, Minoru, and Silvia Fracchi (2007) A review of energy in national MDG reports. New York: United Nations Development Programme. Also available at http://www.energyandenvironment.undp.org/undp/indexAction.cfm?module=Library&action=GetFile&DocumentAttachmentID=2088.

Tan, Celine (2008). No additionality, new conditionality: a critique of the World Bank's proposed climate investment funds. Penang, Malaysia: Third World Network. 30 May.

Third World Network (2008). Some key points on climate change, access to technology and intellectual property rights. Submission to the United Nations Framework Convention on Climate Change. Penang, Malaysia: Third World Network.

Tirpak, Denis, and Helen Adams (2007). Trends in official bilateral and multilateral development assistance in the energy sector: has the DA community responded to the United Nations Climate Change Convention? Paper submitted to the *Climate Policy* special issue on integrating climate change actions into local development, B. Metz and M. T. J. Kok, eds.

_____ (2008). Bilateral and multilateral financial assistance for the energy sector of developing countries. *Climate Policy*, vol. 8, No. 2, pp. 135-151. London: Earthscan.

Toasa, José (2009). Colombia: a new ethanol producer on the rise? WRS-0901. Washington, D. C.: Economic Research Service, United States Department of Agriculture. Available at http://www.ers.usda.gov. January.

Todo, Yasuyuki, and Koji Miyamoto (2006). Knowledge spillovers from foreign direct investment and the role of local R&D activities: evidence from Indonesia. *Economic Development and Cultural Change*, (Chicago, Illinois), vol. 55, No. 1 (October), pp. 173-200.

Toman, Michael A., and Barbora Jemelkova (2003). Energy and economic development: an assessment of the state of knowledge. *The Energy Journal*, vol. 24, No. 4, pp. 93-112.

Tufts University, Fletcher School (2008). Scaling alternative energy: the role of emerging markets. Dialogue synthesis report. 11 April. A joint initiative sponsored by the Center for International Environment and Resource Policy (CIERP) and the Center for Emerging Market Enterprises (CEME) of the Fletcher School, Tufts University.

UNITAID (2008). Annual report 2007. Geneva: World Health Organization.

United Nations (1972). *Report of the United Nations Conference on the Human Environment, Stockholm, 5-16 June 1972*. Sales No. E.73.II.A.14 and corrigendum.

_____ (1992). *Report of the United Nations Conference on Environment and Development, Rio de Janeiro, 3-14 June 1992*, vol. I, *Resolutions Adopted by the Conference*. Sales No. E.93.I.8 and corrigendum. Resolution I, annex I (Rio Declaration on Environment and Development). Resolution I, annex II (Agenda 21).

_____ (1998). Report of the Commission on Sustainable Development on its sixth session (22 December 1997 and 20 April–1 May 1998). *Official Records of the Economic and Social Council, 1998, Supplement No. 9*. E/1998/29.

_____ (2002). *Report of the International Conference on Financing for Development, Monterrey, Mexico, 18-22 March 2002*. Sales No. E.02.II.A.7, Chap I, resolution 1, annex.

_____ (2005). *World Economic and Social Survey 2005: Financing for Development*. Sales No. E.05.II.C.1.

_____ (2006). *World Economic and Social Survey 2006: Diverging Growth and Development*. Sales No. E.06.II.C.1.

_____ (2008). *World Economic and Social Survey 2008: Overcoming Economic Insecurity*. Sales No. E.08.II.C.1.

_____ (2009). Recommendations of the Commission of Experts of the President of the General Assembly on Reforms of the International Monetary and Financial System: note by the President of the General Assembly. A/63/838. 29 April.

United Nations Conference on Trade and Development (UNCTAD)(2002). *Economic Development in Africa: From Adjustment to Poverty Reduction: What is New?* Sales No. E.02.II.D.18.

_____ (2005). Potential uses of structured finance techniques for renewable energy projects in developing countries. Study prepared by the UNCTAD secretariat. 5 December.

_____ (2007). *Least Developed Countries Report 2007: Knowledge, Technological Learning and Innovation for Development*. Sales No. E.07.II.D.8.

United Nations, Department of Economic and Social Affairs (UN/DESA) (2008). Climate change: technology development and technology transfer. Background document prepared for the High-level Conference on Climate Change: Technology Development and Technology Transfer, Beijing, 7 and 8 November 2008.

_____ (2009). A global green New Deal for sustainable development. UN-DESA Policy Brief, No. 12. Available at http://www.un.org/esa/policy/policybriefs/index.htm.

_____, and International Atomic Energy Agency (2007). Energy indicators for sustainable development: country studies on Brazil, Cuba, Lithuania, Mexico, Russian Federation, Slovakia, and Thailand. New York: Department of Economic and Social Affairs of the United Nations Secretariat.

United Nations Development Programme (UNDP) (2007a). *Human Development Report 2007/2008: Fighting Climate Change: Human Solidarity in a Divided World*. Basingstoke, United Kingdom: Palgrave Macmillan.

_____ (2007b). Mainstreaming access to energy services: experiences from three African regional economic communities. Dakar: UNDP Rural Energy for Poverty Reduction Programme.

_____ (2007c). MDG Achievement Fund thematic window for environment and climate change. Available at http://www.undp.org/mdgf/environment.shtml.

United Nations Environment Programme (UNEP) (2009). Global Green New Deal. Policy brief. March. Available at http://www.unep.org/pdf/A_Global_Green_New_Deal_Policy_Brief.pdf.

_____, International Labour Organization, and others (2008). *Green Jobs: Towards Decent Work in a Sustainable, Low-Carbon World*. Nairobi: United Nations Environment Programme. Prepared by Worldwatch Institute, with assistance from Cornell University Global Labor Institute.

United Nations High Commissioner for Refugees (UNHCR) (2008). Climate change, natural disasters and human displacement: a UNHCR perspective. 23 October. Geneva: Office of the United Nations High Commissioner for Refugees.

United Nations Human Settlements Programme (UN-Habitat) (2007). *Global Report on Human Settlements 2007: Enhancing Urban Safety and Security*. London: Earthscan.

_____ (UN-Habitat) (2008). *State of the World's Cities 2008/2009: Harmonious Cities*. London: Earthscan.

United Nations, United Nations Framework Convention on Climate Change (UNFCCC) (2003). Capacity-building in the development and transfer of technologies. Technical paper, FCCC/TP/2003/1. 26 November.

_____ (2008). Investment and financial flows to address climate change: an update. Technical paper. FCCC/TP/2008/7. 26 November.

_____, Subsidiary Body for Scientific and Technological Advice (2006). Synthesis report on technology needs identified by Parties not included in annex I to the Convention: note by the Secretariat. FCCC/SBSTA/2006/INF.1. 21 April.

United States Agency for International Development (2007). From ideas to action: clean energy solutions for Asia to address climate change. Annex 2: India country report. Bangkok: USAID, Regional Development Mission for Asia. Available at http://usaid.eco-asia.org/programs/cdcp/reports/Ideas-to-Action/annexes/Annex%202_India.pdf.

Unruh, Gregory C. (2000). Understanding carbon lock-in. *Energy Policy*, vol. 28, No. 12 (October), pp. 817-830.

Ürge-Vorsatz, Diana, and Bert Metz (2009). Energy efficiency: how far does it get us in controlling climate change? *Energy Efficiency*, vol. 2, No. 2 (May), pp. 87-94.

U.S. Congress, Office of Technology Assessment (OTA) (1991). *Energy in Developing Countries*. OTA-E-486. Washington, D. C.: U.S. Government Printing Office. January.

_____ (1992). *Fueling Development: Energy Technologies for Developing Countries*. OTA-E-516. Washington, D. C.: U.S. Government Printing Office. April.

Vattenfall AB (2007). *Global mapping of greenhouse gas: abatement opportunities up to 2030*. Available at http://www.vattenfall.com/www/ccc/ccc/577730downl/index.jsp.

Weitzman, Martin (2009). Additive damages, fat-tailed climate dynamics, and uncertain discounting. Cambridge, Massachusetts: Faculty of Economics, Harvard University. 27 April. Draft.

Winkler, Harald, ed. (2006). *Energy Policies for Sustainable Development in South Africa: Options for the Future*. Rondebosch, South Africa: Energy Research Centre, University of Cape Town.

_____, and Andrew Marquand (2009). Changing development paths: from an energy-intensive to low-carbon economy in South Africa. *Climate and Development*, vol. 1 No. 1, pp. 47-65.

Wise, Timothy A., and Kevin P. Gallagher (2008). Putting development back into the WTO. In Looking beyond Doha: new thinking on trade policy and development. Brussels: PSE (The Socialist Group in the European Parliament).

Wissenschaftlicher Beirat der Bundesregierung Globale Umweltveränderungen (WBGU) (2009). *Welt im Wandel: Zukunftsfähige Bioenergie und nachhaltige Landnutzung*. Berlin: WBGU. Also available at http://www.wbgu.de/wbgu_download.html.

World Bank (1993). *The East Asian Miracle: Economic Growth and Public Policy, World Bank Policy Research Reports*. New York, New York: Oxford University Press.

_____ (2008a). *International Trade and Climate Change: Economic, Legal, and Institutional Perspectives*. Washington, D. C.: World Bank.

_____ (2008b). Trustee report: financial status of the CIF. CTF/TFC.1/Inf.2. 17 November.

_____ (2009). How will the world finance climate change action? Bali brunch dialogue. 26 April. Washington, D.C.: World Bank.

_____, Commission on Growth and Development (2008). *The Growth Report: Strategies for Sustained Growth and Inclusive Development*. Washington, D.C.: World Bank.

World Health Organization (WHO) (2002). *The World Health Report 2002: Reducing Risks, Promoting Healthy Life*. Geneva: WHO.

_____ (2005a). Climate and health Factsheet. July. Available at http://www.who.int/globalchange/news/fsclimandhealth/en/index.html.

_____ (2005b): *Ecosystems and Human Well-being: Health Synthesis*. A contribution to the Millennium Ecosystem Assessment. Geneva: WHO.

_____ (2006). Burden of disease statistics. Geneva: WHO.

World Intellectual Property Organization (2008). Substantive patent law harmonization. Available at http://www.wipo.int/patent-law/en/harmonization.htm (accessed 28 July 2008).

World Meteorological Organization-International Council for Science (WMO-ICSU) (2009). The state of polar research. Statement from the International Council for Science/World Meteorological Organization Joint Committee for the International Polar Year 2007-2008. Geneva. February.

World Trade Organization (WTO) (1994). *Legal Instruments Embodying the Results of the Uruguay Round of Multilateral Trade Negotiations, done at Marrakesh on 15 April 1994*. Sales No. GATT/1994.7. Geneva: GATT secretariat.

_____ (2001). Declaration on the TRIPS Agreement and public health. Adopted at the Fourth Ministerial Conference of the Word Trade Organization, Doha, 9-14 November 2001. WT/MIN(01)/DEC/2. 20 November.

_____ (2003). Decision of the General Council of 30 August 2003 on the implementation of paragraph 6 of the Doha Declaration on the TRIPS Agreement and public health. WT/MIN(01)/DEC/1.

Wright, T. P. (1936). Factors affecting the costs of airplanes. *Journal of the Aeronautical Sciences*, vol. 3 (February), pp. 122-128.

WWF (2008). Water for life: lessons for climate change adaptation from better management of rivers for people and nature. Available at http://assets.panda.org/downloads/50_12_wwf_climate_change_v2_full_report.pdf.

Yohe, Gary and Richard Moss (2000). Economic sustainability, indicators and climate change. In *Proceedings of the IPCC Expert Meeting on Development, Equity and Sustainability*, Colombo, Sri Lanka. Geneva: Intergovernmental Panel on Climate Change and World Meteorological Organization.

Zabel, G. (2000). Population and energy. August 2000. Available at http://dieoff.org/page199.htm.

Zhang, Zhong Xiang (2007). China is moving away (from) the pattern of "develop first and then treat the pollution". *Energy Policy*, vol. 35, No. 7 (July), pp. 3547-3549.

Litho in United Nations, New York

09-25178—June 2009—5,060

ISBN 978-92-1-109159-5

United Nations publication

Sales No. E.09.II.C.1

E/2009/50/Rev.1

Copyright © United Nations, 2009